JAN 01 $ 37.50

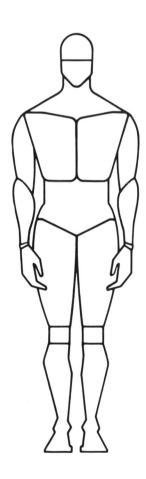

# HUMAN DIMENSION
# & INTERIOR SPACE

## A SOURCE BOOK OF DESIGN REFERENCE STANDARDS

BY **JULIUS PANERO,** AIA, ASID
AND **MARTIN ZELNIK,** AIA, ASID

WHITNEY LIBRARY OF DESIGN
an imprint of Watson-Guptill Publications/New York

## DEDICATION

To that small group of anthropologists specializing in the field of engineering anthropometry, without whose expertise, vision, and sensitivity to the importance of human dimension and its relationship to the design process this book certainly could not have been written.

Copyright © 1979 by Julius Panero and Martin Zelnik

First published 1979 in the United States and Canada by Whitney Library of Design,
an imprint of Watson-Guptill Publications,
a division of Billboard Publications, Inc.,
1515 Broadway, New York, N.Y. 10036

**Library of Congress Cataloging in Publication Data**
Panero, Julius.
  Human dimension & interior space.
  Bibliography: p.
  Includes index.
    1. Architecture—Human factors.   2. Interior
decoration—Human factors.   3. Anthropometry—
Tables, etc. I. Zelnik, Martin, 1939-
joint author. II. Title.
NA2542.4.P356 1979     729     79-20874
ISBN 0-8230-7271-1

Published in Great Britain by The Architectural Press Ltd.,
9 Queen Anne's Gate, London SW1H 9BY
ISBN 0-85139-4574

Manufactured in U.S.A.

First Printing, 1979
11/90

# CONTENTS

# FOREWORD

Over the past 30 years, physical anthropologists have been concerned with the documentation and description of human body size variability and its application to design. A significant problem continues to exist, however, in the communication of such knowledge to the wide variety of potential users, the design community.

The diversity of this group of users is broad, ranging from designers of workspaces such as aircraft cockpits or offices, through pattern makers and clothiers, to designers of respirators and other personal protective equipment. Equally as diverse are the needs of the users. For example, a designer of an office has little use for a dimension such as neck circumference, while a clothier or pattern maker may consider it vital. Furthermore, users often need information about different segments of the population, perhaps about children, coal miners, college students, office workers, factory workers, etc., and each user may require a different type of analysis or data presentation. It is, therefore, extremely helpful for the anthropologist to communicate effectively with each of the many specialists within the specific framework of their particular design problems.

It is thus very gratifying to find that the authors of this book, both experienced professionals in their field, have taken on the complex task of bridging the gap not only by bringing to architects and interior designers much valuable anthropometric information in usable form but, more importantly, by conveying so persuasively the concept that untapped resources of relevant body size information exist and that its use has much potential impact on the improvement of workspace and residential design. In their presentation, the authors strike an excellent balance, avoiding the pitfalls of overwhelming the reader with needless technical complexities and resisting the simple-minded approach which has so often in the past conveyed the mistaken impression that a few tables of summary values will provide the answers to specific design problems.

I have long been an advocate of relating the basic anthropometric data to a specific designer's needs, and the authors' clear treatment for a special audience is particularly gratifying. The real beneficiaries, ultimately, will be office workers, small children, and handicapped persons, to name but a few of the many consumer groups with specialized needs.

John T. McConville, Ph.D.
Anthropology Research Project, Inc.

# ACKNOWLEDGMENTS

Without certain published anthropometric information, this book could not have been written. For this, we would like to express our appreciation to Dr. Howard Stoudt, formerly of the Harvard School of Public Health, and his colleagues, who in conjunction with Jean Roberts of the U.S. Public Health Service prepared a study of the weight, height, and selected body dimensions of adults. This study now constitutes one of the most current and comprehensive sources of published anthropometric data on the civilian population. Our adaptation and metrication of this survey serves as the basis for many of the design reference standards developed in Part C of the book. We would also like to thank Dr. Stoudt, presently a member of the faculty of the department of community health science at Michigan State University, for the additional data he shared with us and for the encouragement he provided during the early stages of the preparation of this book.

With respect to published anthropometric information, we would be remiss in our acknowledgment if we did not mention the three-volume *Anthropometric Source Book,* brilliantly compiled and edited for the National Aeronautics and Space Administration by Dr. John McConville and his colleagues at the Anthropology Research Project, Inc., Yellow Springs, Ohio.

The Aerospace Medical Research Laboratory, Wright-Patterson Air Force Base, Ohio, has also served as a fountainhead of information. We are indebted to Charles E. Clauser, who is presently responsible for the U.S. Air Force's Anthropometry Program, and his colleagues, Dr. Kenneth Kennedy and Milton Alexander, for their comments and encouragement and for making some of their data available to us.

We would also like to express our appreciation to three distinguished human factors engineers whose stimulating articles and books relating to anthropometry and human factors roused our interest and curiosity in investigating the architectural and interior design applications of anthropometric data: Archie Kaplan, Charles Mauro, and Wesley Woodson.

Finally, we would like to thank Carl P. Mason of the Bio-Engineering Research Laboratory of the Veterans Administration Prosthetics

Center; Dr. John Fruin, Research Engineer of The Port of New York and New Jersey Authority and author of *Pedestrian Planning and Design*; and Professor Michael Trencher of the School of Architecture, Pratt Institute, for sharing their technical knowledge with us in connection with certain aspects of our research.

On a more personal note, our amazement and gratitude must be expressed to Jamie Panero, the young son of one of the authors, who with the tenacity of purpose of a graduate research assistant helped in gathering data and was responsible for the metrication of much of the data. A special tribute must also be made to a former student of interior design of both authors, Pamela Kingsbury, who has shouldered the major responsibility for the illustrations, graphics, charts, and layouts. Not only has her technical skill and resourcefulness been of the highest quality, but her unending allegiance to the development of this project has transcended any human understanding of the term "dedication."

# PREFACE

A potential danger in writing a book of this type is dealing with an area of study too large to be treated satisfactorily. Human dimension and interior space, by its very nature, is quite conducive to such an error in judgment. No great leap of the imagination is required to acknowledge the multitude of disciplines implied: ergonomics, anthropometry, biomechanics, architecture, interior design, environmental psychology. The list is almost endless. Each discipline and subareas of those disciplines could in themselves all qualify as legitimate topics for an entire network of books.

The problem, therefore, is to avoid erring in the direction of too large an area of study and risking superficiality or to treat the subject within too narrow a frame of reference by limiting the material too severely. We are hopeful that we have avoided these obvious pitfalls. The measure of success, however, can best be determined within the context of the purpose of this book.

The architectural and interior design professions have an abundance of reference material dealing with general planning and design criteria. Not enough of this material, however, addresses itself specifically to the actual physical fit, or interface, between the human body and the various individual components of interior spaces. Of the available material, much is based almost exclusively on trade practices, many of which are outdated, or on the personal judgments of those preparing the standards. With few exceptions, most reference standards are simply not predicated on enough hard anthropometric data.

This is understandable, given the minimal amount of such data available, the form in which most of these data are presented, the general inaccessibility of such data to the interior designer and architect, and, until very recently, the lack of centralized reference sources for such information. In partial defense, however, of the pragmatic approach underlying the preparation of much of the design standards currently in use, it should be recognized that the use of anthropometric data is no substitute for good design or sound professional judgment. It should be viewed as one of many design tools.

Within recent years and arising out of the pressing need for such information on the part of the equipment designer, industrial designer, and human factors engineer, anthropometric data have become more available. Not all the data are necessarily presented in the form most appropriate for use by the architectural or interior design professions. Nor are all the data necessarily applicable to the nature of the particular design problems peculiar to these professions. Moreover, its availability is still in terms of sources relatively foreign to the architect and interior designer and requires referral to a large variety of such sources for what data there are.

The important fact, however, is that anthropometric data are slowly becoming more available, both on a national and international basis. As the world population continues to grow, as our explorations of outer space increase, as international trade and marketing of services and products expands, and as society generally places more priority on the quality of life, it is expected that the inventory of such data will become even more abundant. Architects and interior designers should avail themselves of these data and become more knowledgeable concerning its applicability to the design process. In addition, they should provide the anthropometrist with input, relative to the type and form of data the profession requires.

In elaborating on the role industrial designers will play in the future development of engineering anthropometry, Mauro indicates the thrust of that role "is in defining their needs in terms that the research anthropometrist can understand." The same should apply to the architect and interior designer.

The general objectives of this book, therefore, are as follows:
1. To develop an awareness on the part of the architect, interior designer, builder, manufacturer, and user of the importance of anthropometry as it relates to human fit and interior space.
2. To provide the architect and interior designer with a basic understanding of anthropometry and the nature, origins, limitations, and proper application of the data involved.
3. To provide the architect and interior designer with a source of the anthropometric data relevant to the nature of those design problems most frequently encountered by those professions and to present those data in an appropriate form.
4. Based on these anthropometric data, to provide the architect and interior designer with a series of graphic design reference standards, involving the interface of the human body with the physical components of some of the prototypical interior spaces in which people live, work, or play.

Accordingly, the book is divided into three major sections. *Part A* familiarizes the architect and interior designer with the elements of anthropometry in terms of theory, limitations, and application. In addition, the special anthropometric problems of physically handicapped and elderly people and of seating are also discussed. *Part B* consists exclusively of hard anthropometric data in the form of tables and related illustrations. *Part C* consists of a series of design reference standards. These standards are in the form of plans and sections of prototypical interior spaces, showing the proper anthropometric relationship between the user and the space.

During the course of developing the necessary research for this book, we found that many of our reasons concerning the need for the architect and interior designer to utilize anthropometric data as a tool in the design process were continually and in some instances, dramatically, reinforced. The urgency for so doing became ever more apparent. We wanted to share some of what we learned and also offer some suggestions for appropriate action that might be taken. Accordingly, the Epilogue contains some jolting examples of how insensitivity to human dimension in the design of various aspects of interior space can result not only in discomfort to the user but, in certain cases, in bodily injury and even death.

# INTRODUCTION

The fascination of philosophers, artists, theoreticians, and architects with human body size dates back many centuries. In the only complete treatise on architecture surviving from antiquity, Vitruvius, who lived in 1st century B.C. Rome, wrote:

> For the human body is so designed by nature that the face, from the chin to the top of the forehead and the lowest roots of the hair, is a tenth part of the whole height; the open hand from the wrist to the tip of the middle finger is just the same; the head from the chin to the crown is an eighth, and with the neck and shoulder from the top of the breast to the lowest roots of the hair is a sixth; from the middle of the breast to the summit of the crown is a fourth. If we take the height of the face itself, the distance from the bottom of the chin to the underside of the nostrils is one third of it; the nose from the underside of the nostrils to a line between the eyebrows is the same; from there to the lowest roots of the hair is also a third, comprising the forehead. The length of the foot is one sixth of the height of the body; of the forearm, one fourth; and the breadth of the breast is also one fourth. The other members, too, have their own symmetrical proportions, and it was by employing them that the famous painters and sculptors of antiquity attained to great and endless renown.
>
> . . . Then again, in the human body the central point is naturally the navel. For if a man be placed flat on his back, with his hands and feet extended, and a pair of compasses centred at his navel, the fingers and toes of his two hands and feet will touch the circumference of a circle described therefrom. And just as the human body yields a circular outline, so too a square figure may be found from it. For if we measure the distance from the soles of the feet to the top of the head, and then apply that measure to the outstretched arms, the breadth will be found to be the same as the height as in the case of plane surfaces which are perfectly square.[1]

Not only was Vitruvius concerned with proportions of the body, but with their metrological implications. In alluding to Greek temple design he tells us, "Moreover, they collected from members of the human body the proportionate dimensions which appear necessary in all building operations, the finger or inch, the palm, the foot, the cubit.[2]

During the Middle Ages, Dionysius, monk of Phourna of Agrapha, wrote of man's body size as "nine heads tall,"[3] and Cennino Cennini,

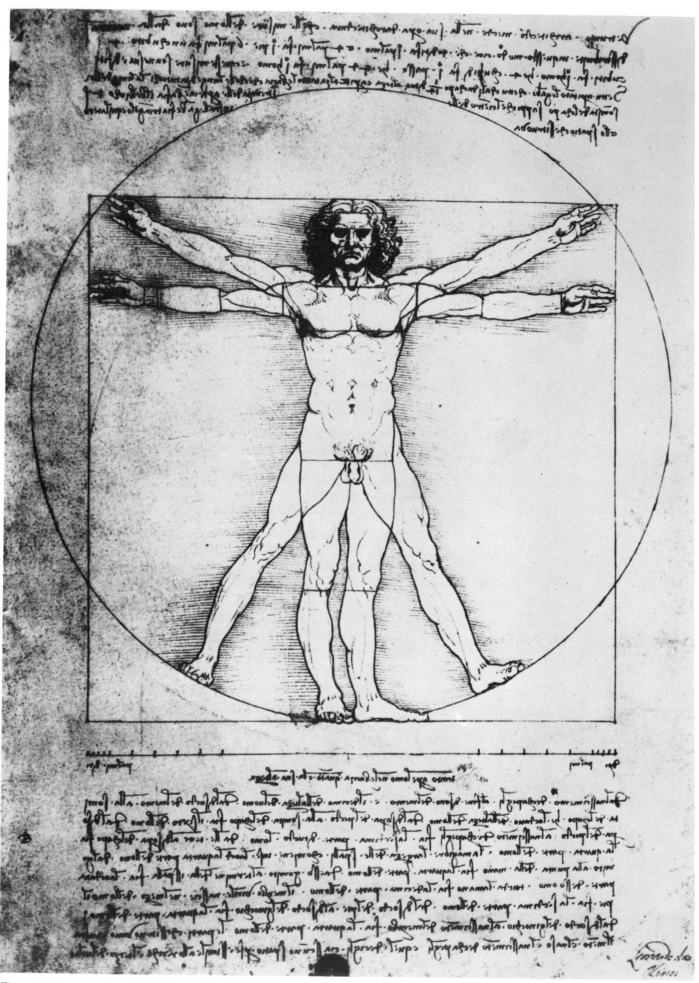

Figure I–1. Leonardo da Vinci's famous drawing of the human figure based on the Vitruvian Norm-Man. Photograph courtesy the Bettmann Archive, Inc.

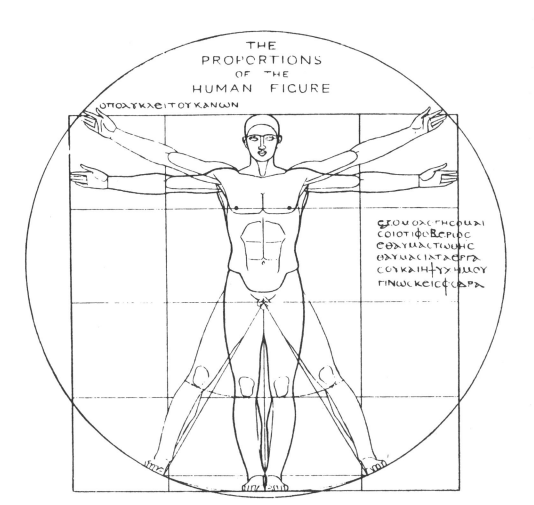

Figure I–2. Vitruvian Man by John Gibson and J. Bonomi, London, 1857.

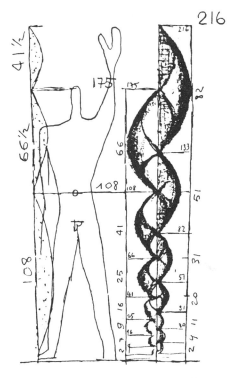

Figure I–3. Modular figure by Le Corbusier.

a 15th-century Italian, described the length of a man as equal to his width with arms extended.[4] During the Renaissance, Leonardo da Vinci created his famous drawing of the human figure, based on the Vitruvian norm-man (Figure I-1). In the mid-19th century John Gibson and J. Bonomi were also to reconstruct the Vitruvian figure (Figure I-2), and later, more than 2000 years after Vitruvius wrote his ten books on architecture, Le Corbusier was to revive interest in the Vitruvian norm with his creation of Modular No. 1 (Figure I-3).

No discussion of body size and proportion, however, would be complete without mention of the so-called Golden Section, the name given in the 19th century to the proportion derived from the divisions of a line into what Euclid in 300 B.C. Greece called "extreme and mean ratio."[5] According to Euclid, a line is cut in such a ratio only when the "whole line is to the greater segment, so is the greater to the less." Although three terms, at least, are required for any proportion, what is unique about the Golden Section is that the third term of the proportion is equal to the sum of the other two.

So fascinating was this notion of the Golden Section that in the early part of the 16th century, Luca Paccoli, a close friend of Leonardo and probably the most famous mathematician of the time, wrote a book about it called *Divina Proportione*[6] (divine proportion) in which he endowed the Golden Section with many varied mystical properties in both science and art. He contended, for example, that he could detect "an aesthetic principle which is found in architectural forms, in the human body, and even in the letters of the Latin alphabet."[7]

It has been claimed that the proportion of the so-called Golden Section is far superior to all other proportions. Actual experiments are said to indicate a preference, on the part of most people, for those proportions closest to Euclid's extreme and mean ratio. While it was employed as a conscious element in architectural design during the Renaissance, the architecture of antiquity, as well as that of the Middle Ages, may also have been designed according to the proportion of the Golden Section. More recently, its most enthusiastic supporter was Le Corbusier, who in 1948 wrote a book dealing with proportions based on it.

The most fascinating observation about the Golden Section, however, involves the human figure. If a horizontal line is drawn through the navel, three different body measurements are produced, as illustrated in Figure I-4. One represents stature, or the distance from the top of the head to the floor. Another represents the distance from the navel to the floor, while the third represents the distance from the top of the head to the navel. It is contended that if actual measurements are substituted for the letters indicated, the ratio of stature to the height of the navel above the floor usually approximates 1.618. The proportion of the three measurements conforms fairly closely to Euclid's extreme and mean ratio.

Despite Vitruvius's attempts to relate the human body to the system of measurements employed by the Greeks in the design of temples, humanity's basic concern with the human figure historically has been more aesthetic than metrological, more involved with proportion than with absolute measurements and function. Over the last several decades, however, concern for human dimensions and body size, as critical factors in the design process, has steadily increased. Nowhere has this concern been greater than in the field of *human factors engineering*, as it is called in the United States, or *ergonomics*, as it is referred to in Europe. It should be noted, however, that concern for body size is only one of several areas of interest to the human factors engineer, or ergonomist, due to the extremely complex nature of those disciplines. According to one definition, "human engineering (human factors engineering, ergonomics, biotechnology) is not a single scientific discipline but a synthesis which integrates the biological sciences—psychology, anthropology, physiology, and medicine—with engineering."[8]

Ergonomics has been defined in one instance as "the technology of work design" that "is based on the human biological sciences: anatomy, physiology and psychology."[9] In another instance, it is defined more simply as "an interdisciplinary science which studies the relationships between people and their environments."[10] Most agree that both terms "human engineering" and "ergonomics" may be used interchangeably, and during the course of this book, both terms will be so used.

The application of human factors engineering has been typically associated with highly complex and limited technological problems in machine and equipment design. The problems have usually involved relatively sophisticated man-machine interface situations: the design of control centers, aircraft cockpits, electronic consoles, and endless numbers and types of military air, ground, and sea vehicles. Yet today human factors engineering relates to the civilian sector as well. The design of consumer products, work environments, transportation vehicles, to name a few, all require human factors input.

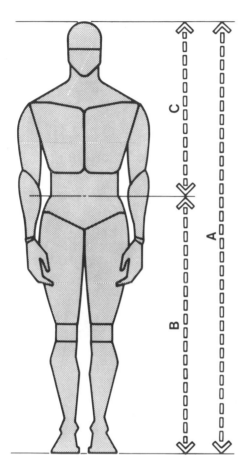

Figure I-4. The human body and the Golden Section.

The field was given enormous impetus during the Second World War due to the compelling need to reconcile human capabilities with the technological sophistication of military equipment. The possibility of human error had to be eliminated. Equipment had to be operated at maximum efficiency under the most trying of circumstances. Problems facing the ergonomist ranged in complexity from a simple control, such as the push button, to complicated console designs for use under battle conditions. More recently, the ergonomist has had to cope with physiological, psychological, and anthropometric (the study of human body measurement, which will be thoroughly discussed in Part A) aspects of design problems inherent in space travel. Of greatest significance, however, was the basic realization and acceptance of the idea that consideration of human factors constituted an integral part of the design process.

Among the most important of these human factors is body size and dimension as it relates to the so-called ergonomic fit, or the *ergofitting*, of the user to the environment—one aspect of the so-called man-machine interface to which the ergonomist constantly alludes.

Most applications of human engineering have, in fact, been in the industrial and military sectors. Unfortunately, the more mundane applications, such as those found in the design of the interior spaces within our homes, offices, health facilities, schools, etc., have been relatively ignored. This is particularly ironic since much of the underlying philosophy of human engineering is based on the premise that everything is designed for people. Where else can the concept of "designing from the man, out" make more sense than in the field of architecture and interior design?

It is the purpose of this book, therefore, to focus on the anthropometric aspects of ergonomics and to apply the related data to the design of interior spaces. The application will take the form of anthropometrically oriented design reference standards structured to ensure a proper ergofitting of people to the interior environments in which they may live, work, or play. These interior environments are all utilized by individuals of varying body sizes, weight, age, and physical condition. On a global basis, users may also reflect a wide range of races, cultures, and ethnic backgrounds.

Despite the variables involved, however, the interface between the user and the designed interior environment, or ergofit, must ensure comfortable, safe, and efficient enjoyment of that environment. Work surface heights in a kitchen, office, or home workshop; allowances for seating around a dining or conference table; heights for shelves in an apartment or library; corridor widths in a home or public building—all must reflect the human factor of body size. In certain situations, we are, for a number of reasons, required to design for a large mixed user population. At the other extreme, we may be obligated to design for a single user. In still other situations, the user may constitute a specific group—young children, elderly people, college students, physically disabled people, etc. It is obvious that if we are to respond responsibly and sensitively to the design needs of the user, we must become more aware of the metrology of body size and its ergonomic implications.

# A HUMAN DIMENSION/

# ANTHROPOMETRICS

# 1 ANTHROPOMETRIC THEORY

## 1.1 ANTHROPOMETRY

People's historic involvement with body size was discussed in the Introduction. However, the science dealing specifically with the measurement of the human body to determine differences in individuals, groups, etc., is termed *anthropometry*. Pioneering work in this field dates back to the Belgian mathematician, Quetlet, who in 1870 published his *Anthropometrie* and is credited not only with founding and formalizing the science, but also with having created the term "anthropometry" itself. The origins of physical anthropology can be traced even further back to the late 18th century and Linne, Buffon, and White, who first developed the science of comparative racial anthropometry.

During the course of time, a significant amount of anthropometric data has been amassed. Unfortunately for the designer, however, the thrust of much of the efforts in this area was for taxonomic purposes, physiological studies, etc., and not primarily for the ergonomic implications of body size. It was not until the 1940s that the need for anthropometric data, generated in a variety of industrial fields, but primarily in the aircraft industry, began to develop and increase. The Second World War naturally provided much of the impetus, and even today it is in the military-industrial sector that much of the anthropometric research is generated. Although the discipline has fallen within the purview of the anthropometrist, anatomist, or ergonomist, it is time for the architect and interior designer to become more aware of the data available and its applicability to the design of interior spaces.

If anthropometry is viewed mainly as exercises in simple measurement and nothing more, one might conclude that the dimensional data could be gathered simply and effortlessly. Nothing, however, could be further from the truth. There are many complicating factors and difficulties involved. One such factor is that body sizes vary with age, sex, race, and even occupational group. For example, Chart 1-1 shows statistics on the statures (body height) of samples from various national groups. The variation in stature is quite significant, ranging from 160.5 cm, or 63.2 in, for the Vietnamese to a high of 179.9 cm, or 70.8 in, for the Belgian—a range of 19.4 cm, or slightly more than 7.5 in.

| Sample | Date | N | Age[a] | Stature Mean | Stature SD |
|---|---|---|---|---|---|
| Republic of Vietnam Armed Forces | 1964 | 2,129 | 27.2 | 160.5 | 5.5 |
| Thailand Armed Forces | 1964 | 2,950 | 24.0 | 163.4 | 5.3 |
| Republic of Korea Army | 1970 | 3,473 | 24.7 | 164.0 | 5.9 |
| Latin America Armed Forces (18 countries) | 1967 | 733 | 23.1 | 166.4 | 6.1 |
| Iran Armed Forces | 1970 | 9,414 | 23.8 | 166.8 | 5.8 |
| Japan JASDF pilots | 1962 | 239 | 24.1 | 166.9 | 4.8 |
| India Army | 1969 | 4,000 | 27.0 | 167.5 | 6.0 |
| Republic of Korea ROKAF pilots | 1961 | 264 | 28.0 | 168.7 | 4.6 |
| Turkey Armed Forces | 1963 | 915 | 24.1 | 169.3 | 5.7 |
| Greece Armed Forces | 1963 | 1,084 | 22.9 | 170.5 | 5.9 |
| Italy Armed Forces | 1963 | 1,358 | 26.5 | 170.6 | 6.2 |
| France Flight personnel | 1955 | 7,084 | 18-45 | 171.3 | 5.8 |
| U.S. Army WWI demobilization | 1921 | 96,596 | 24.9 | 172.0 | 6.7 |
| Australia Army | 1970 | 3,695 | 21.0 | 173.0 | 6.0 |
| U.S. civilian men Nat'l. Health Survey | 1965 | 3,091 | 44.0 | 173.2 | 7.2 |
| U.S. Army WWII separatees | 1951 | 24,508 | 24.3 | 173.9 | 6.4 |
| U.S. Army Ground troops | 1971 | 6,682 | 22.2 | 174.5 | 6.6 |
| U.S. Army Aviators | 1971 | 1,482 | 26.2 | 174.6 | 6.3 |
| Fed. Rep. of Germany Army tank crews | 1965 | 300 | 22.8 | 174.9 | 6.1 |
| U.S. Air Force Flight personnel | 1954 | 4,062 | 27.9 | 175.5 | 6.2 |
| United Kingdom RAF and RN air crew | 1968 | 200 | 28.7 | 177.0 | 6.1 |
| United Kingdom RAF pilots | 1965 | 4,357 | — | 177.2 | 6.2 |
| U.S. Air Force Flight personnel | 1972 | 2,420 | 30.0 | 177.3 | 6.2 |
| Canada RCAF pilots | 1965 | 314 | — | 177.4 | 6.1 |
| Norway Young men | 1964 | 5,765 | 20.0 | 177.5 | 6.0 |
| Belgium Flight personnel | 1954 | 2,450 | 17-50 | 179.9 | 5.8 |

[a] Mean values except where ranges are given.

Chart 1–1. Statistics on the statures in centimeters and certain other characteristics of 26 samples. From Chapanis, *Ethnic Variables in Human Factors Engineering.*

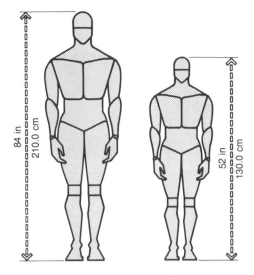

Figure 1–1. Comparison of difference in stature of the tallest Northern Nilote of Southern Sudan with the stature of the smallest Pigmy of Central Africa. Data from Chapanis, *Ethnic Variables in Human Factors Engineering*.

Perhaps an even more dramatic example of ethnic variability, however, is a comparison of the difference in stature of the smallest males on record with the largest, as shown in Figure 1-1. D.F. Roberts notes that the former, the Pigmies of Central Africa, have a mean stature of 143.8 cm, or about 56.6 in, while the tallest males, for whom records are available, are the Northern Nilotes of Southern Sudan, with a mean stature of 182.9 cm, or 72 in—a range of 39.1 cm, or about 15.4 in.[1]

Age is another significant factor in body size. Full growth, with respect to body dimensions, peaks in the late teens and early twenties for males and usually a few years earlier for females. Subsequent to maturity, body dimension for both sexes actually decreases with age, as illustrated in Figure 1-2. In terms of the anthropometry of elderly people, a study in England suggested that body size of elderly women was smaller than the body size of young women. It was also pointed out, however, that to some extent the difference could be attributable not only to the fact that the elderly sample was obviously drawn from an earlier generation but to the aging process itself. Another conclusion of the study was the reduction in upward reach among elderly people.

Socioeconomic factors also impact significantly on body dimensions. The nutrition available to those with higher incomes creates, for example, freedom from childhood disease and contributes to body growth, as illustrated in Figure 1-3. Socioeconomic status also reflects a relationship to the availability of higher education. Accordingly, studies made of college students almost always indicate higher statures than noncollege individuals. Yet, within the same group, variations in body size are so significant that "averages" are not necessarily meaningful or sufficient. To all this must be added such other considerations as the actual physical conditions under which

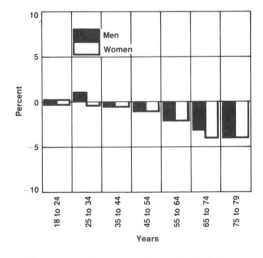

Figure 1–2. Relative change in height with age over the mean for men and women aged 18–24 years. Data from National Health Survey.

Figure 1–3. Bar graphs showing mean height and weight for U.S. children 6 to 11 years by annual family income and education of parents. Data from National Health Survey.

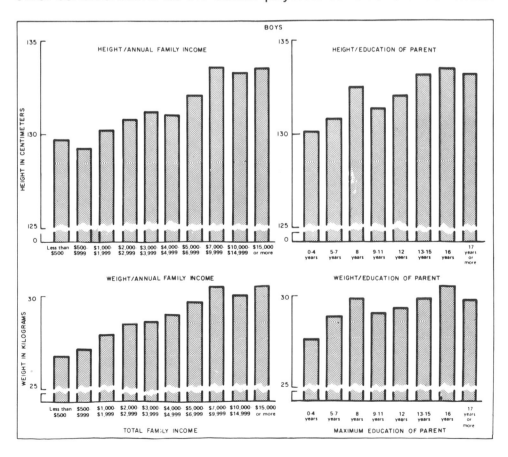

data are recorded. Was the subject clothed or nude? If clothed, was the clothing light or heavy? Was the subject barefooted?

Although there have been some national and international attempts at standardization among anthropometrists, with regard to terminology and definitions, the lack thereof very often complicates the interpretation and significance of the data recorded. Studies, therefore, must often include descriptions of techniques used and diagrams necessary to clearly define the actual points from which measurements were taken. There is no doubt that anthropometric studies are no less sophisticated or tedious than other investigations in the biological sciences. When one considers that the anthropometrist must also be knowledgeable in the area of statistical methodology, the complexity and tediousness of the discipline is underscored even more. It is also obvious that those individuals taking and recording body measurements must be properly trained.

To the interior designer, architect, and industrial designer, however, it should be evident that the same factors that contribute to the complexity and tediousness of the discipline of anthropometry also necessitate a very cautious approach in the application of the data generated. It is essential, therefore, that the designer have some understanding of anthropometrics, its basic vocabulary, the nature of the data available, the forms in which it is usually presented, and the restraints involved in their application.

## 1.2 SOURCES OF DATA

Generally, the collection of anthropometric data is a costly, time-consuming, and relatively cumbersome undertaking, requiring skilled observers, particularly if the objective is to obtain a truly representative national sampling. Accordingly, most of the research in this area has been related to the military rather than the civilian sectors of the world's population. The reasons are obvious. First, it is within these sectors that a compelling need for anthropometric data exists in order to properly equip and clothe the respective armies, navies, and air forces. Second, there exists a national and almost infinite reservoir of available subjects. Third, the funds to implement the studies are committed and made available by the governments involved.

The basic disadvantage in mass military surveys of this kind is usually the restrictions of sex and age. In addition, the measurements have often been limited to height and weight and in many instances have been gathered by unskilled observers. In 1919, however, a survey was made of some 100,000 American troops upon discharge from the service. Reportedly, it was the first study to include measurements other than height and weight.[2] The study was intended for use as a guide in the design of clothing but was never actually used for that. It did, however, during the period between the First and Second World Wars, serve as a standard description of U.S. males.

Most of the early and more successful applications of anthropometry to design actually took place during the Second World War and were predicated on studies prepared by the United States Air Force, the Royal Air Force, and the British Navy. Apparently, this period was a turning point because since that time, the United States, in addition to many other countries, has conducted extensive military anthropometric studies. A 1946 study by Randall, Damon, Benton, and Patt, "Human Body Size in Military Aircraft and Personnel Equipment," has been cited as a major contribution in this area.[3]

Relatively few civilian anthropometric surveys, however, have been taken. Perhaps the most current and complete study of the civilian population of the United States—the National Health Survey—was prepared for the Department of Health, Education, and Welfare (HEW) by Dr. Howard W. Stoudt, Dr. Albert Damon, and Dr. Ross McFarland formerly of the Harvard School of Public Health and Jean Roberts of the U.S. Public Health Service.[4] This study involved a nationwide probability sample of over 7500 nonmilitary and noninstitutionalized people between the ages of 18 and 79 years, of which 6 672 were examined.

Most anthropometric research, nevertheless, is still being done for the military. All branches of the service have active programs, and in many instances will share their data with professionals in the private sector. An excellent example is the three-volume *Anthropometric Source Book* published by the National Aeronautics and Space Administration. This book is probably the most comprehensive source of summarized body size data currently in existence anywhere in the world.[5] Appendix 1 lists military anthropometry laboratories, as well as other national and international sources of anthropometric data. The designer should use the data cautiously and, in instances where the nature of the design problem requires more sophisticated data, consult with a qualified professional in the field of anthropometry.

### 1.3 TYPE OF DATA

Human body dimensions that impact on the design of interior spaces are of two basic types—structural and functional. *Structural* dimensions, sometimes referred to as "static" dimensions, include measurements of the head, torso, and limbs in standard positions. *Functional* dimensions, also referred to as "dynamic" dimensions, as the term suggests, include measurements taken in working positions or during the movement associated with certain tasks. The former are simpler and more readily obtained, while the latter are normally far more complicated. Figures 1-4 through 1-6 illustrate the basic anthropometric instruments usually employed in the measurement of body parts and their use. There are more sophisticated measuring devices and techniques, such as multiple probe contour devices, photometric camera systems, andrometric camera systems, stereophotogrammetry, but their use is not presently widespread.

A glance at any anatomy textbook is sufficient to suggest the endless number of body dimensions possible. One recent publication contains almost one thousand measurements.[6] The number of possibilities and the exotic medical terminology involved can be somewhat intimidating for the designer. For example, the "crinion-menton" is the term for the distance between the hair line in the middle of the forehead and the midpcint of the lower edge of the chin, while the "menton-supramentale" is the distance from the angle between the chin and the lower lip to the lower edge of the chin. Such data might be extremely useful to a designer of a helmet for a pressurized spacesuit, but would be of little value to an interior designer.

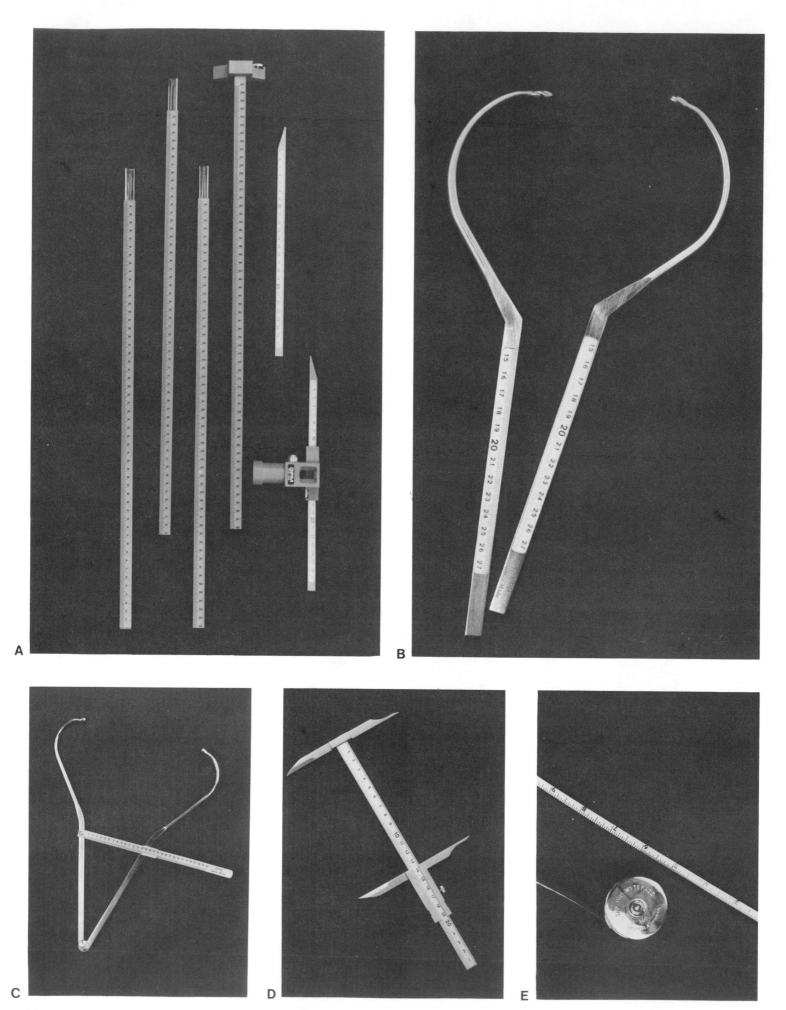

Figure 1–4. A common set of anthropometric instruments (courtesy Pfister Import-Export Inc., 450 Barrel Ave., Carlstadt, N.J. 07072). (a) Anthropometer; (b) curved branches for anthropometer; (c) spreading calipers; (d) sliding compass; (e) anthropometric tape.

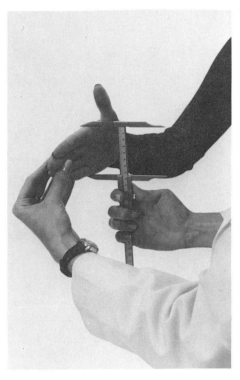

Figure 1–6. Interior design students at the Fashion Institute of Technology illustrating the use of the sliding compass for measuring hand breadth.

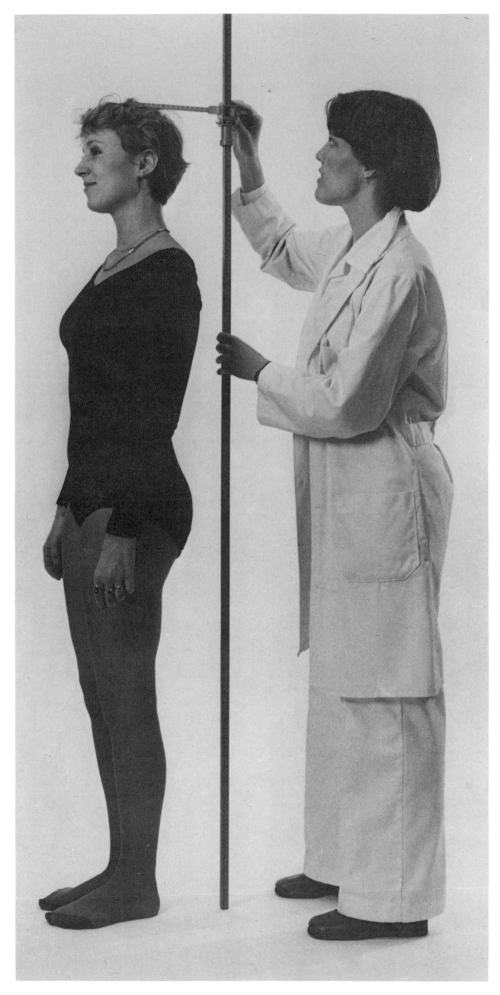

Figure 1–5. Interior design students at the Fashion Institute of Technology illustrating the use of the anthropometer.

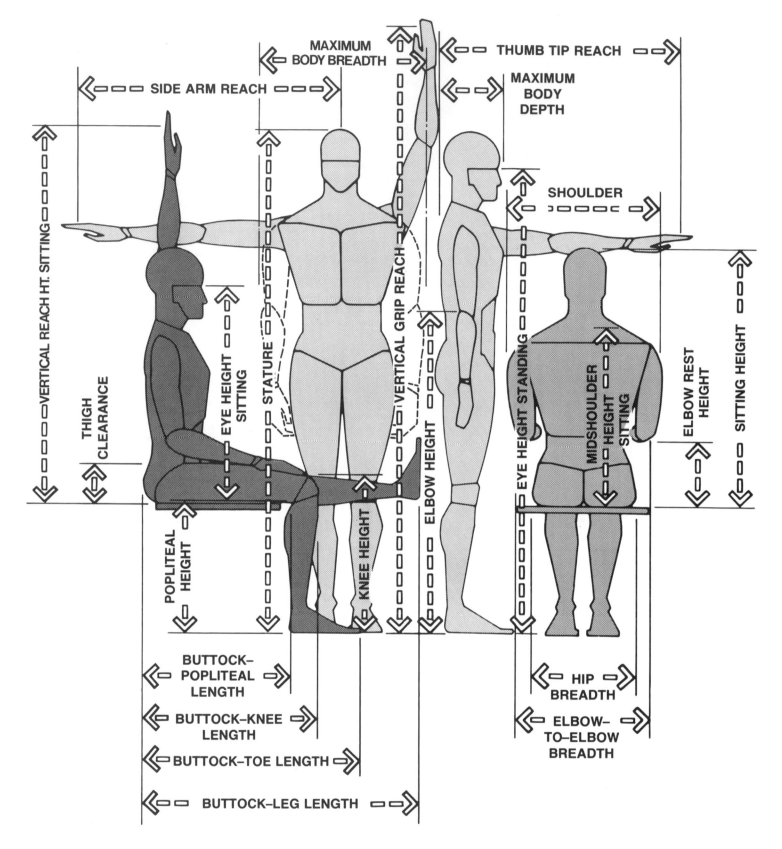

Figure 1–7. Body measurements of most use to the designer of interior spaces.

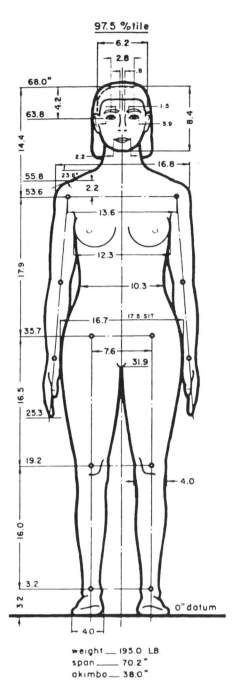

97.5 %tile

weight ___ 195.0 LB
span _____ 70.2"
akimbo ___ 38.0"

Figure 1–8. Anthropometric data of a standing adult female. Drawing from Henry Dreyfuss, *The Measure of Man*, 1978.

Similarly, "interpupillary diameter," the distance between the centers of the pupils, will be of far more value to the designer of optical equipment than to an architect.

Damon et al. contend that "if one wishes to describe a group for human engineering purposes, the ten most important dimensions to obtain are in order: height; weight; sitting height; buttock-knee and buttock-popliteal lengths; breadths across elbows and hips, seated; knee and popliteal heights; and thigh clearance height."[7] These ten measurements are equally essential to the design of interiors.

Figure 1-7 indicates all those body measurements that are of the most significance to the architect, interior designer, or industrial designer. The necessary data for these measurements are developed in the various tables in Part B of this book. Table 1 in Part B, entitled "Metrological Analysis," defines the terms and discusses the application and design implication of the data.

## 1.4 PRESENTATION OF DATA

Generally, anthropometric data for use by the designer may be presented in graphic form, as in the well-known Dreyfuss figure (Figure 1-8), or in a tabular form (Figure 1-9). When data are initially recorded, however, their form, of necessity, is statistically disorganized. Figure 1-10 is an example of a form used to record initial data. Subsequently, the data are then reorganized in a more orderly and logical manner. With regard to anthropometric data, it is usually restructured to indicate frequency, as illustrated in Figure 1-11. Since individual body sizes and measurements vary greatly within any population, it is not practical to design for the entire group. Consequently, statistical distribution of body sizes is of great interest to the designer in establishing design standards and making design decisions.

The restructured array of data in the form of a frequency table, as shown on Figure 1-11, begins to suggest the pattern of distribution. The array of data lists, in order of magnitude from smallest to largest, certain height intervals in inches for army aviators and the corresponding number of instances in which such measurements were observed. Certain information can be immediately noted. The smallest height interval is from 158.8 to 160.5 cm, or 62.5 to 63.2 in, while the tallest interval is between 191.3 and 193 cm, or 75.3 and 76.0 in. It

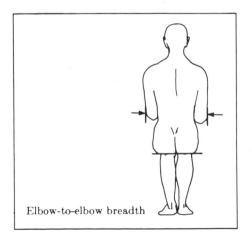

Elbow-to-elbow breadth

ELBOW-TO-ELBOW BREADTH OF U.S. MALE MILITARY AND CIVILIAN SAMPLES

| Population | Percentiles (in.) | | | | | S.D. |
|---|---|---|---|---|---|---|
| | 1st | 5th | 50th | 95th | 99th | |
| Air Force personnel [1] | 14.5 | 15.2 | 17.2 | 19.8 | 20.9 | 1.42 |
| Cadets [2] | 14.4 | 15.1 | 16.7 | 18.4 | 19.1 | - - - - |
| Gunners [2] | 13.9 | 14.6 | 16.4 | 18.2 | 18.9 | - - - - |
| Army personnel: | | | | | | |
| Separatees, white [3] | 14.4 | 15.3 | 17.4 | 20.3 | 21.8 | 1.54 |
| Separatees, Negro [4] | 14.4 | 15.1 | 16.9 | 19.3 | 20.4 | 1.28 |
| Truck and bus drivers [5] | 13.8 | 14.9 | 17.5 | 20.7 | 22.2 | - - - - |

[1] Hertzberg et al. (1954).     [4] USA (1946).
[2] Randall et al. (1946).     [5] McFarland et al. (1958).
[3] Newman and White (1951).

Figure 1–9. Elbow-to-elbow breadth data presented in tabular form with accompanying diagram of human figure to explain measurement. Diagram and table from Van Cott and Kinkale, *Human Engineering Guide to Equipment Design*, 1972, p. 507.

| IF NO REPORT ✓ | REASON FOR NO REPORT | PROCEDURE | RECORDING | CODE |
|---|---|---|---|---|
| | | 9.  Height | [ ] cm.  Height decreased by  Curved Spine [ ]  NO [ ]  Deformed Legs [ ] | |
| | | 10.  Weight | [ ] Lbs. | |

| IF NO REPORT ✓ | REASON FOR NO REPORT | MEASUREMENT | RECORDING IN Cm. | FOR OFFICE USE | CODE |
|---|---|---|---|---|---|
| | | 11.  Sitting height normal | — — — . — | | |
| | | 12.  Sitting height erect | — — — . — | | |
| | | 13.  Knee height* | — — — . — | | |
| | | 14.  Popliteal height | — — — . — | | |
| | | 15.  Thigh clearance height | — — — . — | | |
| | | 16.  Buttock-knee length | — — . — | ✕ | |
| | | 17.  Buttock-popliteal length | — — . — | ✕ | |
| | | 18.  Seat breadth (across hips) | — — . — | ✕ | |
| | | 19.  Elbow-to-elbow breadth | — — . — | ✕ | |
| | | 20.  Elbow rest height | — — — . — | | |

Figure 1–10. An example of a recording form used in an anthropometric study. From National Health Survey.

| Interval | Midpoint | Frequency |
|----------|----------|-----------|
| 62.5–63.2 | 62.85 | 1 |
| 63.3–64.0 | 63.65 | 3 |
| 64.1–64.8 | 64.45 | 3 |
| 64.9–65.6 | 65.25 | 16 |
| 65.7–66.4 | 66.05 | 20 |
| 66.5–67.2 | 66.85 | 47 |
| 67.3–68.0 | 67.65 | 48 |
| 68.1–68.8 | 68.45 | 64 |
| 68.9–69.6 | 69.25 | 73 |
| 69.7–70.4 | 70.05 | 63 |
| 70.5–71.2 | 70.85 | 48 |
| 71.3–72.0 | 71.65 | 43 |
| 72.1–72.8 | 72.45 | 37 |
| 72.9–73.6 | 73.25 | 14 |
| 73.7–74.4 | 74.05 | 10 |
| 74.5–75.2 | 74.85 | 9 |
| 75.3–76.0 | 75.65 | 1 |

Figure 1–11. Example of a frequency table of the standing height in inches of Army aviators. The frequency figures indicate the number of measurements within each interval. From Roebuck, Kroemer, Thomson, *Engineering Anthropometry Methods,* 1975, p. 134.

can also be observed that the number of cases in which these particular extreme high and low measurements occurred were minimal.

The data, however, particularly the nature of the distribution, can be communicated more effectively by means of "column diagrams," or "frequency histograms," as illustrated in Figure 1-12. The heights of the bars vary in order to indicate the frequency or number of cases for each interval, while the width of the bars are equal. It is also possible to use a curve, in lieu of bars, by plotting the frequency against the midpoint for each interval, as shown by the broken line in the figure. This resulting configuration is known as a "frequency polygon."

Despite the variation, the general pattern of distribution of anthropometric data, as with many other types of data, is fairly predictable and approximates the so-called Gaussian distribution. Such distribution, when presented graphically, in terms of frequency of occurrence versus magnitude, usually resembles a bell-shaped symmetrical curve. The significance of the bell-shaped configuration is that the large percentage of the distribution is somewhere in the middle, with a few extremes at either end of the scale, as illustrated in Figure 1-13.

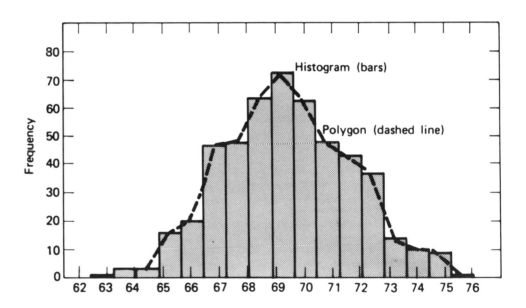

Figure 1–12. Example of a frequency histogram and polygon. From Roebuck, Kroemer, Thomson, *Engineering Anthropometry Methods,* 1975, p. 135.

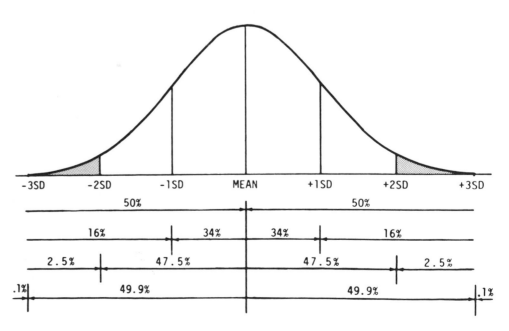

Figure 1–13. Example of areas under a normal curve. Most human dimensions, in a normally distributed group, follow the bell-shaped configuration. A small number of measurements appear at either end of the scale, but most are grouped within the middle portion. Drawing adapted from NASA, *Anthropometric Source Book,* vol. 1.

## 1.5 PERCENTILES

Due to the significant variations in individual body size, "averages" are obviously of little use to the designer and it is necessary, instead, to deal with range. Statistically, it has been shown that human body measurements in any given population will be distributed so that they will fall somewhere in the middle, while a small number of extreme measurements may fall at either end of the spectrum. Since it is impractical to design for the entire population, it is necessary to select a segment from the middle portion. Accordingly, it is fairly common today to omit the extremes at both ends and to deal with 90 percent of the population group.

Most anthropometric data, therefore, are quite often expressed in terms of percentiles. The population is divided, for study purposes, into 100 percentage categories, ranked from least to greatest, with respect to some specific type of body measurement. The first percentile in stature or height, for example, indicates that 99 percent of the study population would have heights of greater dimension. Similarly, a 95th percentile height would indicate that only 5 percent of the study population would have heights greater and that 95 percent of the study population would have the same or lesser heights. Percentiles "indicate the percentage of persons within the population who have a body dimension of a certain size (or smaller)."[8] The *Anthropometric Source Book* published by the National Aeronautics and Space Administration (NASA) defines percentiles in the following manner:

> The definition of the percentiles is fairly simple. For any set of data—the weights of a group of pilots, for example—the first percentile is a value which is, on the one hand, greater than the weights of each of the lightest 1% of the pilots and is, on the other hand, less than the weights of each of the heaviest 99% of these men. Similarly, the second percentile is greater than each of the lightest 2% and less than each of the heaviest 98%. Whatever the value of K—from 1 to 99—the K-th percentile is a value greater than each of the smallest k% of the weights and less than the largest (100 K)%. The 50th percentile, which we encountered among the averages as the median, is a value dividing a set of data into two groups containing the smallest and largest 50% of the values.[9]

A 50th percentile rating represents fairly closely the average value of a dimension for a certain group, but under no circumstances should be misinterpreted as suggesting that the "average man" has the body dimension indicated. This fallacy of the "average man" will be amplified later in Section 2.2.

When dealing with percentiles, two important factors should be kept in mind. Firstly, anthropometric percentiles on actual individuals refer to only one body dimension. This may be stature or sitting height, for example. Secondly, there is no such thing as a 95th percentile or 90th percentile or 5 percentile person. These are mythical figures. An individual having a 50th percentile stature dimension might have a 40th percentile knee height or a 60th percentile hand length, as suggested in Figure 1-14. The graph in Figure 1-15, representing actual data of three individuals, reinforces the mythical aspect of percentile people with respect to all body dimensions. Examination of the graph and its very pronounced angular and uneven path clearly indicates

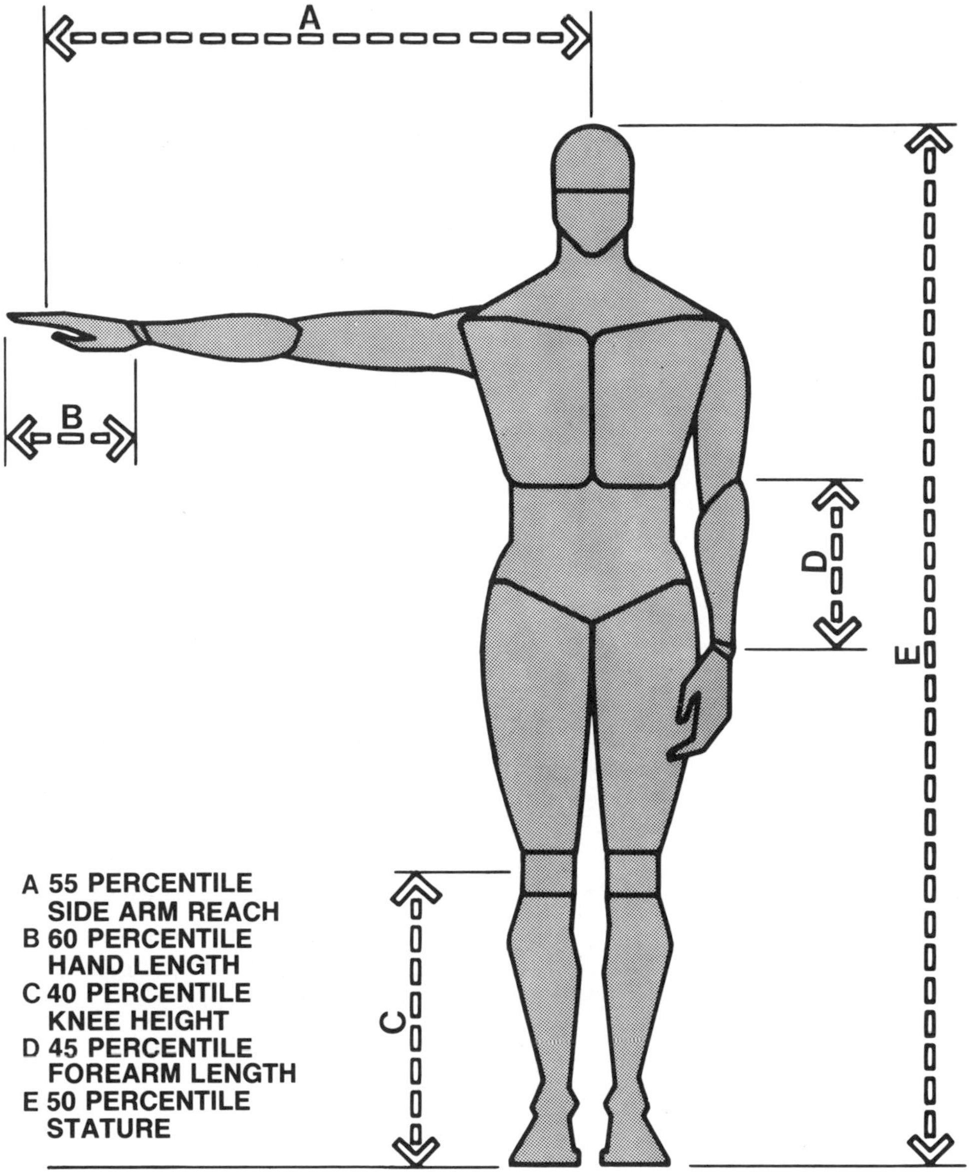

Figure 1–14. Humans are not, in reality, normally distributed in all body dimensions. As the illustration indicates, a person with a 50th percentile stature may well have a 55th percentile side arm reach.

A 55 PERCENTILE SIDE ARM REACH
B 60 PERCENTILE HAND LENGTH
C 40 PERCENTILE KNEE HEIGHT
D 45 PERCENTILE FOREARM LENGTH
E 50 PERCENTILE STATURE

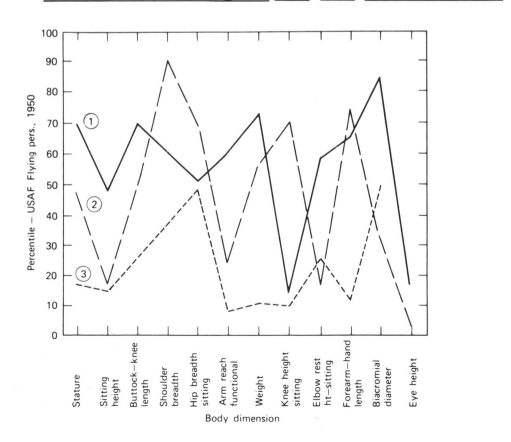

Figure 1–15. A graph indicating the percentiles for the various body dimensions of three actual individuals. Each graph line represents one person. Note that the individual represented by the solid line, for example, shows a 70th percentile buttock-knee length, a 15th percentile knee-height sitting, and a 60th percentile shoulder height. If all the body dimensions were equivalent to the same percentile, that fact would be shown in a straight horizontal line across the graph. Drawing from Roebuck, Kroemer, Thomson, *Engineering Anthropometry Methods,* 1975, p. 172.

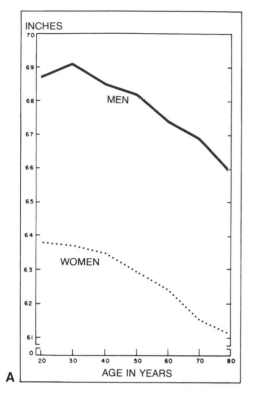

**A**

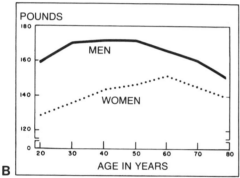

**B**

Figure 1–16. (*a*) The graph indicates that men as a group are generally taller than women as a group and that the height of both men and women decreases with age. From National Health Survey. (*b*) The graph indicates that men as a group are heavier than women as a group and that the body weight of both men and women decreases with age. From National Health Survey.

that each of the three individuals has a differing percentile ranking for each of the body dimensions shown.

## 1.6 VARIABILITY AND RELIABILITY

As discussed earlier in this section, a number of factors can cause significant variations in human body size. Individuals from one part of the country may be taller and heavier than those from another part. A socioeconomic study has indicated a significant difference in stature between people having different occupations. A comparison in stature between truck drivers and research workers, for example, indicated that the latter, as a group, were taller than the former. The military, as a group, differs anthropometrically from the civilian population.[10] Men within the same group are usually taller and heavier than the women within that group, and elderly people differ in body size from the middle-aged (Figure 1-16). Moreover, measurements of general body sizes within a country may change over a period of time. American soldiers in the Second World War were proven to be taller and heavier than soldiers of the First World War (Figure 1-17). It has been demonstrated that ethnicity is also an extremely significant factor in body size. This has been an area of such growing concern and interest to ergonomists the world over that in 1972 the first international symposium on "natural and cultural variables in human factors engineering" was held in The Netherlands under the auspices of the North Atlantic Treaty Organization. Body size was one of five topics discussed. Papers delivered at that symposium revealed some very substantial anthropometric differences among the various populations of the world.

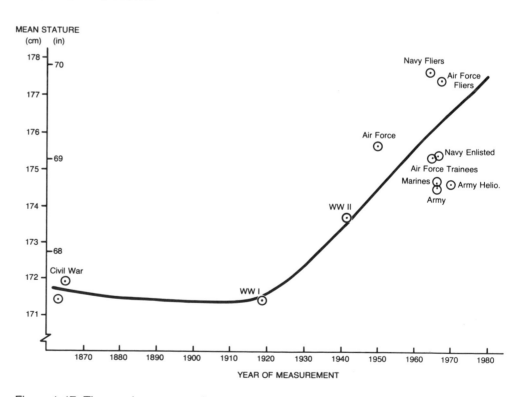

Figure 1–17. The graph compares the mean stature for young U.S. males with the year of measurement. The trend, referred to as "secular change," indicates a growth in the stature of U.S. males from generation to generation. A publication of the National Center for Health Statistics (Hammill et al., 1976), however, concludes that the secular growth trend appears to have stopped in American children born after 1955–1956. Graph adapted from NASA, *Anthropometric Source Book,* vol. 1.

# 2 ANTHROPOMETRIC DATA/

# APPLICATION

## 2.1 APPROPRIATENESS

It is essential, due to the many variables involved, that the data selected be appropriate to the user of the space or furniture to be designed. It becomes necessary, therefore, for the intended user population to be properly defined in terms of such factors as age, sex, occupation, and ethnicity. If the user is an individual, or constitutes a very small group, it may, in certain situations, be feasible to develop your own primary anthropometric data by actually having individual body measurements taken. Surely, if one is prepared to take the time to be fitted for a dress or a suit, one should be willing to spend the time to be fitted for an interior environment or components of that environment, particularly since, in most cases, the latter will reflect a far greater financial investment. The measurements, in the event individual data are generated, should, however, be taken with proper instruments by a trained observer. In situations where specific body dimensions or other data for a particular user population are unavailable, and both time and funds prevent undertaking sophisticated studies, an engineering anthropometrist can be consulted to discuss the statistical methods of obtaining the necessary information.

## 2.2 "AVERAGE MAN" FALLACY

As suggested previously, a very serious error in the application of data is to assume that the 50th percentile dimensions represent the measurements of an "average man" and to create a design to accommodate 50th percentile data. The fallacy in such an assumption is that by prior definition 50 percent of the group may suffer. There simply is no "average man." Depending on the nature of the design problem, the design should usually be conceived to accommodate the 5th or the 95th percentile, so that the greatest portion of the population is served.

Dr. H. T. E. Hertzberg, one of the country's most distinguished research physical anthropologists, in discussing the so-called average man, indicated, "there is really no such thing as an 'average' man or woman. There are men who are average in weight, or in stature, or in

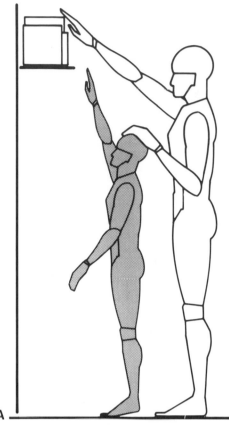

A

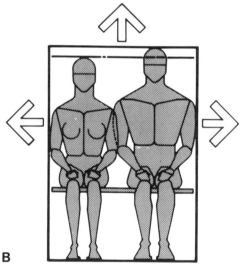

B

Figure 2–1. (a) People of smaller body dimensions and, correspondingly, the lower-range percentile data should be used to establish dimensions where reach is the determining factor. (b) Larger-size people and, correspondingly, the high percentile range data should be used in establishing clearance dimensions.

sitting height, but the men who are average in two dimensions constitute only about 7 percent of the population; those in three, only about 3 percent; those in four, less than 2 percent. There are no men average in as few as 10 dimensions. Therefore, the concept of the 'average' man is fundamentally incorrect, because no such creature exists. Work places to be efficient should be designed according to the measured range of body size."[1]

## 2.3 REACH, CLEARANCE, AND ADJUSTABILITY

The selection of appropriate anthropometric data is based on the nature of the particular design problem under consideration. If the design requires the user to reach from a seated or standing position, the 5th percentile data should be utilized. Such data for arm reach indicates that 5 percent of the population would have an arm reach of short (or shorter) dimension, while 95 percent of the population, the overwhelming majority, would have longer arm reaches. If the design in a reach situation can accommodate the user with the shortest arm reach, obviously it will function for the users with longer reaches as well; it is equally obvious that the opposite is not true, as shown in Figure 2.1a.

In designs where clearance is the primary consideration, the larger or 95th percentile data should be used. The logic is simple. If the design will allow adequate clearance for the users with the largest body size, it would also allow clearance for those users with smaller body size. Here, too, it can be seen from Figure 2-1b that the opposite is not true.

In other situations it may be desirable to provide the design with a built-in adjustment capability. Certain chair types, adjustable shelves, etc., are examples of such. The range of adjustment should be based on the anthropometrics of the user, the nature of the task, and the physical or mechanical limitations involved. The range should allow the design to accommodate at least 90 percent of the user population involved, or more.

It should be noted that all the foregoing examples were used primarily to illustrate the basic logic underlying the selection of the body dimensions involved and the particular percentiles to be accommodated. Wherever possible, however, it is naturally more desirable to accommodate the greatest percentage of the user population. In this regard, there is no substitute for common sense. If a shelf can just as easily be placed an inch or two lower, without significantly impacting on other design or cost factors, thereby accommodating 98 or 99 percent of the user population, obviously that is the correct design decision.

## 2.4 THE HIDDEN DIMENSIONS

Applied anthropometry can serve as an extremely helpful tool in the design process, if used intelligently and within the larger perspective of all the other human factors that impact on that process. In fitting the body to the environment, the factors involved in the tailoring of that fit cannot be limited to measurements and distances in the absolute sense of the meaning of those terms. Distance and, by exten-

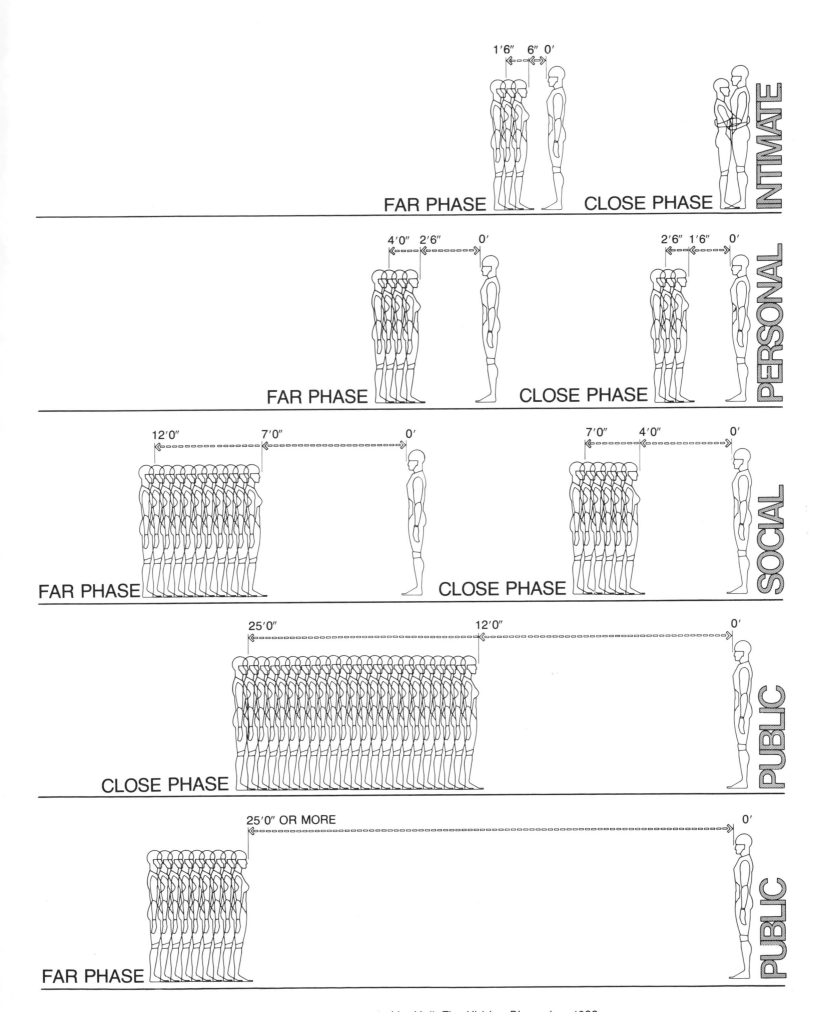

INTIMATE

FAR PHASE — 1'6" 6" 0' — CLOSE PHASE

PERSONAL

4'0" 2'6" 0'
FAR PHASE

2'6" 1'6" 0'
CLOSE PHASE

SOCIAL

12'0" 7'0" 0'
FAR PHASE

7'0" 4'0" 0'
CLOSE PHASE

PUBLIC

25'0" 12'0" 0'
CLOSE PHASE

PUBLIC

25'0" OR MORE 0'
FAR PHASE

Figure 2–2. Graphic illustration of the distance zones suggested by Hall, *The Hidden Dimension*, 1966.

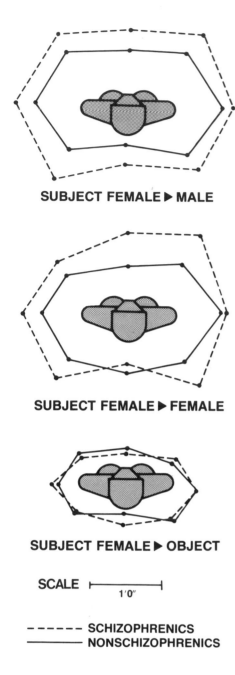

**SUBJECT FEMALE ▶ MALE**

**SUBJECT FEMALE ▶ FEMALE**

**SUBJECT FEMALE ▶ OBJECT**

SCALE ├─────┤
1'0"

- - - - - SCHIZOPHRENICS
───────── NONSCHIZOPHRENICS

Figure 2–3. Horowitz et al. "body buffer zone." The diagrams depict the mean of the approach of the subjects over a three-day period. Although the schizophrenic group had a significantly greater buffer zone area, both groups approached the inanimate object more closely than the animate object. No significant difference between approaches to male or female was found in either group. One of the hypotheses emerging from the finding was that "an area of personal space appears to surround every individual, which seems to be reproducible and may be regarded as an immediate 'body-buffer zone.'" Adapted from *Archives of General Psychiatry.*

sion, clearance and space generally have many other more sophisticated and subtle connotations.

There are, as Hall suggests, "hidden dimensions." To assume that people's boundaries begin and end with the skin is to fail to "grasp the significance of the many elements that contribute to man's sense of space." Hall, by way of example, contends that people function within four "distance" zones, each of which has a "near" and "far" phase. The zone selected for use at any one time is predicated on the nature of the activity or social transaction in progress.[2] Figure 2-2 illustrates the zones referred to by Hall as well as the activities usually associated with each.

Some years ago, Horowitz et al. contended that each human being has an internal projection of the space immediately around him or her. They termed the space the "body buffer zone" and suggested that its size, shape, and penetrability were related to the immediate interpersonal events and the individual's psychological and cultural history. Individuals, they held, tend to keep a characteristic distance between themselves and other people and inanimate objects. This contention was demonstrated in an experiment they conducted at a U.S. naval hospital. Under the pretext that their equilibrium was to be studied, subjects were instructed to either "walk over to Smith (or a hatrack that was intentionally located in the area) while we check your equilibrium." In actuality, however, measurements of the distance left between the subjects and the person or hatrack, after completing their approach across the room, were taken. The subjects were taken from two groups. One consisted of 19 patients with an established diagnosis of schizophrenia. The other group were nonschizophrenic people of similar backgrounds. The results revealed that both groups approached the hatrack significantly closer than they did the person. In addition, the tests indicated that when approaching another person, there was definitely an area beyond which they would not go,[3] as indicated in Figure 2-3.

Dr. John J. Fruin, in studying pedestrian movements and "queuing," talks of "touch," "no-touch," "personal comfort," and "circulation" zones, as illustrated in Figures 2-4 through 2-7.[4] The term "flight distance" has been used to describe the distance that organisms usually place between themselves and other organisms. Sommer studied "personal distance" and observed interaction between subjects seated around a table in terms of their particular locations around that table. Figure 2-8 shows the seating arrangement. It was observed that the greatest frequency of conversation occurred across the corners AB, AH, EF, and ED.[5]

## 2.5 PEOPLE IN MOTION

In an article dealing with design and human locomotion, Archie Kaplan writes:

> Movement is the natural state of man and the basis of his being. Human life represents no static state; from the blink of an eye to top speed running, in sleep or wakefulness, man is in motion. . . .[6]

With this in mind, it should be recognized that in addition to the psychological factors, the dynamics of space also affect people's inter-

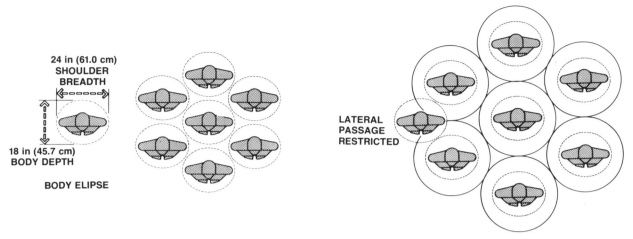

Figure 2–4 (left). Illustration of Fruin's "touch zone" based on a "body elipse" buffer zone with a minor axis related to body depth and a major axis related to shoulder breadth, allowing a queuing area of 3 sq ft, or 0.29 sq m, per person. Below this boundary the frequency of body contact between pedestrians is increased. Figures 2-4 to 2-7 adapted from Fruin, *Pedestrian Planning and Design,* 1971. Figure 2–5 (right). Illustration of Fruin's "no touch zone," based on an expanded interperson spacing of 36 in, or 91.4 cm, and a 7 sq ft, or 0.65 sq m, area per person. Fruin contends that body contact can be avoided between 3 and 7 sq ft, or 0.29 to 0.65 sq m, per person.

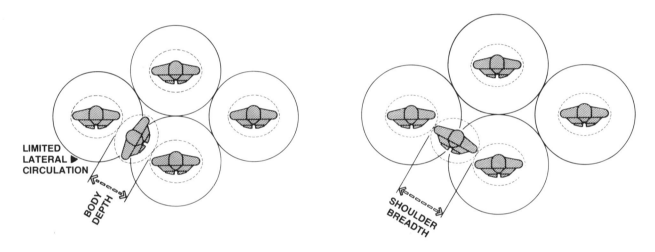

Figure 2–6 (left). Illustration of Fruin's "personal comfort zone," expanding the body buffer zone to a 42-in, or 106.7-cm, diameter and a 10-sq ft, or 0.93-sq m, area. A full body depth separates standees, allowing for limited lateral circulation by moving sideways. Figure 2–7 (right). Illustration of Fruin's "circulation zone," expanding the body buffer zone to a 48-in or 121.9-cm, diameter and 13-sq ft, or 1.21-sq m, area. Fruin contends that 10 to 13 sq ft, or 0.93 to 1.21 sq m, per person would allow circulation without disturbing others.

Figure 2–8. Sommer's experiment at the Saskatchewan Hospital involved a seating arrangement as shown at right. It was observed that greater interaction between people occurred across the corners AB, AH, EF, and ED. Adapted from *Sociometry.*

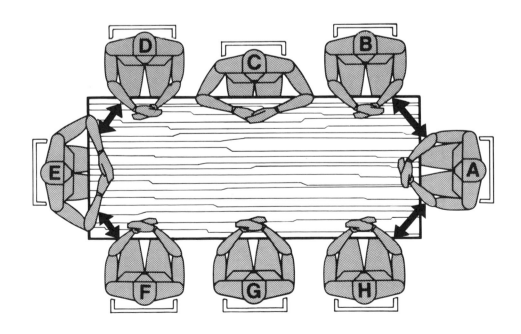

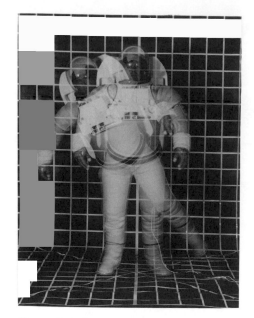

Figure 2–9. *Spatial envelope* defined by body movement in performance of a simple task. Photograph courtesy National Aeronautics and Space Administration.

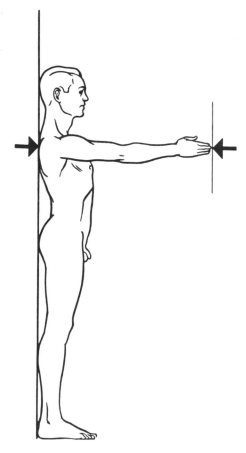

Figure 2–10. Classic anthropometric diagram representing arm reach. From Damon, Stoudt, McFarland, *The Human Body in Equipment Design,* 1966, p. 96.

face with the environment. People, as Kaplan suggests, are constantly in motion. Even when not engaged in a particular activity or task, the human body is never really completely still or at rest, and even when considered to be rigid, the body will, in fact, sway to some extent in all directions. The body is always pliable and can stretch. Limbs can rotate and twist, and electrical energy from body muscles can be harnessed to operate machines. One dramatic example of the relative pliability and elasticity of the human body is the change it undergoes during weightlessness. National Aeronautics and Space Administration data indicate that astronauts "grow" about 3 percent in height during the first few days in a zero-gravity environment. This increase typically amounts to about 5 cm, or 2 in. This increase is caused primarily by a lengthening of the spinal column due to the contraction and expansion of the intervertebral discs. Upon reexposure to one gravity, the process is reversed and the body returns to normal.[7]

Changes in height, however, are not limited to zero gravity conditions. Such changes are also observed on earth after a person has been in a reclining horizontal posture for a period of time, such as when sleeping, and then assumes a standing position. The human body is, by its nature, a dynamic organism.

By contrast, however, much of the anthropometric data available are based on static measurements taken of samples of larger populations in various positions (i.e., standing, sitting, with limbs extended, etc.). The static nature of most of the data is usually related more to the anticipated body positions at the completion of a task rather than the flow of body movements involved at arriving at those final positions. Figure 2-9 illustrates the "spatial envelope" defined by body movement in the performance of a simple task.

In the application of hard-lined anthropometric data, therefore, the designer must somehow reconcile the static nature of the data with the reality of the dynamic aspects of body movements. At the very least, he must be aware of the inherent limitations of the data. By way of example, Figure 2-10 illustrates the classic anthropometric diagram associated with arm reach measurement. It is such hard data on which the maximum distance of a shelf, or perhaps of a control, might be located to accommodate a majority of users. What other factors could impact on the dynamics and/or the geometrics of the activity? Surely the capability of the human body to stretch as well as the idiosyncrasies of the individual user's body posture will affect body movement to some degree. In addition, what about the user's actual body positions and motions immediately preceding the flow of movements associated with the execution of a specific task? The position of the body as well as the momentum generated by the body movements preceding that task are certainly bound to affect the user's reach.

Anthropometric space requirements for walking clearances constitute yet another excellent example of the importance of body movement and its implications in the design process. Human stride and gait affect the clearances to be allowed between people and physical obstructions. Tables, unfortunately, do not reflect these factors. However, very little published research in this particular area is available.

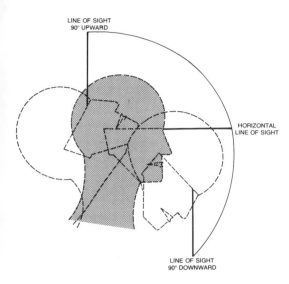

LINE OF SIGHT
90° UPWARD

HORIZONTAL
LINE OF SIGHT

LINE OF SIGHT
90° DOWNWARD

Figure 2–11. Range of head movements in the vertical plane increases area of visibility. From *Human Factors Engineering,* 1977.

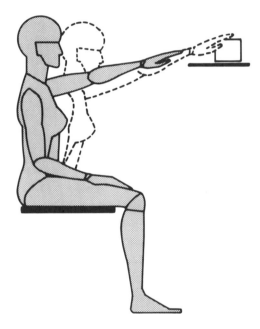

Figure 2–12. The ability to lean forward, even slightly, increases functional reach.

Sitting, all too often, is viewed as a task that is essentially static in nature. Nothing could be further from the truth. The act of sitting, in actuality, involves almost continuous repositioning in order to respond to the demands of the various activities to be performed in that position. Moreover, one cannot deal exclusively with the body in the seated position. The movements involved in getting into and out of the seat must be considered. Also, the entire sitting process must be perceived within a continuum of motion.

On balance, then, given all the other variables involved, many of which have yet to be defined or measured, the designer should not always interpret the anthropometric data too literally. Any attempt to simulate graphically and in two dimensions the dynamic patterns of body movements, which by their very nature involve time, space, and three dimensions, is bound to lose something in the translation.

## 2.6 RANGE OF JOINT MOTION

It is obvious that the extent to which the body's joints can move or rotate will impact greatly on the individual's interface with the physical environment. Movement of the head, for example, as illustrated in Figure 2-11, will greatly increase the area of visibility. The ability to lean forward, as illustrated in Figure 2-12, will increase functional reach, as will the ability to kneel or to stand on one's toes. It is helpful, therefore, if not essential, that the designer have some knowledge of the range of joint motion.

The angle formed by two body segments or by one such segment and a vertical or horizontal plane usually defines the range of joint motion at any given time. The total range is measured by the angle formed between the two most extreme positions possible, given the normal constraints of bone and muscle structure. The methodologies, devices, and techniques necessary for accurately measuring the range of motion of body joints are numerous and vary in complexity from a goniometer, a simple protractor-like device, to highly sophisticated photographic techniques. Joint motion can be more clearly understood when considered in terms of the body linkage system shown in Figure 2-13. The links are theoretically viewed as straight line distances between centers of joint rotation.

Movable joints are divided into three general types. The first involves a single plane freedom of motion in one direction only from a starting position. Termed hinge joints, the elbow and the knee are typical examples. The second involves motion in two planes originating from a zero starting position. This type of motion is typified by the wrist. The third type of joint, the so-called ball and socket, allows three dimensional, or rotary, motion as in the shoulder or hip.

The types of joint movement of particular concern to the designer are flexion, extension, abduction, adduction, medial rotation, lateral rotation, pronation, and supination. This classic terminology is defined and illustrated in Table 9 in Part B of this book. Several factors can affect the range of joint motion. Sex is a significant factor. A study in this regard indicates that women, in general, exceed men in range of joint motion measurements at all joints except the knee.[8] The widest range of joint motion in both sexes, as would be expected, is found

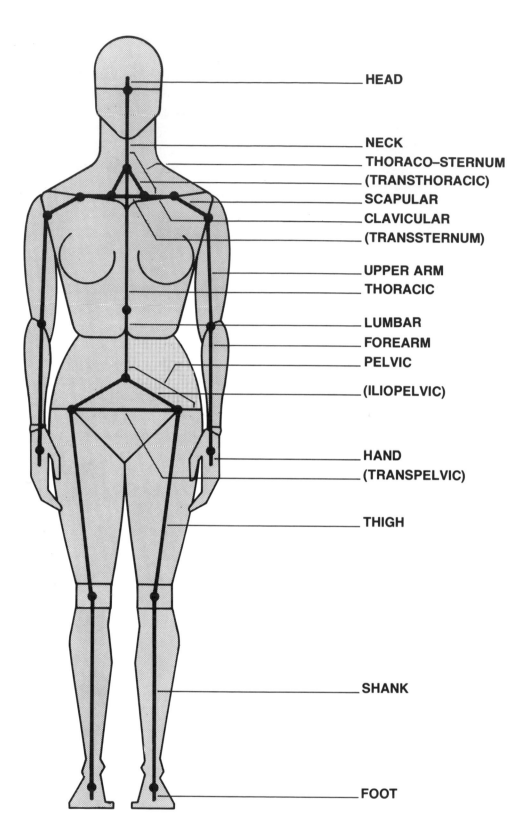

HEAD

NECK
THORACO–STERNUM
(TRANSTHORACIC)
SCAPULAR
CLAVICULAR
(TRANSSTERNUM)

UPPER ARM
THORACIC

LUMBAR
FOREARM
PELVIC

(ILIOPELVIC)

HAND
(TRANSPELVIC)

THIGH

SHANK

FOOT

Figure 2–13. Body linkage system.
Adapted from linkage system diagram,
*Anthropometric Source Book,* vol. 1.

among the most slender, while the least range of motion is found among the fattest. Age, by itself, surprisingly, does not dramatically decrease or otherwise inhibit joint motion. It has been observed that between the first and seventh decades the mobility of joints decreases by approximately 10 percent, with very little of that change occurring after puberty. It should be noted, however, that arthritis, which usually increases in incidence after middle age, will result in a general decrease in average joint mobility of any population.

## 2.7 RESTRAINTS

It is important here to caution the student, the interior designer, or the architect against viewing the anthropometric data presented as information so precise and so "scientifically correct" as to be infallible. It is stressed that anthropometry, at least at its present stage of development, is not so exact a science as one might wish. The data should be viewed, however, as one of many sources of information or tools available to the designer of interior space. The danger is for the designer to substitute tabular data for common sense, function, or design sensitivity, which are all essential parts of the creative design process. While the authors of this book have provided as much anthropometric information as could be accumulated considering the state of the art, more information is constantly being produced, and undoubtedly, some may not be included here. This is due to the incipient nature of the science of anthropometry and the lack of a significant number of professionals involved in research in the area. In fact, there is a vast amount of data yet unavailable, particularly with respect to children and physically disabled and elderly people. In addition, more information about functional dimensions is needed.

Finally, to place the use of the data presented in ultimate perspective, one should consider the three-dimensional dynamics of "man in motion," the psychological aspects of space and the user, and the proxemic factors involved. Obviously, physical body size is only one of a vast number of human factors that impact on establishing the dimensions of interior spaces.

# 3 ELDERLY AND PHYSICALLY DISABLED PEOPLE

## 3.1 ELDERLY PEOPLE

It was noted in the Introduction that most available anthropometric data are related to military populations and, of consequence, are generally restricted in terms of age and sex. The National Health Survey of the U.S. Public Health Service is probably the first large-scale study prepared with respect to civilian populations and is based on a national sampling of Americans between the ages of 18 and 79. If information regarding the civilian population generally appears to be limited, however, anthropometric data for specific segments of the population, such as aged people, is sparser still.

When one considers that there are now close to 20 million Americans over the age of 65, with the number increasing yearly, it becomes apparent that the need for anthropometric data for this segment of the population is critical. Moreover, the data are essential if we are to respond sensitively in designing the interior spaces in which elderly people are to function.

Some data are available and some conclusions have been drawn. The most significant findings are as follows:

1. Older people of both sexes tend to be shorter than younger people. To a certain degree, however, the difference may be accounted for because the older individuals are obviously representative of an earlier generation, while recent studies indicate that body sizes generally are increasing. It has also been suggested that the decreases might be due to the selective survival of short, light people—an extremely interesting speculation.

2. Reach measurements of older people are shorter than those of younger people. There is also considerable variability in the degree to which the reach of elderly people is impaired due to the incidence of arthritis and other joint movement limitations. This is particularly true of vertical grip reach.

The basic problem with most of the available anthropometric data is the small size of the group studied. For example, data on "the functional anthropometry of old men" (Chart 3-1) prepared by Damon and Stoudt[1] and "the functional anthropometry of elderly women" (Chart 3-2 and Figure 3-1) prepared by D. F. Roberts[2] were based on 133 subjects and 78 subjects, respectively. Perhaps the best available data, which are in a percentile form required by the designer, are given in the National Health Survey, which includes data up to age 79. These data are included in Part B.

| Measurement | Number | Mean | SD | Percentiles | | | | | | |
|---|---|---|---|---|---|---|---|---|---|---|
| | | | | 1st | 5th | 10th | 50th | 90th | 95th | 99th |
| Weight (lb) | 130 | 152.49 | 23.19 | 112 | 119 | 124 | 151 | 184 | 192 | 204 |
| Stature | 119 | 66.28 | 2.09 | 61.6 | 63.3 | 63.7 | 66.1 | 69.3 | 69.9 | 70.3 |
| Sitting height, erect | 119 | 34.77 | 1.21 | 32.5 | 33.0 | 33.2 | 34.7 | 36.5 | 37.0 | 37.2 |
| Sitting height, normal | 131 | 33.42 | 1.45 | 29.7 | 31.0 | 31.6 | 33.4 | 35.2 | 35.9 | 36.5 |
| Trunk height, sitting | 131 | 22.57 | 1.24 | 19.8 | 20.5 | 20.9 | 22.7 | 24.3 | 24.5 | 24.9 |
| Knee height, sitting | 132 | 21.19 | 0.85 | 19.4 | 19.9 | 20.1 | 21.2 | 22.3 | 22.6 | 23.4 |
| Popliteal height, sitting | 131 | 17.31 | 0.83 | 15.4 | 15.7 | 16.3 | 17.2 | 18.4 | 18.6 | 19.2 |
| Span | 120 | 68.50 | 2.76 | 63.3 | 64.2 | 64.8 | 68.5 | 71.5 | 72.7 | 75.7 |
| Span akimbo | 121 | 35.69 | 1.52 | 32.4 | 33.4 | 33.8 | 35.7 | 37.3 | 37.9 | 39.4 |
| Forward arm reach | 118 | 34.21 | 1.51 | 31.2 | 31.7 | 32.3 | 34.2 | 36.1 | 37.0 | 38.4 |
| Shoulder–elbow length | 131 | 14.53 | 0.66 | 13.4 | 13.5 | 13.7 | 14.5 | 15.3 | 15.6 | 16.4 |
| Elbow–middle finger length | 130 | 18.27 | 0.71 | 16.9 | 17.2 | 17.4 | 18.3 | 19.3 | 19.5 | 20.4 |
| Buttock–popliteal length | 131 | 18.57 | 1.00 | 16.5 | 16.9 | 17.4 | 18.5 | 19.8 | 20.3 | 21.1 |
| Buttock–knee length | 132 | 23.26 | 0.96 | 21.0 | 21.8 | 22.1 | 23.2 | 24.6 | 25.0 | 25.4 |
| Head length | 133 | 7.74 | 0.25 | 7.1 | 7.3 | 7.4 | 7.7 | 8.0 | 8.1 | 8.3 |
| Face length | 127 | 4.96 | 0.27 | 4.4 | 4.6 | 4.6 | 5.0 | 5.3 | 5.5 | 5.6 |
| Nose length | 133 | 2.37 | 0.14 | 2.0 | 2.1 | 2.2 | 2.4 | 2.5 | 2.6 | 2.7 |
| Ear length | 132 | 2.94 | 0.19 | 2.5 | 2.6 | 2.7 | 2.9 | 3.2 | 3.3 | 3.4 |
| Hand length | 130 | 7.41 | 0.31 | 6.7 | 7.0 | 7.0 | 7.4 | 7.8 | 8.0 | 8.2 |
| Foot length | 132 | 10.24 | 0.39 | 9.2 | 9.7 | 9.8 | 10.2 | 10.8 | 10.9 | 11.3 |
| Biacromial breadth | 133 | 14.90 | 0.64 | 13.3 | 13.7 | 14.1 | 14.9 | 15.7 | 15.9 | 16.3 |
| Bideltoid breadth | 129 | 17.07 | 0.90 | 15.3 | 15.6 | 15.8 | 17.0 | 18.2 | 18.5 | 19.1 |
| Chest breadth | 133 | 11.64 | 0.81 | 9.9 | 10.2 | 10.6 | 11.7 | 12.7 | 13.0 | 13.4 |
| Elbow-to-elbow breadth, sitting | 132 | 17.81 | 1.32 | 15.0 | 15.5 | 16.2 | 17.8 | 19.3 | 20.1 | 21.0 |
| Bi-iliac breadth | 132 | 12.28 | 0.67 | 10.9 | 11.2 | 11.4 | 12.3 | 13.2 | 13.5 | 13.9 |
| Hip breadth, sitting | 131 | 14.87 | 0.94 | 13.2 | 13.5 | 13.7 | 14.8 | 16.1 | 16.7 | 17.2 |
| Knee-to-knee breadth, sitting | 129 | 8.07 | 0.52 | 7.3 | 7.5 | 7.6 | 8.0 | 8.5 | 8.7 | 10.1 |
| Head breadth | 133 | 6.07 | 0.20 | 5.6 | 5.8 | 5.8 | 6.1 | 6.3 | 6.4 | 6.5 |
| Face breadth | 132 | 5.55 | 0.23 | 5.1 | 5.2 | 5.3 | 5.6 | 5.8 | 5.9 | 6.1 |
| Nose breadth | 131 | 1.57 | 0.15 | 1.3 | 1.4 | 1.4 | 1.6 | 1.8 | 1.9 | 2.0 |
| Ear breadth | 122 | 1.47 | 0.12 | 1.2 | 1.3 | 1.4 | 1.5 | 1.6 | 1.7 | 1.8 |
| Hand breadth | 129 | 3.32 | 0.15 | 3.0 | 3.1 | 3.1 | 3.3 | 3.5 | 3.6 | 3.7 |
| Foot breadth | 119 | 3.93 | 0.19 | 3.5 | 3.6 | 3.7 | 3.9 | 4.2 | 4.3 | 4.3 |
| Chest depth | 133 | 9.58 | 0.78 | 7.9 | 8.2 | 8.5 | 9.6 | 10.6 | 10.8 | 11.2 |
| Abdominal depth | 126 | 10.83 | 1.32 | 8.4 | 8.6 | 9.1 | 10.8 | 12.4 | 13.2 | 14.0 |
| Chest circumference, rest | 133 | 37.87 | 2.98 | 32.0 | 33.3 | 33.7 | 37.9 | 41.3 | 42.0 | 46.0 |
| Chest circumference, insp. | 130 | 38.42 | 2.92 | 32.6 | 33.5 | 34.6 | 38.4 | 42.1 | 42.9 | 46.9 |
| Chest circumference, exp. | 130 | 37.28 | 3.00 | 31.5 | 32.0 | 33.3 | 37.4 | 40.9 | 42.1 | 44.9 |
| Waist circumference | 108 | 35.46 | 3.68 | 28.5 | 30.2 | 30.7 | 35.2 | 40.2 | 42.1 | 44.1 |
| Upper arm circumference | 133 | 11.28 | 1.11 | 8.9 | 9.5 | 9.8 | 11.4 | 12.8 | 13.0 | 14.0 |
| Calf circumference, right | 110 | 13.50 | 1.07 | 11.6 | 12.0 | 12.2 | 13.4 | 14.8 | 15.2 | 16.2 |
| Calf circumference, left | 109 | 13.48 | 1.01 | 11.7 | 11.9 | 12.1 | 13.4 | 14.8 | 15.4 | 15.8 |
| Head circumference | 133 | 22.34 | 0.72 | 21.0 | 21.3 | 21.5 | 22.4 | 23.2 | 23.3 | 23.8 |
| Triceps skinfold (mm) | 133 | 11.36 | 4.22 | 4.2 | 5.9 | 6.7 | 10.6 | 17.1 | 19.0 | 24.2 |
| Subscapular skinfold (mm) | 133 | 16.18 | 6.76 | 5.9 | 7.0 | 8.5 | 15.5 | 24.8 | 26.7 | 43.2 |
| Grip strength, right (lb) | 118 | 63.49 | 17.33 | 27.8 | 41.2 | 45.6 | 62.4 | 87.3 | 90.8 | 102.1 |
| Grip strength, left (lb) | 119 | 58.77 | 18.10 | 38.6 | 41.0 | 43.2 | 61.3 | 79.4 | 84.4 | 97.9 |

Chart 3–1. Functional anthropometry of elderly men. From Damon and Stoudt, "The Functional Anthropometry of Old Men," *Human Factors,* 1963, p. 488.

|   |   | M* | SD* | n* |
|---|---|---|---|---|
|   | age | 71–65 yr | 7–51 | 78 |
|   | weight | 132–68 lb | 29–74 | 76 |
| A | stature with shoes | 61–16 in | 2–50 | 77 |
|   | stature without shoes | 60–06 in | 2–45 | 78 |
| B | eye height, standing | 55–54 in | 2–66 | 78 |
| C | acromial height, standing | 49–48 in | 2–14 | 78 |
| D | elbow height, standing | 36–73 in | 1–89 | 78 |
|   | heel height | 1–13 in | 0–44 | 77 |

*Sitting on a 17–in chair*

|   |   | in | | |
|---|---|---|---|---|
| a | elbow height above seat | 7–57 | 1–21 | 78 |
| b | vertex height above seat | 31–27 | 1–43 | 78 |
| c | eye height above seat | 26–82 | 1–47 | 78 |
| d | occiput height above seat | 28–09 | 1–44 | 78 |
| e | height of shoulder blades above seat | 15–68 | 1–09 | 78 |
| f | height to acromion above seat | 20–67 | 1–23 | 78 |
| g | popliteal height from floor | 15–15 | 0–85 | 78 |
| h | height to top of knee from floor | 18–83 | 0–87 | 78 |
| i | height of top of thighs above seat | 4–96 | 0–90 | 78 |
| j | distance from front of knee to sacral plane | 22–04 | 1–36 | 78 |
| k | distance from popliteal angle to sacral plane | 18–46 | 1–14 | 78 |
| l | distance from heel to sacral plane | 36–76 | 1–78 | 78 |
| m | width of thighs | 14–74 | 1–55 | 78 |
| n | bideltoid width | 16–26 | 1–17 | 78 |
| o | horizontal distance from back of thorax to gripped pencil, arm horizontal | 28–56 | 1–67 | 78 |
| p | horizontal distance from back of thorax to gripped pencil, arm straight, hand 11 in above seat | 25–35 | 1–84 | 78 |

*Standing*

|   |   | in | | |
|---|---|---|---|---|
| q | distance from abdomen to gripped pencil, arm horizontal | 18–54 | 2–40 | 77 |
| r | distance from abdomen to gripped pencil, hand on 34–in table | 13–96 | 2–34 | 77 |
| s | maximum comfortable upward reach | 71–67 | 3–43 | 78 |
| t | maximum comfortable upward reach with 14–in obstruction | 67–04 | 3–89 | 77 |
| u | fist carrying height at side | 27–58 | 1–87 | 78 |
| v | fist carrying height with 14–in obstruction | 32–43 | 2–07 | 77 |
| w | radius of chalk circle, right hand, arm straight | 19–29 | 1–55 | 77 |
|   | grip diameter—index finger | 1–34 | 0–15 | 76 |
|   | grip diameter—middle finger | 1–56 | 0–17 | 77 |
|   | grip strength | 13–95 kg | 4–29 | 76 |

*M = mean; SD = standard deviation; n = no. in sample.

Chart 3–2. Functional anthropometry of elderly women. From Roberts, "Functional Anthropometry of Elderly Women," *Ergonomics* 3 (1960), pp. 321-327.

Figure 3–1. Figures illustrating body measurements indicated in Chart 3.2. From Roberts, "Functional Anthropometry of Elderly Women," *Ergonomics* 3 (1960), pp. 321-327.

| CATEGORY | NUMBER OF INDIVIDUALS |
|---|---|
| VISUAL: | |
| 25% vision loss | 4,105,000 |
| 50% vision loss | 184,000 |
| 75% vision loss | 618,000 |
| 100% vision loss | 483,000 |
| | 5,390,000 |
| ORTHOPEDIC AIDS: | |
| Wheelchairs | 409,000 |
| Crutches | 443,000 |
| Canes | 2,156,000 |
| Walkers | 404,000 |
| Braces | 1,102,000 |
| Artificial Limbs | 172,000 |
| Special Shoes | 2,337,000 |
| | 7,023,000 |
| AUDITORY: | |
| Deaf | 1,800,000 |
| Hard of Hearing | 18,300,000 |
| | 20,100,000 |
| CARDIO-VASCULAR: | 7,600,000 |
| RESPIRATORY: | 14,500,000 |
| MENTAL RETARDATION: | 5,120,000 |
| ARTHRITIS: | 18,300,000 |
| AGING: Over age 65 | 7,000,000 |
| CHILDHOOD: Ages 5-12 | 32,550,000 |
| PREGNANCY: | 3,730,000 |
| TOTAL = | 121,313,000 |
| Total U.S. population = | 215,000,000 |

Chart 3–3. Distribution of disabilities by category. From Selim, *Barrier Free Design,* 1977.

## 3.2 PHYSICALLY DISABLED PEOPLE

The problem of physically disabled people coping with the man-made environment is a massive one. The U.S. Department of Health, Education, and Welfare estimated in 1970 that some 69 million people in the United States alone are physically limited.[3] Chart 3-3 shows a distribution of disabilities by category compiled by the Michigan Center for a Barrier-Free Environment from the sources indicated. It underscores the magnitude of the problem on a national basis. On a cosmopolitan basis, figures place the worldwide physically disabled population at 400 million, of which over 75 percent are left to their own devices.

To solve all the problems of all the physically disabled people with respect to their interface with physical barriers is obviously an interdisciplinary undertaking that transcends the scope of this book. However, the anthropometrics involved can be introduced here; they will be explored further in Part C.

## 3.3 CHAIRBOUND PEOPLE

There are no large-scale data on the anthropometrics of chairbound people. Such a study would be quite difficult in view of the many variables involved: the types of disabilities, the limbs or segments of the bodies involved, the extent of paralysis, the degree of muscle dysfunction, the cumulative effect on overall limb mobility due to chair confinement, etc. All would have to be considered. For study purposes, therefore, the assumption has been made that where limb mobility has not been impaired, the range of movement would approximate that of able-bodied people.

It is, however, important that in determining appropriate reach, clearance, and other dimensions, the individual and the wheelchair be viewed together. This requires some knowledge of the anatomy of the wheelchair itself. Figure 3-2 provides some basic and useful data on this.

With regard to the anthropometrics involved, there are many diagrams in circulation illustrating body measurements of men and women in wheelchairs. Caution should be exercised in interpreting, and subsequently applying, the data indicated. In many instances, the reach dimensions are qualified to indicate a so-called average dimension. This notion of average was discussed in Section 2.2 and proved to be fallacious. If reach is a critical factor in the particular design, it is essential to base the design on those body dimensions representative of the lower range of the population, not the average. Consequently, the 5th percentile arm reach data should be used. If the design were based on the so-called average reach, half of the chairbound users simply could not function.

Figure 3-3, Chart 3-4, and Figure 3-4 illustrate the anthropometrics of chairbound people. What should be noted, however, is that most wheelchairs are not built to keep the body in an erect position. Accordingly, body parts are not strictly vertical or horizontal. In describing the geometrics involved, Dr. Herman L. Kamenetz states:

From this imagined posture only the ankles keep their position of 90 degrees. The legs are lifted by about 15 degrees so that the knees assume

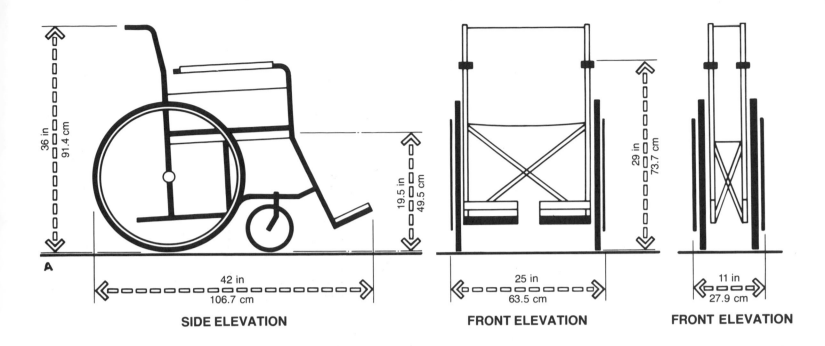

**SIDE ELEVATION**

36 in
91.4 cm

42 in
106.7 cm

19.5 in
49.5 cm

**FRONT ELEVATION**

29 in
73.7 cm

25 in
63.5 cm

**FRONT ELEVATION**

11 in
27.9 cm

—————— TURNING RADIUS BASED ON
MOVING WHEELS IN OPPOSITE
DIRECTIONS AND PIVOTING
ABOUT CENTER

□□□□□□ TURNING RADIUS BASED ON
LOCKING ONE WHEEL AND
TURNING THE OTHER WITH
THE PIVOT POINT ON THE
LOCKED WHEEL

**ALTERNATE WHEELCHAIR
TURNING RADII**

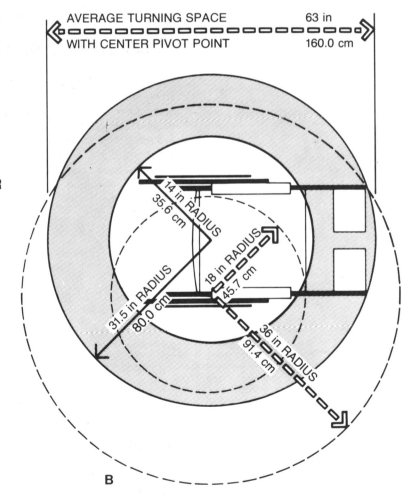

AVERAGE TURNING SPACE 63 in
WITH CENTER PIVOT POINT 160.0 cm

14 in
35.6 cm RADIUS

18 in RADIUS
45.7 cm

31.5 in RADIUS
80.0 cm

36 in RADIUS
91.4 cm

B

Figure 3–2. (*a*) Wheelchair dimensions. The source of the dimensions shown is the American National Standards Institute (ANSI Pub. A117–1961, Revalidated 1971). The measurements indicated, however, vary with model and manufacturer, and each chair should be measured individually. The length of the chair is of particular importance since it determines the turning radius. It is essential also, when calculating clearances, to allow for the protrusion of the feet beyond the edge of the footrests. ANSI contends that the collapsible model wheelchair of tubular metal construction with plastic upholstery for back and seat is the one most commonly used and falls within the dimensions indicated. (*b*) Alternate wheelchair turning radii.

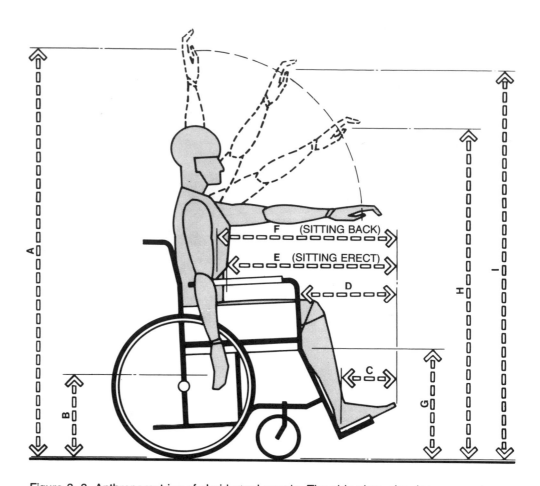

Figure 3-3. Anthropometrics of chairbound people. The side view, showing user and chair, indicates some of the more critical anthropometric measurements for both men and women. All reach dimensions are based on 2.5 percentile data to accommodate those users with smaller body sizes. It is recommended that since the female body size is smaller than the male, the female dimensions be used for the design of all reach situations. Dimensions involving clearance problems are based on 97.5 percentile data. Since the male body size is larger, the dimensions for men should be used to satisfy clearance requirements. The figure and data were adapted from Goldsmith's *Designing for the Disabled,* 1963, and were based on measurements obtained from British and American studies.

|   | MALE | | FEMALE | |
|---|---|---|---|---|
|   | in | cm | in | cm |
| A | 62.25 | 158.1 | 56.75 | 144.1 |
| B | 16.25 | 41.3 | 17.5 | 44.5 |
| C | 8.75 | 22.2 | 7.0 | 17.8 |
| D | 18.5 | 47.0 | 16.5 | 41.9 |
| E | 25.75 | 65.4 | 23.0 | 58.4 |
| F | 28.75 | 73.0 | 26.0 | 66.0 |
| G | 19.0 | 48.3 | 19.0 | 48.3 |
| H | 51.5 | 130.8 | 47.0 | 119.4 |
| I | 58.25 | 148.0 | 53.24 | 135.2 |

Chart 3-4. Data accompanying Figure 3-3.

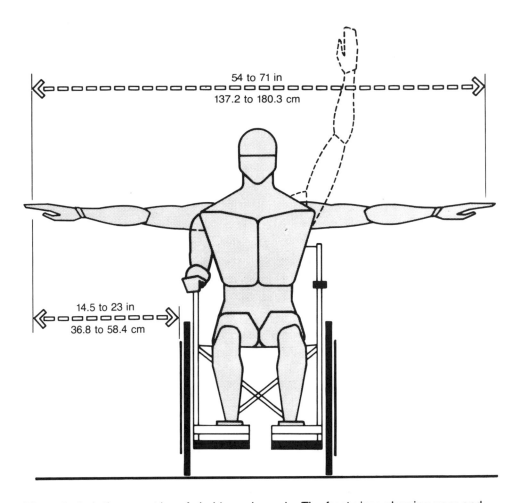

Figure 3–4. Anthropometrics of chairbound people. The front view, showing user and chair, also indicates some of the more critical anthropometric measurements. The source of the bilateral horizontal reach dimensions with both arms extended to each side, shoulder high, was the American National Standards Institute (ANSI Pub. A117-1961, Revalidated 1971). It should be noted that no data were available with regard to sex or precise percentile grouping.

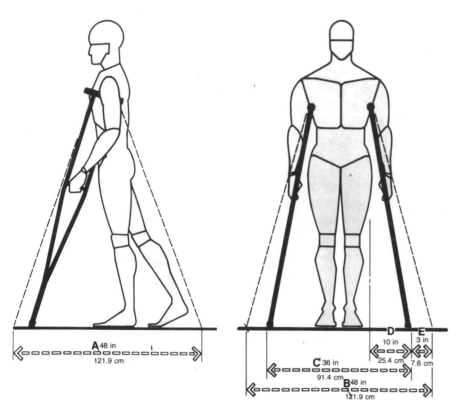

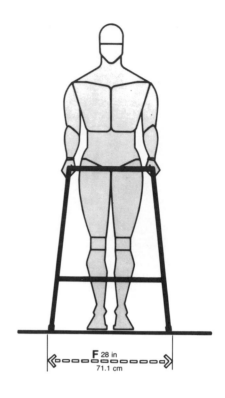

A 48 in
121.9 cm

D
10 in
25.4 cm

E
3 in
7.6 cm

C 36 in
91.4 cm

B 48 in
121.9 cm

F 28 in
71.1 cm

Figure 3–5. Crutches. The mode, gait, and speed of the user is impeded significantly by the use of crutches. Changes of grade and circulation up or down stairs are extremely difficult and in some situations almost impossible. The limited use of the user's lower extremities as well as manipulation and placement of crutches significantly limit the leverage that he or she can develop, particularly as may be required in opening or closing doors and getting in and out of seats. The critical dimensions that impact on clearance include crutch swing (A), walking crutch swing (B), standing crutch span (C), body crutch span (D), and body crutch swing (E). For users with severe arthritis and cerebral palsy, the clearances indicated may have to be increased.

Figure 3–6. Walker. The clearance required by a user employing the aid of a walker is more easily defined by the inherent nature of the device and method of operation. The front view of the user indicates a minimum of 28 in (F), or 71.1 cm.

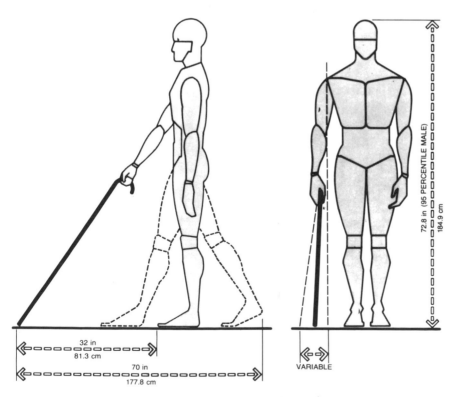

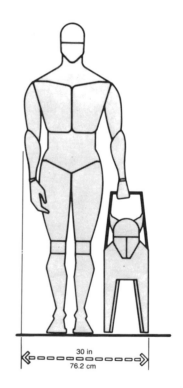

32 in
81.3 cm

70 in
177.8 cm

72.8 in (95 PERCENTILE MALE)
184.9 cm

VARIABLE

30 in
76.2 cm

Figure 3–7. Canes. Canes may be utilized by someone who is blind, who has an injured limb, or who might be suffering from a host of afflictions such as varying degrees of aging, arthritis, cerebral palsy, diabetes, multiple sclerosis, and other maladies. The blind user, however, because of the nature of the disability, would require the maximum space for clearance. The side and front views of the user indicate the clearance allowances required.

Figure 3–8. Seeing-eye dog. Given the many variables involved, the precise combined clearance data for user and dog are difficult to establish. A clearance of 30 in, or 76.2 cm, however, would constitute the very minimum allowance.

an angle of about 105 degrees, and the back reclines by about 10 degrees, which results in an angle at the hip joints of about 100 degrees. Finally, the body being kept in this relationship of its parts to one another, the entire chair is as though it were tilted backward by about 5 degrees, so that the seat is 5 degrees from the horizontal, the legs 20 degrees, and the back 15 degrees from the vertical.[4]

If the user's impairment permits him or her to assume an erect position, the incline of the chair back notwithstanding, standard anthropometric data for arm reach would be adequate, given the nature of the task and degree of fit involved.

If, however, arm reach is based on the back being in an inclined position, 15° from the vertical, the standard anthropometric arm reach data would have to be modified accordingly. It should be noted that measurement of standard arm reach is taken with the back erect and with the subject seated on a horizontal plane.

## 3.4 AMBULANT DISABLED PEOPLE

For ambulant disabled people, it is necessary to consider those users functioning with crutches (Figure 3.5), walkers (Figure 3.6), canes (Figure 3.7), and seeing-eye dogs (Figure 3.8). All these aids become, in essence, a functional part of the individual's body. Accordingly, both aid and user should in almost every instance be viewed as a single entity. For design purposes it is useful to know something not only of the anthropometry involved, but of the total spatial considerations.

# 4 ANTHROPOMETRICS OF SEATING

The design of seating can be traced at least to antiquity. The stool, for example, had already been developed into a valued article of furniture by the Egyptians as far back as 2050 B.C. and the chair as far back as 1600 B.C.[1] Despite its ubiquity and long history, however, seating is still one of the most poorly designed elements of interior space. Industrial designer Neils Diffrient has said that "Chair design is the acid test for designers."[2] One of the major difficulties in the design of seating is that sitting is, quite frequently, viewed as a static activity while, in actuality, it is a rather dynamic one. Accordingly, the application of static two-dimensional data, alone, to solve a dynamic three-dimensional problem, involving biomechanical considerations, is not a valid design approach. Paradoxically, a chair that is anthropometrically correct may not necessarily be comfortable as well. If the design, however, is simply not responsive at all to human dimensions and body size, there is no question that the seating will, in fact, be uncomfortable.

Another difficulty is that very little data are available with respect to the biomechanics of chair design and practically no research has been published with respect to "comfort." All that can be provided in this section, as well as in Part C, are some broad guidelines, basic concepts, and recommendations.

## 4.1 THE DYNAMICS OF SITTING

The dynamics of sitting can be more clearly illustrated by studying the mechanics of the support system and the general bone structure involved. According to Tichauer, "The axis of support of the seated torso is a line in a coronal plane passing through the projection of the lowest point of the ischial tuberosities on the surface of the seat."[3] Figures 4-1 and 4-2 show the tuberosities. Branton makes two observations in this regard. The first is that, when sitting, about 75 percent of the total body weight is supported on only 4 square inches (sq in), or 26 sq cm, of these tuberosities.[4] This constitutes an exceptionally heavy load, distributed over a relatively small area, and as a result, very high compressive stresses are exerted on the areas of the buttocks beneath. Tichauer indicated that these stresses have been estimated at 85 to 100 pounds per square inch (psi).[5] Other data have

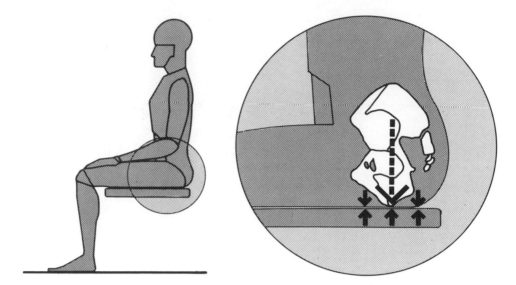

Figure 4–1. A sectional view of the seated figure showing the ischial tuberosities.

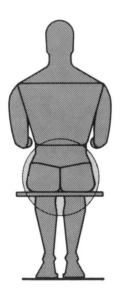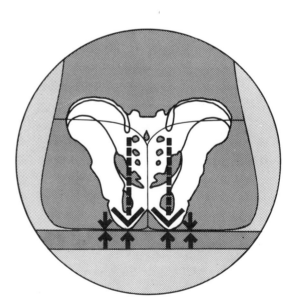

Figure 4–2. An enlarged posterior sectional view of the ischial tuberosities.

shown the compression pressures on the areas of the skin between the buttocks and a hard seat pan as high as 40 to 60 psi and the pressure a few inches away as only about 4 psi.[6] These pressures cause fatigue and discomfort and result in a change in the sitter's posture in an attempt to alleviate the condition. Prolonged sitting, without change in posture, under the compressive pressures cited may cause ischemia, or an interference in the blood circulation, resulting in aches, pains, and possible numbness.

It becomes obvious that the design of seating should provide for the distribution of the body weight supported by the ischial tuberosities over a larger area. Proper padding on the seat pan can accomplish this. It is apparent, too, that the design of the seating should also permit the sitter to change posture when necessary to alleviate discomfort. In this regard, proper anthropometric data are essential in determining the proper measurements and clearances required.

Branton's second observation is that, structurally, the tuberosities form a two-point support system which is inherently unstable.[7] The seat pan alone, therefore, is not sufficient for stabilization. Theoretically, the legs, feet, and back, in contact with surfaces other than the seat pan, should produce the necessary equilibrium. This would presuppose that the center of gravity was directly over the tuberosities. The center of gravity of the upright seated body, however, is actually located outside the body, about 1 in, or 2.5 cm, in front of the navel, as indicated in Figure 4-3. The combination of the two-point support system, in addition to the position of the center of gravity, has led Branton to suggest a scheme "in which a system of masses is inherently unstable on the seat."[8] He further suggests that if the system is to remain as stable as it normally appears to be, some internally active (muscular) forces must be assumed to be at work.

Given the many body postures assumed during any sitting period, in addition to the muscular activity involved, even when the body seems to be at rest, sitting is not the static type of activity it frequently is conceived to be. According to Branton, "the sitting body, therefore, is not merely an inert bag of bones dumped for a time in the seat, but a live organism in a dynamic state of continuous activity."[9]

It has also been contended that the many postures assumed while sitting are attempts to use the body as a lever system in an effort to counterbalance the weights of the head and trunk. Stretching the legs forward and locking the knee joints, for example, enlarges the base of the body's mass and reduces the effort of other muscles to stabilize the trunk. Other postures, such as holding up the chin with the hand while the elbow rests on the armrest or the lap, or supporting the head by leaning it against the headrest, are still other examples of the body's attempt at stabilization, providing relief to the muscle system and, in turn, alleviating discomfort. More significantly, these changes in posture occur without deliberation. Branton attempts to explain this phenomenon by suggesting the existence of an "internal 'posture program,' which enables the body to strike a running compromise between its twin needs for stability and variety."[10]

Of particular significance to the designer is the importance of the lo-

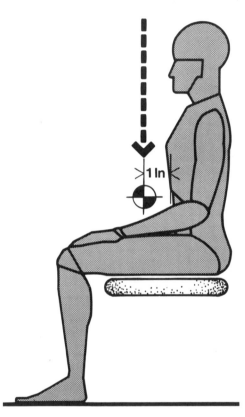

Figure 4-3. Center of gravity of the upright seated figure.

cation of back-, head-, and armrests as well as their size and configuration, since it is these elements of the chair or seat that function as stabilizers. If the seat does not provide for proper body stabilization, the user must stabilize himself by assuming the various postures mentioned earlier. This requires the expenditure of additional energy due to the muscular effort involved and increases discomfort.

## 4.2 ANTHROPOMETRIC CONSIDERATIONS

In view of the elusive nature of sitter comfort and the fact that sitting is more of a dynamic activity than a static one, the relative importance of an anthropometrically oriented approach to seating design has occasionally been challenged. Although, as mentioned earlier, there is no guarantee that an anthropometrically correct chair will be comfortable, there seems to be general agreement that the design must, nevertheless, be based on properly selected anthropometric data. If it is not, there is little doubt that the seating design will cause the user discomfort. The essential anthropometric dimensions for seating design are shown in Figure 4-4 and Chart 4.1.

It should also be noted, however, that the data cannot be applied in a vacuum. In establishing chair dimensions, the anthropometric aspects must be related to the biomechanical demands involved. It was demonstrated previously, for example, that body stabilization involved not only the seat pan, but the legs, feet, and back in contact with other surfaces. In addition, some muscular force was also required. If, through improper anthropometric design, the chair did not allow the majority of users to, in fact, have foot or back contact with other surfaces, body instability would be increased and additional muscular force would have to be introduced in order to maintain proper equilibrium. The greater the degree of muscular force or control required, the greater the fatigue and discomfort.

It is necessary, therefore, that the designer become familiar with the anthropometric considerations involved in the design of seating and their relationship to the biomechanical and ergonomic imperatives implied. To deal with one without knowledge of the others is to solve only a part of the design problem. In this regard the generally accepted basic dimensions required in the design of seating include seat height, seat depth, seat width, backrest height, and armrest height and spacing.

## 4.3 SEAT HEIGHT

One of the basic considerations in the design of seating is the height of the top of the seat surface above the floor. If the seating surface is too high, the underside of the thigh becomes compressed, as illustrated in Figure 4-5. This can cause considerable discomfort as well as a restriction in blood circulation. If the height of the seat does not permit the soles of the feet proper contact with the floor surface, body stability is weakened. If the height of the seat is too low (Figure 4-6), the legs may become extended and positioned forward. The feet then are deprived of any stability. By and large, however, a tall person would be far more comfortable using a chair with a low seat height than a short person using a chair with a seat height that is too high.

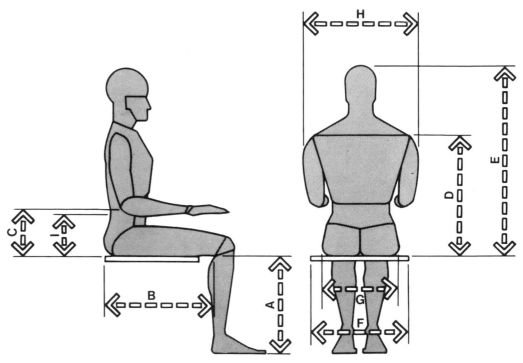

Figure 4–4. Key anthropometric dimensions required for chair design.

| | MEN | | | | WOMEN | | | |
| | Percentile | | | | Percentile | | | |
| | 5 | | 95 | | 5 | | 95 | |
| MEASUREMENT | in | cm | in | cm | in | cm | in | cm |
|---|---|---|---|---|---|---|---|---|
| **A** Popliteal Height | 15.5 | 39.4 | 19.3 | 49.0 | 14.0 | 35.6 | 17.5 | 44.5 |
| **B** Buttock-Popliteal Length | 17.3 | 43.9 | 21.6 | 54.9 | 17.0 | 43.2 | 21.0 | 53.3 |
| **C** Elbow Rest Height | 7.4 | 18.8 | 11.6 | 29.5 | 7.1 | 18.0 | 11.0 | 27.9 |
| **D** Shoulder Height | 21.0 | 53.3 | 25.0 | 63.5 | 18.0 | 45.7 | 25.0 | 63.5 |
| **E** Sitting Height Normal | 31.6 | 80.3 | 36.6 | 93.0 | 29.6 | 75.2 | 34.7 | 88.1 |
| **F** Elbow-to-Elbow Breadth | 13.7 | 34.8 | 19.9 | 50.5 | 12.3 | 31.2 | 19.3 | 49.0 |
| **G** Hip Breadth | 12.2 | 31.0 | 15.9 | 40.4 | 12.3 | 31.2 | 17.1 | 43.4 |
| **H** Shoulder Breadth | 17.0 | 43.2 | 19.0 | 48.3 | 13.0 | 33.0 | 19.0 | 48.3 |
| **I** Lumbar Height | See Note. | | | | | | | |

Note: No published anthropometric studies concerning lumbar height can be located. A British study [H-D. Darcus and A.G.M. Weddel, *British Medical Bulletin* 5 (1947), pp. 31–37], however, gives a 90 percent range of 8 to 12 in, or 20.3 to 30.5 cm, for British men. Diffrient (*Humanscale 1/2/3*) indicates that the center of forward curvature of the lumbar region for adults is located about 9 to 10 in, or 22.9 to 25.4 cm, above the compressed seat cushion.

Chart 4–1. Selected body dimensions, taken from Tables 2 and 3 of Part B, useful in the design of seating. Little detailed published data are available with regard to lumbar heights. Estimates, however, vary from a range of 8 to 12 in, or 20.3 to 30.5 cm, and 9 to 10 in, or 22.9 to 25.4 cm.

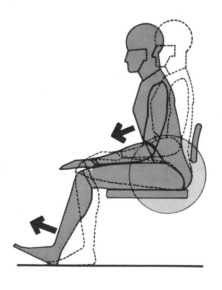

Figure 4–5. A seat surface placed too high causes the thigh to become compressed and blood circulation to be constricted. In addition, the soles of the feet are not permitted proper contact with the floor surface, thus weakening body stability.

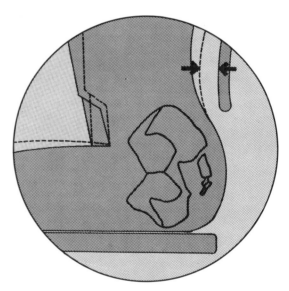

Figure 4–6. A seat surface located too low may cause the legs to become extended and positioned forward, depriving them of any stability. In addition the movement of the body forward will also cause the back to slide away from the backrest and deprive the sitter of proper lumbar support.

Anthropometrically, the popliteal height (the distance taken vertically from the floor to the underside of the portion of the thigh just behind the knee) should be the measurement in the tables used as reference in establishing the proper seat height. The lower range of the table, such as the 5th percentile data, would be appropriate since these will serve the segment of the population with the smallest body dimension. The rationale, as discussed earlier, is that a seat height that will accommodate a person with a smaller popliteal height measurement will also accommodate one with a larger measurement. Chart 4-1 indicates a 5th percentile popliteal height of 15.5 in, or 39.4 cm, for men and 14.0, or 35.6 cm, for women. The measurements, however, were recorded with the examinee stripped to the waist, pockets emptied, without shoes, and wearing a knee-length examining gown—hardly the kind of attire most people normally wear while sitting. It is necessary, therefore, to compensate for these conditions by increasing the measurements accordingly.

Since the items of clothing as well as the shoes are a function of climate, time of day, location, socioeconomic class, age, culture, and fashion, it is obvious that the factor to be added is, at best, an educated guess or reasonable approximation. Given the dangers involved in making the seat height too high, it would make sense to be conservative in estimating this factor and to err on the smaller side. It is suggested, therefore, that 1.5 in, or 3.8 cm, be added to both measurements; the figures then become 17 and 15.5, or 43.2 and 39.4 cm, respectively. These figures, however, could just as easily be increased if boots or very high heels were assumed to be the footwear. Similarly, the figures would be smaller if the user were lounging at home in slippers and a bathrobe. Given the great variation possible in popliteal height due exclusively to attire, not to mention body size, a very strong argument can be presented for adjustability in all chair types. It should be noted that in determining seat height the type, resiliency, and sag of padding or upholstery should be considered. Moreover, when the chair is used in conjunction with a table, desk, or other work surface, or footrest, seat height dimensions can vary. These conditions, as well as others involving the anthropometrics of seating, will be examined graphically in Part C.

## 4.4 SEAT DEPTH

Another basic consideration in chair design is the depth of the seat. If the depth is too great, the front surface or edge of the seat will press into the area just behind the knees, cutting off circulation to the legs and feet as shown in Figure 4-7. The compression of the tissues will also cause irritation and discomfort. A greater danger, still, is the possibility of blood clotting, or thrombophlebitis, if the user does not change body position. To alleviate the discomfort in the legs, the user may move his buttocks forward, in which case his back becomes unsupported, body stability is weaker, and greater muscular force is required to maintain equilibrium. The result is fatigue, discomfort, and back pain. Too shallow a seat depth (Figure 4-8) may result in an awkward situation where the user has the sensation of falling off the front of the chair. In addition, a shallow seat depth will also result in a lack of support of the lower thighs.

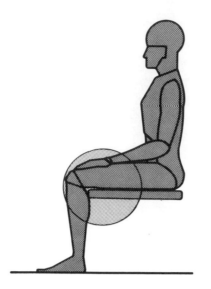
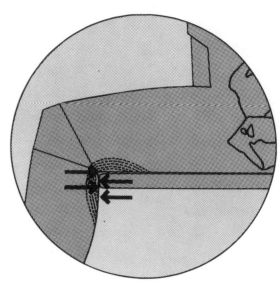

Figure 4–7. If the depth of the seat is too great, the seat front will press into the area just behind the knee, causing discomfort and problems with blood circulation.

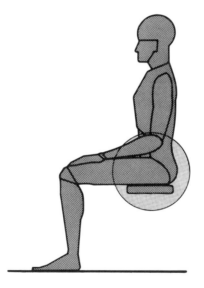
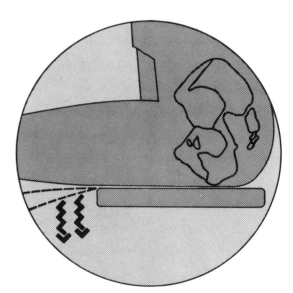

Figure 4–8. A shallow seat depth will deprive the sitter of proper support under the thighs. It may also give the sitter the sensation of tipping off the chair.

Anthropometrically, the buttock-popliteal length (the horizontal distance from the rearmost surface of the buttock to the back of the lower leg) is the measurement in the tables to be used to establish the proper seat depth.

Chart 4-1 indicates a 5th percentile buttock-popliteal length of 17.3 in, or 43.9 cm, for men and 17.0 in, or 43.2 cm, for women, while the smallest measurement indicated in Table 2K in Part B is the 1st percentile female data, with a measurement of 16.1 in, or 40.9 cm. Accordingly, a depth of seat measurement that exceeds about 16 in, or 40.6 cm simply would not accommodate the very small user, while a seat depth of 17 in, or 43.2 cm, for an easy chair, however, would accommodate about 95 percent of all users.

## 4.5 BACKREST

Although the size, configuration, and location of the backrest is one of the most important considerations necessary to ensure a proper fit between user and chair, it is also the most difficult component to dimension in reference to published anthropometric data. Despite the availability of those body measurements required in dimensioning

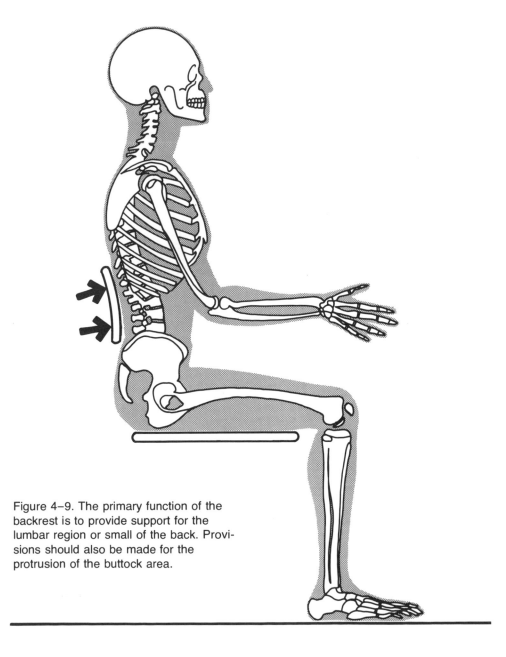

Figure 4–9. The primary function of the backrest is to provide support for the lumbar region or small of the back. Provisions should also be made for the protrusion of the buttock area.

basic chair parts, such as seat height, seat depth, seat width, and armrest heights, there is a paucity of data relating specifically to the lumbar region and spinal curvature. Accordingly, it will be necessary to limit discussion of the backrest to guidelines and some generalizations.

There appears to be general agreement that the primary function of the backrest is to provide support for the lumbar region, or small of the back (Figure 4-9). This is the concave lower portion which extends approximately from the waist to about the middle of the back. The configuration of the backrest, therefore, should to some extent accommodate the spinal profile, particularly in the lumbar area, as shown in Figure 4-10. Caution should be exercised, however, not to provide so close a fit as to prevent the user from shifting body position.

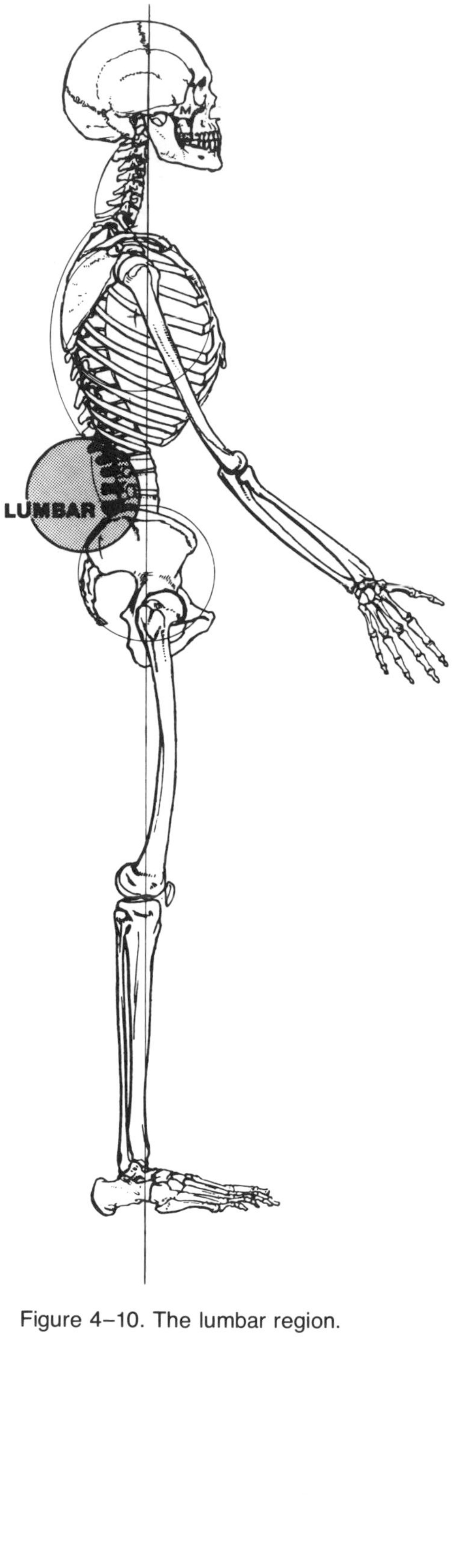

The overall height of the backrest may vary depending on the type and intended use of the chair involved. It may be just sufficient to provide lumbar support and little more, as in the case of the typical secretarial chair; or it may extend all the way to the back of the head or nape of the neck, as in easy chairs or reclining chairs, or possibly somewhere in between, as in general purpose seating. Provisions should also be made for necessary clearance to allow space for the protrusion of the buttock area. This clearance may take the form of an open area or recess between the seat surface and the lumbar support. Soft padding in this area will also accommodate the protrusion in the buttock region.

## 4.6 ARMRESTS

Armrests serve several functions. They support the weight of the arms and assist the user in lowering himself into the seat or in pushing or raising himself out of the seat. If the chair is used in conjunction with some work task, for instance, one involving the manipulation of sensitive console dials or controls the armrest can also function to steady the arm during the performance of the particular activities. Anthropometrically, several factors must be taken into consideration in sizing and locating the armrests. For the height of the armrest, the elbow rest height would appear to be the proper anthropometric reference measurement to apply. This measurement is the dimension from the tip of the elbow to the seat surface. The decision to be made is the particular percentile data to be selected.

But consider the problem of one user with a large body breadth dimension as opposed to another extremely slender person with a relatively small body breadth dimension, who both have identical elbow rest height measurements. It has been observed in such cases that the user with the narrow body breadth would require higher armrests, because as the arms swing outward to connect with the armrest, the vertical distance from the elbow to the seat increases. Since no basic relationship exists between transverse measurements and those in the vertical plane, it has been suggested that the armrest should accommodate the higher range elbow rest height. Those users with shorter elbow rest heights can use the armrests by abducting the arms or raising the shoulders. However, if the armrest is too high, the user may have to force or lever the trunk out of the chair and round

Figure 4–10. The lumbar region.

LUMBAR

the shoulders, resulting in fatigue and discomfort due to the muscular activity generated. Chart 4-1 shows the highest measurement for elbow rest height to be the 95th percentile male data, or 11.6 in, or 29.5 cm. Such an armrest height would, in fact, be uncomfortable for most people. The 70th percentile data would appear to be an optimal high range limitation and the 5th percentile the low limit. Most sources, therefore, recommend an armrest height between 7 and 10 in, or 17.8 and 25.4 cm.

## 4.7 CUSHIONING

The purpose of cushioning is essentially to distribute the pressure, due to the weight of the body at the point of interface, over a larger surface area. The danger, however, is for the designer to assume that the more opulent, deeper, and softer the cushioning, the greater the degree of comfort. This simply is not the case. All too often it is the very seating that appears overstuffed that, in fact, can provide the most discomfort, fatigue, and pain. Where the bone structures are closest to the skin are the areas of greatest potential discomfort due to the compressive stresses imposed on the body tissue. The ischial tuberosities in the buttock area mentioned previously are an excellent example of a sensitive area, in which the importance and need for proper cushioning is shown.

If cushioning is not properly designed, it is possible that relief from compressive stress may be obtained at the expense of body stability. Branton suggests that a state could be reached whereby the cushioning could deprive the body structure of support altogether. The body would "flounder about" in the soft mass of cushioning with only the feet resting on the floor, thereby increasing the burden of body stabilization on internal muscular activity.[11]

Still another source of discomfort may develop if the body weight causes the front end of the seat cushion to elevate, placing pressure on the bottom of the thigh and the nerves in that area. Similarly, if the body sinks too deeply into the cushioning, the sides and possibly the rear portions of the seat cushion may also elevate, producing additional pressures on the various parts of the body involved. In addition, the deeper the body sinks into the chair, the more effort is required to get out of the chair.

It is obvious that hard, flat seats are uncomfortable for extended use. It has also been suggested that excessively deep, soft cushioning can result in extreme discomfort. Although more research is required to objectively study the entire notion of sitter comfort, certain guidelines for proper cushioning have been suggested. Diffrient recommends that, for comfort, an average padded seat would have about 1.5 in, or 3.8 cm, of medium foam padding over .5 in, or 1.3 cm, of firm closed-cell padding, or a total of about 2 in, or 5.1 cm, with a maximum allowable seat compression of about 1.5 in. The seat compression allowance is based on a 172-lb, or 78-kg, male. For every 30 lb, or 13.6 kg, less, .25 in, or 6.4 mm, should be deducted. For every additional 30 lb, .25 in should be added.[12] Croney recommends a depression of about ½ in, or 13 mm.[13] Damon et al. suggest that 1 to 2 in, or 2.5 to 5.1 cm, of compression would suffice.[14]

# B HUMAN DIMENSION/ ANTHROPOMETRIC TABLES

As discussed in Part A, there is a paucity of anthropometric data appropriate in both content and form, specifically for use by the designers and builders of interior space. Much of the data available were not originally gathered with either the designer or the builder necessarily in mind. Accordingly, a large portion of the information in circulation is limited in use, since it usually reflects a specific population, age group, and sex not at all representative of the customary design market. In most instances, with the exception of the National Health Survey, the population is military, the age between 18 and 45 years, and the sex male—hardly a typical cross section of the broad market served by the architectural and interior design professions. To find all the data useful to the designer within a single reference source is almost impossible.

After some research, an inventory of nearly one hundred anthropometric studies involving almost one thousand different body measurements was compiled. It was then necessary to scan this inventory and filter out for presentation that information of most value to the architect and interior designer. In certain instances, it was necessary to modify the original form of the data so that they might be used more efficiently by designers. Moreover, in all cases where metric units were not indicated, necessary conversions were made. Where appropriate, diagrams and figures were drawn to further illustrate and explain the data. The result is the nine tables shown on the following pages.

Every effort has been made to review all the data for errors and inconsistencies. The quantity of statistics, the many different sources, the lack of control over methodologies employed, the metrication involved, the reproduction process, and the secondary nature of some of the material, however, make it impossible for the accuracy or consistency of all the data to be unconditionally guaranteed. In instances where the user requires more precise information with respect to various aspects of the data, the measuring techniques employed, or a more accurate description of the population involved, it is suggested he or she refer to the original sources. For this reason, the sources from which all the data for each table were extracted are cited at the beginning of each table or set of tables.

The user is also cautioned against the selection and application of data without first familiarizing himself with some of the fundamentals and basic theory discussed in the earlier section of the book. Data can be misleading and if used improperly can result in serious design errors. Finally, the user is cautioned that statistical data of itself is no substitute for common sense and prudent design analysis.

The data indicated in the tables that follow have been based on measurements taken of nude subjects or subjects wearing thin hospital gowns, who are either barefooted or wearing paper slippers. It is essential, therefore, that appropriate allowances be made for garments, shoes, and hats. These allowances may vary, depending on season, particular environment, sex, and even current fashion. In most cases these allowances will add to the body dimensions, but extremely heavy and bulky outerware, for example, may decrease reach measurements and the range of joint motion.

Although the tolerances and interface problems faced by the architect or interior designer will normally not be so complex or sophisticated as some of the military applications, the effect of clothing on human dimension and interior space is still an important factor. Sound judgment and common sense must be exercised by the designer in determining what body measurements will be affected and by how much. Reach and clearance are the essential factors to be considered. The following are allowances suggested for some of the more standard items of clothing and the more significant body dimensions affected. Each design situation, however, should be viewed individually. In some cases it may be necessary for the designer to develop additional allowance factors, appropriate to the specific design requirements and the critical body dimensions involved.

| CLOTHING TYPE | ALLOWANCE | | MOST IMPORTANT BODY DIMEN-SIONS AFFECTED |
|---|---|---|---|
| Men's suit | .50 in | 1.3 cm | Body depth |
| | .75-1.0 in | 1.9-2.5 cm | Body breadth |
| Women's suit or dress | .25-.50 in | 0.6-1.3 cm | Body depth |
| | .50-.75 in | 1.3-1.9 cm | Body breadth |
| Winter outerware including basic suit or dress | 2.0 in | 5.1 cm | Body depth |
| | 3.0-4.0 in | 7.6-10.2 cm | Body breadth |
| | 1.75-2.0 in | 4.4-5.1 cm | Thigh clearance |
| Men's heels | 1.0-1.5 in | 2.5-3.8 cm | Stature, eye height, knee height sitting , popliteal height |
| Women's heels | 1.0-3.0 in | 2.5-7.6 cm | Stature, eye height, knee height sitting , popliteal height |
| Men's shoes | 1.25-1.5 in | 3.2-3.8 cm | Foot length |
| Women's shoes | .5-.75 in | 1.3-1.9 cm | Foot length |
| Gloves | .25-.50 in | 0.6-1.3 cm | Hand length, hand breadth |

# **1** METROLOGICAL ANALYSIS

## DESCRIPTION

The anthropometric data reflected in the other tables (2 through 8) involve certain specific structural and functional measurements. The proper use of this information requires some knowledge of the nature of these measurements. Table 1 includes the generally accepted anthropometric terms for the various measurements, their definitions, information regarding their particular applicability and use, general factors to be considered, and indications as to whether 5th or 95th percentile data should be selected.

The user is cautioned not to view all the definitions as necessarily representing precise technical descriptions of the specific measuring techniques used, since those techniques may differ slightly with each survey. The definitions are, however, reasonably accurate and representative, particularly in terms of the nature of their intended usage by architects or interior designers. If unique design situations make a more precise definition critical, refer to the original survey upon which the data are based.

## SOURCE

No single authority was consulted for all the definitions provided. Various sources of reference, however, were consulted, including Albert Damon, Howard W. Stoudt, Ross McFarland, *The Human Body in Equipment Design* (Cambridge, Mass.: Harvard University Press, 1971); Wesley Woodson and Donald W. Conover, *Human Engineering Guide for Equipment Designers,* 2d ed. (Berkeley and Los Angeles: University of California Press, 1964); and *Anthropometric Source Book, vol. 2: A Handbook of Anthropometric Data,* NASA Reference Publication 1024, July 1978. In some instances, the exact wording of the definitions was used; in other instances, abbreviated versions were employed; and in still other instances where definitions were not readily available, the terms were defined by the authors.

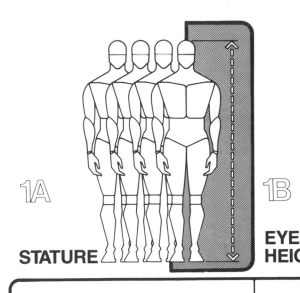

## STATURE

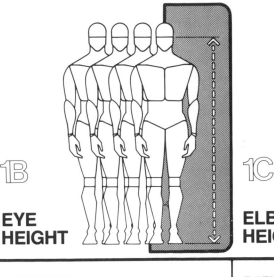

## EYE HEIGHT

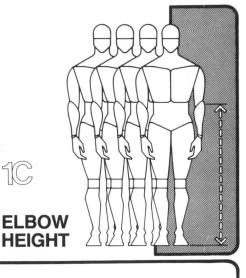

## ELBOW HEIGHT

### DEFINITION

Stature is the vertical distance from the floor to the top of the head, measured while the subject stands erect, looking straight ahead.

### APPLICABILITY

These data are useful in establishing minimum heights of openings and doors. Normally, however, building codes and/or the standard manufactured sizes of doors and frames are more than adequate to accommodate at least 99 percent of the user population. The data can be more useful in determining the minimum distances of overhead obstructions from the floor.

### CONSIDERATIONS

Measurements are usually taken without shoes. Accordingly, appropriate compensation in the data should be made.

### PERCENTILE SELECTION

Since clearance is the operative functional factor, the upper percentile range should be accommodated. Because ceiling heights are usually never critical dimensions, the designer should accommodate as close to 100 percent of the population as possible.

### DEFINITION

Eye height is the vertical distance from the floor to the inner corner of the eye, measured with the subject looking straight ahead and standing erect.

### APPLICABILITY

These data can be helpful in establishing sight lines in such facilities as theaters, auditoriums, conference rooms and in the placement of sign-age and other visual material. They can also be useful in establishing heights of privacy screens and low or open plan office partitions.

### CONSIDERATIONS

Approximately 2.5 cm, or 1 in, should be added for men's shoes and 7.6 cm, or 3 in, for women's shoes, since measurements are normally taken with the subject barefooted. These data should be used in conjunction with neck flexion and rotation data, as well as sight angle information, to establish the range of visual field under varying conditions and head angles.

### PERCENTILE SELECTION

Percentile selection will depend on a variety of factors. If, for example, the design problem involves determining the height of a partition or screen to ensure privacy of the person behind the screen, then screen height should relate to the eye height of the taller person (95th percentile or above). The logic is that if a tall person cannot see over the screen, then surely a short person cannot see over it. If the design problem, instead, is to allow a person to look over a screen, the reverse logic would hold true. The height of the screen should relate to the eye height of the shorter person (5th percentile or less). If a short person can see over the screen, then a tall person will be able to as well.

### DEFINITION

Elbow height is the distance measured vertically from the floor to the depression formed at the elbow where the forearm meets the upper arm.

### APPLICABILITY

Elbow height data are essential in establishing comfortable heights for work counters, vanities, kitchen counters, work benches, and other work surfaces used while standing. Too often, heights of such surfaces have been established by chance, rule of thumb, or "trade practice." Scientific studies, however, place the most comfortable height at 3 in, or 7.6 cm, below elbow height, while a ballpark figure for a rest surface is of 1 to 1½ in, or 2.5 to 3.8 cm, below elbow height.

### CONSIDERATIONS

The nature of activity should be considered in establishing height. In many instances this will take precedence over the suggested "elbow height less 3 in" (7.6 cm) recommendation.

### PERCENTILE SELECTION

Assuming the work surface height is at the recommended 3 in, or 7.6 cm, below elbow height, a range from 38 in, or 96.5 cm (reflecting the 5th percentile measurement), to 43 in, or 109.2 cm (reflecting the 95th percentile measurement), should accommodate the middle 90 percent of the male user population. In view of the smaller elbow height 5th percentile dimension for females, a range from 35 in, or 88.9 cm, to 43 in, or 109.2 cm, is necessary to accommodate both sexes. These figures are all tentative, however, because of the number of variables involved, i.e., the specific function to be performed and differing opinions as to optimal height.

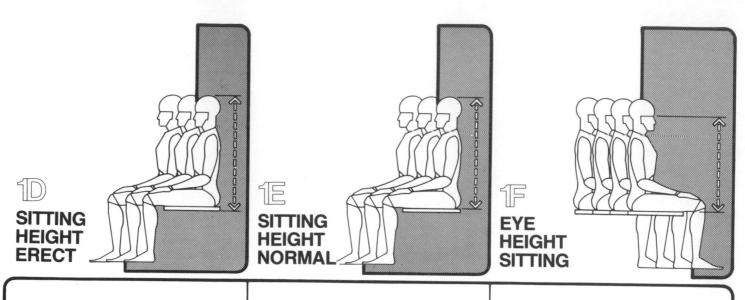

| 1D SITTING HEIGHT ERECT | 1E SITTING HEIGHT NORMAL | 1F EYE HEIGHT SITTING |

## DEFINITION
Sitting height erect is the vertical distance from the sitting surface to the top of the head with the subject sitting erect.

## APPLICATION
This measurement would be helpful in determining the allowable height of obstructions from the surface of a seat or, by adding the seat height, the height of the obstruction above the floor. Bunk bed arrangements and innovative space-saving designs, such as where the area under a loft bed is utilized as an eating or work area, could be predicated upon these critical data. The heights of low privacy partitions in offices or other spaces could also be established with the use of these measurements, as could the height of booth partitions in eating and drinking spaces.

## CONSIDERATIONS
The slope of the seat, resiliency of the upholstery, clothing, and body movements getting in and out of the seat are all important factors to consider.

## PERCENTILE SELECTION
The 95th percentile data are more appropriate due to the clearance factor involved.

## DEFINITION
Sitting height normal is the vertical distance from the sitting surface to the top of the head, measured with the subject sitting relaxed.

## APPLICATION
This measurement would be helpful in determining minimum height of obstructions from the surface of a seat or, by adding the seat height, the minimum height of the obstruction above the floor. Bunk bed arrangements and innovative space-saving designs, such as where the area under a loft bed is utilized as an eating or work area, could be predicated upon these critical data. The heights of low privacy partitions in offices or other spaces could also be established with the use of these measurements, as could the height of booth partitions in eating and drinking spaces.

## CONSIDERATIONS
The slope of the seat, resiliency of the upholstery, clothing, and the body movements getting in and out of the seat are all important factors to consider.

## PERCENTILE SELECTION
The 95th percentile data are more appropriate due to the clearance factor involved.

## DEFINITION
Eye height is the vertical distance from the inner corner of the eye to the sitting surface.

## APPLICATION
The primary value of this measurement would be in determining sight lines and optimum fields of vision where visibility is one of the central design considerations, such as in theaters, auditoriums, lecture rooms, and other interior spaces in which audiovisual activities are required.

## CONSIDERATIONS
The range of head and eye movement discussed elsewhere in the book should be considered, as well as the resiliency of the seat upholstery, the height of the seat above the floor, and provisions for adjustability.

## PERCENTILE SELECTION
Providing proper adjustability can permit a range of accommodation from 5th to 95th percentile or greater.

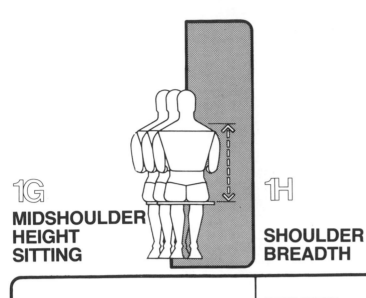
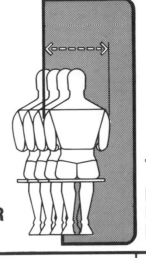
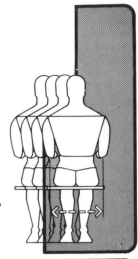

## 1G MIDSHOULDER HEIGHT SITTING

### DEFINITION
Shoulder height is the distance taken vertically from the sitting surface to a point on the shoulder midway between the neck and acromion.

### APPLICABILITY
These data are of most use in the design of tight work spaces in vehicle design and of limited use to the architect or interior designer. They can be of some help, however, in determining obstructions to visibility in the planning of spaces where audiovisual activities take place and perhaps in determining heights of seating booth and other similar design situations.

### CONSIDERATIONS
The resiliency of the chair upholstery should be considered.

### PERCENTILE SELECTION
Since clearance is the operative design factor, 95th percentile data should be used.

## 1H SHOULDER BREADTH

### DEFINITION
Shoulder breadth is the maximum horizontal distance across the deltoid muscles.

### APPLICABILITY
Shoulder breadth data are most useful to the interior designer or architect in helping to establish allowances for seating around tables and for row seating in theaters and auditoriums. They can also be useful in establishing clearances for circulation in public and private spaces.

### CONSIDERATIONS
These data should be used cautiously in view of the many variables that can be involved. Allowances for clothing should be made, with 7.9 mm, or 5/16 in, for light clothing and about 7.6 cm, or 3 in, for heavy clothing. It should also be noted that the space required across the shoulder is increased by movements of the trunk and shoulder.

### PERCENTILE SELECTION
Since clearance is the operative design factor, 95th percentile data should be used.

## 1 ELBOW-TO-ELBOW BREADTH

### DEFINITION
Elbow to elbow is the distance across the lateral surfaces of the elbows measured with elbows flexed and resting lightly against the body with the forearms extended horizontally.

### APPLICABILITY
These data could be helpful in determining allowances for seating around conference tables, dining tables, counters, card or game tables.

### CONSIDERATIONS
These should be used in conjunction with shoulder breadth measurements as required.

### PERCENTILE
Since clearance is the operative design factor, 95th percentile data should be used.

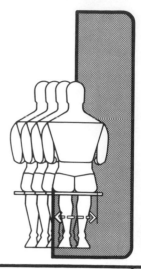

# HIP BREADTH

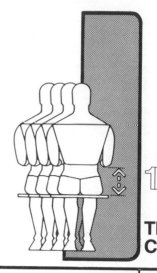

# ELBOW REST HEIGHT

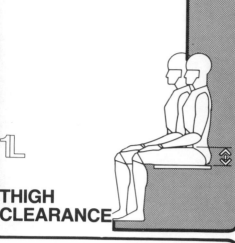

# THIGH CLEARANCE

### DEFINITION
Hip breadth is the breadth of the body as measured across the widest portion of the hips. Note that a hip breadth measurement can also be taken with the subject in a standing position, in which case the definition would be the maximum breadth of the lower torso. The data in subsequent tables, however, refer to the sitting position as indicated.

### APPLICABILITY
These data could be extremely helpful in determining allowances for inside chair width dimensions, bar and counter seating, perch-type office stools.

### CONSIDERATIONS
Depending on the particular application, these data should be used in conjunction with elbow to elbow and shoulder breadth dimensions as required.

### PERCENTILE
Since clearance is the operative design factor, 95th percentile data should be used.

### DEFINITION
Elbow rest height is the height from the top of the sitting surface to the bottom of the tip of the elbow.

### APPLICABILITY
These data, together with other appropriate data and considerations, could be helpful in determining heights of armrests, work counters, desks, tables, special equipment.

### CONSIDERATIONS
Resiliency of the chair upholstery, slope of seat, and body posture should all be taken into consideration.

### PERCENTILE SELECTION
Elbow rest height is really neither a clearance situation nor a reach situation, particularly when an armrest is involved. The intent is for the arm to rest comfortably on a surface. Data around the 50th percentile would be appropriate. In any event a range between 14 and 27.9 cm, or 5½ and 11 in, should suit most users.

### DEFINITION
Thigh clearance is the distance taken vertically from a sitting surface to the top of the thigh at the point where the thigh and the abdomen intersect.

### APPLICABILITY
These data are critical in the design of interior elements such as counters, desks, conference tables, cabinetwork, or furniture that may require the user, while seated, to position his or her legs under the work surface. More specifically, the data are essential in order to establish the dimension of any apron or drawers situated directly below the work surface so that adequate clearance will be allowed between the top of the thigh and the bottom of any obstruction above it.

### CONSIDERATIONS
In determining the maximum dimensions mentioned above, several other factors must also be considered such as popliteal height and the resiliency of the upholstery of the chair.

### PERCENTILE SELECTION
Since clearance is the operative design factor, 95th percentile data should be used.

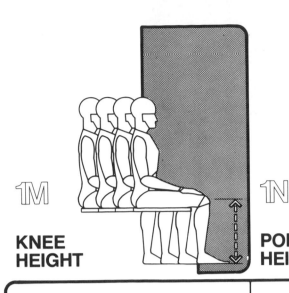

## KNEE HEIGHT

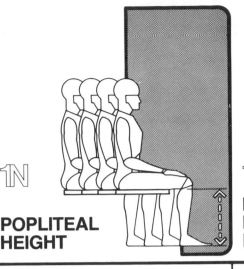

## POPLITEAL HEIGHT

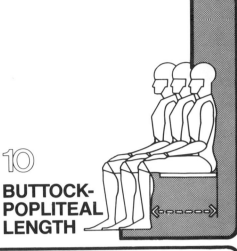

## BUTTOCK-POPLITEAL LENGTH

### DEFINITION
Knee height is the vertical distance from the floor to the midpoint of the kneecap.

### APPLICABILITY
These data are critical in establishing the distance from the floor to the underside of a desk, table, or counter, particularly where the seated user is required to have his lower body partially under the furniture. How close the seated user will be located to the object will dictate if the knee height dimension alone or the thigh clearance measurement will be the determining factor.

### CONSIDERATIONS
The height of the seat as well as the resiliency of the upholstery should also be considered.

### PERCENTILE SELECTION
To ensure clearance, 95th percentile data should be used.

### DEFINITION
Popliteal height is the distance, taken vertically, from the floor to the underside of the portion of the thigh just behind the knee while the subject is seated with body erect. The knees and ankles are usually perpendicular, with the bottom of the thigh and the back of the knees barely touching the sitting surface.

### APPLICABILITY
These data are critical in establishing the height of seating surfaces above the floor, particularly the highest point on the front of the seat.

### CONSIDERATIONS
In applying the data, it is necessary to take into consideration the resiliency of the upholstered seat surface.

### PERCENTILE SELECTION
In establishing seat height, 5th percentile data should be used. Pressure on the underside of the thigh is one of the causes of user discomfort. This condition occurs when the height of the seat is too great. A seat height that will accommodate the user with the smaller popliteal height will also suit the user with greater popliteal height.

### DEFINITION
Buttock-popliteal length is the horizontal distance from the rearmost surface of the buttock to the back of the lower leg.

### APPLICABILITY
These data are useful in connection with seating design, particularly location of legs, vertical surfaces of the front of benches, banquettes, etc., as well as determination of seat lengths.

### CONSIDERATIONS
The angle of the seat should be considered.

### PERCENTILE SELECTION
The 5th percentile data should be used. These will accommodate the greatest number of users: those with shorter buttock-popliteal lengths as well as those with greater lengths. If 95th percentile data are used, the design will accommodate the users with the larger measurements only, but not those with the smaller measurements.

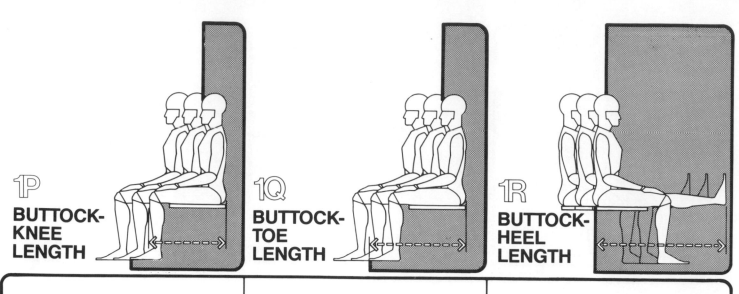

## 1P BUTTOCK-KNEE LENGTH

### DEFINITION
Buttock-knee length is the horizontal distance from the rearmost surface of the buttocks to the front of the kneecaps.

### APPLICABILITY
These data can be useful in determining the proper distance from the back of a seat to any physical obstruction or objects located in front of the knees. Fixed seating in auditoriums, theaters, and places of worship are space types where this would apply.

### CONSIDERATIONS
The buttock-knee length dimension is less than the buttock-toe length. If no toe space is provided in the equipment, furniture, or other interior elements positioned in front of the seat, the buttock-toe length measurement must be used to allow for proper clearance.

### PERCENTILE SELECTION
Since clearance is the operative design factor, 95th percentile data should be used.

## 1Q BUTTOCK-TOE LENGTH

### DEFINITION
Buttock-toe length is the horizontal distance from the rearmost surface of the buttocks to the tip of the toe.

### APPLICABILITY
These data can be useful in determining the proper distance from the back of a seat to any physical obstruction or objects located in front of the knees. Fixed seating in auditoriums, theaters, and places of worship are space types in which this would apply.

### CONSIDERATIONS
If toe space is provided in the equipment, furniture, or other interior elements positioned in front of the knee and spacing is critical, the buttock-knee length may be used, instead, in helping to determine proper clearances.

### PERCENTILE SELECTION
Since clearance is the operative design factor, 95th percentile data should be used.

## 1R BUTTOCK-HEEL LENGTH

### DEFINITION
Buttock-heel length is the horizontal distance from the base of the heel to a wall against which the subject sits erect with his leg maximally extended forward along the sitting surface. This is sometimes referred to as buttock-leg length.

### APPLICABILITY
These data generally would have limited applicability for the interior designer, with the exception of determining space requirements for lounge and informal seating arrangements. The data might, for example, be useful in determining combined space requirements for chair and ottoman arrangements as well as physical therapy or exercise equipment and space.

### CONSIDERATIONS
The extent to which the buttock-leg length might be increased by any specialized footgear should be reflected in the clearances allowed in the design. In all cases about 1 in, or 2.5 cm, should be added for men's shoes and about 3 in, or 7.6 cm, for women's shoes.

### PERCENTILE SELECTION
Since clearance is the operative design factor, 95th percentile data should be used.

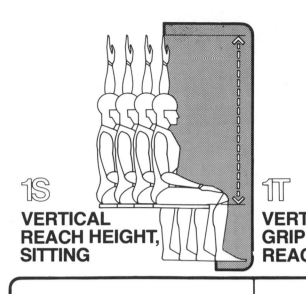

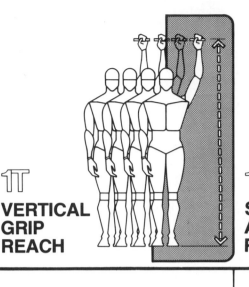

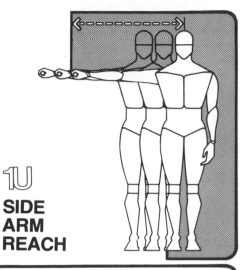

# 1S
## VERTICAL REACH HEIGHT, SITTING

# 1T
## VERTICAL GRIP REACH

# 1U
## SIDE ARM REACH

### DEFINITION
Vertical reach is the height above the sitting surface of the tip of the middle finger when the arm, hand, and fingers are extended vertically.

### APPLICABILITY
This measurement would be of primary value in establishing the location of overhead controls, buttons, etc., and accordingly would be of more use to an equipment designer.

### CONSIDERATIONS
Angle of seat and resiliency of upholstery should be considered.

### PERCENTILE SELECTION
The 5th percentile would be most appropriate. If a user with the shortest reach is accommodated, the one with the longest reach will be accommodated.

### DEFINITION
Vertical grip reach is usually measured from the floor to the top of a bar grasped in the right hand while the subject stands erect and the hand within which the bar is grasped is raised as high as it can be conveniently without experiencing discomfort or strain.

### APPLICABILITY
Perhaps the most useful application of these data is in establishing maximum heights above the floor for switches, controls, levers, handles, book shelves, hat shelves, etc.

### CONSIDERATIONS
Measurements are usually taken without shoes. Accordingly, appropriate compensation in the data should be made.

### PERCENTILE SELECTION
The operative functional factor is reach. If the higher percentile data are used, the design will accommodate those users with the greatest reach, but the user population with the smaller overhead reach will not be accommodated. A design based on the lower percentile range, however, will accommodate not only the smaller, but the larger user.

### DEFINITION
Side arm reach is the distance from the center line of the body to the outside surface of a bar grasped in the right hand while the subject stands erect and the arm is conveniently outstretched horizontally without experiencing discomfort or strain.

### APPLICABILITY
This measurement would prove more useful to the equipment designer in locating controls. It can be useful to the architect or interior designer, however, in the design of specialized spaces, such as hospital interiors or laboratories. If the user were in a seated position, the dimension, although possibly slightly changed, would still be useful in locating a bookshelf located to the side.

### CONSIDERATIONS
If the activity involved requires the use of any specialized handgear, gloves, or any device that by its nature would extend the user's normal reach, the extent to which the reach may be increased should be taken into consideration.

### PERCENTILE SELECTION
Since the operative functional factor is reach, this constitutes a classic situation where the users with the smallest arm reach dimension should be accommodated. Accordingly, 5th percentile data should be utilized.

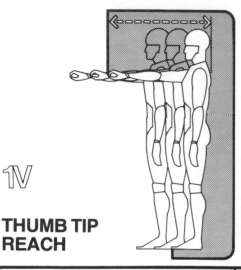

# 1V
## THUMB TIP REACH

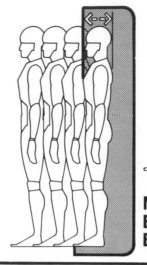

# 1X
## MAXIMUM BODY DEPTH

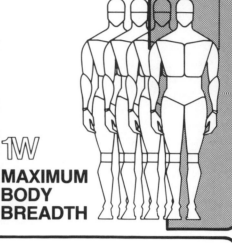

# 1W
## MAXIMUM BODY BREADTH

### DEFINITION
Thumb tip reach is the distance from the wall to the tip of the thumb measured with the subject's shoulders against the wall, his arm extended forward, and his index finger touching the tip of his thumb.

### APPLICABILITY
Perhaps the primary value of these data is in establishing a maximum dimension for obstructions over which a user might be compelled to reach to grasp an object or operate a piece of equipment. An example of such a design situation might be shelving over a workcounter or cabinets fastened to low office partitions in front of a desk.

### CONSIDERATIONS
The specific nature of the operation or task should be considered.

### PERCENTILE SELECTION
Since the operative functional factor is reach, this constitutes a classic situation where the users with the smallest arm reach dimension should be accommodated. Accordingly, 5th percentile data should be utilized.

### DEFINITION
Maximum body depth is the horizontal distance between the most anterior point on the body to the most posterior. Anterior points are usually located on the chest or abdomen while the posterior points are usually found in the buttock or shoulder region.

### APPLICABILITY
Although of more value to an equipment designer, this information could be useful to the architect in providing necessary clearances in extremely tight spaces or queuing situations.

### CONSIDERATIONS
Type of clothing, sex of user, and hidden dimension, discussed in Section A, should all be considered.

### PERCENTILE SELECTION
The 95th percentile data would be most appropriate.

### DEFINITION
Maximum body breadth is the maximum distance, including arms, across the body.

### APPLICABILITY
This measurement would be useful in planning aisle widths, corridor widths, door or access opening widths, public assembly areas, etc.

### CONSIDERATIONS
Type of clothing, stride and other body movements, as well as hidden dimensions, discussed in Section A, should be considered.

### PERCENTILE SELECTION
The 95th percentile data would be most appropriate.

# 2 ADULT MALE AND FEMALE

# WEIGHT AND STRUCTURAL BODY DIMENSIONS

## DESCRIPTION

This table is probably the most comprehensive and current source of available adult civilian anthropometric data. Prepared by Dr. Howard Stoudt, Dr. Albert Damon, and Dr. Ross McFarland formerly of the Harvard School of Public Health, in conjunction with Jean Roberts of the U.S. Public Health Service, it provides detailed body measurements for both sexes and is broken down by age categories (18–24, 25–34, 35–44, 45–54, 55–64, 65–74, and 75–79) as well as by percentiles. In addition to weight, eleven different body measurements are given: stature, sitting height erect, sitting height normal, elbow rest height, thigh clearance height, knee height, popliteal height, buttock-popliteal length, buttock-knee length, elbow-to-elbow breadth, and seat breadth. Proper allowances for clothing and shoes should be added to all data.

## SOURCE

Howard W. Stoudt, Albert Damon, Ross McFarland, and Jean Roberts, "National Health Survey 1962: Weight, Height and Selected Body Dimensions of Adults, United States 1960–1962" (Washington, D.C.: U.S. Government Printing Office, Public Health Service Publication no. 1000 Series 11, no. 8, June 1965).

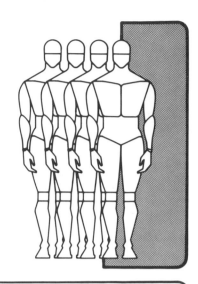

2A

## WEIGHT

| | | 18 to 79 (Total) | | 18 to 24 Years | | 25 to 34 Years | | 35 to 44 Years | | 45 to 54 Years | | 55 to 64 Years | | 65 to 74 Years | | 75 to 79 Years | |
|---|---|---|---|---|---|---|---|---|---|---|---|---|---|---|---|---|---|
| | | lb | kg | lb | kg | lb | kg | lb | kg | lb | kg | lb | kg | lb | kg | lb | kg |
| **99** | MEN | 241 | 109.3 | 231 | 104.8 | 248 | 112.5 | 244 | 110.7 | 241 | 109.3 | 230 | 104.3 | 225 | 102.0 | 212 | 96.2 |
| | WOMEN | 236 | 107.0 | 218 | 98.9 | 239 | 108.4 | 238 | 108.0 | 240 | 108.9 | 244 | 110.7 | 214 | 97.1 | 205 | 93.0 |
| **95** | **MEN** | **212** | **96.2** | **214** | **97.1** | **223** | **101.2** | **219** | **99.3** | **219** | **99.3** | **213** | **96.6** | **207** | **93.9** | **198** | **89.8** |
| | **WOMEN** | **199** | **90.3** | **170** | **77.1** | **191** | **86.6** | **204** | **92.5** | **205** | **93.0** | **211** | **95.7** | **196** | **88.9** | **193** | **87.5** |
| **90** | MEN | 205 | 93.0 | 193 | 87.5 | 208 | 94.3 | 207 | 93.9 | 209 | 94.8 | 203 | 92.1 | 198 | 89.8 | 191 | 86.6 |
| | WOMEN | 182 | 82.6 | 157 | 71.2 | 173 | 78.5 | 184 | 83.5 | 190 | 86.2 | 195 | 88.5 | 183 | 83.0 | 178 | 80.7 |
| **80** | MEN | 190 | 86.2 | 180 | 81.6 | 195 | 88.5 | 193 | 87.5 | 194 | 88.0 | 190 | 86.2 | 183 | 83.0 | 170 | 77.1 |
| | WOMEN | 164 | 74.4 | 145 | 65.8 | 152 | 68.9 | 165 | 74.8 | 171 | 77.6 | 176 | 79.8 | 169 | 76.7 | 162 | 73.5 |
| **70** | MEN | 181 | 82.1 | 171 | 77.6 | 185 | 83.9 | 184 | 83.5 | 185 | 83.9 | 180 | 81.6 | 172 | 78.0 | 161 | 73.0 |
| | WOMEN | 152 | 68.9 | 137 | 62.1 | 143 | 64.9 | 153 | 69.4 | 158 | 71.7 | 165 | 74.8 | 160 | 72.6 | 155 | 70.3 |
| **60** | MEN | 173 | 78.5 | 164 | 74.4 | 177 | 80.3 | 177 | 80.3 | 178 | 80.7 | 172 | 78.0 | 166 | 75.3 | 150 | 68.0 |
| | WOMEN | 144 | 65.3 | 131 | 59.4 | 136 | 61.7 | 144 | 65.3 | 149 | 67.6 | 154 | 69.9 | 151 | 68.5 | 147 | 66.7 |
| **50** | MEN | 166 | 75.3 | 157 | 71.2 | 169 | 76.7 | 171 | 77.6 | 171 | 77.6 | 165 | 74.8 | 161 | 73.0 | 146 | 66.2 |
| | WOMEN | 137 | 62.1 | 126 | 57.2 | 130 | 59.0 | 137 | 62.1 | 143 | 64.9 | 146 | 66.2 | 145 | 65.8 | 137 | 62.1 |
| **40** | MEN | 159 | 72.1 | 151 | 68.5 | 162 | 73.5 | 164 | 74.4 | 163 | 73.9 | 158 | 71.7 | 153 | 69.4 | 141 | 64.0 |
| | WOMEN | 131 | 59.4 | 122 | 55.3 | 125 | 56.7 | 131 | 59.4 | 137 | 62.1 | 140 | 63.5 | 138 | 62.6 | 127 | 57.6 |
| **30** | MEN | 152 | 68.9 | 145 | 65.8 | 154 | 69.9 | 158 | 71.7 | 156 | 70.8 | 151 | 68.5 | 146 | 66.2 | 137 | 62.1 |
| | WOMEN | 125 | 56.7 | 117 | 53.1 | 120 | 54.4 | 125 | 56.7 | 130 | 59.0 | 134 | 60.8 | 132 | 59.9 | 119 | 54.0 |
| **20** | MEN | 144 | 65.3 | 140 | 63.5 | 146 | 66.2 | 151 | 68.5 | 149 | 67.6 | 143 | 64.9 | 138 | 62.6 | 132 | 59.9 |
| | WOMEN | 118 | 53.5 | 111 | 50.3 | 114 | 51.7 | 119 | 54.0 | 122 | 55.3 | 129 | 58.5 | 125 | 56.7 | 113 | 51.3 |
| **10** | MEN | 134 | 60.8 | 131 | 59.4 | 136 | 61.7 | 141 | 64.0 | 139 | 63.0 | 131 | 59.4 | 126 | 57.2 | 120 | 54.4 |
| | WOMEN | 111 | 50.3 | 104 | 47.2 | 107 | 48.5 | 113 | 51.3 | 113 | 51.3 | 120 | 54.4 | 114 | 51.7 | 105 | 47.6 |
| **5** | **MEN** | **126** | **57.2** | **124** | **56.2** | **129** | **58.5** | **134** | **60.8** | **131** | **59.4** | **123** | **55.8** | **117** | **53.1** | **107** | **48.5** |
| | **WOMEN** | **104** | **47.2** | **99** | **44.9** | **102** | **46.3** | **109** | **49.4** | **106** | **48.1** | **112** | **50.8** | **106** | **48.1** | **95** | **43.1** |
| **1** | MEN | 112 | 50.8 | 115 | 52.2 | 114 | 51.7 | 121 | 54.9 | 116 | 52.6 | 112 | 50.8 | 99 | 44.9 | 99 | 44.9 |
| | WOMEN | 93 | 42.2 | 91 | 41.3 | 92 | 41.7 | 100 | 45.4 | 95 | 43.1 | 95 | 43.1 | 92 | 41.7 | 74 | 33.6 |

**Adult Male and Female Weight* in Pounds and Kilograms by Age, Sex, and Selected Percentiles†**

*All measurements were made with the examinee stripped to the waist and without shoes, but wearing paper slippers and a lightweight, knee-length examining gown. Men's trouser pockets were emptied.
†Measurement below which the indicated percent of people in the given age group fall.

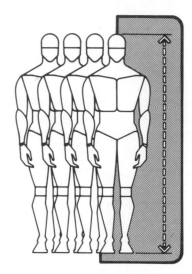

2B

## STATURE

### Adult Male and Female Stature* in Inches and Centimeters by Age, Sex and Selected Percentiles†

| Percentile | | 18 to 79 (Total) in | cm | 18 to 24 Years in | cm | 25 to 34 Years in | cm | 35 to 44 Years in | cm | 45 to 54 Years in | cm | 55 to 64 Years in | cm | 65 to 74 Years in | cm | 75 to 79 Years in | cm |
|---|---|---|---|---|---|---|---|---|---|---|---|---|---|---|---|---|---|
| 99 | MEN | 74.6 | 189.5 | 74.8 | 190.0 | 76.0 | 193.0 | 74.1 | 188.2 | 74.0 | 188.0 | 73.5 | 186.7 | 72.0 | 182.9 | 72.6 | 184.4 |
| 99 | WOMEN | 68.8 | 174.8 | 69.3 | 176.0 | 69.0 | 175.3 | 69.0 | 175.3 | 68.7 | 174.5 | 68.7 | 174.5 | 67.0 | 170.2 | 68.2 | 173.2 |
| 95 | **MEN** | **72.8** | **184.9** | **73.1** | **185.7** | **73.8** | **187.5** | **72.5** | **184.2** | **72.7** | **184.7** | **72.2** | **183.4** | **70.9** | **180.1** | **70.5** | **179.1** |
| 95 | **WOMEN** | **67.1** | **170.4** | **67.9** | **172.5** | **67.3** | **170.9** | **67.2** | **170.7** | **67.2** | **170.7** | **66.6** | **169.2** | **65.5** | **166.4** | **64.9** | **164.8** |
| 90 | MEN | 71.8 | 182.4 | 72.4 | 183.9 | 72.7 | 184.7 | 71.7 | 182.1 | 71.7 | 182.1 | 71.0 | 180.3 | 70.2 | 178.3 | 69.5 | 176.5 |
| 90 | WOMEN | 66.4 | 168.7 | 66.8 | 169.7 | 66.6 | 169.2 | 66.6 | 169.2 | 66.1 | 167.9 | 65.6 | 166.6 | 64.7 | 164.3 | 64.5 | 163.8 |
| 80 | MEN | 70.6 | 179.3 | 70.9 | 180.1 | 71.4 | 181.4 | 70.7 | 179.6 | 70.5 | 179.1 | 69.8 | 177.3 | 68.9 | 175.0 | 68.1 | 173.0 |
| 80 | WOMEN | 65.1 | 165.4 | 65.9 | 167.4 | 65.7 | 166.9 | 65.5 | 166.4 | 64.8 | 164.6 | 64.3 | 163.3 | 63.7 | 161.8 | 63.6 | 161.5 |
| 70 | MEN | 69.7 | 177.0 | 70.1 | 178.1 | 70.5 | 179.1 | 70.0 | 177.8 | 69.5 | 176.5 | 68.8 | 174.8 | 68.3 | 173.5 | 67.0 | 170.2 |
| 70 | WOMEN | 64.4 | 163.6 | 65.0 | 165.1 | 64.9 | 164.8 | 64.7 | 164.3 | 64.1 | 162.8 | 63.6 | 161.5 | 62.8 | 159.5 | 62.8 | 159.5 |
| 60 | MEN | 68.8 | 174.8 | 69.3 | 176.0 | 69.8 | 177.3 | 69.2 | 175.8 | 68.8 | 174.8 | 68.3 | 173.5 | 67.5 | 171.5 | 66.6 | 169.2 |
| 60 | WOMEN | 63.7 | 161.8 | 64.5 | 163.8 | 64.4 | 163.6 | 64.1 | 162.8 | 63.4 | 161.0 | 62.9 | 159.8 | 62.1 | 157.7 | 62.3 | 158.2 |
| 50 | MEN | 68.3 | 173.5 | 68.6 | 174.2 | 69.0 | 175.3 | 68.6 | 174.2 | 68.3 | 173.5 | 67.6 | 171.7 | 66.8 | 169.7 | 66.2 | 168.1 |
| 50 | WOMEN | 62.9 | 159.8 | 63.9 | 162.3 | 63.7 | 161.8 | 63.4 | 161.0 | 62.8 | 159.5 | 62.3 | 158.2 | 61.6 | 156.5 | 61.8 | 157.0 |
| 40 | MEN | 67.6 | 171.7 | 67.9 | 172.5 | 68.4 | 173.7 | 68.1 | 173.0 | 67.7 | 172.0 | 66.8 | 169.7 | 66.2 | 168.1 | 65.0 | 165.1 |
| 40 | WOMEN | 62.4 | 158.5 | 63.0 | 160.0 | 62.9 | 159.8 | 62.8 | 159.5 | 62.3 | 158.2 | 61.8 | 157.0 | 61.1 | 155.2 | 61.3 | 155.7 |
| 30 | MEN | 66.8 | 169.7 | 67.1 | 170.4 | 67.7 | 172.0 | 67.3 | 170.9 | 66.9 | 169.9 | 66.0 | 167.6 | 65.5 | 166.4 | 64.2 | 163.1 |
| 30 | WOMEN | 61.8 | 157.0 | 62.3 | 158.2 | 62.4 | 158.5 | 62.2 | 158.0 | 61.7 | 156.7 | 61.3 | 155.7 | 60.2 | 152.9 | 60.1 | 152.7 |
| 20 | MEN | 66.0 | 167.6 | 66.5 | 168.9 | 66.8 | 169.7 | 66.4 | 168.7 | 66.1 | 167.9 | 64.7 | 164.3 | 64.8 | 164.6 | 63.3 | 160.8 |
| 20 | WOMEN | 61.1 | 155.2 | 61.6 | 156.5 | 61.8 | 157.0 | 61.4 | 156.0 | 60.9 | 154.7 | 60.6 | 153.9 | 59.5 | 151.1 | 59.0 | 149.9 |
| 10 | MEN | 64.5 | 163.8 | 65.4 | 166.1 | 65.5 | 166.4 | 65.2 | 165.6 | 64.8 | 164.6 | 63.7 | 161.8 | 64.1 | 162.8 | 62.0 | 157.5 |
| 10 | WOMEN | 59.8 | 151.9 | 60.7 | 154.2 | 60.6 | 153.9 | 60.4 | 153.4 | 59.8 | 151.9 | 59.4 | 150.9 | 58.3 | 148.1 | 57.3 | 145.5 |
| 5 | **MEN** | **63.6** | **161.5** | **64.3** | **163.3** | **64.4** | **163.6** | **64.2** | **163.1** | **64.0** | **162.6** | **62.9** | **159.8** | **62.7** | **159.3** | **61.3** | **155.7** |
| 5 | **WOMEN** | **59.0** | **149.9** | **60.0** | **152.4** | **59.7** | **151.6** | **59.6** | **151.4** | **59.1** | **150.1** | **58.4** | **148.3** | **57.5** | **146.1** | **55.3** | **140.5** |
| 1 | MEN | 61.7 | 156.7 | 62.6 | 159.0 | 62.6 | 159.0 | 62.3 | 158.2 | 62.3 | 158.2 | 61.2 | 155.4 | 60.8 | 154.4 | 57.7 | 146.6 |
| 1 | WOMEN | 57.1 | 145.0 | 58.4 | 148.3 | 58.1 | 147.6 | 57.6 | 146.3 | 57.3 | 145.5 | 56.0 | 142.2 | 55.8 | 141.7 | 46.8 | 118.9 |

*Height, without shoes. See Table 1A for definition of stature.
†Measurement below which the indicated percent of people in the given age group fall.

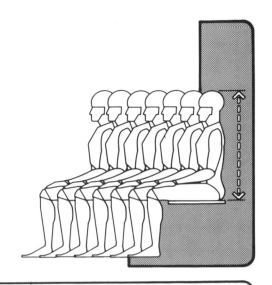

## 2C
## SITTING HEIGHT ERECT

| | | 18 to 79 (Total) | | 18 to 24 Years | | 25 to 34 Years | | 35 to 44 Years | | 45 to 54 Years | | 55 to 64 Years | | 65 to 74 Years | | 75 to 79 Years | |
|---|---|---|---|---|---|---|---|---|---|---|---|---|---|---|---|---|---|
| | | in | cm | in | cm | in | cm | in | cm | in | cm | in | cm | in | cm | in | cm |
| **99** | MEN | 38.9 | 98.8 | 39.1 | 99.3 | 39.0 | 99.1 | 38.9 | 98.8 | 38.9 | 98.8 | 38.7 | 98.3 | 37.7 | 95.8 | 37.6 | 95.5 |
| | WOMEN | 36.6 | 93.0 | 36.7 | 93.2 | 36.8 | 93.5 | 36.8 | 93.5 | 36.4 | 92.5 | 36.4 | 92.5 | 35.8 | 90.9 | 35.7 | 90.7 |
| **95** | **MEN** | **38.0** | **96.5** | **38.3** | **97.3** | **38.4** | **97.5** | **38.0** | **96.5** | **38.0** | **96.5** | **37.7** | **95.8** | **36.9** | **93.7** | **36.7** | **93.2** |
| | **WOMEN** | **35.7** | **90.7** | **35.9** | **91.2** | **35.5** | **90.9** | **35.8** | **90.9** | **35.6** | **90.4** | **35.4** | **89.9** | **34.5** | **87.6** | **34.8** | **88.4** |
| **90** | MEN | 37.6 | 95.5 | 37.8 | 96.0 | 37.3 | 96.3 | 37.7 | 95.8 | 37.6 | 95.5 | 37.1 | 94.2 | 36.5 | 92.7 | 36.1 | 91.7 |
| | WOMEN | 35.2 | 89.4 | 35.4 | 89.9 | 34.9 | 90.2 | 35.4 | 89.9 | 35.0 | 88.9 | 34.8 | 88.4 | 33.9 | 86.1 | 34.0 | 86.4 |
| **80** | MEN | 36.9 | 93.7 | 37.1 | 95.8 | 36.9 | 94.7 | 37.1 | 95.8 | 36.9 | 93.7 | 36.6 | 93.0 | 35.9 | 91.2 | 35.3 | 89.7 |
| | WOMEN | 34.6 | 87.9 | 34.8 | 88.4 | 34.5 | 88.6 | 34.8 | 88.4 | 34.6 | 87.9 | 39.2 | 86.9 | 33.4 | 84.8 | 33.3 | 84.6 |
| **70** | MEN | 36.5 | 92.7 | 36.7 | 93.2 | 36.5 | 93.7 | 36.7 | 93.2 | 36.5 | 92.7 | 36.1 | 91.7 | 35.5 | 90.2 | 34.9 | 88.6 |
| | WOMEN | 34.2 | 86.9 | 34.4 | 87.4 | 34.1 | 87.6 | 34.4 | 87.4 | 34.1 | 86.6 | 33.8 | 85.9 | 32.9 | 83.6 | 32.8 | 83.3 |
| **60** | MEN | 36.0 | 91.4 | 36.3 | 92.2 | 36.1 | 92.7 | 36.3 | 92.2 | 36.0 | 91.4 | 35.7 | 90.7 | 35.1 | 89.2 | 34.6 | 87.9 |
| | WOMEN | 33.8 | 85.9 | 34.0 | 86.4 | 33.8 | 86.6 | 34.1 | 86.6 | 33.8 | 85.9 | 33.4 | 84.8 | 32.6 | 82.8 | 32.5 | 82.6 |
| **50** | MEN | 35.7 | 90.7 | 35.9 | 91.2 | 36.1 | 91.7 | 36.0 | 91.4 | 35.7 | 90.7 | 35.3 | 89.7 | 34.8 | 88.4 | 34.3 | 87.1 |
| | WOMEN | 33.4 | 84.8 | 33.7 | 85.6 | 33.8 | 85.9 | 33.7 | 85.6 | 33.5 | 85.1 | 33.0 | 83.8 | 32.2 | 81.8 | 32.1 | 81.5 |
| **40** | MEN | 35.3 | 89.7 | 35.4 | 89.9 | 35.7 | 90.7 | 35.6 | 90.4 | 35.3 | 89.7 | 35.0 | 88.9 | 34.4 | 87.4 | 34.1 | 86.6 |
| | WOMEN | 33.1 | 84.1 | 33.4 | 84.8 | 33.4 | 84.8 | 33.4 | 84.8 | 33.2 | 84.3 | 32.7 | 83.1 | 31.9 | 81.0 | 31.6 | 80.3 |
| **30** | MEN | 34.9 | 88.6 | 35.0 | 88.9 | 35.3 | 88.6 | 35.2 | 89.4 | 35.0 | 89.4 | 34.5 | 88.9 | 34.1 | 87.6 | 33.6 | 85.3 |
| | WOMEN | 32.6 | 82.8 | 33.0 | 83.8 | 33.1 | 82.8 | 33.1 | 89.1 | 32.8 | 83.3 | 32.3 | 82.0 | 31.5 | 80.0 | 31.1 | 79.0 |
| **20** | MEN | 34.4 | 87.4 | 34.5 | 87.6 | 34.9 | 87.1 | 34.8 | 88.4 | 34.5 | 87.6 | 34.1 | 86.6 | 33.7 | 85.6 | 33.2 | 84.3 |
| | WOMEN | 32.2 | 81.8 | 32.6 | 82.8 | 32.6 | 81.5 | 32.6 | 82.8 | 32.3 | 82.8 | 31.9 | 81.0 | 31.0 | 78.7 | 30.4 | 77.2 |
| **10** | MEN | 33.8 | 85.9 | 34.0 | 86.4 | 34.3 | 86.1 | 34.2 | 86.9 | 34.1 | 86.6 | 33.3 | 84.6 | 33.1 | 84.1 | 32.4 | 82.3 |
| | WOMEN | 31.4 | 79.8 | 32.1 | 81.5 | 32.1 | 78.8 | 32.1 | 81.5 | 31.7 | 80.5 | 31.2 | 79.2 | 30.3 | 77.0 | 29.2 | 74.2 |
| **5** | **MEN** | **33.2** | **84.3** | **33.3** | **84.6** | **33.9** | **82.6** | **33.7** | **85.6** | **33.5** | **85.1** | **32.9** | **83.6** | **32.5** | **82.6** | **31.8** | **80.8** |
| | **WOMEN** | **30.9** | **78.5** | **31.4** | **79.8** | **31.4** | **78.8** | **31.5** | **80.0** | **31.2** | **79.2** | **30.7** | **78.0** | **29.7** | **75.4** | **28.1** | **71.4** |
| **1** | MEN | 31.9 | 81.0 | 31.8 | 80.8 | 32.5 | 82.6 | 32.2 | 81.8 | 32.8 | 83.3 | 31.4 | 79.8 | 31.3 | 79.5 | 27.7 | 70.4 |
| | WOMEN | 29.5 | 74.9 | 30.4 | 77.2 | 30.3 | 77.0 | 30.3 | 77.0 | 30.1 | 76.5 | 30.0 | 76.2 | 28.6 | 72.6 | 17.8 | 45.2 |

**Adult Male and Female Sitting Height Erect\* in Inches and Centimeters by Age, Sex, and Selected Percentiles†**

\*See Table 1D for definition of sitting height erect.
†Measurement below which the indicated percent of people in the given age group fall.

# 2D
## SITTING HEIGHT NORMAL

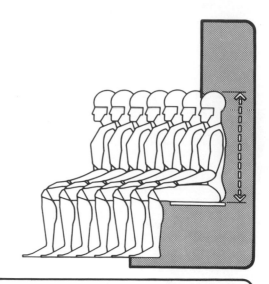

**Adult Male and Female Sitting Height Normal\* in Inches and Centimeters by Age, Sex, and Selected Percentiles†**

| | | 18 to 79 (Total) | | 18 to 24 Years | | 25 to 34 Years | | 35 to 44 Years | | 45 to 54 Years | | 55 to 64 Years | | 65 to 74 Years | | 75 to 79 Years | |
|---|---|---|---|---|---|---|---|---|---|---|---|---|---|---|---|---|---|
| | | in | cm | in | cm | in | cm | in | cm | in | cm | in | cm | in | cm | in | cm |
| **99** | MEN | 37.6 | 95.5 | 37.8 | 96.0 | 37.8 | 96.0 | 37.7 | 95.8 | 37.7 | 95.8 | 36.9 | 93.7 | 36.4 | 92.5 | 36.7 | 93.2 |
| | WOMEN | 35.7 | 90.7 | 35.7 | 90.7 | 35.9 | 91.2 | 35.8 | 90.9 | 35.5 | 90.2 | 35.4 | 89.9 | 34.9 | 88.6 | 35.0 | 88.9 |
| **95** | **MEN** | 36.6 | 93.0 | 36.7 | 93.2 | 36.8 | 93.5 | 36.7 | 93.2 | 36.7 | 93.2 | 36.0 | 91.4 | 35.7 | 90.7 | 35.8 | 90.9 |
| | **WOMEN** | 34.7 | 88.1 | 34.8 | 88.4 | 34.9 | 88.6 | 34.9 | 88.6 | 34.6 | 87.9 | 34.4 | 87.4 | 33.9 | 86.1 | 33.4 | 84.8 |
| **90** | MEN | 35.9 | 91.2 | 36.0 | 91.4 | 36.3 | 92.2 | 36.2 | 91.9 | 36.0 | 91.4 | 35.6 | 90.4 | 35.1 | 89.2 | 35.2 | 89.4 |
| | WOMEN | 34.1 | 86.6 | 34.3 | 87.1 | 34.5 | 87.6 | 34.4 | 87.4 | 34.0 | 86.4 | 33.8 | 85.9 | 33.1 | 84.1 | 32.8 | 83.3 |
| **80** | MEN | 35.3 | 89.7 | 35.4 | 89.9 | 35.6 | 90.4 | 35.5 | 90.2 | 35.5 | 90.2 | 35.0 | 88.9 | 34.6 | 87.9 | 34.6 | 87.9 |
| | WOMEN | 33.6 | 85.3 | 33.7 | 85.6 | 33.8 | 85.9 | 33.8 | 85.9 | 33.5 | 85.1 | 33.2 | 84.3 | 32.5 | 82.6 | 32.3 | 82.0 |
| **70** | MEN | 34.8 | 88.4 | 34.9 | 88.6 | 35.1 | 89.2 | 34.9 | 88.6 | 35.0 | 88.9 | 34.6 | 87.9 | 34.1 | 86.6 | 34.1 | 86.6 |
| | WOMEN | 33.1 | 84.1 | 33.4 | 84.8 | 33.4 | 84.8 | 33.3 | 84.6 | 33.0 | 83.8 | 32.8 | 83.3 | 31.9 | 81.0 | 31.8 | 80.8 |
| **60** | MEN | 34.5 | 87.6 | 34.5 | 87.6 | 34.8 | 88.4 | 34.6 | 87.9 | 34.6 | 87.9 | 34.3 | 87.1 | 33.8 | 85.9 | 33.7 | 85.6 |
| | WOMEN | 32.7 | 83.1 | 33.0 | 83.8 | 33.0 | 83.8 | 32.9 | 83.6 | 32.7 | 83.1 | 32.4 | 82.3 | 31.6 | 80.3 | 31.4 | 79.8 |
| **50** | MEN | 34.1 | 86.6 | 34.2 | 86.9 | 34.4 | 87.4 | 34.3 | 87.1 | 34.2 | 86.9 | 33.9 | 86.1 | 33.4 | 84.8 | 33.3 | 84.6 |
| | WOMEN | 32.3 | 82.0 | 32.6 | 82.8 | 32.6 | 82.8 | 32.6 | 82.8 | 32.3 | 82.0 | 32.1 | 81.5 | 31.2 | 79.2 | 31.0 | 78.7 |
| **40** | MEN | 33.7 | 85.6 | 33.8 | 85.9 | 34.0 | 86.4 | 34.0 | 86.4 | 33.8 | 85.9 | 33.5 | 85.1 | 33.1 | 84.1 | 32.9 | 83.6 |
| | WOMEN | 31.9 | 81.0 | 32.3 | 82.0 | 32.3 | 82.0 | 32.3 | 82.0 | 32.0 | 81.3 | 31.7 | 80.5 | 30.8 | 78.2 | 30.6 | 77.7 |
| **30** | MEN | 33.3 | 84.6 | 33.3 | 84.6 | 33.6 | 85.3 | 33.5 | 85.1 | 33.4 | 84.8 | 33.2 | 84.3 | 32.7 | 83.1 | 32.5 | 82.6 |
| | WOMEN | 31.5 | 80.0 | 31.9 | 81.0 | 31.9 | 81.0 | 31.9 | 81.0 | 31.5 | 80.0 | 31.3 | 79.5 | 30.4 | 77.2 | 30.1 | 76.5 |
| **20** | MEN | 32.9 | 83.6 | 32.9 | 83.6 | 33.2 | 84.3 | 33.1 | 84.1 | 32.9 | 83.6 | 32.6 | 82.8 | 32.4 | 82.3 | 32.1 | 81.5 |
| | WOMEN | 31.0 | 78.7 | 31.3 | 79.5 | 31.4 | 79.8 | 31.4 | 79.8 | 31.1 | 79.0 | 30.8 | 78.2 | 30.0 | 76.2 | 29.2 | 74.2 |
| **10** | MEN | 32.2 | 81.8 | 32.3 | 82.0 | 32.6 | 82.8 | 32.4 | 82.3 | 32.3 | 82.0 | 31.8 | 80.8 | 31.9 | 81.0 | 30.7 | 78.0 |
| | WOMEN | 30.2 | 76.7 | 30.6 | 77.7 | 30.7 | 78.0 | 30.8 | 78.2 | 30.3 | 77.0 | 30.2 | 76.7 | 29.3 | 74.4 | 27.6 | 70.1 |
| **5** | **MEN** | 31.6 | 80.3 | 31.9 | 81.0 | 32.1 | 81.5 | 32.0 | 81.3 | 31.8 | 80.8 | 31.3 | 79.5 | 31.2 | 79.2 | 29.8 | 75.7 |
| | **WOMEN** | 29.6 | 75.2 | 30.1 | 76.5 | 30.1 | 76.5 | 30.2 | 76.7 | 29.7 | 75.4 | 29.7 | 75.4 | 28.7 | 72.9 | 27.1 | 68.8 |
| **1** | MEN | 30.4 | 77.2 | 30.5 | 77.5 | 31.0 | 78.7 | 30.8 | 78.2 | 30.8 | 78.2 | 30.2 | 76.7 | 30.1 | 76.5 | 26.7 | 67.8 |
| | WOMEN | 28.2 | 71.6 | 29.2 | 74.2 | 28.9 | 73.4 | 29.2 | 74.2 | 28.7 | 72.9 | 28.3 | 71.9 | 27.0 | 68.6 | 14.8 | 37.6 |

\*See Table 1E for definition of sitting height normal.
†Measurement below which the indicated percent of people in the given age group fall.

## 2E

## ELBOW-TO-ELBOW BREADTH

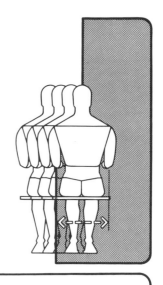

### Adult Male and Female Elbow-to-Elbow Breadth* in Inches and Centimeters by Age, Sex, and Selected Percentiles†

| | | 18 to 79 (Total) | | 18 to 24 Years | | 25 to 34 Years | | 35 to 44 Years | | 45 to 54 Years | | 55 to 64 Years | | 65 to 74 Years | | 75 to 79 Years | |
|---|---|---|---|---|---|---|---|---|---|---|---|---|---|---|---|---|---|
| | | in | cm | in | cm | in | cm | in | cm | in | cm | in | cm | in | cm | in | cm |
| **99** | MEN | 21.4 | 54.4 | 20.8 | 52.8 | 21.4 | 54.4 | 21.5 | 54.6 | 21.8 | 55.4 | 22.0 | 55.9 | 21.0 | 53.3 | 20.7 | 52.6 |
| | WOMEN | 21.2 | 53.8 | 20.0 | 50.8 | 20.6 | 52.3 | 21.5 | 54.6 | 21.7 | 55.1 | 21.8 | 55.4 | 20.8 | 52.8 | 19.8 | 50.3 |
| **95** | **MEN** | **19.9** | **50.5** | **19.4** | **49.3** | **19.7** | **50.0** | **20.0** | **50.8** | **20.0** | **50.8** | **20.0** | **50.8** | **19.9** | **50.5** | **19.5** | **49.5** |
| | **WOMEN** | **19.3** | **40.9** | **16.9** | **42.9** | **18.3** | **46.5** | **19.3** | **49.0** | **19.7** | **50.0** | **20.2** | **51.3** | **19.7** | **50.0** | **19.1** | **48.5** |
| **90** | MEN | 19.0 | 48.3 | 18.2 | 46.2 | 18.8 | 47.8 | 19.2 | 48.8 | 19.2 | 48.8 | 19.3 | 49.0 | 19.3 | 49.0 | 18.7 | 47.5 |
| | WOMEN | 18.3 | 46.5 | 16.0 | 40.6 | 17.3 | 43.9 | 18.2 | 46.2 | 18.7 | 47.5 | 19.3 | 49.0 | 18.8 | 47.8 | 18.1 | 46.0 |
| **80** | MEN | 18.1 | 46.0 | 17.2 | 43.7 | 17.8 | 45.2 | 18.3 | 46.5 | 18.4 | 46.7 | 18.3 | 46.5 | 18.5 | 47.0 | 17.8 | 45.2 |
| | WOMEN | 17.1 | 43.4 | 15.1 | 38.4 | 15.8 | 40.1 | 16.9 | 42.9 | 17.6 | 44.7 | 18.2 | 46.2 | 17.9 | 45.5 | 17.5 | 44.5 |
| **70** | MEN | 17.5 | 44.5 | 16.5 | 41.9 | 17.3 | 43.9 | 17.7 | 45.0 | 17.8 | 45.2 | 17.7 | 45.0 | 17.8 | 45.2 | 17.1 | 43.4 |
| | WOMEN | 16.3 | 41.4 | 14.6 | 37.1 | 15.2 | 38.6 | 16.0 | 40.6 | 16.8 | 42.7 | 17.4 | 44.2 | 17.4 | 44.2 | 16.9 | 42.9 |
| **60** | MEN | 17.0 | 43.2 | 15.9 | 40.4 | 16.8 | 42.7 | 17.2 | 43.7 | 17.3 | 43.9 | 17.2 | 43.7 | 17.3 | 43.9 | 16.7 | 42.4 |
| | WOMEN | 15.6 | 39.6 | 14.2 | 36.1 | 14.7 | 37.3 | 15.5 | 39.4 | 16.0 | 40.6 | 16.8 | 42.7 | 16.9 | 42.9 | 16.3 | 41.4 |
| **50** | MEN | 16.5 | 41.9 | 15.4 | 39.1 | 16.3 | 41.4 | 16.7 | 42.4 | 16.8 | 42.7 | 16.7 | 42.4 | 16.8 | 42.7 | 16.4 | 41.7 |
| | WOMEN | 15.1 | 38.4 | 13.8 | 35.1 | 14.2 | 36.1 | 14.9 | 37.8 | 15.5 | 39.4 | 16.3 | 41.4 | 16.4 | 41.7 | 15.7 | 39.9 |
| **40** | MEN | 16.0 | 40.6 | 15.0 | 38.1 | 15.9 | 40.4 | 16.3 | 41.4 | 16.3 | 41.4 | 16.1 | 40.9 | 16.3 | 41.4 | 16.0 | 40.6 |
| | WOMEN | 14.6 | 37.1 | 13.4 | 34.0 | 13.8 | 35.1 | 14.5 | 36.8 | 15.1 | 38.4 | 15.8 | 40.1 | 16.0 | 40.6 | 15.3 | 38.9 |
| **30** | MEN | 15.5 | 39.4 | 14.5 | 36.8 | 15.4 | 39.1 | 15.9 | 40.4 | 15.9 | 40.4 | 15.6 | 39.6 | 15.9 | 40.4 | 15.5 | 39.4 |
| | WOMEN | 14.1 | 35.8 | 13.1 | 33.3 | 13.5 | 34.3 | 14.1 | 35.8 | 14.6 | 37.1 | 15.2 | 38.6 | 15.5 | 39.4 | 14.7 | 37.3 |
| **20** | MEN | 15.0 | 38.1 | 14.1 | 35.8 | 15.0 | 38.1 | 15.3 | 38.9 | 15.3 | 38.9 | 15.2 | 38.6 | 15.3 | 38.9 | 14.9 | 37.8 |
| | WOMEN | 13.5 | 34.3 | 12.6 | 32.0 | 13.1 | 33.3 | 13.6 | 34.5 | 14.1 | 35.8 | 14.7 | 37.3 | 14.9 | 37.8 | 14.2 | 36.1 |
| **10** | MEN | 14.3 | 36.1 | 13.4 | 34.0 | 14.2 | 36.1 | 14.6 | 37.1 | 14.6 | 37.1 | 14.5 | 36.8 | 14.6 | 37.1 | 14.3 | 36.3 |
| | WOMEN | 12.9 | 32.8 | 12.1 | 30.7 | 12.5 | 31.8 | 13.1 | 33.3 | 13.3 | 33.8 | 14.0 | 35.6 | 14.2 | 36.1 | 13.5 | 34.3 |
| **5** | **MEN** | **13.7** | **34.8** | **13.1** | **33.3** | **13.7** | **34.8** | **14.1** | **35.8** | **14.1** | **35.8** | **14.1** | **35.8** | **14.0** | **35.6** | **14.0** | **35.6** |
| | **WOMEN** | **12.3** | **31.2** | **11.7** | **29.7** | **12.2** | **31.0** | **12.5** | **31.8** | **12.7** | **32.3** | **13.4** | **34.0** | **13.7** | **34.8** | **13.1** | **33.3** |
| **1** | MEN | 13.0 | 33.0 | 12.3 | 31.2 | 13.1 | 33.3 | 13.1 | 33.3 | 13.2 | 33.5 | 13.2 | 33.5 | 13.2 | 33.5 | 12.4 | 31.5 |
| | WOMEN | 11.4 | 29.0 | 11.0 | 27.9 | 11.4 | 29.0 | 11.7 | 29.7 | 11.6 | 29.5 | 12.3 | 31.2 | 12.4 | 31.5 | 12.3 | 31.2 |

*See Table 1I for definition of elbow-to-elbow breadth.
†Measurement below which the indicated percent of people in the given age group fall.

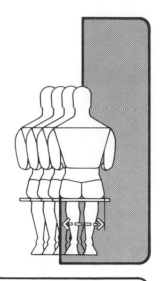

# 2F

## HIP
## BREADTH

| | | 18 to 79 (Total) | | 18 to 24 Years | | 25 to 34 Years | | 35 to 44 Years | | 45 to 54 Years | | 55 to 64 Years | | 65 to 74 Years | | 75 to 79 Years | |
|---|---|---|---|---|---|---|---|---|---|---|---|---|---|---|---|---|---|
| **Adult Male and Female Hip Breadth\* in Inches and Centimeters by Age, Sex, and Selected Percentiles†** | | in | cm | in | cm | in | cm | in | cm | in | cm | in | cm | in | cm | in | cm |
| **99** | MEN | 17.0 | 43.2 | 17.3 | 43.9 | 17.4 | 44.2 | 17.1 | 43.4 | 16.9 | 42.9 | 16.9 | 42.9 | 16.6 | 42.2 | 16.5 | 41.9 |
| | WOMEN | 18.8 | 47.8 | 18.4 | 46.7 | 19.0 | 48.3 | 19.2 | 48.8 | 19.0 | 48.3 | 18.7 | 47.5 | 18.2 | 46.2 | 17.1 | 43.4 |
| **95** | **MEN** | **15.9** | **40.4** | **15.8** | **40.1** | **16.0** | **40.6** | **15.9** | **40.4** | **16.0** | **40.6** | **15.9** | **40.4** | **15.7** | **39.9** | **15.5** | **39.4** |
| | **WOMEN** | **17.1** | **43.4** | **15.9** | **40.4** | **16.8** | **42.7** | **17.3** | **43.9** | **17.6** | **44.7** | **17.4** | **44.2** | **17.3** | **43.9** | **16.8** | **42.7** |
| **90** | MEN | 15.5 | 39.4 | 15.0 | 38.1 | 15.6 | 39.6 | 15.6 | 39.6 | 15.7 | 39.9 | 15.6 | 39.6 | 15.1 | 38.4 | 14.9 | 37.8 |
| | WOMEN | 16.4 | 41.7 | 15.4 | 39.1 | 16.0 | 40.6 | 16.5 | 41.9 | 16.7 | 42.4 | 16.8 | 42.7 | 16.7 | 42.4 | 16.5 | 41.9 |
| **80** | MEN | 14.9 | 37.8 | 14.6 | 37.1 | 14.9 | 37.8 | 15.0 | 38.1 | 15.1 | 38.4 | 15.0 | 38.1 | 14.7 | 37.3 | 14.5 | 36.8 |
| | WOMEN | 15.6 | 39.6 | 14.8 | 37.6 | 15.3 | 38.9 | 15.7 | 39.9 | 15.8 | 40.1 | 16.0 | 40.6 | 15.9 | 40.4 | 15.8 | 40.1 |
| **70** | MEN | 14.6 | 37.1 | 14.1 | 35.8 | 14.6 | 37.1 | 14.7 | 37.3 | 14.8 | 37.6 | 14.6 | 37.1 | 14.5 | 36.8 | 14.2 | 36.1 |
| | WOMEN | 15.1 | 38.4 | 14.4 | 36.6 | 14.8 | 37.6 | 15.1 | 38.4 | 15.4 | 39.1 | 15.6 | 39.6 | 15.4 | 39.1 | 15.0 | 38.1 |
| **60** | MEN | 14.3 | 36.3 | 13.8 | 35.1 | 14.3 | 36.3 | 14.4 | 36.6 | 14.5 | 36.8 | 14.3 | 36.3 | 14.2 | 36.1 | 13.9 | 35.3 |
| | WOMEN | 14.7 | 37.3 | 14.1 | 35.3 | 14.4 | 36.6 | 14.8 | 37.6 | 15.0 | 38.1 | 15.1 | 38.4 | 14.9 | 37.8 | 14.5 | 36.8 |
| **50** | MEN | 14.0 | 35.6 | 13.5 | 34.3 | 14.0 | 35.6 | 14.1 | 35.8 | 14.2 | 36.1 | 14.0 | 35.6 | 13.9 | 35.3 | 13.6 | 34.5 |
| | WOMEN | 14.3 | 36.3 | 13.8 | 35.1 | 14.0 | 35.6 | 14.5 | 36.8 | 14.6 | 37.1 | 14.7 | 37.3 | 14.6 | 37.1 | 14.0 | 35.6 |
| **40** | MEN | 13.7 | 34.8 | 13.3 | 33.8 | 13.7 | 34.8 | 13.8 | 35.1 | 13.9 | 35.3 | 13.7 | 34.8 | 13.6 | 34.5 | 13.4 | 34.0 |
| | WOMEN | 14.0 | 35.6 | 13.5 | 34.3 | 13.7 | 34.8 | 14.2 | 36.1 | 14.2 | 36.1 | 14.3 | 36.3 | 14.3 | 36.3 | 13.7 | 34.8 |
| **30** | MEN | 13.4 | 34.0 | 13.0 | 33.0 | 13.4 | 34.0 | 13.5 | 34.3 | 13.5 | 34.3 | 13.4 | 34.0 | 13.4 | 34.0 | 13.2 | 33.5 |
| | WOMEN | 13.6 | 34.5 | 13.2 | 33.5 | 13.4 | 34.0 | 13.8 | 35.1 | 13.8 | 35.1 | 13.9 | 35.3 | 14.0 | 35.6 | 13.3 | 33.8 |
| **20** | MEN | 13.1 | 33.3 | 12.6 | 32.0 | 13.1 | 33.3 | 13.3 | 33.8 | 13.2 | 33.5 | 13.1 | 33.3 | 13.1 | 33.3 | 12.9 | 32.8 |
| | WOMEN | 13.3 | 33.8 | 12.8 | 32.5 | 13.1 | 33.3 | 13.4 | 34.0 | 13.4 | 34.0 | 13.6 | 34.5 | 13.5 | 34.3 | 13.0 | 33.0 |
| **10** | MEN | 12.5 | 31.8 | 12.5 | 31.0 | 12.5 | 31.8 | 12.9 | 32.8 | 12.6 | 32.0 | 12.6 | 32.0 | 12.6 | 32.0 | 12.4 | 31.5 |
| | WOMEN | 12.7 | 32.3 | 12.3 | 31.2 | 12.6 | 32.0 | 12.9 | 32.8 | 13.0 | 33.0 | 13.2 | 33.5 | 12.9 | 32.8 | 12.2 | 31.0 |
| **5** | **MEN** | **12.2** | **31.0** | **12.0** | **30.5** | **12.2** | **31.0** | **12.4** | **31.5** | **12.2** | **31.0** | **12.2** | **31.0** | **12.2** | **31.0** | **12.1** | **30.7** |
| | **WOMEN** | **12.3** | **31.2** | **12.1** | **30.7** | **12.2** | **31.0** | **12.4** | **31.5** | **12.4** | **31.5** | **12.9** | **32.8** | **12.4** | **31.5** | **11.7** | **29.7** |
| **1** | MEN | 11.5 | 29.2 | 11.3 | 28.7 | 11.7 | 29.7 | 12.0 | 30.5 | 11.5 | 29.2 | 11.6 | 29.5 | 11.4 | 29.0 | 11.4 | 29.0 |
| | WOMEN | 11.7 | 29.7 | 11.3 | 28.7 | 11.5 | 29.2 | 12.0 | 30.5 | 12.0 | 30.5 | 12.1 | 30.7 | 12.1 | 30.7 | 9.8 | 24.9 |

\*See Table 1J for definition of hip breadth.
†Measurement below which the indicated percent of people in the given age group fall.

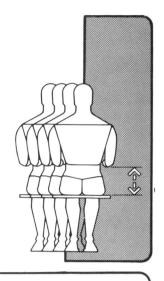

## 2G
**ELBOW
REST
HEIGHT**

| | Adult Male and Female Elbow Rest Height* in Inches and Centimeters by Age, Sex, and Selected Percentiles† | 18 to 79 (Total) | | 18 to 24 Years | | 25 to 34 Years | | 35 to 44 Years | | 45 to 54 Years | | 55 to 64 Years | | 65 to 74 Years | | 75 to 79 Years | |
|---|---|---|---|---|---|---|---|---|---|---|---|---|---|---|---|---|---|
| | | in | cm | in | cm | in | cm | in | cm | in | cm | in | cm | in | cm | in | cm |
| **99** | MEN | 12.5 | 31.8 | 12.8 | 32.5 | 12.6 | 32.0 | 12.6 | 32.0 | 12.0 | 24.1 | 12.2 | 23.6 | 11.9 | 22.9 | 11.0 | 21.8 |
| | WOMEN | 11.9 | 30.2 | 11.8 | 30.0 | 11.9 | 30.2 | 12.0 | 30.5 | 12.1 | 30.7 | 11.9 | 30.2 | 11.3 | 28.7 | 10.7 | 27.2 |
| **95** | **MEN** | **11.6** | **29.5** | **11.9** | **30.2** | **11.7** | **29.7** | **11.8** | **30.0** | **11.5** | **30.5** | **11.4** | **30.0** | **10.9** | **27.7** | **10.6** | **26.9** |
| | **WOMEN** | **11.0** | **27.9** | **10.8** | **27.4** | **11.1** | **28.2** | **11.3** | **28.7** | **11.0** | **27.9** | **10.9** | **27.7** | **10.2** | **25.9** | **10.0** | **25.4** |
| **90** | MEN | 11.0 | 27.9 | 11.4 | 30.0 | 11.1 | 28.2 | 11.3 | 28.7 | 11.0 | 27.9 | 10.9 | 27.7 | 10.6 | 26.9 | 10.2 | 25.9 |
| | WOMEN | 10.7 | 27.2 | 10.5 | 26.7 | 10.8 | 27.4 | 10.8 | 27.4 | 10.7 | 27.2 | 10.6 | 26.9 | 9.8 | 24.9 | 9.8 | 24.9 |
| **80** | MEN | 10.6 | 26.9 | 10.7 | 27.2 | 10.7 | 27.2 | 10.7 | 27.2 | 10.5 | 26.7 | 10.4 | 26.4 | 10.0 | 25.4 | 9.7 | 24.6 |
| | WOMEN | 10.1 | 25.7 | 9.9 | 25.1 | 10.3 | 26.2 | 10.3 | 26.2 | 10.3 | 26.2 | 10.0 | 25.4 | 9.5 | 24.1 | 9.4 | 22.9 |
| **70** | MEN | 10.2 | 25.9 | 10.3 | 26.2 | 10.3 | 26.2 | 10.4 | 26.4 | 10.1 | 25.7 | 9.9 | 25.1 | 9.6 | 24.4 | 9.3 | 23.6 |
| | WOMEN | 9.7 | 24.6 | 9.6 | 24.4 | 9.9 | 25.1 | 9.9 | 25.1 | 9.9 | 25.1 | 9.6 | 24.4 | 9.1 | 23.1 | 9.1 | 23.1 |
| **60** | MEN | 9.8 | 24.9 | 9.9 | 25.1 | 10.0 | 25.4 | 10.0 | 25.4 | 9.8 | 24.9 | 9.6 | 24.4 | 9.3 | 23.6 | 8.9 | 22.6 |
| | WOMEN | 9.5 | 24.1 | 9.4 | 23.9 | 9.6 | 24.4 | 9.7 | 24.6 | 9.6 | 24.4 | 9.3 | 23.6 | 8.8 | 22.4 | 8.7 | 22.1 |
| **50** | MEN | 9.5 | 24.1 | 9.6 | 24.4 | 9.7 | 24.6 | 9.7 | 24.6 | 9.6 | 24.4 | 9.3 | 23.6 | 9.0 | 22.9 | 8.6 | 21.8 |
| | WOMEN | 9.2 | 23.4 | 9.1 | 23.1 | 9.3 | 23.6 | 9.4 | 23.9 | 9.3 | 23.6 | 9.0 | 22.9 | 8.5 | 21.6 | 8.4 | 21.3 |
| **40** | MEN | 9.2 | 23.4 | 9.4 | 23.9 | 9.4 | 23.9 | 9.4 | 23.9 | 9.3 | 23.6 | 9.0 | 22.9 | 8.7 | 22.1 | 8.2 | 20.8 |
| | WOMEN | 8.9 | 22.6 | 8.8 | 22.4 | 9.1 | 23.1 | 9.2 | 23.4 | 9.0 | 22.9 | 8.6 | 21.8 | 8.2 | 20.8 | 8.0 | 20.3 |
| **30** | MEN | 8.9 | 22.6 | 9.1 | 23.1 | 9.1 | 23.1 | 9.1 | 23.1 | 9.1 | 23.1 | 8.6 | 21.8 | 8.4 | 21.3 | 7.8 | 19.8 |
| | WOMEN | 8.5 | 21.6 | 8.5 | 21.6 | 8.7 | 22.1 | 8.9 | 22.6 | 8.7 | 21.8 | 8.3 | 21.1 | 7.8 | 19.8 | 7.7 | 19.6 |
| **20** | MEN | 8.5 | 21.6 | 8.6 | 21.8 | 8.7 | 22.1 | 8.7 | 22.1 | 8.7 | 22.1 | 8.3 | 21.1 | 8.0 | 20.3 | 7.5 | 19.1 |
| | WOMEN | 8.2 | 20.8 | 8.2 | 20.8 | 8.4 | 21.3 | 8.5 | 21.6 | 8.3 | 21.1 | 8.0 | 20.3 | 7.4 | 18.8 | 7.4 | 18.8 |
| **10** | MEN | 8.0 | 20.3 | 8.1 | 20.6 | 8.3 | 21.1 | 8.2 | 20.8 | 8.2 | 20.8 | 7.7 | 19.6 | 7.4 | 18.8 | 7.1 | 18.0 |
| | WOMEN | 7.6 | 19.3 | 7.6 | 19.3 | 8.0 | 20.3 | 8.0 | 20.3 | 7.8 | 19.8 | 7.4 | 18.8 | 7.0 | 17.5 | 7.0 | 17.5 |
| **5** | **MEN** | **7.4** | **18.8** | **7.6** | **19.3** | **8.0** | **20.3** | **7.8** | **19.8** | **7.7** | **19.6** | **7.2** | **18.3** | **7.1** | **18.0** | **6.5** | **16.5** |
| | **WOMEN** | **7.1** | **18.0** | **7.2** | **18.3** | **7.4** | **18.8** | **7.5** | **19.1** | **7.3** | **19.8** | **7.1** | **18.0** | **6.4** | **16.3** | **6.4** | **16.3** |
| **1** | MEN | 6.3 | 16.0 | 6.3 | 16.0 | 7.0 | 17.8 | 6.5 | 16.5 | 7.0 | 17.8 | 6.0 | 17.8 | 6.1 | 15.5 | 5.7 | 14.5 |
| | WOMEN | 6.1 | 15.5 | 6.2 | 15.7 | 6.1 | 15.5 | 6.7 | 17.0 | 6.4 | 16.3 | 6.4 | 16.3 | 5.4 | 13.7 | 2.8 | 7.1 |

*See Table 1K for definition of elbow rest height.
†Measurement below which the indicated percent of people in the given age group fall.

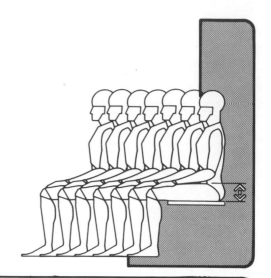

# 2H

## THIGH CLEARANCE

| | | 18 to 79 (Total) | | 18 to 24 Years | | 25 to 34 Years | | 35 to 44 Years | | 45 to 54 Years | | 55 to 64 Years | | 65 to 74 Years | | 75 to 79 Years | |
|---|---|---|---|---|---|---|---|---|---|---|---|---|---|---|---|---|---|
| | | in | cm | in | cm | in | cm | in | cm | in | cm | in | cm | in | cm | in | cm |
| **99** | MEN | 7.7 | 19.6 | 7.7 | 19.6 | 7.9 | 20.1 | 7.8 | 19.8 | 7.1 | 18.0 | 7.4 | 18.8 | 7.0 | 17.8 | 7.2 | 18.3 |
| | WOMEN | 7.7 | 19.6 | 7.0 | 17.8 | 7.7 | 19.6 | 7.8 | 19.8 | 7.7 | 19.6 | 8.3 | 21.1 | 7.0 | 17.8 | 6.9 | 17.5 |
| **95** | **MEN** | **6.9** | **17.5** | **6.9** | **17.5** | **7.0** | **17.8** | **7.0** | **17.8** | **6.9** | **17.5** | **6.8** | **17.3** | **6.7** | **17.0** | **6.6** | **16.8** |
| | **WOMEN** | **6.9** | **17.5** | **6.7** | **17.0** | **6.9** | **17.5** | **7.0** | **17.8** | **6.9** | **17.5** | **6.9** | **17.5** | **6.6** | **16.8** | **6.5** | **16.5** |
| **90** | MEN | 6.7 | 17.0 | 6.8 | 17.3 | 6.9 | 17.5 | 6.8 | 17.3 | 6.7 | 17.0 | 6.6 | 16.8 | 6.5 | 16.5 | 6.1 | 15.5 |
| | WOMEN | 6.6 | 16.8 | 6.3 | 16.0 | 6.6 | 16.8 | 6.7 | 17.0 | 6.6 | 16.8 | 6.6 | 16.8 | 6.2 | 15.7 | 6.1 | 15.5 |
| **80** | MEN | 6.4 | 16.3 | 6.4 | 16.3 | 6.6 | 16.8 | 6.5 | 16.5 | 6.3 | 16.0 | 6.1 | 15.5 | 6.0 | 15.2 | 5.8 | 14.7 |
| | WOMEN | 6.0 | 15.2 | 5.9 | 15.0 | 6.0 | 15.2 | 6.3 | 16.0 | 6.1 | 15.5 | 6.0 | 15.2 | 5.9 | 15.0 | 5.8 | 14.7 |
| **70** | MEN | 6.0 | 15.2 | 6.1 | 15.5 | 6.3 | 16.0 | 6.2 | 15.7 | 6.0 | 15.2 | 5.9 | 15.0 | 5.8 | 14.7 | 5.6 | 14.2 |
| | WOMEN | 5.8 | 14.7 | 5.7 | 14.5 | 5.8 | 14.7 | 5.9 | 15.0 | 5.9 | 15.0 | 5.8 | 14.7 | 5.7 | 14.5 | 5.6 | 14.2 |
| **60** | MEN | 5.8 | 14.7 | 5.9 | 15.0 | 6.0 | 15.2 | 6.0 | 15.2 | 5.8 | 14.7 | 5.7 | 14.5 | 5.6 | 14.2 | 5.4 | 13.7 |
| | WOMEN | 5.6 | 14.2 | 5.5 | 14.0 | 5.6 | 14.2 | 5.7 | 14.5 | 5.7 | 14.5 | 5.6 | 14.2 | 5.5 | 14.0 | 5.4 | 13.7 |
| **50** | MEN | 5.7 | 14.5 | 5.7 | 14.5 | 5.8 | 14.7 | 5.8 | 14.7 | 5.6 | 14.2 | 5.5 | 14.0 | 5.4 | 13.7 | 5.2 | 13.2 |
| | WOMEN | 5.4 | 13.7 | 5.4 | 13.7 | 5.4 | 13.7 | 5.5 | 14.0 | 5.5 | 14.0 | 5.4 | 13.7 | 5.3 | 13.5 | 5.2 | 13.2 |
| **40** | MEN | 5.5 | 14.0 | 5.5 | 14.0 | 5.6 | 14.2 | 5.6 | 14.2 | 5.5 | 14.0 | 5.3 | 13.5 | 5.3 | 13.5 | 5.0 | 13.0 |
| | WOMEN | 5.2 | 13.2 | 5.2 | 13.2 | 5.2 | 13.2 | 5.3 | 13.5 | 5.3 | 13.5 | 5.2 | 13.2 | 5.1 | 13.0 | 4.9 | 12.4 |
| **30** | MEN | 5.3 | 13.5 | 5.3 | 13.5 | 5.4 | 13.7 | 5.4 | 13.7 | 5.3 | 13.5 | 5.2 | 13.2 | 5.1 | 13.0 | 4.7 | 11.9 |
| | WOMEN | 5.1 | 13.0 | 5.0 | 13.0 | 5.1 | 13.0 | 5.1 | 13.0 | 5.1 | 13.0 | 5.0 | 13.0 | 4.9 | 12.4 | 4.7 | 11.9 |
| **20** | MEN | 5.1 | 13.0 | 5.1 | 13.0 | 5.2 | 13.2 | 5.2 | 13.2 | 5.1 | 13.0 | 4.9 | 12.4 | 4.8 | 12.2 | 4.5 | 11.4 |
| | WOMEN | 4.7 | 11.9 | 4.7 | 11.9 | 4.7 | 11.9 | 4.9 | 12.4 | 4.8 | 12.2 | 4.7 | 11.9 | 4.6 | 11.7 | 4.4 | 11.2 |
| **10** | MEN | 4.7 | 11.9 | 4.7 | 11.9 | 4.9 | 12.4 | 5.0 | 13.0 | 4.9 | 12.4 | 4.5 | 11.4 | 4.4 | 11.2 | 4.2 | 10.7 |
| | WOMEN | 4.3 | 10.9 | 4.3 | 10.9 | 4.9 | 12.4 | 4.4 | 11.2 | 4.4 | 11.2 | 4.3 | 10.9 | 4.2 | 10.7 | 4.1 | 10.4 |
| **5** | **MEN** | **4.3** | **10.9** | **4.3** | **10.9** | **4.5** | **11.4** | **4.4** | **11.2** | **4.2** | **10.7** | **4.2** | **10.7** | **4.2** | **10.7** | **4.1** | **10.4** |
| | **WOMEN** | **4.1** | **10.4** | **4.1** | **10.4** | **4.2** | **10.7** | **4.2** | **10.7** | **4.1** | **10.4** | **4.1** | **10.4** | **4.1** | **10.4** | **4.0** | **10.1** |
| **1** | MEN | 4.1 | 10.4 | 4.1 | 10.4 | 4.1 | 10.4 | 4.1 | 10.4 | 4.0 | 10.1 | 4.0 | 10.1 | 4.0 | 10.1 | 3.9 | 9.9 |
| | WOMEN | 3.8 | 9.7 | 3.6 | 9.1 | 4.0 | 10.1 | 4.0 | 10.1 | 3.5 | 8.9 | 3.5 | 8.9 | 3.4 | 8.6 | 3.2 | 8.1 |

\*See Table 1L for definition of thigh clearance.
†Measurement below which the indicated percent of people in the given age group fall.

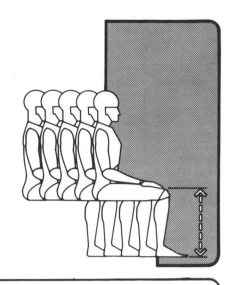

# KNEE HEIGHT

**Adult Male and Female Knee Height\* in Inches and Centimeters by Age, Sex, and Selected Percentiles†**

| | | 18 to 79 (Total) | | 18 to 24 Years | | 25 to 34 Years | | 35 to 44 Years | | 45 to 54 Years | | 55 to 64 Years | | 65 to 74 Years | | 75 to 79 Years | |
|---|---|---|---|---|---|---|---|---|---|---|---|---|---|---|---|---|---|
| | | in | cm | in | cm | in | cm | in | cm | in | cm | in | cm | in | cm | in | cm |
| **99** | MEN | 24.1 | 61.2 | 23.9 | 60.7 | 24.6 | 62.5 | 24.4 | 70.0 | 23.9 | 60.7 | 24.0 | 61.0 | 23.7 | 61.0 | 23.3 | 59.9 |
| | WOMEN | 22.4 | 56.9 | 22.7 | 57.7 | 22.5 | 57.2 | 22.4 | 56.9 | 22.5 | 57.2 | 21.9 | 55.6 | 22.0 | 55.9 | 21.5 | 54.6 |
| **95** | **MEN** | **23.4** | **59.4** | **23.4** | **59.4** | **23.7** | **61.0** | **23.4** | **59.4** | **23.3** | **59.9** | **23.1** | **58.7** | **22.9** | **58.7** | **22.7** | **57.7** |
| | **WOMEN** | **21.5** | **54.6** | **21.6** | **54.9** | **21.6** | **54.9** | **21.5** | **54.6** | **21.6** | **54.9** | **21.4** | **54.4** | **21.0** | **53.3** | **20.9** | **53.1** |
| **90** | MEN | 22.9 | 58.7 | 22.9 | 58.7 | 23.3 | 59.9 | 22.9 | 58.7 | 22.8 | 57.9 | 22.8 | 57.9 | 22.5 | 57.2 | 22.2 | 56.4 |
| | WOMEN | 21.0 | 53.3 | 21.0 | 53.3 | 21.0 | 53.3 | 21.0 | 53.3 | 21.0 | 53.3 | 20.9 | 53.1 | 20.7 | 52.6 | 20.7 | 52.6 |
| **80** | MEN | 22.4 | 57.0 | 22.5 | 57.2 | 22.7 | 57.7 | 22.5 | 57.2 | 22.4 | 57.0 | 22.2 | 56.4 | 21.9 | 55.6 | 21.7 | 55.1 |
| | WOMEN | 20.5 | 52.1 | 20.6 | 52.3 | 20.6 | 52.3 | 20.6 | 52.3 | 20.5 | 52.1 | 20.4 | 51.8 | 20.1 | 51.1 | 20.2 | 51.3 |
| **70** | MEN | 22.0 | 55.9 | 22.1 | 56.1 | 22.2 | 56.4 | 22.1 | 56.1 | 22.0 | 55.9 | 21.8 | 55.4 | 21.6 | 54.9 | 21.4 | 54.4 |
| | WOMEN | 20.1 | 51.1 | 20.3 | 51.6 | 20.3 | 51.6 | 20.2 | 51.3 | 20.1 | 51.1 | 20.0 | 50.8 | 19.8 | 50.3 | 19.9 | 50.5 |
| **60** | MEN | 21.7 | 55.1 | 21.8 | 55.4 | 21.9 | 55.6 | 21.8 | 55.4 | 21.7 | 55.1 | 21.4 | 54.4 | 21.3 | 54.1 | 21.0 | 53.3 |
| | WOMEN | 19.8 | 50.3 | 20.0 | 50.8 | 20.0 | 50.8 | 19.9 | 50.5 | 19.8 | 50.3 | 19.7 | 50.0 | 19.5 | 49.5 | 19.6 | 49.8 |
| **50** | MEN | 21.4 | 54.4 | 21.5 | 54.6 | 21.6 | 54.9 | 21.5 | 54.6 | 21.4 | 54.4 | 21.1 | 53.6 | 21.0 | 53.3 | 20.7 | 52.6 |
| | WOMEN | 19.6 | 49.8 | 19.7 | 50.0 | 19.7 | 50.0 | 19.6 | 49.8 | 19.5 | 49.5 | 19.5 | 49.5 | 19.2 | 48.8 | 19.4 | 49.3 |
| **40** | MEN | 21.1 | 53.6 | 21.2 | 53.8 | 21.3 | 54.1 | 21.2 | 53.5 | 21.1 | 53.6 | 20.8 | 52.8 | 20.7 | 52.6 | 20.4 | 51.8 |
| | WOMEN | 19.3 | 49.0 | 19.5 | 49.5 | 19.4 | 49.3 | 19.4 | 49.3 | 19.2 | 48.8 | 19.2 | 48.8 | 19.0 | 48.3 | 19.2 | 48.8 |
| **30** | MEN | 20.7 | 52.6 | 20.8 | 52.8 | 21.1 | 53.6 | 20.8 | 52.8 | 20.7 | 52.6 | 20.5 | 52.1 | 20.5 | 52.1 | 20.0 | 50.8 |
| | WOMEN | 19.1 | 48.5 | 19.2 | 48.8 | 19.2 | 48.8 | 19.1 | 48.5 | 19.0 | 48.3 | 19.0 | 48.3 | 18.7 | 47.5 | 18.9 | 48.0 |
| **20** | MEN | 20.4 | 51.8 | 20.5 | 52.1 | 20.6 | 52.3 | 20.4 | 51.8 | 20.3 | 51.6 | 20.2 | 51.3 | 20.2 | 51.3 | 19.6 | 49.8 |
| | WOMEN | 18.6 | 47.2 | 18.9 | 48.0 | 18.8 | 47.8 | 18.8 | 47.8 | 18.5 | 47.0 | 18.6 | 47.2 | 18.4 | 46.7 | 18.4 | 46.7 |
| **10** | MEN | 20.0 | 50.8 | 20.1 | 51.1 | 20.2 | 51.3 | 20.0 | 50.8 | 19.9 | 50.5 | 19.6 | 49.8 | 19.9 | 50.5 | 19.2 | 48.8 |
| | WOMEN | 18.2 | 46.2 | 18.4 | 46.7 | 18.3 | 46.5 | 18.3 | 46.5 | 18.1 | 46.0 | 18.2 | 46.2 | 18.1 | 46.0 | 18.0 | 45.7 |
| **5** | **MEN** | **19.3** | **49.0** | **19.4** | **49.3** | **19.8** | **50.3** | **19.4** | **49.3** | **19.3** | **49.0** | **19.1** | **48.5** | **19.2** | **48.8** | **19.0** | **48.3** |
| | **WOMEN** | **17.9** | **45.5** | **18.1** | **46.0** | **18.0** | **45.7** | **18.0** | **45.7** | **17.6** | **44.7** | **17.8** | **45.2** | **17.8** | **45.2** | **17.3** | **43.9** |
| **1** | MEN | 18.3 | 46.5 | 18.3 | 46.5 | 19.0 | 48.3 | 18.4 | 46.7 | 18.2 | 46.2 | 18.1 | 46.0 | 18.2 | 46.2 | 18.0 | 45.7 |
| | WOMEN | 17.1 | 43.4 | 17.3 | 43.9 | 17.2 | 43.7 | 17.2 | 43.7 | 17.1 | 43.4 | 16.6 | 42.2 | 17.1 | 43.4 | 16.3 | 41.4 |

\*See Table 1M for definition of knee height.
†Measurement below which the indicated percent of people in the given age group fall.

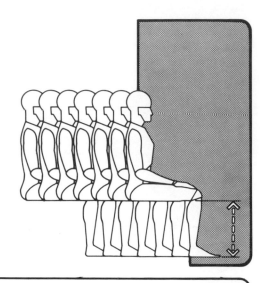

## 2J

## POPLITEAL HEIGHT

| | | 18 to 79 (Total) | | 18 to 24 Years | | 25 to 34 Years | | 35 to 44 Years | | 45 to 54 Years | | 55 to 64 Years | | 65 to 74 Years | | 75 to 79 Years | |
|---|---|---|---|---|---|---|---|---|---|---|---|---|---|---|---|---|---|
| | | in | cm | in | cm | in | cm | in | cm | in | cm | in | cm | in | cm | in | cm |
| **99** | MEN | 20.0 | 50.8 | 20.4 | 51.8 | 20.6 | 52.3 | 19.9 | 50.5 | 19.9 | 50.5 | 19.8 | 50.3 | 19.8 | 50.3 | 19.3 | 49.0 |
| | WOMEN | 18.0 | 45.7 | 18.5 | 47.0 | 18.2 | 46.2 | 17.9 | 45.5 | 18.3 | 46.5 | 17.9 | 45.5 | 17.9 | 45.5 | 17.8 | 45.2 |
| **95** | **MEN** | **19.3** | **49.0** | **19.6** | **49.8** | **19.7** | **50.0** | **19.1** | **48.5** | **19.1** | **48.5** | **19.0** | **48.3** | **18.9** | **48.0** | **18.4** | **46.7** |
| | **WOMEN** | **17.5** | **44.5** | **17.8** | **45.2** | **17.5** | **44.5** | **17.5** | **44.5** | **17.5** | **44.5** | **17.1** | **43.4** | **17.0** | **43.2** | **17.2** | **43.7** |
| **90** | MEN | 18.8 | 47.8 | 19.0 | 48.3 | 19.2 | 48.8 | 18.8 | 47.8 | 18.6 | 47.2 | 18.6 | 47.2 | 18.4 | 46.7 | 17.9 | 45.5 |
| | WOMEN | 17.0 | 43.2 | 17.4 | 44.2 | 17.0 | 43.2 | 17.0 | 43.2 | 17.0 | 43.2 | 16.8 | 42.7 | 16.8 | 42.7 | 16.9 | 42.9 |
| **80** | MEN | 18.2 | 46.2 | 18.5 | 47.0 | 18.6 | 47.2 | 18.2 | 46.2 | 17.9 | 45.5 | 18.0 | 45.7 | 17.8 | 45.2 | 17.4 | 44.2 |
| | WOMEN | 16.6 | 42.2 | 16.9 | 42.9 | 16.7 | 42.4 | 16.6 | 42.2 | 16.6 | 42.2 | 16.4 | 41.7 | 16.3 | 41.4 | 16.6 | 42.2 |
| **70** | MEN | 17.8 | 45.2 | 18.0 | 45.7 | 18.1 | 46.0 | 17.8 | 45.2 | 17.7 | 45.0 | 17.7 | 45.0 | 17.6 | 44.7 | 17.0 | 43.2 |
| | WOMEN | 16.3 | 41.4 | 16.6 | 42.2 | 16.4 | 41.7 | 16.3 | 41.4 | 16.2 | 41.1 | 16.1 | 40.9 | 15.9 | 40.4 | 16.2 | 41.1 |
| **60** | MEN | 17.6 | 44.7 | 17.7 | 45.0 | 17.8 | 45.2 | 17.6 | 44.7 | 17.5 | 44.5 | 17.4 | 44.2 | 17.3 | 43.9 | 16.8 | 42.7 |
| | WOMEN | 16.0 | 40.6 | 16.4 | 41.7 | 16.1 | 40.9 | 16.0 | 40.6 | 15.9 | 40.4 | 15.7 | 39.9 | 15.6 | 39.6 | 15.9 | 40.4 |
| **50** | MEN | 17.3 | 43.9 | 17.5 | 44.5 | 17.5 | 44.5 | 17.3 | 43.9 | 17.2 | 43.7 | 17.1 | 43.4 | 17.1 | 43.4 | 16.6 | 42.2 |
| | WOMEN | 15.7 | 39.9 | 16.1 | 40.9 | 15.8 | 40.1 | 15.7 | 39.9 | 15.5 | 39.4 | 15.4 | 39.1 | 15.3 | 38.9 | 15.6 | 39.6 |
| **40** | MEN | 17.0 | 43.2 | 17.2 | 43.7 | 17.3 | 43.9 | 17.0 | 43.2 | 17.0 | 43.2 | 16.9 | 42.9 | 16.8 | 42.7 | 16.4 | 41.7 |
| | WOMEN | 15.4 | 39.1 | 15.8 | 40.1 | 15.6 | 39.6 | 15.4 | 39.1 | 15.2 | 38.6 | 15.0 | 38.1 | 15.0 | 38.1 | 15.4 | 39.1 |
| **30** | MEN | 16.7 | 42.4 | 17.0 | 43.2 | 17.0 | 43.2 | 16.7 | 42.4 | 16.7 | 42.4 | 16.5 | 41.9 | 16.5 | 41.9 | 16.2 | 41.1 |
| | WOMEN | 15.1 | 38.4 | 15.5 | 39.4 | 15.3 | 38.9 | 15.1 | 38.4 | 14.9 | 37.8 | 14.7 | 37.3 | 14.7 | 37.3 | 15.1 | 38.4 |
| **20** | MEN | 16.4 | 41.7 | 16.6 | 42.2 | 16.6 | 42.2 | 16.4 | 41.7 | 16.3 | 41.4 | 16.2 | 41.1 | 16.2 | 41.1 | 15.9 | 40.4 |
| | WOMEN | 14.7 | 37.3 | 15.2 | 38.6 | 15.0 | 38.1 | 14.7 | 37.3 | 14.5 | 36.8 | 14.4 | 36.6 | 14.4 | 36.6 | 14.6 | 37.1 |
| **10** | MEN | 16.0 | 40.6 | 16.2 | 41.1 | 16.2 | 41.1 | 16.1 | 40.9 | 16.0 | 40.6 | 15.8 | 40.1 | 15.6 | 39.6 | 15.4 | 39.1 |
| | WOMEN | 14.2 | 36.1 | 14.6 | 37.1 | 14.4 | 36.6 | 14.2 | 36.1 | 14.2 | 36.1 | 14.1 | 35.8 | 14.1 | 35.8 | 14.1 | 35.8 |
| **5** | **MEN** | **15.5** | **39.3** | **16.0** | **40.6** | **16.0** | **40.6** | **15.6** | **39.6** | **15.5** | **39.4** | **15.3** | **38.9** | **15.2** | **38.6** | **15.2** | **38.6** |
| | **WOMEN** | **14.0** | **35.6** | **14.2** | **36.1** | **14.1** | **35.8** | **14.0** | **35.6** | **13.8** | **35.1** | **13.6** | **34.5** | **13.9** | **35.3** | **13.5** | **34.3** |
| **1** | MEN | 14.9 | 37.8 | 15.2 | 38.6 | 15.1 | 38.4 | 15.0 | 38.1 | 14.7 | 37.3 | 14.9 | 37.8 | 14.2 | 36.1 | 15.0 | 38.1 |
| | WOMEN | 13.1 | 33.3 | 13.5 | 34.3 | 13.2 | 33.5 | 13.1 | 33.3 | 13.1 | 33.3 | 13.1 | 33.3 | 13.0 | 33.0 | 9.6 | 24.4 |

**Adult Male and Female Popliteal Height\* in Inches and Centimeters by Age, Sex, and Selected Percentiles†**

*See Table 1N for definition of popliteal height.
†Measurement below which the indicated percent of people in the given age group fall.

# BUTTOCK-POPLITEAL LENGTH

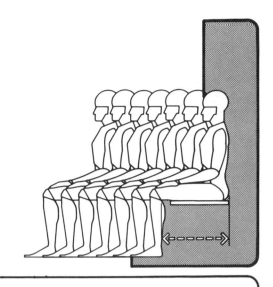

## Adult Male and Female Buttock-Popliteal Length* in Inches and Centimeters by Age, Sex, and Selected Percentiles†

| | | 18 to 79 (Total) | | 18 to 24 Years | | 25 to 34 Years | | 35 to 44 Years | | 45 to 54 Years | | 55 to 64 Years | | 65 to 74 Years | | 75 to 79 Years | |
|---|---|---|---|---|---|---|---|---|---|---|---|---|---|---|---|---|---|
| | | in | cm | in | cm | in | cm | in | cm | in | cm | in | cm | in | cm | in | cm |
| **99** | MEN | 22.7 | 57.7 | 22.9 | 58.2 | 23.1 | 58.7 | 22.7 | 57.7 | 22.0 | 55.9 | 22.2 | 56.4 | 21.9 | 55.6 | 22.1 | 56.1 |
| | WOMEN | 22.0 | 55.9 | 21.9 | 55.6 | 21.9 | 55.6 | 22.4 | 56.9 | 22.0 | 55.9 | 22.0 | 55.9 | 21.9 | 55.6 | 20.8 | 52.8 |
| **95** | **MEN** | **21.6** | **54.9** | **21.6** | **54.9** | **21.9** | **55.6** | **21.8** | **55.4** | **21.5** | **54.6** | **21.5** | **54.6** | **20.9** | **53.1** | **21.2** | **53.8** |
| | **WOMEN** | **21.0** | **53.3** | **21.1** | **53.6** | **21.0** | **53.3** | **21.1** | **53.6** | **20.9** | **53.1** | **21.0** | **53.3** | **20.9** | **53.1** | **20.0** | **50.8** |
| **90** | MEN | 21.0 | 53.3 | 21.0 | 53.3 | 21.4 | 54.4 | 21.1 | 53.6 | 20.9 | 53.1 | 20.9 | 53.1 | 20.7 | 52.6 | 20.8 | 52.8 |
| | WOMEN | 20.6 | 52.3 | 20.6 | 52.3 | 20.5 | 52.1 | 20.7 | 52.6 | 20.6 | 52.3 | 20.5 | 52.1 | 20.4 | 51.8 | 19.9 | 50.5 |
| **80** | MEN | 20.5 | 52.1 | 20.5 | 52.1 | 20.8 | 52.8 | 20.6 | 52.3 | 20.5 | 52.1 | 20.4 | 51.8 | 20.3 | 51.6 | 20.2 | 51.3 |
| | WOMEN | 19.9 | 50.5 | 19.8 | 50.3 | 19.9 | 50.5 | 20.0 | 50.8 | 20.0 | 50.8 | 19.9 | 50.5 | 19.8 | 50.3 | 19.6 | 49.8 |
| **70** | MEN | 20.1 | 51.1 | 20.0 | 50.8 | 20.4 | 51.8 | 20.1 | 51.1 | 20.1 | 51.1 | 20.0 | 50.8 | 19.9 | 50.5 | 19.7 | 50.0 |
| | WOMEN | 19.5 | 49.5 | 19.5 | 49.5 | 19.5 | 49.5 | 19.6 | 49.8 | 19.6 | 49.8 | 19.5 | 49.5 | 19.4 | 49.3 | 19.3 | 49.0 |
| **60** | MEN | 19.8 | 50.3 | 19.7 | 50.0 | 20.0 | 50.8 | 19.8 | 50.3 | 19.7 | 50.0 | 19.7 | 50.0 | 19.6 | 49.8 | 19.2 | 48.8 |
| | WOMEN | 19.2 | 48.8 | 19.1 | 48.5 | 19.2 | 48.8 | 19.3 | 49.0 | 19.3 | 49.0 | 19.2 | 48.8 | 19.1 | 48.5 | 19.0 | 48.3 |
| **50** | MEN | 19.5 | 49.0 | 19.5 | 49.0 | 19.6 | 49.8 | 19.5 | 49.0 | 19.5 | 49.0 | 19.4 | 49.3 | 19.3 | 49.0 | 18.9 | 48.0 |
| | WOMEN | 18.9 | 48.0 | 18.8 | 47.8 | 18.9 | 48.0 | 18.9 | 48.0 | 18.9 | 48.0 | 18.9 | 48.0 | 18.8 | 47.8 | 18.7 | 47.5 |
| **40** | MEN | 19.2 | 48.8 | 19.2 | 48.8 | 19.3 | 49.0 | 19.2 | 48.8 | 19.2 | 48.8 | 19.0 | 48.3 | 19.0 | 48.3 | 18.6 | 47.2 |
| | WOMEN | 18.6 | 47.2 | 18.5 | 47.0 | 18.6 | 47.2 | 18.6 | 47.2 | 18.6 | 47.2 | 18.6 | 47.2 | 18.5 | 47.0 | 18.3 | 46.5 |
| **30** | MEN | 18.8 | 47.8 | 19.0 | 48.3 | 19.0 | 48.3 | 18.9 | 48.0 | 18.8 | 47.8 | 18.6 | 47.2 | 18.6 | 47.2 | 18.3 | 46.5 |
| | WOMEN | 18.2 | 46.2 | 18.1 | 46.0 | 18.3 | 46.5 | 18.3 | 46.5 | 18.2 | 46.2 | 18.3 | 46.5 | 18.2 | 46.2 | 18.0 | 45.7 |
| **20** | MEN | 18.4 | 46.7 | 18.5 | 47.0 | 18.5 | 47.0 | 18.5 | 47.0 | 18.3 | 46.5 | 18.2 | 46.2 | 18.3 | 46.5 | 17.9 | 45.5 |
| | WOMEN | 17.9 | 45.5 | 17.7 | 45.0 | 18.0 | 45.7 | 18.0 | 45.7 | 17.8 | 45.2 | 18.0 | 47.2 | 17.8 | 45.2 | 17.6 | 44.7 |
| **10** | MEN | 17.9 | 45.5 | 18.0 | 45.7 | 18.1 | 46.0 | 18.0 | 45.7 | 17.8 | 45.2 | 17.6 | 44.7 | 17.8 | 45.2 | 17.3 | 43.9 |
| | WOMEN | 17.3 | 43.9 | 17.2 | 43.7 | 17.3 | 43.9 | 17.4 | 44.2 | 17.3 | 43.9 | 17.4 | 44.2 | 17.3 | 43.9 | 17.2 | 43.7 |
| **5** | **MEN** | **17.3** | **43.9** | **17.4** | **44.2** | **17.6** | **44.7** | **17.4** | **44.2** | **17.4** | **44.2** | **17.2** | **43.7** | **17.3** | **43.9** | **17.0** | **43.2** |
| | **WOMEN** | **17.0** | **43.2** | **16.9** | **42.9** | **17.0** | **43.2** | **17.1** | **43.4** | **17.0** | **43.2** | **17.1** | **43.4** | **16.9** | **42.9** | **17.0** | **43.2** |
| **1** | MEN | 16.5 | 41.9 | 16.5 | 41.9 | 16.6 | 42.1 | 16.5 | 41.9 | 17.0 | 43.2 | 16.4 | 41.7 | 16.3 | 41.4 | 16.2 | 41.1 |
| | WOMEN | 16.1 | 40.9 | 16.1 | 40.9 | 16.1 | 40.9 | 16.2 | 41.1 | 15.8 | 40.1 | 16.1 | 40.9 | 16.1 | 40.9 | 14.7 | 37.3 |

*See Table 10 for definition of buttock-popliteal length.
†Measurement below which the indicated percent of people in the given age group fall.

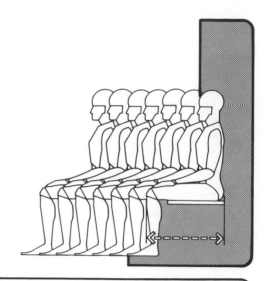

## 2L
## BUTTOCK-KNEE LENGTH

### Adult Male and Female Buttock-Knee Length* in Inches and Centimeters by Age, Sex, and Selected Percentiles†

| | | 18 to 79 (Total) | | 18 to 24 Years | | 25 to 34 Years | | 35 to 44 Years | | 45 to 54 Years | | 55 to 64 Years | | 65 to 74 Years | | 75 to 79 Years | |
|---|---|---|---|---|---|---|---|---|---|---|---|---|---|---|---|---|---|
| | | in | cm | in | cm | in | cm | in | cm | in | cm | in | cm | in | cm | in | cm |
| **99** | MEN | 26.3 | 66.8 | 26.5 | 67.3 | 26.8 | 68.1 | 26.2 | 66.5 | 26.1 | 66.3 | 25.8 | 65.5 | 25.9 | 65.8 | 24.9 | 63.2 |
| | WOMEN | 25.7 | 65.3 | 25.6 | 65.0 | 25.6 | 65.0 | 25.9 | 65.8 | 25.5 | 64.8 | 25.7 | 65.3 | 25.9 | 65.8 | 24.7 | 62.7 |
| **95** | **MEN** | **25.2** | **64.0** | **25.4** | **64.5** | **25.7** | **65.3** | **25.1** | **63.8** | **25.2** | **64.0** | **24.9** | **63.2** | **24.8** | **63.0** | **24.7** | **62.7** |
| | **WOMEN** | **24.6** | **62.5** | **24.6** | **62.5** | **24.6** | **62.5** | **24.7** | **62.7** | **24.6** | **62.5** | **24.7** | **62.7** | **24.6** | **62.5** | **23.9** | **60.7** |
| **90** | MEN | 24.8 | 63.0 | 24.9 | 63.2 | 25.0 | 64.0 | 24.8 | 63.0 | 24.8 | 63.0 | 24.6 | 62.5 | 24.4 | 62.0 | 24.4 | 62.0 |
| | WOMEN | 24.0 | 61.0 | 23.9 | 60.7 | 24.0 | 61.0 | 24.0 | 61.0 | 24.1 | 61.2 | 24.0 | 61.0 | 23.9 | 60.7 | 23.5 | 59.7 |
| **80** | MEN | 24.4 | 62.0 | 24.4 | 62.0 | 24.6 | 62.5 | 24.4 | 62.0 | 24.4 | 62.0 | 24.1 | 61.2 | 23.9 | 60.7 | 23.9 | 60.7 |
| | WOMEN | 23.4 | 59.4 | 23.3 | 59.2 | 23.5 | 59.7 | 23.5 | 59.7 | 23.5 | 59.7 | 23.4 | 59.4 | 23.4 | 59.4 | 22.9 | 58.2 |
| **70** | MEN | 23.9 | 60.7 | 23.9 | 60.7 | 24.2 | 61.5 | 24.0 | 61.0 | 24.0 | 61.0 | 23.7 | 60.2 | 23.6 | 59.9 | 23.3 | 59.2 |
| | WOMEN | 22.9 | 58.2 | 22.9 | 58.2 | 23.0 | 58.4 | 23.0 | 58.4 | 22.9 | 58.2 | 22.9 | 58.2 | 22.9 | 58.2 | 22.6 | 57.4 |
| **60** | MEN | 23.6 | 59.9 | 23.6 | 59.9 | 23.9 | 60.7 | 23.7 | 60.2 | 23.7 | 60.2 | 23.4 | 59.4 | 23.3 | 59.2 | 22.9 | 58.2 |
| | WOMEN | 22.6 | 57.4 | 22.5 | 57.2 | 22.7 | 57.7 | 22.7 | 55.7 | 22.6 | 57.4 | 22.6 | 57.4 | 22.6 | 57.4 | 22.4 | 56.9 |
| **50** | MEN | 23.3 | 59.2 | 23.3 | 59.2 | 23.6 | 59.9 | 23.4 | 59.4 | 23.4 | 59.4 | 23.1 | 58.7 | 23.0 | 58.4 | 22.6 | 57.4 |
| | WOMEN | 22.4 | 56.9 | 22.2 | 56.4 | 22.4 | 56.9 | 22.5 | 57.2 | 22.4 | 56.9 | 22.3 | 56.6 | 22.2 | 56.4 | 22.2 | 56.4 |
| **40** | MEN | 23.0 | 58.4 | 23.0 | 58.4 | 23.3 | 59.2 | 23.1 | 58.7 | 23.1 | 58.7 | 22.8 | 57.9 | 22.7 | 57.7 | 22.3 | 56.6 |
| | WOMEN | 22.1 | 56.1 | 21.9 | 55.6 | 22.1 | 56.1 | 22.2 | 56.4 | 22.1 | 56.1 | 22.0 | 55.9 | 21.9 | 55.6 | 21.9 | 55.6 |
| **30** | MEN | 22.7 | 57.7 | 22.7 | 57.7 | 22.9 | 58.2 | 22.7 | 57.7 | 22.7 | 57.7 | 22.4 | 56.9 | 22.4 | 56.9 | 22.0 | 55.9 |
| | WOMEN | 21.7 | 55.1 | 21.6 | 54.9 | 21.8 | 55.4 | 21.9 | 55.6 | 21.7 | 55.1 | 21.7 | 55.1 | 21.5 | 54.6 | 21.4 | 54.4 |
| **20** | MEN | 22.3 | 56.6 | 22.3 | 56.6 | 22.5 | 57.2 | 22.4 | 56.9 | 22.4 | 56.9 | 22.1 | 56.1 | 22.2 | 56.4 | 21.6 | 54.9 |
| | WOMEN | 21.3 | 54.1 | 21.3 | 54.1 | 21.4 | 54.4 | 21.5 | 54.6 | 21.3 | 54.1 | 21.3 | 54.1 | 21.2 | 53.8 | 21.0 | 53.3 |
| **10** | MEN | 21.8 | 55.4 | 21.9 | 55.6 | 22.1 | 56.1 | 21.9 | 55.6 | 21.9 | 55.6 | 21.5 | 54.6 | 21.5 | 54.6 | 21.2 | 53.8 |
| | WOMEN | 20.9 | 53.1 | 20.8 | 52.8 | 21.0 | 53.3 | 21.1 | 53.6 | 20.9 | 53.1 | 20.9 | 53.1 | 20.6 | 52.3 | 20.3 | 51.6 |
| **5** | **MEN** | **21.3** | **54.1** | **21.3** | **54.1** | **21.6** | **54.9** | **21.3** | **54.1** | **21.3** | **54.1** | **21.2** | **53.8** | **21.0** | **53.3** | **21.0** | **53.3** |
| | **WOMEN** | **20.4** | **51.8** | **20.3** | **51.6** | **20.5** | **52.1** | **20.5** | **52.1** | **20.3** | **51.6** | **20.3** | **51.6** | **20.2** | **51.3** | **19.9** | **50.5** |
| **1** | MEN | 20.3 | 51.6 | 20.4 | 51.8 | 20.8 | 52.8 | 20.3 | 51.6 | 20.4 | 51.8 | 19.6 | 49.8 | 20.1 | 51.1 | 20.2 | 51.3 |
| | WOMEN | 19.5 | 49.5 | 19.3 | 49.0 | 20.0 | 51.0 | 20.0 | 51.0 | 19.4 | 49.3 | 19.4 | 49.3 | 19.4 | 49.3 | 18.5 | 47.0 |

*See Table 1P for definition of buttock-knee length.
†Measurement below which the indicated percent of people in the given age group fall.

# 3 ADULT MALE AND FEMALE

## MISCELLANEOUS STRUCTURAL BODY DIMENSIONS

### DESCRIPTION

Certain selected male and female structural measurements not previously included within the scope of Table 2 are presented in this table. Only 5th and 95th percentile data are indicated since these were deemed to be more useful for design purposes.

### SOURCE

**A, B, D, E, G Male Data:** U.S. Air Force Flying Personnel, 1967; Churchill, Kikta, and Churchill, Aerospace Medical Research Laboratories, Wright-Patterson Air Force Base, Ohio, 1967.

**A, E Female Data:** Air Force Women, 1968; Clauser, et al., *Anthropometry of Air Force Women*, Technical Report 70-5, Aerospace Medical Research Laboratories, Wright-Patterson Air Force Base, Ohio, 1972.

**B, D, G Female Data:** Airline Stewardesses, 1971; Snow, Reynolds, and Allgood, *Anthropometry of Airline Stewardesses*, Department of Transportation, Report no. FAA-AM-2, FAA Office of Aviation Medicine, Civil Aeromedical Institute, Oklahoma City, Okla., 1975.

**C Male Data:** U.S. Air Force Flying Personnel, 1950; Hertzberg, Daniels, and Churchill, *Anthropometry of Flying Personnel, 1950*, Technical Report no. 52-321, Wright Air Development Center, Wright-Patterson Air Force Base, Ohio, 1954.

**C Female Data:** VonCott and Kinkade, *Human Engineering Guide to Equipment Design* (Washington, D.C.: American Institutes for Research), p. 495.

**F Male and Female Data:** Woodson and Conover, *Human Engineering Guide for Equipment Designers,* 2d ed. (Berkeley and Los Angeles: University of California Press, 1964), pp. 5–16, 5–17, 5–18, 5–19.

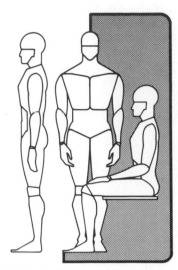

# 3

## MISCELLANEOUS STRUCTURAL BODY DIMENSIONS

| Adult Male and Female Miscellaneous Structural Body Dimensions in Inches and Centimeters by Age and Selected Percentiles | | | | | | | | | | | | | | |
|---|---|---|---|---|---|---|---|---|---|---|---|---|---|---|
| | | A | | B | | C | | D | | E | | F | | G | |
| | | in | cm | in | cm | in | cm | in | cm | in | cm | in | cm | in | cm |
| **95** | MEN | 36.2 | 91.9 | 47.3 | 120.1 | 68.6 | 174.2 | 20.7 | 52.6 | 27.3 | 69.3 | 37.0 | 94.0 | 33.9 | 86.1 |
| | WOMEN | 32.0 | 81.3 | 43.6 | 110.7 | 64.1 | 162.8 | 17.0 | 43.2 | 24.6 | 62.5 | 37.0 | 94.0 | 31.7 | 80.5 |
| **5** | MEN | 30.8 | 78.2 | 41.3 | 104.9 | 60.8 | 154.4 | 17.4 | 44.2 | 23.7 | 60.2 | 32.0 | 81.3 | 30.0 | 76.2 |
| | WOMEN | 26.8 | 68.1 | 38.6 | 98.0 | 56.3 | 143.0 | 14.9 | 37.8 | 21.2 | 53.8 | 27.0 | 68.6 | 28.1 | 71.4 |

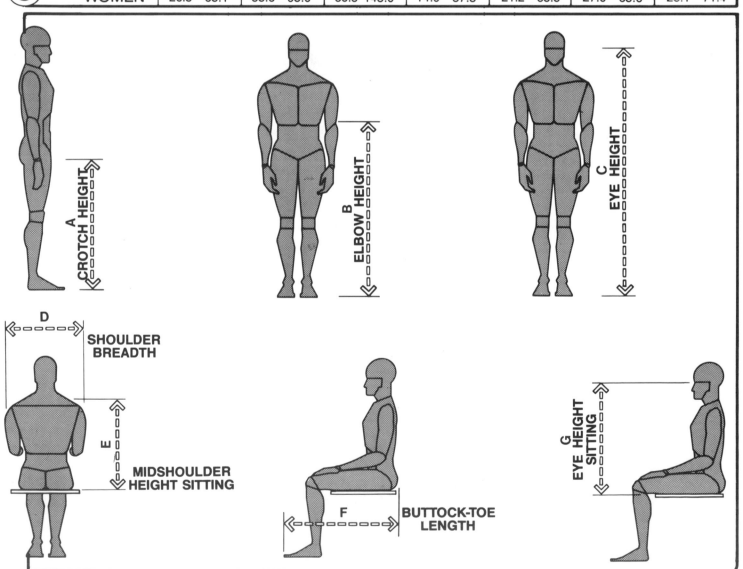

A CROTCH HEIGHT

B ELBOW HEIGHT

C EYE HEIGHT

D SHOULDER BREADTH

E MIDSHOULDER HEIGHT SITTING

F BUTTOCK-TOE LENGTH

G EYE HEIGHT SITTING

# 4 ADULT MALE AND FEMALE

# FUNCTIONAL BODY DIMENSIONS

## DESCRIPTION

Table 4 provides functional dimensions for males and females not included within the scope of Table 2. Only 5th and 95th percentile measurements are indicated since these were deemed to be the most useful for design purposes.

## SOURCE

**A Male Data:** U.S. Air Force Flying Personnel, 1967; Churchill, Kikta, and Churchill, Aerospace Medical Research Laboratories, Wright-Patterson Air Force Base, Ohio, 1967.

**A, D, F Female Data:** Air Force Women, 1968; Clauser, et al., *Anthropometry of Air Force Women*, Technical Report 70-5, Aerospace Medical Research Laboratories, Wright-Patterson Air Force Base, Ohio, 1972.

**B, D Male Data:** U.S. Air Force Flying Personnel, 1950; Hertzberg, Daniels, and Churchill, *Anthropometry of Flying Personnel, 1950*, Technical Report no. 52-321, Wright Air Development Center, Wright-Patterson Air Force Base, Ohio, 1954.

**B, E Female and E Male Data:** Woodson and Conover, *Human Engineering Guide for Equipment Designers,* 2d ed. (Berkeley and Los Angeles: University of California Press, 1964), pp. 5–16, 5–17, 5–18, 5–19.

**C Male Data:** Snow and Snyder, *Anthropometry of Air Traffic Control Trainees*, Report no. AM 65-26 (September 1965), Federal Aviation Agency, Oklahoma City, Okla.

**C Female Data:** Airline Stewardesses, 1971; Snow, Reynolds, and Allgood, *Anthropometry of Airline Stewardesses*, Department of Transportation, Report no. FAA-AM-2, FAA Office of Aviation Medicine, Civil Aeromedical Institute, Oklahoma City, Okla., 1975.

**F Male Data:** Hertzberg, et al., *The Anthropometry of Working Positions*, Report no. WADC TR-54-520, Wright-Patterson Air Force Base, Ohio, 1956.

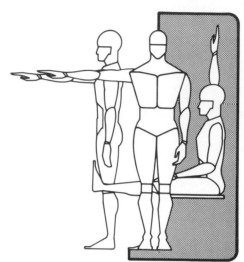

# 4

## FUNCTIONAL
## BODY
## DIMENSIONS

| | | A | | B | | C | | D | | E | | F | |
|---|---|---|---|---|---|---|---|---|---|---|---|---|---|
| Adult Male and Female Functional Body Dimensions in Inches and Centimeters by Age, Sex, and Selected Percentiles | | in | cm | in | cm | in | cm | in | cm | in | cm | in | cm |
| **95** | MEN | 38.3 | 97.3 | 46.1 | 117.1 | 51.6 | 131.1 | 35.0 | 88.9 | 39.0 | 86.4 | 88.5 | 224.8 |
| | WOMEN | 36.3 | 92.2 | 49.0 | 124.5 | 49.1 | 124.7 | 31.7 | 80.5 | 38.0 | 96.5 | 84.0 | 213.4 |
| **5** | MEN | 32.4 | 82.3 | 39.4 | 100.1 | 59.0 | 149.9 | 29.7 | 75.4 | 29.0 | 73.7 | 76.8 | 195.1 |
| | WOMEN | 29.9 | 75.9 | 34.0 | 86.4 | 55.2 | 140.2 | 26.6 | 67.6 | 27.0 | 68.6 | 72.9 | 185.2 |

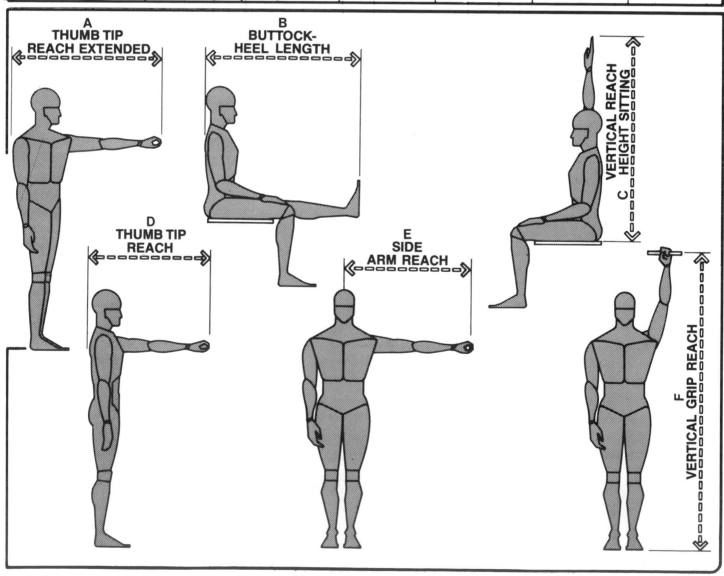

**A THUMB TIP REACH EXTENDED**

**B BUTTOCK-HEEL LENGTH**

**C HEIGHT SITTING** / **VERTICAL REACH**

**D THUMB TIP REACH**

**E SIDE ARM REACH**

**F VERTICAL GRIP REACH**

# 5 ADULT MALE AND FEMALE

## PROJECTED 1985 BODY DIMENSIONS

### DESCRIPTION

In Part A, secular changes in the body size of populations, over periods of time, were discussed. It was noted, for example, that the body size of Second World War inductees was greater than that of First World War inductees. A recent study by the U.S. Department of Health, Education, and Welfare, taken in 1971–1974, indicates that relatively more men and women are taller than those examined in the National Health Survey of 1960–1962. Fifty-one percent of the men in the recent survey were 175.3 cm, or 69 in, or taller as compared with 38 percent in the 1960–1962 survey. Recognizing the significance of secular change, as well as the length of the research and development cycle associated with the design and production of various equipment—a process typical of certain industries—projections of future body measurements can at times prove extremely useful. At the very least the inclusion of certain projections in these tables can, to some degree, complete the spectrum of anthropometric data available to the architect and interior designer. Table 5 includes such projections. Selected anticipated female and male structural body measurements for the year 1985 are shown. Only 5th and 95th percentile measurements are indicated since they were deemed to be most useful for design purposes.

The male measurements reflect extrapolations made on the basis of data from a number of surveys of U.S. Air Force (USAF) and U.S. Navy Flying Personnel conducted between 1950 and 1973. The data were restricted to those from commissioned officers in the 23–25 age range. The female measurements were estimated from a 1968 Air Force Women's survey. Unfortunately, there was no corresponding large group of surveys on which to study secular changes in dimensions of female officers. Proper allowances for clothing and shoes should be added to all data.

### SOURCE

*Anthropometric Source Book, Volume I: Anthropometry for Designers*, NASA reference publication 1024, National Aeronautics and Space Administration, Scientific and Technical Information Office, July 1978.

## 5

## PROJECTED 1985
## BODY DIMENSIONS

| | Weight | | A | | B | | C | | D | | E | | F | | G | |
|---|---|---|---|---|---|---|---|---|---|---|---|---|---|---|---|---|
| | lb | kg | in | cm | in | cm | in | cm | in | cm | in | cm | in | cm | in | cm |
| **95** MEN | 215.4 | 97.7 | 47.6 | 120.9 | 61.3 | 155.7 | 74.3 | 188.6 | 34.4 | 87.4 | 34.1 | 86.5 | 7.5 | 19.1 | 39.0 | 99.0 |
| WOMEN | 165.1 | 74.9 | 42.8* | 108.7 | 55.7 | 141.4 | 68.0 | 172.8 | 31.7 | 80.6 | 31.3 | 79.6 | 5.9 | 14.9 | 36.0 | 91.5 |
| **5** MEN | 143.7 | 65.2 | 41.5 | 105.5 | 53.7 | 136.5 | 66.2 | 168.2 | 29.3 | 74.3 | 30.1 | 76.4 | 5.7 | 14.5 | 34.8 | 88.5 |
| WOMEN | 104.5 | 47.4 | 38.0* | 96.5 | 48.4 | 122.9 | 60.0 | 152.3 | 26.7 | 67.7 | 27.4 | 69.5 | 4.1 | 10.4 | 32.0 | 81.2 |

| | H | | I | | J | | K | | L | | M | | N | | O | |
|---|---|---|---|---|---|---|---|---|---|---|---|---|---|---|---|---|
| | in | cm | in | cm | in | cm | in | cm | in | cm | in | cm | in | cm | in | cm |
| **95** MEN | 23.7 | 60.3 | 18.8 | 47.8 | 21.7 | 55.1 | 25.7 | 65.4 | 20.8 | 52.9 | 11.7 | 29.7 | 27.4 | 69.6 | 16.6 | 42.2 |
| WOMEN | 21.4* | 54.3 | 17.4 | 44.2 | 20.7 | 52.7 | 24.4 | 62.0 | 18.4 | 46.8 | 10.7 | 27.1 | 24.8 | 63.1 | 16.4 | 41.6 |
| **5** MEN | 20.5 | 52.1 | 15.9 | 40.4 | 18.3 | 46.4 | 22.2 | 56.4 | 17.5 | 44.4 | 8.3 | 21.0 | 23.9 | 60.6 | 13.5 | 34.4 |
| WOMEN | 18.4* | 46.7 | 14.9 | 37.8 | 17.2 | 43.7 | 21.0 | 53.3 | 15.2 | 38.6 | 7.6 | 19.2 | 21.3 | 54.2 | 13.9 | 35.4 |

**Adult Male and Female Projected 1985 Body Dimensions in Inches and Centimeters by Sex and Selected Percentiles**

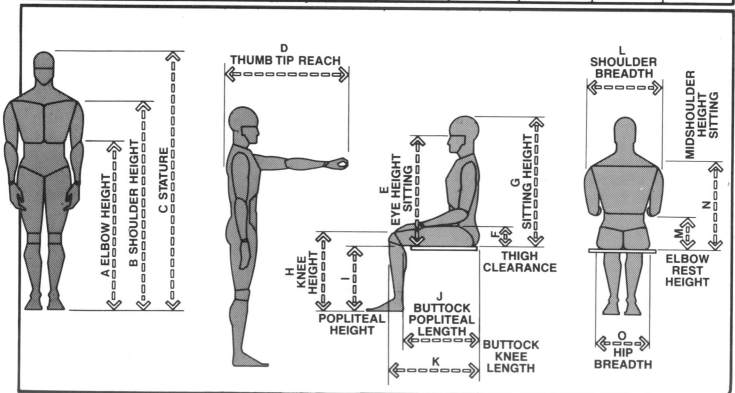

*Data estimated from regression equations.

# 6 ADULT MALE WORKING POSITIONS

## DESCRIPTION

Table 6 provides various 5th and 95th percentile body dimensions of kneeling, crawling, and prone positions not included in the data indicated in the other tables. This information is useful to the architect and interior designer in the planning of mechanical and utility spaces, exercise rooms, physical therapy spaces, and other similar areas. Proper allowances for clothing and shoes should be added to all data.

## SOURCE

*Human Factors Engineering,* 3d ed., AFSC Design Handbook 1-3/1 January 1977, Department of the Air Force, Headquarters Air Force Systems Command Andrews AFB, DC 20334, p. 8. The data used from AFSC DH 1-3 was, in turn, extracted from H. T. E. Hertzberg, I. Emanuel, and M. Alexander, *The Anthropometry of Working Positions,* WADC-TR-54-520 [Yellow Springs, Ohio: Antioch College, August 1956 (DDC N° AD 110573)]; and Albert Damon, Howard W. Stoudt, Ross McFarland, *The Human Body in Equipment Design* (Cambridge, Mass.: Harvard University Press, 1971), pp. 134–136.

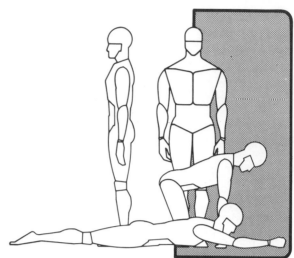

# 6

## WORKING
## POSITIONS

| Adult Male Working Positions in Inches and Centimeters and by Selected Percentiles* | | A | B | C | D | E | F | G | H |
|---|---|---|---|---|---|---|---|---|---|
| **95** | in | 22.8 | 13.0 | 48.1 | 34.5 | 95.8 | 16.4 | 58.2 | 30.5 |
| | cm | 57.9 | 33.0 | 122.2 | 87.6 | 243.3 | 41.7 | 147.8 | 77.5 |
| **5** | in | 18.8 | 10.1 | 37.6 | 29.7 | 84.7 | 12.3 | 49.3 | 26.2 |
| | cm | 47.8 | 25.7 | 95.5 | 75.4 | 215.1 | 31.2 | 125.2 | 66.5 |

*A and B from Damon, Stoudt, McFarland, *The Human Body in Equipment Design.* C through H from *Human Factors Engineering.*

# 7 CHILDREN AGES 6 TO 11

# WEIGHT AND STRUCTURAL BODY DIMENSIONS

## DESCRIPTION

To date, very little anthropometric data have been available to the designer with regard to functional body measurements of infants and children. Such information is vital to the proper design of juvenile furniture and preschool, school, and other interior environments for use by children. What makes the need for such data even more critical is that the element of safety as well as comfort is at stake. There is a strong relationship between improperly designed furniture and accidental death and injury to children. Cases of strangulation and neck impingement in cribs and high chairs, for example, are not uncommon. Table 7 provides some anthropometric data in the form of body measurements of children from 6 to 11 years of age in the United States from 1963 to 1965. Although the measurements are structural rather than functional, they should be useful to the designer. (The measurements were converted from centimeters to inches, which explains why there are some discrepancies within the tables.) Proper allowances for clothing and shoes should be added to all data.

For additional anthropometric data concerning infants and children, a 1975 study prepared by Snyder, Spencer, Owings, and Schneider, all of the University of Michigan, for the Society of Automotive Engineers, entitled *Anthropometry of U.S. Infants and Children*, is highly recommended.

## SOURCE

Robert M. Malina, Peter V. V. Hamill, and Stanley Lemeshow, *National Health Examination Survey: Selected Body Measurements of Children 6–11 Years, 1963–1965* (Washington, D.C.: U.S. Government Printing Office, Vital and Health Statistics Series 11, no. 123, DHEW publication no. (HSM) 73-1605.

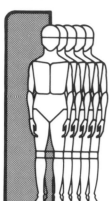

## 7A
## WEIGHT

| %ile | Sex | 6 Years lb | 6 Years kg | 7 Years lb | 7 Years kg | 8 Years lb | 8 Years kg | 9 Years lb | 9 Years kg | 10 Years lb | 10 Years kg | 11 Years lb | 11 Years kg |
|---|---|---|---|---|---|---|---|---|---|---|---|---|---|
| 95 | **BOYS** | **61.7** | **28.0** | **69.4** | **31.5** | **80.2** | **36.4** | **95.9** | **43.5** | **99.2** | **45.0** | **116.8** | **53.0** |
| 95 | **GIRLS** | **61.7** | **28.0** | **69.4** | **31.5** | **84.2** | **38.2** | **100.5** | **45.6** | **110.0** | **49.9** | **127.9** | **58.0** |
| 90 | BOYS | 57.3 | 26.0 | 65.0 | 29.5 | 74.7 | 33.9 | 84.9 | 38.5 | 92.6 | 42.0 | 107.1 | 48.6 |
| 90 | GIRLS | 56.9 | 25.8 | 65.5 | 29.7 | 76.1 | 34.5 | 92.2 | 41.8 | 100.5 | 45.6 | 114.9 | 52.1 |
| 75 | BOYS | 52.2 | 23.7 | 58.6 | 26.6 | 65.7 | 29.8 | 74.7 | 33.9 | 80.5 | 36.5 | 91.9 | 41.7 |
| 75 | GIRLS | 51.1 | 23.2 | 58.2 | 26.4 | 66.1 | 30.0 | 76.3 | 34.6 | 87.1 | 39.5 | 99.2 | 45.0 |
| 50 | BOYS | 47.6 | 21.6 | 53.1 | 24.1 | 59.7 | 27.1 | 65.5 | 29.7 | 71.9 | 32.6 | 80.7 | 36.6 |
| 50 | GIRLS | 46.5 | 21.1 | 51.8 | 23.5 | 58.9 | 26.7 | 65.7 | 29.8 | 75.4 | 34.2 | 84.2 | 38.2 |
| 25 | BOYS | 43.7 | 19.8 | 48.9 | 22.2 | 54.0 | 24.5 | 59.1 | 26.8 | 64.8 | 29.4 | 73.0 | 33.1 |
| 25 | GIRLS | 42.3 | 19.2 | 47.0 | 21.3 | 52.5 | 23.8 | 58.6 | 26.6 | 64.4 | 29.2 | 73.6 | 33.4 |
| 10 | BOYS | 40.1 | 18.2 | 45.0 | 20.4 | 49.8 | 22.6 | 54.0 | 24.5 | 58.9 | 26.7 | 65.4 | 30.1 |
| 10 | GIRLS | 38.8 | 17.6 | 43.0 | 19.5 | 47.8 | 21.7 | 53.6 | 24.3 | 57.8 | 26.2 | 65.7 | 29.8 |
| 5 | **BOYS** | **38.4** | **17.4** | **42.8** | **19.4** | **47.4** | **21.5** | **51.1** | **23.2** | **56.2** | **25.5** | **63.0** | **28.6** |
| 5 | **GIRLS** | **36.2** | **16.4** | **41.2** | **18.7** | **45.2** | **20.5** | **50.5** | **22.9** | **54.9** | **24.9** | **62.6** | **28.4** |

*Weight of Children in Pounds and Kilograms by Age, Sex, and Selected Percentiles*

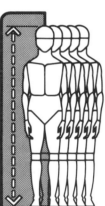

## 7B
## STATURE

| %ile | Sex | 6 Years in | 6 Years cm | 7 Years in | 7 Years cm | 8 Years in | 8 Years cm | 9 Years in | 9 Years cm | 10 Years in | 10 Years cm | 11 Years in | 11 Years cm |
|---|---|---|---|---|---|---|---|---|---|---|---|---|---|
| 95 | **BOYS** | **50.4** | **128.0** | **52.9** | **134.4** | **54.8** | **139.3** | **57.2** | **145.4** | **59.6** | **151.3** | **61.8** | **157.0** |
| 95 | **GIRLS** | **49.9** | **126.7** | **52.2** | **132.7** | **54.8** | **139.3** | **58.0** | **147.4** | **60.4** | **153.4** | **62.9** | **159.7** |
| 90 | BOYS | 49.5 | 125.7 | 51.9 | 131.8 | 54.1 | 137.3 | 56.5 | 143.5 | 58.5 | 148.5 | 60.7 | 154.3 |
| 90 | GIRLS | 49.2 | 125.0 | 51.5 | 130.7 | 54.0 | 137.2 | 57.0 | 144.8 | 59.1 | 150.2 | 62.2 | 158.0 |
| 75 | BOYS | 48.0 | 122.0 | 50.4 | 128.0 | 52.6 | 133.7 | 55.2 | 140.1 | 56.9 | 144.6 | 59.2 | 150.4 |
| 75 | GIRLS | 47.9 | 121.6 | 50.2 | 127.4 | 52.5 | 133.4 | 55.2 | 140.1 | 57.4 | 145.7 | 60.2 | 152.8 |
| 50 | BOYS | 46.7 | 118.5 | 49.0 | 124.4 | 51.2 | 130.0 | 53.4 | 135.6 | 55.4 | 140.6 | 57.4 | 145.8 |
| 50 | GIRLS | 46.3 | 117.7 | 48.7 | 123.6 | 51.0 | 129.6 | 53.3 | 135.4 | 55.5 | 141.0 | 58.0 | 147.4 |
| 25 | BOYS | 45.3 | 115.1 | 47.6 | 120.8 | 49.7 | 126.3 | 51.7 | 131.4 | 53.6 | 136.2 | 55.6 | 141.2 |
| 25 | GIRLS | 45.0 | 114.4 | 47.1 | 119.7 | 49.4 | 125.5 | 51.5 | 130.8 | 53.5 | 135.9 | 56.3 | 143.0 |
| 10 | BOYS | 44.0 | 111.8 | 46.4 | 117.8 | 48.5 | 123.3 | 50.0 | 127.0 | 51.7 | 131.4 | 54.0 | 137.2 |
| 10 | GIRLS | 43.5 | 110.6 | 45.8 | 116.3 | 47.8 | 121.4 | 50.0 | 127.1 | 52.0 | 132.0 | 54.7 | 138.9 |
| 5 | **BOYS** | **43.6** | **110.7** | **45.5** | **115.6** | **47.4** | **120.3** | **49.1** | **124.6** | **50.9** | **129.3** | **53.0** | **134.6** |
| 5 | **GIRLS** | **42.6** | **108.3** | **44.8** | **113.7** | **46.9** | **119.1** | **49.0** | **124.4** | **51.0** | **129.5** | **53.3** | **135.4** |

*Stature of Children in Inches and Centimeters by Age, Sex, and Selected Percentiles*

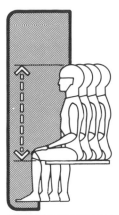

# 7C

## SITTING HEIGHT ERECT

| Sitting Height Erect of Children in Inches and Centimeters by Age, Sex, and Selected Percentiles | | | | | | | | | | | | | |
|---|---|---|---|---|---|---|---|---|---|---|---|---|---|
| | | 6 Years | | 7 Years | | 8 Years | | 9 Years | | 10 Years | | 11 Years | |
| | | in | cm | in | cm | in | cm | in | cm | in | cm | in | cm |
| **95** | **BOYS** | **27.4** | **69.5** | **28.2** | **71.7** | **29.2** | **74.1** | **30.2** | **76.6** | **30.9** | **78.5** | **31.7** | **80.6** |
| | **GIRLS** | **27.1** | **68.8** | **28.1** | **71.3** | **28.9** | **73.3** | **30.1** | **76.4** | **31.1** | **79.1** | **32.8** | **83.4** |
| **90** | BOYS | 26.9 | 68.3 | 27.8 | 70.6 | 28.8 | 73.2 | 29.7 | 75.5 | 30.4 | 77.2 | 31.3 | 79.5 |
| | GIRLS | 26.7 | 67.9 | 27.7 | 70.3 | 28.5 | 72.4 | 29.6 | 75.3 | 30.6 | 77.6 | 32.0 | 81.4 |
| **75** | BOYS | 26.2 | 66.5 | 27.0 | 68.7 | 28.1 | 71.3 | 29.0 | 73.6 | 29.6 | 75.2 | 30.5 | 77.5 |
| | GIRLS | 25.9 | 65.8 | 26.9 | 68.2 | 27.8 | 70.7 | 28.9 | 73.3 | 29.8 | 75.6 | 31.0 | 78.7 |
| **50** | BOYS | 25.5 | 64.7 | 26.4 | 67.1 | 27.3 | 69.3 | 28.1 | 71.4 | 28.8 | 73.1 | 29.7 | 75.4 |
| | GIRLS | 25.2 | 64.1 | 26.1 | 66.3 | 27.0 | 68.6 | 27.9 | 70.8 | 28.9 | 73.4 | 30.0 | 76.1 |
| **25** | BOYS | 24.7 | 62.8 | 25.6 | 65.1 | 26.5 | 67.3 | 27.2 | 69.2 | 28.0 | 71.0 | 28.9 | 73.3 |
| | GIRLS | 24.4 | 62.1 | 25.2 | 64.1 | 26.2 | 66.5 | 27.0 | 68.7 | 27.3 | 70.7 | 29.1 | 73.8 |
| **10** | BOYS | 24.1 | 61.1 | 25.0 | 63.5 | 25.8 | 65.5 | 26.3 | 66.8 | 27.2 | 69.0 | 28.1 | 71.3 |
| | GIRLS | 23.7 | 60.1 | 24.5 | 62.3 | 25.4 | 64.4 | 26.3 | 66.7 | 27.1 | 68.8 | 28.2 | 71.6 |
| **5** | **BOYS** | **23.7** | **60.2** | **24.6** | **62.4** | **25.4** | **64.5** | **25.9** | **65.9** | **26.5** | **67.4** | **27.6** | **70.1** |
| | **GIRLS** | **23.1** | **58.8** | **24.1** | **61.2** | **24.8** | **63.1** | **25.8** | **65.5** | **26.7** | **67.8** | **27.4** | **69.7** |

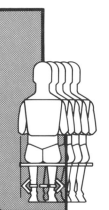

# 7D

## ELBOW-TO-ELBOW BREADTH

| Elbow-to-Elbow Breadth of Children in Inches and Centimeters by Age, Sex, and Selected Percentiles | | | | | | | | | | | | | |
|---|---|---|---|---|---|---|---|---|---|---|---|---|---|
| | | 6 Years | | 7 Years | | 8 Years | | 9 Years | | 10 Years | | 11 Years | |
| | | in | cm | in | cm | in | cm | in | cm | in | cm | in | cm |
| **95** | **BOYS** | **11.3** | **28.8** | **11.9** | **30.2** | **12.4** | **31.6** | **13.7** | **34.7** | **13.5** | **34.4** | **14.7** | **37.3** |
| | **GIRLS** | **11.1** | **28.1** | **11.6** | **29.5** | **12.4** | **31.6** | **13.5** | **34.2** | **14.2** | **36.1** | **14.7** | **37.4** |
| **90** | BOYS | 11.0 | 28.0 | 11.5 | 29.2 | 11.9 | 30.1 | 12.6 | 32.1 | 12.8 | 32.6 | 13.7 | 34.9 |
| | GIRLS | 10.6 | 26.9 | 11.1 | 28.3 | 11.7 | 29.7 | 12.5 | 31.7 | 13.1 | 33.4 | 13.9 | 35.2 |
| **75** | BOYS | 10.6 | 26.8 | 10.9 | 27.6 | 11.3 | 28.6 | 11.6 | 29.5 | 12.0 | 30.5 | 12.6 | 32.1 |
| | GIRLS | 10.0 | 25.4 | 10.4 | 26.4 | 10.9 | 27.7 | 11.3 | 28.8 | 12.0 | 30.4 | 12.6 | 32.1 |
| **50** | BOYS | 10.0 | 25.3 | 10.3 | 26.2 | 10.6 | 26.8 | 10.8 | 27.5 | 11.2 | 28.5 | 11.7 | 29.7 |
| | GIRLS | 9.4 | 24.0 | 9.7 | 24.6 | 10.1 | 25.7 | 10.4 | 26.5 | 10.9 | 27.7 | 11.5 | 29.2 |
| **25** | BOYS | 9.3 | 23.7 | 9.6 | 24.5 | 10.0 | 25.3 | 10.2 | 25.9 | 10.6 | 27.0 | 11.0 | 27.9 |
| | GIRLS | 8.9 | 22.5 | 9.1 | 23.1 | 9.5 | 24.1 | 9.8 | 24.8 | 10.1 | 25.7 | 10.6 | 26.8 |
| **10** | BOYS | 8.9 | 22.5 | 9.1 | 23.1 | 9.4 | 23.8 | 9.6 | 24.4 | 10.0 | 25.3 | 10.4 | 26.5 |
| | GIRLS | 8.4 | 21.4 | 8.7 | 22.0 | 8.8 | 22.3 | 9.3 | 23.5 | 9.5 | 24.2 | 10.0 | 25.3 |
| **5** | **BOYS** | **8.5** | **21.7** | **8.8** | **22.3** | **9.1** | **23.1** | **9.3** | **23.5** | **9.6** | **24.3** | **10.1** | **25.6** |
| | **GIRLS** | **8.3** | **21.0** | **8.4** | **21.3** | **8.4** | **21.4** | **9.1** | **23.0** | **9.2** | **23.4** | **9.6** | **24.5** |

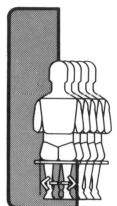

## 7E
## HIP BREADTH

| | | 6 Years | | 7 Years | | 8 Years | | 9 Years | | 10 Years | | 11 Years | |
|---|---|---|---|---|---|---|---|---|---|---|---|---|---|
| | | in | cm | in | cm | in | cm | in | cm | in | cm | in | cm |
| **95** | **BOYS** | 9.3 | 23.5 | 9.6 | 24.5 | 10.4 | 26.3 | 11.3 | 28.8 | 11.4 | 28.9 | 12.0 | 30.6 |
| | **GIRLS** | 9.3 | 23.7 | 10.1 | 25.7 | 10.6 | 26.9 | 11.5 | 29.2 | 12.3 | 31.2 | 13.3 | 33.8 |
| **90** | BOYS | 8.9 | 22.6 | 9.3 | 23.6 | 9.8 | 24.9 | 10.6 | 26.8 | 10.8 | 27.5 | 11.5 | 29.3 |
| | GIRLS | 9.0 | 22.8 | 9.7 | 24.6 | 10.2 | 25.9 | 11.0 | 28.0 | 11.6 | 29.5 | 12.4 | 31.6 |
| **75** | BOYS | 8.5 | 21.5 | 8.8 | 22.4 | 9.3 | 23.5 | 9.7 | 24.7 | 10.1 | 25.6 | 10.7 | 27.3 |
| | GIRLS | 8.5 | 21.7 | 9.0 | 22.9 | 9.6 | 24.4 | 10.1 | 25.7 | 10.7 | 27.3 | 11.3 | 28.8 |
| **50** | BOYS | 8.1 | 20.5 | 8.4 | 21.3 | 8.8 | 22.3 | 9.2 | 23.3 | 9.5 | 24.1 | 10.0 | 25.5 |
| | GIRLS | 8.1 | 20.5 | 8.5 | 21.6 | 9.0 | 22.8 | 9.3 | 23.6 | 9.9 | 25.2 | 10.5 | 26.6 |
| **25** | BOYS | 7.7 | 19.5 | 8.0 | 20.3 | 8.3 | 21.2 | 8.7 | 22.1 | 8.9 | 22.7 | 9.4 | 23.9 |
| | GIRLS | 7.6 | 19.4 | 8.0 | 20.4 | 8.4 | 21.4 | 8.8 | 22.4 | 9.2 | 23.4 | 9.8 | 24.9 |
| **10** | BOYS | 7.3 | 18.6 | 7.6 | 19.4 | 8.0 | 20.2 | 8.3 | 21.0 | 8.5 | 21.7 | 8.9 | 22.7 |
| | GIRLS | 7.3 | 18.5 | 7.6 | 19.4 | 8.0 | 20.3 | 8.4 | 21.3 | 8.7 | 22.1 | 9.1 | 23.2 |
| **5** | **BOYS** | 7.1 | 18.1 | 7.5 | 19.1 | 7.7 | 19.6 | 8.0 | 20.3 | 8.3 | 21.1 | 8.7 | 22.1 |
| | **GIRLS** | 7.1 | 18.1 | 7.4 | 18.7 | 7.8 | 19.7 | 8.1 | 20.6 | 8.4 | 21.3 | 8.8 | 22.3 |

Hip Breadth of Children in Inches and Centimeters by Age, Sex, and Selected Percentiles

## 7F
## THIGH CLEARANCE

| | | 6 Years | | 7 Years | | 8 Years | | 9 Years | | 10 Years | | 11 Years | |
|---|---|---|---|---|---|---|---|---|---|---|---|---|---|
| | | in | cm | in | cm | in | cm | in | cm | in | cm | in | cm |
| **95** | **BOYS** | 4.3 | 11.0 | 4.6 | 11.7 | 5.0 | 12.6 | 5.5 | 13.9 | 5.4 | 13.7 | 5.8 | 14.7 |
| | **GIRLS** | 4.5 | 11.5 | 4.8 | 12.2 | 5.1 | 12.9 | 5.4 | 13.8 | 5.6 | 14.3 | 5.9 | 14.9 |
| **90** | BOYS | 4.2 | 10.7 | 4.5 | 11.4 | 4.7 | 11.9 | 5.1 | 12.9 | 5.2 | 13.1 | 5.5 | 13.9 |
| | GIRLS | 4.3 | 10.8 | 4.5 | 11.5 | 4.9 | 12.4 | 5.2 | 13.3 | 5.4 | 13.6 | 5.6 | 14.3 |
| **75** | BOYS | 3.9 | 9.9 | 4.1 | 10.5 | 4.4 | 11.2 | 4.6 | 11.7 | 4.7 | 11.9 | 5.0 | 12.8 |
| | GIRLS | 3.9 | 10.0 | 4.1 | 10.5 | 4.4 | 11.3 | 4.6 | 11.8 | 5.0 | 12.6 | 5.2 | 13.1 |
| **50** | BOYS | 3.6 | 9.1 | 3.8 | 9.6 | 4.1 | 10.3 | 4.2 | 10.7 | 4.4 | 11.1 | 4.6 | 11.6 |
| | GIRLS | 3.6 | 9.2 | 3.8 | 9.6 | 4.1 | 10.3 | 4.2 | 10.7 | 4.5 | 11.4 | 4.7 | 11.9 |
| **25** | BOYS | 3.3 | 8.3 | 3.5 | 8.8 | 3.7 | 9.4 | 3.9 | 9.8 | 4.0 | 10.1 | 4.2 | 10.6 |
| | GIRLS | 3.3 | 8.4 | 3.5 | 8.8 | 3.7 | 9.4 | 3.9 | 9.8 | 4.1 | 10.3 | 4.2 | 10.7 |
| **10** | BOYS | 3.0 | 7.7 | 3.2 | 8.2 | 3.5 | 8.8 | 3.6 | 9.1 | 3.7 | 9.3 | 3.9 | 9.8 |
| | GIRLS | 3.1 | 7.8 | 3.2 | 8.2 | 3.4 | 8.7 | 3.6 | 9.1 | 3.7 | 9.4 | 4.0 | 10.1 |
| **5** | **BOYS** | 2.9 | 7.4 | 3.1 | 7.9 | 3.3 | 8.3 | 3.3 | 8.4 | 3.5 | 9.0 | 3.7 | 9.3 |
| | **GIRLS** | 2.9 | 7.4 | 3.1 | 8.0 | 3.2 | 8.2 | 3.3 | 8.5 | 3.5 | 9.0 | 3.7 | 9.4 |

Thigh Clearance of Children in Inches and Centimeters by Age, Sex, and Selected Percentiles

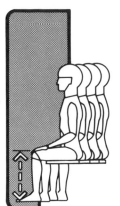

# 7G
## KNEE HEIGHT

| Knee Height of Children in Inches and Centimeters by Age, Sex, and Selected Percentiles | | 6 Years | | 7 Years | | 8 Years | | 9 Years | | 10 Years | | 11 Years | |
|---|---|---|---|---|---|---|---|---|---|---|---|---|---|---|
| | | in | cm | in | cm | in | cm | in | cm | in | cm | in | cm |
| 95 | BOYS | 15.6 | 39.7 | 16.6 | 42.2 | 17.2 | 43.8 | 18.4 | 46.7 | 19.1 | 48.6 | 20.0 | 50.9 |
| | GIRLS | 15.6 | 39.7 | 16.4 | 41.6 | 17.4 | 44.3 | 18.6 | 47.3 | 19.4 | 49.3 | 20.2 | 51.2 |
| 90 | BOYS | 15.3 | 38.8 | 16.3 | 41.3 | 16.9 | 42.9 | 18.0 | 45.6 | 18.7 | 47.5 | 19.6 | 49.8 |
| | GIRLS | 15.2 | 38.7 | 16.0 | 40.7 | 17.0 | 43.3 | 18.1 | 46.1 | 18.8 | 47.8 | 19.8 | 50.3 |
| 75 | BOYS | 14.7 | 37.4 | 15.6 | 39.6 | 16.4 | 41.7 | 17.2 | 43.8 | 18.1 | 45.9 | 19.0 | 48.2 |
| | GIRLS | 14.7 | 37.3 | 15.6 | 39.5 | 16.5 | 41.8 | 17.5 | 44.4 | 18.3 | 46.4 | 19.0 | 48.3 |
| 50 | BOYS | 14.1 | 35.9 | 15.0 | 38.2 | 15.8 | 40.2 | 16.7 | 42.4 | 17.4 | 44.3 | 18.2 | 46.3 |
| | GIRLS | 14.1 | 35.9 | 14.9 | 37.8 | 15.8 | 40.1 | 16.7 | 42.3 | 17.5 | 44.4 | 18.3 | 46.6 |
| 25 | BOYS | 13.6 | 34.6 | 14.4 | 36.7 | 15.2 | 38.6 | 16.0 | 40.7 | 16.7 | 42.4 | 17.5 | 44.4 |
| | GIRLS | 13.6 | 34.5 | 14.4 | 36.5 | 15.2 | 38.5 | 15.9 | 40.5 | 16.7 | 42.4 | 17.6 | 44.8 |
| 10 | BOYS | 13.2 | 33.5 | 14.0 | 35.5 | 14.7 | 37.3 | 15.4 | 39.1 | 16.0 | 40.7 | 16.9 | 42.8 |
| | GIRLS | 13.0 | 33.1 | 13.9 | 35.2 | 14.6 | 37.2 | 15.4 | 39.1 | 16.0 | 40.7 | 16.9 | 43.0 |
| 5 | BOYS | 13.0 | 32.9 | 13.7 | 34.8 | 14.3 | 36.3 | 15.0 | 38.1 | 15.6 | 39.7 | 16.4 | 41.7 |
| | GIRLS | 12.8 | 32.4 | 13.5 | 34.3 | 14.3 | 36.3 | 15.0 | 38.2 | 15.6 | 39.6 | 16.6 | 42.1 |

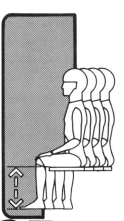

# 7H
## POPLITEAL HEIGHT

| Popliteal Height of Children in Inches and Centimeters by Age, Sex, and Selected Percentiles | | 6 Years | | 7 Years | | 8 Years | | 9 Years | | 10 Years | | 11 Years | |
|---|---|---|---|---|---|---|---|---|---|---|---|---|---|---|
| | | in | cm | in | cm | in | cm | in | cm | in | cm | in | cm |
| 95 | BOYS | 12.8 | 32.6 | 13.6 | 34.6 | 14.1 | 35.8 | 15.0 | 38.0 | 15.6 | 39.7 | 16.3 | 41.3 |
| | GIRLS | 12.6 | 32.1 | 13.4 | 34.0 | 14.1 | 35.8 | 15.1 | 38.4 | 15.7 | 39.8 | 16.4 | 41.7 |
| 90 | BOYS | 12.4 | 31.6 | 13.3 | 33.7 | 13.9 | 35.2 | 14.6 | 37.2 | 15.4 | 39.0 | 15.9 | 40.4 |
| | GIRLS | 12.4 | 31.4 | 13.1 | 33.3 | 13.7 | 34.9 | 14.8 | 37.6 | 15.4 | 39.1 | 16.0 | 40.7 |
| 75 | BOYS | 12.0 | 30.5 | 12.8 | 32.4 | 13.3 | 33.9 | 14.1 | 35.7 | 14.7 | 37.4 | 15.4 | 39.1 |
| | GIRLS | 11.9 | 30.2 | 12.6 | 32.0 | 13.3 | 33.7 | 14.1 | 35.7 | 14.7 | 37.4 | 15.5 | 39.3 |
| 50 | BOYS | 11.5 | 29.3 | 12.2 | 31.1 | 12.9 | 32.7 | 13.5 | 34.3 | 14.1 | 35.9 | 14.7 | 37.3 |
| | GIRLS | 11.4 | 29.0 | 12.0 | 30.6 | 12.8 | 32.5 | 13.5 | 34.2 | 14.0 | 35.6 | 14.8 | 37.5 |
| 25 | BOYS | 11.0 | 28.0 | 11.7 | 29.7 | 12.3 | 31.3 | 13.0 | 32.9 | 13.5 | 34.4 | 14.1 | 35.7 |
| | GIRLS | 10.9 | 27.7 | 11.5 | 29.3 | 12.2 | 31.1 | 12.8 | 32.6 | 13.4 | 34.1 | 14.1 | 35.7 |
| 10 | BOYS | 10.6 | 26.9 | 11.3 | 28.6 | 11.9 | 30.1 | 12.4 | 31.5 | 13.0 | 33.0 | 13.6 | 34.5 |
| | GIRLS | 10.4 | 26.5 | 11.1 | 28.2 | 11.7 | 29.6 | 12.3 | 31.3 | 12.8 | 32.6 | 13.5 | 34.2 |
| 5 | BOYS | 10.4 | 26.3 | 11.1 | 28.1 | 11.5 | 29.2 | 12.1 | 30.8 | 12.7 | 32.2 | 13.3 | 33.7 |
| | GIRLS | 10.2 | 26.0 | 10.8 | 27.4 | 11.5 | 29.1 | 11.9 | 30.3 | 12.5 | 31.8 | 13.1 | 33.3 |

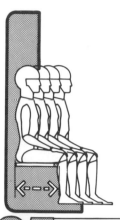

# 7I

## BUTTOCK-POPLITEAL LENGTH

| Buttock-Popliteal Length of Children in Inches and Centimeters by Age, Sex, and Selected Percentiles | | | | | | | | | | | | | |
|---|---|---|---|---|---|---|---|---|---|---|---|---|---|
| | | 6 Years | | 7 Years | | 8 Years | | 9 Years | | 10 Years | | 11 Years | |
| | | in | cm | in | cm | in | cm | in | cm | in | cm | in | cm |
| **95** | **BOYS** | 14.7 | 37.4 | 15.3 | 38.9 | 16.6 | 42.2 | 17.7 | 45.0 | 18.3 | 46.5 | 19.0 | 48.3 |
| | **GIRLS** | 15.2 | 38.6 | 15.9 | 40.3 | 17.0 | 43.1 | 17.8 | 45.2 | 18.8 | 47.7 | 19.9 | 50.5 |
| **90** | BOYS | 14.1 | 35.7 | 15.0 | 38.0 | 15.8 | 40.1 | 16.8 | 42.7 | 17.4 | 44.3 | 18.3 | 46.4 |
| | GIRLS | 14.6 | 37.0 | 15.2 | 38.5 | 16.2 | 41.1 | 17.2 | 43.8 | 18.0 | 45.8 | 19.2 | 48.7 |
| **75** | BOYS | 13.3 | 33.7 | 14.1 | 35.7 | 14.9 | 37.8 | 15.7 | 39.9 | 16.5 | 41.9 | 17.2 | 43.7 |
| | GIRLS | 13.5 | 34.4 | 14.4 | 36.5 | 15.2 | 38.6 | 16.2 | 41.2 | 17.2 | 43.6 | 18.0 | 45.7 |
| **50** | BOYS | 12.6 | 31.9 | 13.3 | 33.8 | 14.1 | 35.8 | 15.0 | 38.2 | 15.6 | 39.7 | 16.4 | 41.7 |
| | GIRLS | 12.8 | 32.6 | 13.6 | 34.6 | 14.4 | 36.6 | 15.3 | 38.9 | 16.2 | 41.2 | 17.0 | 43.1 |
| **25** | BOYS | 12.0 | 30.4 | 12.8 | 32.4 | 13.5 | 34.3 | 14.3 | 36.3 | 14.9 | 37.8 | 15.6 | 39.7 |
| | GIRLS | 12.2 | 31.1 | 13.0 | 32.8 | 13.8 | 35.1 | 14.6 | 37.2 | 15.4 | 39.1 | 16.1 | 40.9 |
| **10** | BOYS | 11.5 | 29.3 | 12.3 | 31.2 | 13.0 | 33.1 | 13.7 | 34.7 | 14.3 | 36.2 | 15.0 | 38.2 |
| | GIRLS | 11.7 | 29.7 | 12.4 | 31.6 | 13.2 | 33.5 | 13.9 | 35.4 | 14.6 | 37.0 | 15.4 | 39.2 |
| **5** | **BOYS** | 11.3 | 28.6 | 12.0 | 30.4 | 12.7 | 32.3 | 13.4 | 34.1 | 13.9 | 35.3 | 14.5 | 36.9 |
| | **GIRLS** | 11.3 | 28.8 | 12.0 | 30.6 | 12.9 | 32.7 | 13.5 | 34.3 | 14.1 | 35.8 | 15.0 | 38.1 |

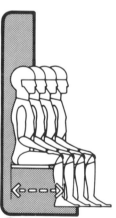

# 7J

## BUTTOCK-KNEE LENGTH

| Buttock-Knee Length of Children in Inches and Centimeters by Age, Sex, and Selected Percentiles | | | | | | | | | | | | | |
|---|---|---|---|---|---|---|---|---|---|---|---|---|---|
| | | 6 Years | | 7 Years | | 8 Years | | 9 Years | | 10 Years | | 11 Years | |
| | | in | cm | in | cm | in | cm | in | cm | in | cm | in | cm |
| **95** | **BOYS** | 16.4 | 41.6 | 17.6 | 44.6 | 18.3 | 46.5 | 19.5 | 49.5 | 20.1 | 51.0 | 21.1 | 53.7 |
| | **GIRLS** | 16.5 | 41.9 | 17.5 | 44.4 | 18.7 | 47.6 | 19.9 | 50.5 | 20.7 | 52.7 | 22.0 | 55.9 |
| **90** | BOYS | 16.1 | 40.8 | 17.1 | 43.4 | 17.9 | 45.4 | 18.9 | 47.9 | 19.7 | 50.1 | 20.7 | 52.5 |
| | GIRLS | 16.2 | 41.2 | 17.1 | 43.5 | 18.3 | 46.4 | 19.4 | 49.4 | 20.2 | 51.4 | 21.6 | 54.8 |
| **75** | BOYS | 15.4 | 39.1 | 16.4 | 41.6 | 17.2 | 43.8 | 18.2 | 46.2 | 19.0 | 48.2 | 19.9 | 50.5 |
| | GIRLS | 15.6 | 39.6 | 16.5 | 41.9 | 17.5 | 44.5 | 18.6 | 47.3 | 19.5 | 49.5 | 20.5 | 52.1 |
| **50** | BOYS | 14.7 | 37.4 | 15.7 | 39.9 | 16.5 | 41.8 | 17.4 | 44.2 | 18.2 | 46.3 | 19.0 | 48.3 |
| | GIRLS | 14.9 | 37.9 | 15.8 | 40.1 | 16.7 | 42.5 | 17.6 | 44.7 | 18.6 | 47.3 | 19.5 | 49.5 |
| **25** | BOYS | 14.1 | 35.7 | 15.0 | 38.1 | 15.8 | 40.2 | 16.5 | 41.9 | 17.4 | 44.2 | 18.2 | 46.2 |
| | GIRLS | 14.2 | 36.1 | 15.0 | 38.2 | 15.9 | 40.5 | 16.8 | 42.6 | 17.6 | 44.7 | 18.6 | 47.3 |
| **10** | BOYS | 13.2 | 33.6 | 14.2 | 36.1 | 14.8 | 37.6 | 15.6 | 39.7 | 16.3 | 41.5 | 17.4 | 44.1 |
| | GIRLS | 13.2 | 33.5 | 14.1 | 35.7 | 15.2 | 38.6 | 15.9 | 40.4 | 16.7 | 42.3 | 17.8 | 45.2 |
| **5** | **BOYS** | 12.4 | 31.5 | 13.3 | 33.7 | 14.1 | 35.7 | 14.8 | 37.7 | 15.7 | 39.8 | 16.6 | 42.2 |
| | **GIRLS** | 12.7 | 32.2 | 13.5 | 34.2 | 14.6 | 37.1 | 15.2 | 38.6 | 15.9 | 40.5 | 17.2 | 43.7 |

# 8 MALE HEAD, FACE HAND, AND FOOT DIMENSIONS

## DESCRIPTION

The table provides 5th and 95th percentile dimensions of the male head, face, hand, and foot. Although of greater value to the designer of clothing and equipment, the hand and foot dimensions could also prove quite useful to the architect and interior designer. Applications would include security grilles, gratings, access and vision panels, recreational equipment, commercial or residential shoe storage arrangements and devices, and special spaces for physically disabled people. Proper allowances for clothing and shoes should be added to all data.

## SOURCE

*Human Factors Engineering,* 3d ed., AFSC Design Handbook 1-31 January 1977, Department of the Air Force, Headquarters Air Force Systems Command Andrews AFB, DC 20334, p. 6.

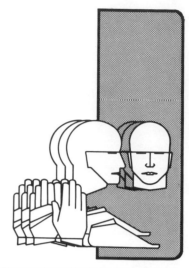

# 8

## HEAD, FACE, HAND, AND FOOT DIMENSIONS

| Adult Male Head, Face, Hand, and Foot Dimensions in Inches and Centimeters and by Selected Percentiles | | | | | | | | | | |
|---|---|---|---|---|---|---|---|---|---|---|
| | | A | B | C* | D | E | F | G | H | I |
| **95** | in | 5.0 | 6.50 | 23.59 | 5.13 | 8.27 | 2.71 | 5.94 | 5.98 | 8.07 |
| | cm | 12.7 | 16.5 | 59.9 | 13.0 | 21.0 | 6.9 | 15.1 | 15.2 | 20.5 |
| **5** | in | 4.1 | 5.80 | 21.74 | 4.35 | 7.39 | 2.24 | 5.27 | 5.26 | 7.00 |
| | cm | 10.4 | 14.7 | 55.2 | 11.0 | 18.8 | 5.7 | 13.4 | 13.4 | 17.8 |
| | | J | K | L(*) | M(*) | N | O | P | Q(*) | R |
| **95** | in | 4.63 | 3.78 | 9.11 | 10.95 | 11.44 | 8.42 | 4.18 | 10.62 | 2.87 |
| | cm | 11.8 | 9.6 | 23.1 | 27.8 | 29.1 | 21.4 | 10.6 | 27.0 | 7.3 |
| **5** | in | 3.92 | 3.24 | 7.89 | 9.38 | 9.89 | 7.18 | 3.54 | 9.02 | 2.40 |
| | cm | 10.0 | 8.2 | 20.0 | 23.8 | 25.1 | 18.2 | 9.0 | 22.9 | 6.1 |

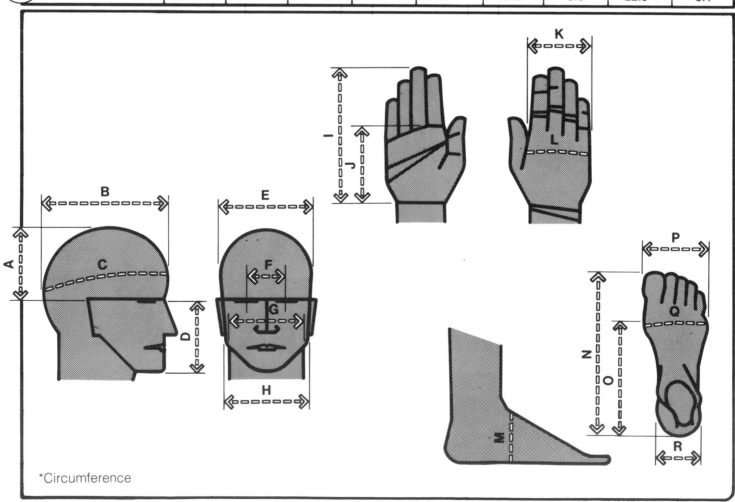

*Circumference

# 9 JOINT MOTION

## DESCRIPTION

The study, measurement, and evaluation of the ranges of joint motion is a complex and relatively sophisticated science. Measuring techniques have not been completely perfected and some yet remain to be devised. Research with respect to certain aspects of the dynamics involved, particularly in terms of the interaction of two or more joints or muscles, is still in its early stages. The data available are scarce, and information specifically related to large samplings of the civilian population practically nonexistent. Table 9 includes what information is available concerning ranges of joint motion relative to the neck, spine, shoulder, elbow, hip, knee, wrist, fingers, ankle, and foot. Most of the data, however, are based on a military population and are concerned primarily with the simple movement of a single joint and not with the effect of one upon the other. Proper allowances for clothing and shoes should be added to all data.

## SOURCE

*Human Factors Engineering,* 3d ed., AFSC Design Handbook 1-3, January 1977, Department of the Air Force, Headquarters Air Force Systems Command, Andrews AFB, DC 20334, pp. 16–17.

## JOINT MOTION TERMINOLOGY[1]

**Flexion:** bending or decreasing the angle between the parts of the body. Supplementing the more commonly measured arm and leg flexions, several kinds of flexion have been identified to meet special descriptive needs. These are *trunk lateral* flexion in which the trunk segments move so as to decrease the angle between them and the right thigh; *radial* flexion, which refers to the movement of the thumb side of the hand toward the radial side of the forearm segments; and *ulnar* flexion, which refers to the opposite side of the hand's movement toward the ulnar side of the forearm segment.

**Extension:** straightening or increasing the angle between the parts of the body. It is generally defined as the return from flexion. When a joint is extended beyond the normal range of its movement, the movement becomes known as "hyperextension."

**Abduction:** movement of a body segment away from the midline of the body or body part to which it is attached.

**Adduction:** movement of a body segment or segment combination toward the midline of the body or body part to which it is attached.

**Medial rotation:** turning toward the midline of the body.

**Lateral rotation:** turning away from the midline of the body.

**Pronation:** rotating the forearm so that the palm faces downward.

**Supination:** rotating the forearm so that the palm faces upward.

**Eversion:** rotation of the foot which lifts its lateral border to turn the sole or plantar surface outward.

**Inversion:** lifting the medial border of the foot to turn the sole inward.

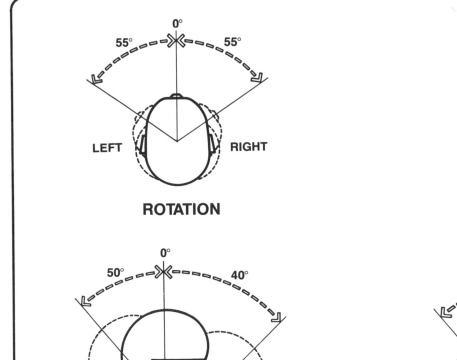

**ROTATION**

**HYPEREXTENSION
AND FLEXION**

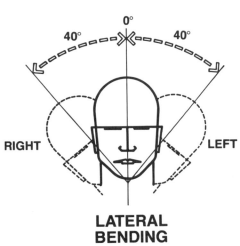

**LATERAL
BENDING**

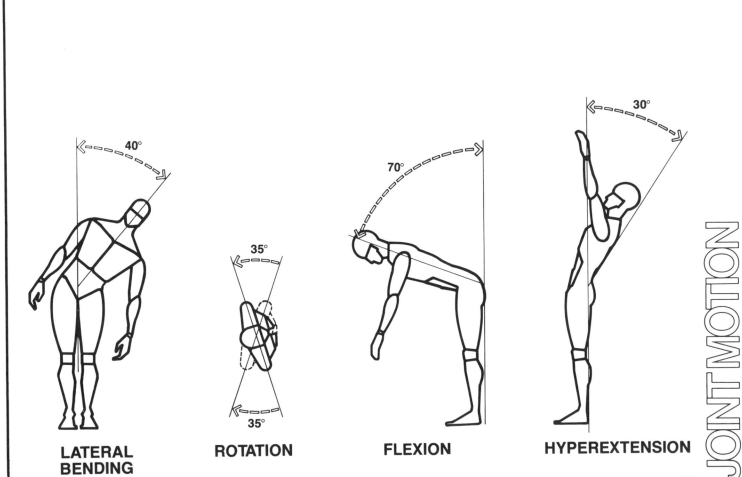

**LATERAL
BENDING**

**ROTATION**

**FLEXION**

**HYPEREXTENSION**

# SHOULDER

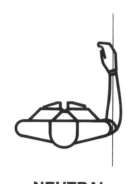

**NEUTRAL**

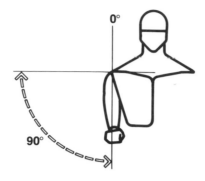

**ABDUCTION**

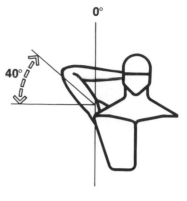

**ELEVATION**

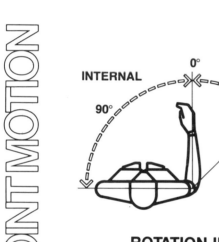

**ROTATION IN
NEUTRAL POSITION**

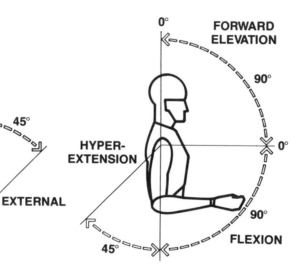

**HYPEREXTENSION
AND FLEXION**

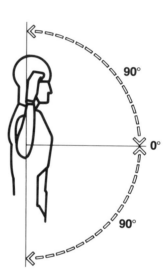

**ROTATION IN
ABDUCTION**

# ELBOW / FOREARM

**NEUTRAL
EXTENSION**

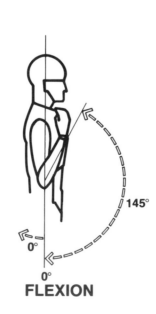

**FLEXION**

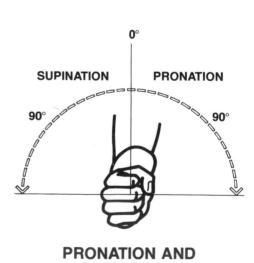

**PRONATION AND
SUPINATION**

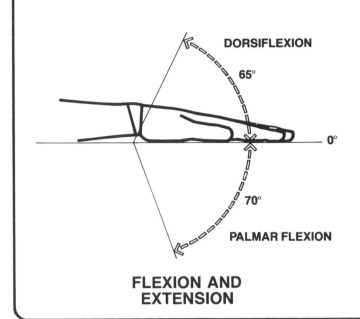

**DORSIFLEXION**

65°

0°

70°

**PALMAR FLEXION**

## FLEXION AND EXTENSION

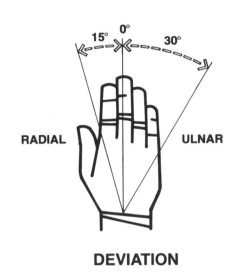

15° 0° 30°

**RADIAL**     **ULNAR**

## DEVIATION

# FINGERS

0°

## NEUTRAL

0°

## HYPEREXTENSION

## NEUTRAL

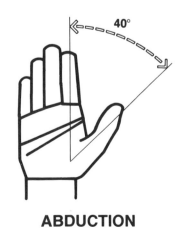

40°

## ABDUCTION

## OPPOSITION

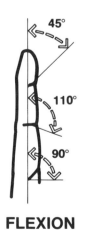

45°

110°

90°

## FLEXION

# HIP

**NEUTRAL EXTENSION**

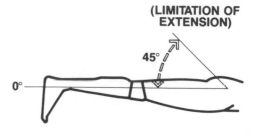

(LIMITATION OF EXTENSION)

0°

45°

**HYPEREXTENSION**

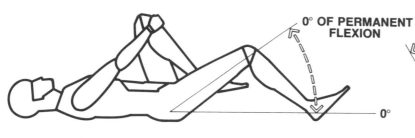

0° OF PERMANENT FLEXION

0°

**PERMANENT FLEXION**

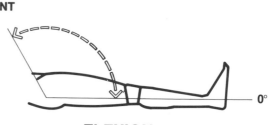

0°

**FLEXION**

## JOINT MOTION

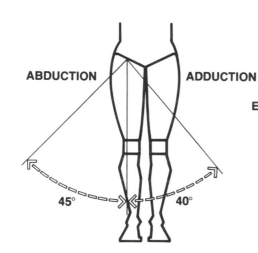

ABDUCTION  ADDUCTION

45°  40°

**ABDUCTION AND ADDUCTION**

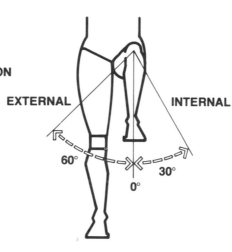

EXTERNAL  INTERNAL

60°  30°

0°

**ROTATION IN FLEXION**

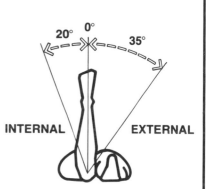

20°  0°  35°

INTERNAL  EXTERNAL

**ROTATION IN EXTENSION**

# KNEE

## JOINT MOTION

NEUTRAL EXTENSION

0°

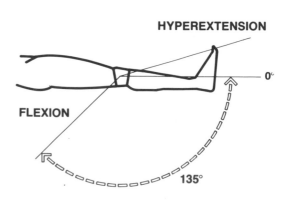

HYPEREXTENSION

0°

FLEXION

135°

**HYPEREXTENSION AND FLEXION**

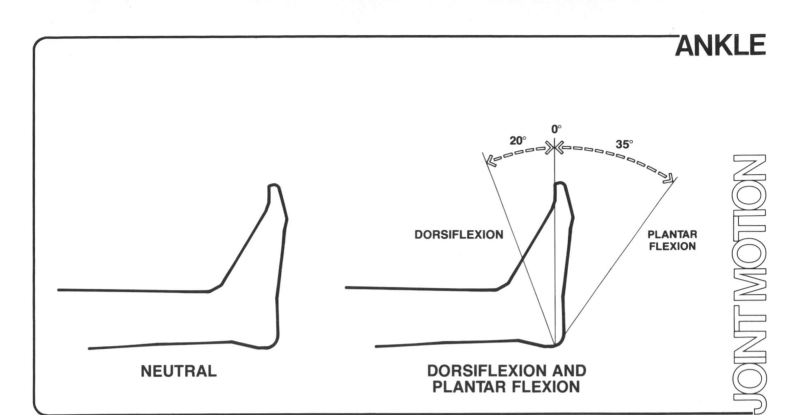

**NEUTRAL**

**DORSIFLEXION AND PLANTAR FLEXION**

# FOOT

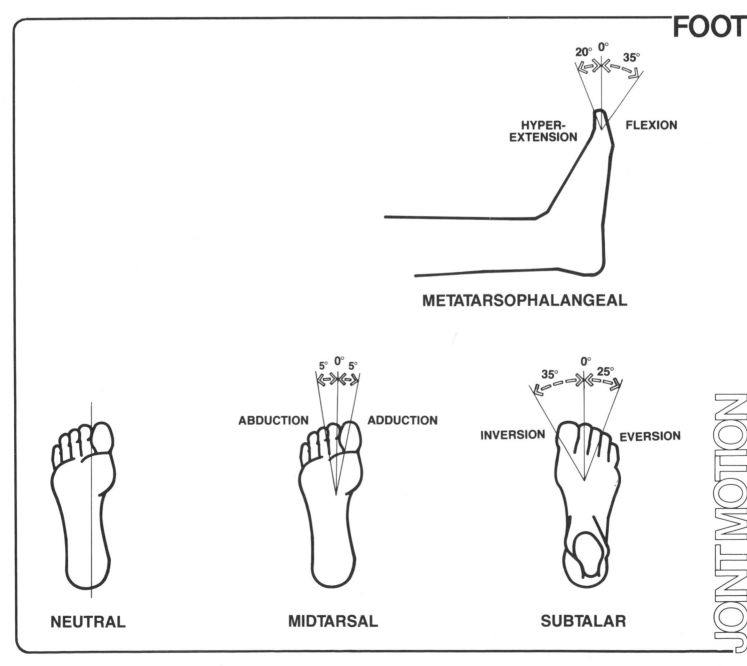

**METATARSOPHALANGEAL**

**NEUTRAL**

**MIDTARSAL**

**SUBTALAR**

# C INTERIOR SPACE/

# BASIC DESIGN REFERENCE STANDARDS

The promise of easy answers associated with packaged solutions, rules of thumb, standards, and other presumably painless and time-saving devices is understandably an appealing one. In certain situations, reliance on such sources may be perfectly appropriate. In problems dealing with such human factors as the interface between the human body and the designed environment, however, the use of such sources should be discouraged. The great variety of body sizes and dimensions to be contended with and the almost infinite number of interface scenarios possible make reliance on such sources sometimes dangerous, often inappropriate, and usually unwise. In those instances where so-called standards or rules of thumb may, in fact, be appropriate, it is still more useful to understand the underlying concepts, process, and rationale than to unquestioningly apply them with only the end results in mind.

## INTENT

In anticipation that the term "design reference standards," the title given to this section, should in any way be misconstrued to suggest the promise of a handbook of ready-made design solutions, it is necessary that the purpose of this section be made clear. It is definitely not intended that the drawings on the following pages be viewed as design solutions. They should serve simply as models or reference standards in the development of a more anthropometrically based approach to preliminary design, especially in areas involving the interface between the human body and various design components of interior space. The two areas of interface most commonly encountered in the average interior design or architectural practice and the two explored in this book are essentially of a physical and a visual nature. The physical usually involves problems of clearance and reach. The visual involves the field of vision in both the horizontal and the vertical planes. Both are a function, directly or indirectly, of human dimension and the range of joint motion. To intelligently resolve these problems, the designer needs some basic knowledge of anthropometry, in terms of both theory and application and an available data bank of body sizes and dimensions. The former was the subject of Part A, the latter the subject of Part B.

## THE DRAWINGS

The drawings that follow identify various classic problems of interface commonly encountered in the design of certain prototypical interior spaces. By referring to the particular illustrations and the accompanying drawing text, the designer will be able to undertake his or her own individual analysis of any problem involving human dimension and the quality of interface. To more clearly explain the logic involved and to underscore the anthropometric aspect of the process, it should be noted that each drawing contains certain dimensional arrows drawn in solid line with code numbers written above. The numbers represent certain standard body measurements.

## THE MATRICES

The legend for translating these numbers into particular anthropometric measurements is contained both in the master matrix at the beginning of each section and in the matrix at the beginning of each subsection. The dimension line indicates where the measurement is taken. The following observations should make the use of the matrix easier. One column lists the 24 body measurements. The other column lists the various types of interior spaces. The circular symbols indicate those specific measurements that are most significant in the design of a particular space type. The darkened circles signify that the measurement should be of the person having a larger body size. The circles shown in outline indicate that the measurement should be of a person having a smaller body size. The half darkened circles suggest that both large and small body size data be considered. The extended arrows identify the tables in Part B in which the related body measurements can be found. The matrix at the beginning of each subsection lists only those measurements relevant to that subsection. The other column lists the basic activities involved, while the symbols indicate those specific measurements most relevant to a particular activity.

## THE CHARTS

The arrows shown in broken line, with a letter above, indicate other dimensional criteria that have been determined in order to comfortably accommodate the designated body measurements. The charts on each page are keyed to the letters and show the dimensions in both English and metric systems.

Through the careful use of these drawings, tables, matrices, charts, and text as a model, the designer of interior space should be able to establish the dimensional requirements necessary to respond to the anthropometric demands inherent in any type of interface situation that includes the human body and that space. Preliminary design assumptions so developed are sure to be far more responsive to human dimension than arbitrary or often outdated standards or rules of thumb.

| TABLE | WORK | GENERAL PURPOSE | EXECUTIVE | EASY CHAIR | DRAFTING | BANQUETTE | SEATING TYPES — ANTHROPOMETRIC DATA |
|---|---|---|---|---|---|---|---|
| | | | | | | | 1 STATURE |
| | | | | | | | 2 EYE HEIGHT |
| | | | | | | | 3 ELBOW HEIGHT |
| | | | | | | | 4 SITTING HEIGHT ERECT |
| | | | | | | | 5 SITTING HEIGHT NORMAL |
| | | | | | | | 6 EYE HEIGHT SITTING |
| | | | | | | | 7 MIDSHOULDER HEIGHT SITTING |
| | | | | | | | 8 SHOULDER BREADTH |
| | | | | | | | 9 ELBOW-TO-ELBOW BREADTH |
| 1J,2F | | | ● | ● | | | 10 HIP BREADTH |
| 1K,2G | | | ● | ● | | | 11 ELBOW REST HEIGHT |
| | | | | | | | 12 THIGH CLEARANCE |
| | | | | | | | 13 KNEE HEIGHT |
| 1N,2J | ● | ● | ● | ● | ● | ● | 14 POPLITEAL HEIGHT |
| 1O,2K | ● | ● | ● | ● | ● | | 15 BUTTOCK-POPLITEAL LENGTH |
| 1P,2L | | | | | ● | | 16 BUTTOCK-KNEE LENGTH |
| | | | | | | | 17 BUTTOCK-TOE LENGTH |
| 1R,4B | | | ● | | | | 18 BUTTOCK-HEEL LENGTH |
| | | | | | | | 19 VERTICAL REACH HEIGHT SITTING |
| | | | | | | | 20 VERTICAL GRIP REACH |
| | | | | | | | 21 SIDE ARM REACH |
| | | | | | | | 22 THUMB TIP REACH |
| | | | | | | | 23 MAXIMUM BODY DEPTH |
| 1X,6A | | | ● | ● | ● | ● | 24 MAXIMUM BODY BREADTH |

The design of seating, more than any other element of interior space, involves the elusive quality of user comfort. Since relatively little research in this area has been undertaken, conflicting recommendations abound for many of the dimensions involved. The measurements indicated in the drawings on the following pages, therefore, reflect basic anthropometric requirements and, within reasonable parameters, generally accepted notions of comfort. The intent of the diagrams is to indicate some of the more basic critical dimensional requirements necessary to ensure a reasonable interface between the human body and the seat and to establish an intelligent point of departure for the design process. Part of this process, it should be noted, involves the fabrication of full-size mockups and prototypes, whereby function, esthetics, and user comfort can be properly evaluated and design modifications made accordingly.

In many instances, seating is directly related to a table, desk, counter, or a variety of special worksurfaces. However, the diagrams in this section deal exclusively with the seat itself. The proper relationship between the seat and other elements is included in those other sections appropriate to the activity involved. For example, the desk/chair relationship is included in Section 3 dealing with office spaces; situations involving visibility and lines of sight from a seated position are covered in the section on the design of audiovisual spaces. The seating types included in the diagrams are executive chairs, secretarial chairs, general purpose chairs, drafting stools, and banquettes. The critical dimensions examined include seat height, seat depth, seat width, seat angle, armrest height and spacing, and backrest dimensions and slope.

It should be noted that the dimensions shown are taken from the compressed seat padding or cushion surface. In the design of seating, the relative resiliency and compressive qualities of the cushion are therefore extremely important. Recommended seat compression allowance varies, according to the source consulted, from ½ to 2 in, or 1.3 to 5.1 cm, and is obviously a function of both the material used and the manner in which the padding is detailed. Section 4 of Part A deals in greater detail with the question of cushioning and with the general theory of seating design. This section should be consulted prior to the application of any of the recommended dimensional information shown in the following diagrams.

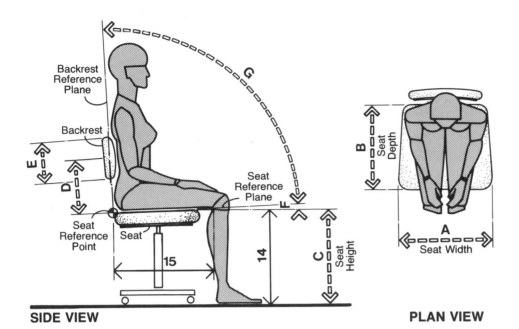

**SIDE VIEW**

**WORK OR SECRETARIAL CHAIR**

**PLAN VIEW**

# 1 SEATING

The top diagram shows the more critical measurements to be considered in the design of the typical work or secretarial chair. To function properly, its design must be responsive to human dimension. Anthropometrically, the two most important measurements are buttock-popliteal length and popliteal height. Provision for support of the lumbar region by proper location of a backrest is essential for a successful design.

The element of sitter comfort, however, is an elusive quality that defies translation into simple dimensions. This factor alone, in addition to the considerable variation in human body size, demands the exercise of a great deal of personal judgment in establishing proper chair dimensions. Currently used recommendations may vary, but they all work and are generally responsive to anthropometric requirements. For the most part, they are also within reasonable range of each other. The authors felt it would be interesting, therefore, in addition to stating their own dimensional suggestions, to present in the form of a chart recommendations from a variety of respected sources. It should be recognized, however, that the primary intent of the data presented is to provide the designer with a basis for initial preliminary design assumptions and mockups—not a final design solution.

It is also suggested that the reader refer to Part A, Section 4, and the following pages of this section for additional information related to the theoretical aspects of chair design. A good deal of that is applicable to all chair types.

## CRITICAL WORK CHAIR MEASUREMENTS

| SOURCE | A SEAT WIDTH | | B SEAT DEPTH | | C SEAT HEIGHT | | D C.L. OF BACKREST HEIGHT FROM SEAT SURFACE | | E BACKREST HEIGHT | | F ANGLE OF TILT OF SEAT SURFACE | G ANGLE OF BACKREST |
|---|---|---|---|---|---|---|---|---|---|---|---|---|
| | in | cm | in | cm | in | cm | in | cm | in | cm | degrees | degrees |
| 1 CRONEY | 17 | 43.2 | 13.5-15 | 33.6-38.1 | 14-19 | 35.6-48.2 | 5-7.5 | 12.7-19.0 | 4-8 | 10.2-20.3 | 0°-5° or 3°-5° | 95°-115° |
| 2 DIFFRIENT | 16 min. | 40.6 | 15-16 | 38.1-40.6 | 13.6-20.6 | 34.5-52.3 | 9-10 | 22.9-25.4 | 6-9 | 15.2-22.9 | 0°-5° | 95° |
| 3 DREYFUSS | 15 | 38.1 | 12-15 | 30.5-38.1 | 15-18 | 38.1-45.7 | 7-11 | 17.8-27.9 | 5.1-8 | 12.9-20.3 | 0°-5° | 95°-105° |
| 4 GRANDJEAN | 15.75 | 40.0 | 15.75 | 40.0 | 14.9-20.8 | 37.8-52.8 | | | 7.9-11.8 | 20-30 | 3°-5° | Adjustable |
| 5 PANERO-ZELNIK | 17-19 | 43.2-48.3 | 15.5-16 | 39.4-40.6 | 14-20 | 35.6-50.8 | 8-10 | 19.2-25.4 | 6-9 | 15.2-22.9 | 0°-5° | 95°-105° |
| 6 WOODSON-CONOVER | 15 | 38.1 | 12-15 | 30.5-38.1 | 15-18 | 38.1-45.7 | 7-10 | 17.8-25.4 | 6-8 | 15.24-20.32 | 3°-5° | 20° |

(1) John Croney, *Anthropometrics for Designers*, p. 147; (2) Niels Diffrient et al., *Humanscale*, Guide 2B; (3) Henry Dreyfuss, *The Measure of Man*, Sheet O, Dwg. 2; (4) Etienne Grandjean, *Ergonomics of the Home*, pp. 126, 127; (5) Authors; (6) W.E. Woodson and Donald Conover, *Human Engineering Guide for Equipment Designers*, p. 2-142 (see Selected Bibliography for additional information).

# 1 SEATING

The top diagram shows dimensions for a general purpose chair intended for brief periods of use. A 17-in, or 43.2-cm, seat height will accommodate most adults, except very small females, who may require a 16-in, or 40.6-cm, and in extreme cases, even a 14-in, or 35.6-cm, seat height. A smaller user, however, can function with a greater seat height by using a footrest.

The bottom diagram shows the dimensions for an executive chair, a type intended for a longer duration of use. The buttock-popliteal length governs the seat depth. This length, for 95 percent of both men and women, is 17-in, or 43.2-cm, or more. A seat depth not exceeding that should, therefore, accommodate a large majority of users. The very large person, however, would find that such a depth might leave a substantial portion of his thigh unsupported, while a very small person would find that the edge of the seat might dig into the tissue behind his or her knee.

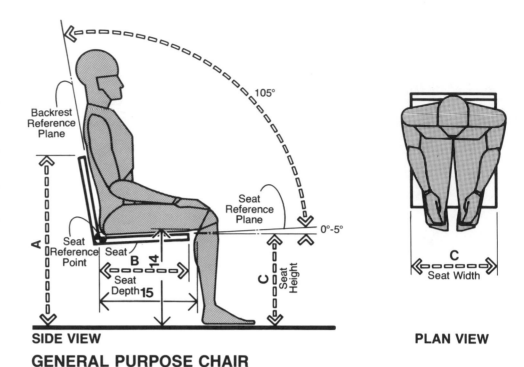

**SIDE VIEW**

**GENERAL PURPOSE CHAIR**

**PLAN VIEW**

|   | in | cm |
|---|---|---|
| **A** | 31–33 | 78.7–83.8 |
| **B** | 15.5–16 | 39.4–40.6 |
| **C** | 16–17 | 40.6–43.2 |
| **D** | 17–24 | 43.2–61.0 |
| **E** | 0–6 | 0.0–15.2 |
| **F** | 15.5–18 | 39.4–45.7 |
| **G** | 8–10 | 20.3–25.4 |
| **H** | 12 | 30.5 |
| **I** | 18–20 | 45.7–50.8 |
| **J** | 24–28 | 61.0–71.1 |
| **K** | 23–29 | 58.4–73.7 |

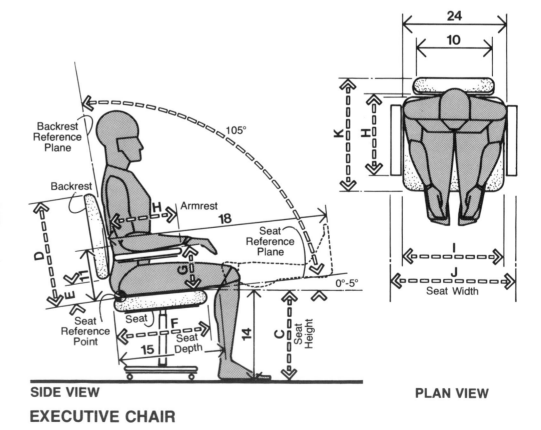

**SIDE VIEW**

**EXECUTIVE CHAIR**

**PLAN VIEW**

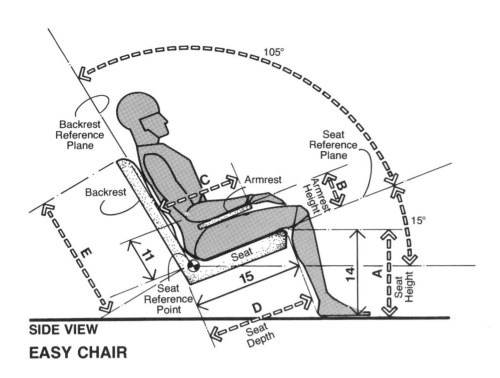

**SIDE VIEW**

**EASY CHAIR**

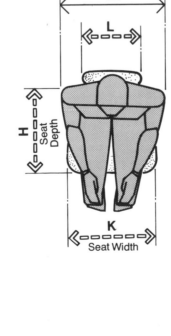

**SIDE VIEW**

**DRAFTING CHAIR / STOOL**

**PLAN VIEW**

The easy chair, shown in the drawing at the top, is a difficult chair type to design, or establish guidelines for, since it is primarily intended for relaxation and comfort—qualities which are highly personal. Nevertheless, the drawing offers some basic dimensions for use in making preliminary design assumptions. The following suggestions should also prove helpful: (1) The angle formed by thighs and trunk should not be less than 105°. Angles significantly less than this will cause discomfort. (2) Design should allow the user to change body posture. (3) The front edge of the seat should be rounded to prevent irritation. (4) The backrest should provide lumbar support by following the spinal contour in the lumbar region. (5) The seat surface should tilt backwards. Too severe an angle, however, may cause a person difficulty in getting up from the chair, particularly for elderly people. A seat angle of about 15° should be adequate. (6) If the angle formed by the backrest with the vertical exceeds 30°, provisions for a headrest will be required in the form of a separate design element or extension of the backrest itself. (7) Armrests should be padded and designed horizontally or at the same angle as the seat surface. The drawing at the bottom provides basic dimensional information for the design of a drafting stool, which is similar in many respects to the secretarial chair.

| | in | cm |
|---|---|---|
| **A** | 16–17 | 40.6–43.2 |
| **B** | 8.5–9 | 21.6–22.9 |
| **C** | 10–12 | 25.4–30.5 |
| **D** | 16.5–17.5 | 41.9–44.5 |
| **E** | 18–24 | 45.7–61.0 |
| **F** | 6–9 | 15.2–22.9 |
| **G** | 10 adjust. | 25.4 adjust. |
| **H** | 15.5–16 | 39.4–40.6 |
| **I** | 12 max. | 30.5 max. |
| **J** | 30 adjust. | 76.2 adjust. |
| **K** | 15 | 38.1 |
| **L** | 12–14 | 30.5–35.6 |

# 1 SEATING

The drawings at the bottom show the basic dimensions for the design of banquette seating. The lack of armrests makes it difficult to define seat boundaries. The user, therefore, tends to establish his own territory by assuming a desired sitting posture and placing personal articles next to him, such as a briefcase, purse, or package. Since the nature of this type of seating can permit some form of body contact, hidden dimensions and personal space also play an important part in how close the users sharing the banquette will sit.

Because of the many hidden psychological factors involved, the actual efficiency of this seating type in terms of capacity is questionable. The diagrams indicate two possible seating situations, each dictated by the anthropometrics involved. One arrangement is based on the premise that the user's elbows will be extended, possibly in conjunction with some activity, such as reading, or simply as an attempt to stake out additional territory, as would be the case in the strategic positioning of some personal article on the seat. In this situation it would be reasonable to assume that each user would take up about 30 in, or 76.2 cm, of space. The other diagram shows a more compact seating arrangement. The diagram at the top shows a section through a typical banquette.

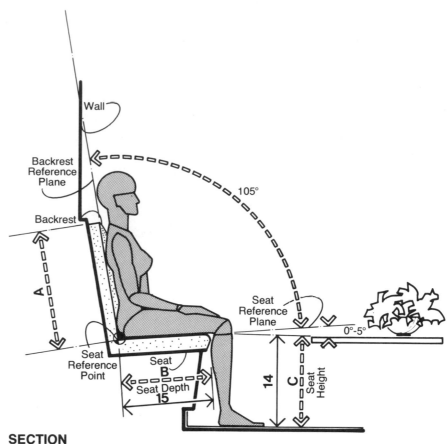

**SECTION**
## BANQUETTE SEATING

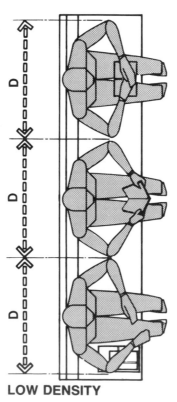

**LOW DENSITY**

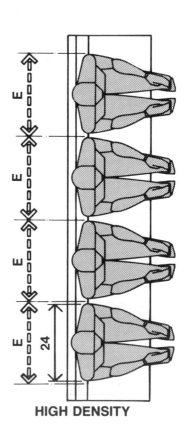

**HIGH DENSITY**

## BANQUETTE SEATING

|   | in | cm |
|---|------|---------|
| A | 18–24 | 45.7–61.0 |
| B | 15.5–16 | 39.4–40.6 |
| C | 16–17 | 40.6–43.2 |
| D | 30 | 76.2 |
| E | 24 | 61.0 |

# 2 RESIDENTIAL SPACES

## ANTHROPOMETRIC DATA

| TABLE | 2.1 LIVING SPACES | 2.2 DINING SPACES | 2.3 SLEEPING SPACES | 2.4 COOKING SPACES | 2.5 BATHROOMS | # | SPACE |
|---|---|---|---|---|---|---|---|
| 1A,2B | | | ◕ | ◕ | | 1 | STATURE |
| 1B,3C | ◐ | | ● | ◐ | ◐ | 2 | EYE HEIGHT |
| 1C,3B | | | ◐ | ◐ | | 3 | ELBOW HEIGHT |
| 1D,2C | | | ● | ● | | 4 | SITTING HEIGHT ERECT |
| | | | | | | 5 | SITTING HEIGHT NORMAL |
| 1F,3G | ◐ | ◐ | ◐ | ● | | 6 | EYE HEIGHT SITTING |
| | | | | | | 7 | MIDSHOULDER HEIGHT SITTING |
| | | | | | | 8 | SHOULDER BREADTH |
| | | | | | | 9 | ELBOW-TO-ELBOW BREADTH |
| 1J,2F | ● | | | | ● | 10 | HIP BREADTH |
| | | | | | | 11 | ELBOW REST HEIGHT |
| 1L,2H | | ● | ● | ● | | 12 | THIGH CLEARANCE |
| 1M,2I | | ● | ● | | | 13 | KNEE HEIGHT |
| 1N,2J | | ◐ | ◐ | | | 14 | POPLITEAL HEIGHT |
| 1O,2K | ◐ | | | | | 15 | BUTTOCK-POPLITEAL LENGTH |
| 1P,2L | | ● | ● | ● | | 16 | BUTTOCK-KNEE LENGTH |
| 1Q,3F | ◐ | | | | | 17 | BUTTOCK-TOE LENGTH |
| 1R,4B | ◐ | | | | ◐ | 18 | BUTTOCK-HEEL LENGTH |
| 1S,4C | | | | | ○ | 19 | VERTICAL REACH HEIGHT SITTING |
| 1T,4F | | | | ○ | ○ | 20 | VERTICAL GRIP REACH |
| 1U,4E | | | | | ○ | 21 | SIDE ARM REACH |
| 1V,4D | | ○ | | ○ | ○ | 22 | THUMB TIP REACH |
| 1W,6B | ● | ● | ● | ● | | 23 | MAXIMUM BODY DEPTH |
| 1X,6A | ● | ● | ● | ● | ◐ | 24 | MAXIMUM BODY BREADTH |

The variety of human activity that occurs within residential spaces, whether they be studio apartments, two- and three-bedroom cooperatives, or suburban houses, is formidable. It is within this single environment that people sleep, dine, relax, meditate, entertain and are entertained, make love, do housework, read, cook, bathe, are conceived, and in some cases are born or die. It is also within these spaces that people spend at least half of their waking hours and are subjected to most of the physical injuries they are likely to sustain during the course of their lifetime. The impressive number and diversity of functions that must take place within this single environment, the extended period of time that people spend within it, and their vulnerability to fatigue and accidents give the quality of their interface with that environment added significance. Another factor that makes the quality of interface even more critical is the decrease in the size of residential spaces available on today's market due to the increasing costs of both construction and land. As a consequence of these external economic factors, it becomes necessary in many cases to maximize the utilization of existing space to the greatest degree possible. In some instances this involves innovative ways of perceiving both the problem and the design solution. For example, it may be necessary to explore the use of overhead space, to have a single portion of the space perform several functions, or to creatively recycle space, formerly used for a different purpose, to accommodate a residential function. The text and illustrations to follow deal with human dimension and residential space in terms of the major functions that must be accommodated.

# 2.1 LIVING SPACES

| TABLE | LOUNGING | CIRCULATION | BAR/STORAGE | ACTIVITIES — ANTHROPOMETRIC DATA |
|---|---|---|---|---|
| 1B,3C | | | ◑ | 2 EYE HEIGHT |
| 1F,3G | ◑ | | | 6 EYE HEIGHT SITTING |
| 1J,2F | ● | | | 10 HIP BREADTH |
| 1O,2K | ◑ | | | 15 BUTTOCK-POPLITEAL LENGTH |
| 1Q,3F | ◑ | | | 17 BUTTOCK-TOE LENGTH |
| 1R,4B | ◑ | | | 18 BUTTOCK-HEEL LENGTH |
| 1W,6B | | | ● | 23 MAXIMUM BODY DEPTH |
| 1X,6A | ● | ● | | 24 MAXIMUM BODY BREADTH |

The various activities and elements of furniture usually associated with living spaces result in many levels of interface between the human body and the physical components of the space. The most obvious is between the user and the chair or sofa. In this regard seat height must take into consideration popliteal height, while seat depth must be responsive to buttock-popliteal length. Circulation around seating elements must accommodate maximum body breadth, while the location of a coffee table in relation to a chair should be responsive to human reach dimensions. The height at which a painting is hung on a wall should be determined in relationship to eye height. The possibilities are almost endless and the drawings on the following pages explore only a few of the many design situations that require knowledge of human dimensions. The matrix above indicates some of the anthropometric measurements to take into consideration to ensure the proper levels of interface.

# 2.1 LIVING SPACES

The drawings here examine the relationship of female and male body dimensions to sofa seating, in order to determine how much space the seated body requires. The anthropometric measurements of major interest here are maximum body breadth and buttock-popliteal length.

The top drawing deals with male dimensions; based on 95th percentile data, the maximum body breadth dimension is 22.8 in, or 57.9 cm, with a nude subject. Allowing for clothing and some body movement as well as change in posture and position, a minimum dimension of 28 in, or 71.1 cm, is suggested as a width allowance for a seated person. The overall dimension, therefore, includes the individual width allowances and the width of a sofa arm construction, which obviously can vary depending on personal design preference. A range of 3 to 6 in, or 7.6 to 15.2 cm, is suggested. Using the buttock-popliteal length of the smaller person and adding a similar allowance of 6 to 9 in, or 15.2 to 22.9 cm, for backrest construction as well as a minimum zone in front of the sofa for foot movement, an overall depth dimension of 42 to 48 in, or 106.7 to 121.9 cm, is suggested. The rationale for the drawing at the bottom dealing with female data is the same. The information should prove not only useful in providing a keener insight into the general relationship between body size and furniture but of specific value in establishing preliminary design assumptions for institutional seating in spaces designed exclusively for the use of males or of females. In spaces where seating is to be used by both sexes, the larger dimensions should apply.

| | in | cm |
|---|---|---|
| A | 42–48 | 106.7–121.9 |
| B | 6–9 | 15.2–22.9 |
| C | 3–6 | 7.6–15.2 |
| D | 28 | 71.1 |
| E | 62–68 | 157.5–172.7 |
| F | 90–96 | 228.6–243.8 |
| G | 40–46 | 101.6–116.8 |
| H | 26 | 66.0 |
| I | 58–64 | 147.3–162.6 |
| J | 84–90 | 213.4–228.6 |

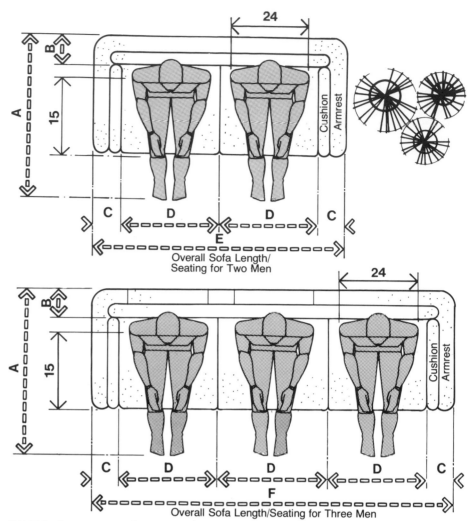

**SOFA SEATING / MALES**

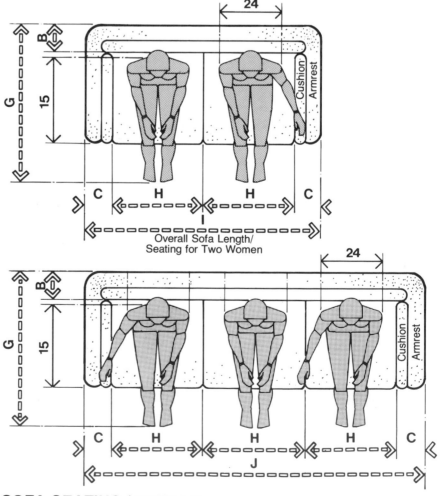

**SOFA SEATING / FEMALE**

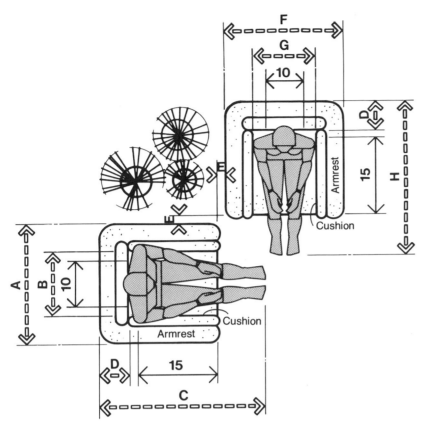

**CORNER LOUNGE CHAIR SEATING/
MALE AND FEMALE**

The top drawing examines the relationship of the female and male body dimensions to arm chair seating in order to determine the amount of space the seated body requires. The rationale is similar to that in dealing with sofa seating, outlined on the preceding page.

The bottom drawing is not intended to suggest a specific layout for a conversational grouping, and therefore should not be taken literally. Nor is it suggested that special female and male seating be provided in the same living space. The drawing is essentially informative and its purpose is to suggest allowances for comfortable circulation relative to corner lounge seating situations. The key consideration anthropometrically is maximum body breadth data. Since clearance is involved, the data related to the larger person rather than the smaller should be used.

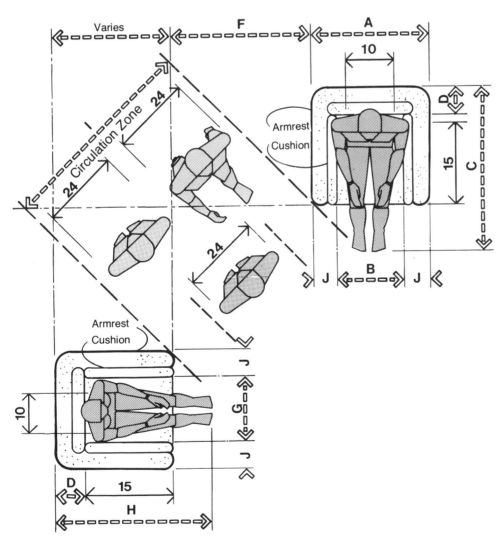

**CORNER LOUNGE SEATING WITH CIRCULATION**

|   | in | cm |
|---|----|----|
| **A** | 34–40 | 86.4–101.6 |
| **B** | 28 | 71.1 |
| **C** | 42–48 | 106.7–121.9 |
| **D** | 6–9 | 15.2–22.9 |
| **E** | 3 | 7.6 |
| **F** | 32–38 | 81.3–96.5 |
| **G** | 26 | 66.0 |
| **H** | 40–46 | 101.6–116.8 |
| **I** | 48–60 | 121.9–152.4 |
| **J** | 3–6 | 7.6–15.2 |

# 2.1 LIVING SPACES

The drawings at the top and center deal with the major clearances involved in lounge or conversational seating. The top drawing is based on a conversational grouping in which the clearance between the front of the seat and the edge of the table is limited between 16 and 18 in, or 40.6 and 45.7 cm. This clearance may require some degree of body contact or side-stepping for circulation and access. Anthropometrically, however, it does accommodate human reach, permitting the seated person access to the coffee table without rising. The drawing also suggests a dimensional range for verbal conversation. The center drawing illustrates a similar furniture arrangement that would permit circulation with full head-on access. The clearance indicated, however, to permit such access would make it impossible for most people to reach the coffee table from a seated position. This could be extremely undesirable in terms of food, beverages, and cigarettes. Given the choice between full head-on access and the accommodation of reach, the authors opt for reach and recommend the smaller clearance.

The bottom drawing suggests an overall allowance for easy chair or reclining chair seating, including footrest. The buttock-leg length of the larger person is the most significant anthropometric measurement in establishing this clearance. It should also be noted that the height of the footrest is also a function of seat height. The footrest should be a few inches below the height of the seat.

| | in | cm |
|---|---|---|
| A | 84–112 | 213.4–284.5 |
| B | 13–16 | 33.0–40.6 |
| C | 58–80 | 147.3–203.2 |
| D | 16–18 | 40.6–45.7 |
| E | 14–17 | 35.6–43.2 |
| F | 12–18 | 30.5–45.7 |
| G | 30–36 | 76.2–91.4 |
| H | 12–16 | 30.5–40.6 |
| I | 60–68 | 152.4–172.7 |
| J | 54–62 | 137.2–157.5 |

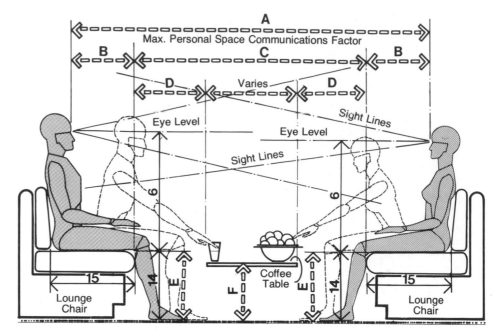

**LOUNGE SEATING / CLEARANCES**

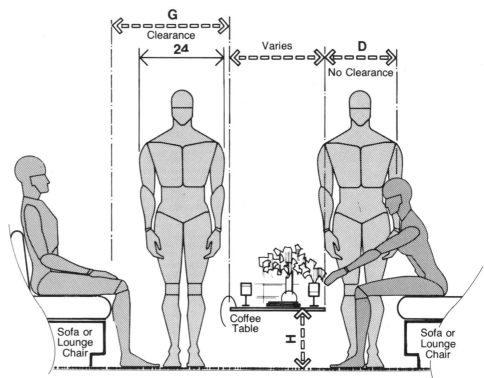

**LOUNGE SEATING / CLEARANCE RELATIONSHIPS**

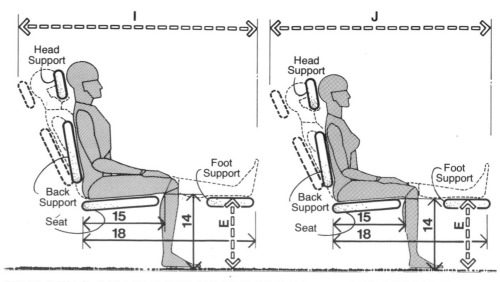

**RECLINING CHAIR WITH FOOTREST / MALE AND FEMALE**

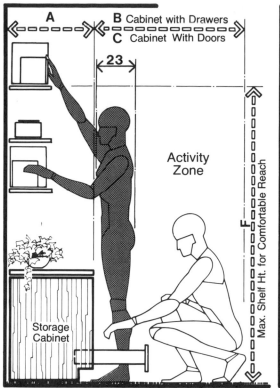

**WALL UNIT / ACCESS BY MALE**

**WALL UNIT/ ACCESS BY FEMALE**

The drawings on this page illustrate the relationship of human dimension and accessibility to low and high storage or furniture usually associated with living spaces. The configuration of the furniture is not intended as a realistic illustration of any specific element of furniture, but rather as a general representation of furniture types normally found in a living space. In situations where the user is not a known entity, either in terms of sex or body size, the body size data of the smaller person should govern. In the event the user is known, dimensions more appropriate to that body size should be used where practical. It should be noted that for each sex two dimensions are shown on the drawing. In each case the lower figure is based on 5th percentile body size data and the larger on 95th percentile data.

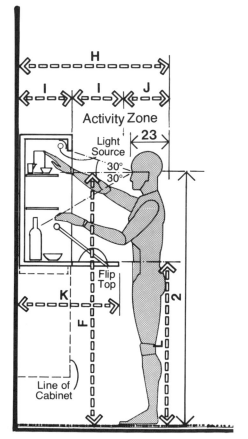

**WALL-MOUNTED BAR UNIT/ ACCESS BY MALE**

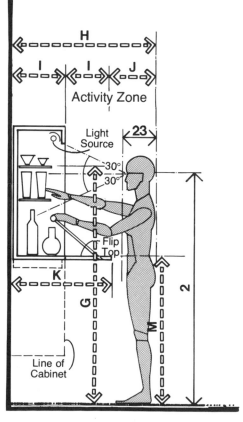

**WALL-MOUNTED BAR UNIT/ ACCESS BY FEMALE**

|   | in | cm |
|---|---|---|
| **A** | 18–24 | 45.7–61.0 |
| **B** | 48–58 | 121.9–147.3 |
| **C** | 36–40 | 91.4–101.6 |
| **D** | 46–52 | 116.8–132.08 |
| **E** | 30–36 | 76.2–91.4 |
| **F** | 72 | 182.9 |
| **G** | 69 | 175.3 |
| **H** | 42–50 | 106.7–127.0 |
| **I** | 12–16 | 30.5–40.6 |
| **J** | 18 | 45.7 |
| **K** | 24–32 | 61.0–81.3 |
| **L** | 39–42 | 99.1–106.7 |
| **M** | 36–39 | 91.4–99.1 |

# 2.1 LIVING SPACES

The top drawing illustrates the relationship between human dimension and the display of art work. Eye height is the significant anthropometric body measurement here. It should be noted, however, that the visual angle in which small detail can be sharply defined without rotating the eyes is only about 1°. Therefore, the drawing should be used as a basis for preliminary design assumptions about art work generally, and even in viewing the art work shown here, a certain amount of scanning or eye rotation is required. In addition, the horizontality of the line of sight is theoretical. Most of the time the body and head are in a relaxed position and the line of sight is slightly below the horizontal. A more detailed discussion of the visual and anthropometric considerations regarding the viewing of displays can be found in Section 9 in Part C. The bottom drawing provides some useful information concerning human dimension and the clearances required for coat removal.

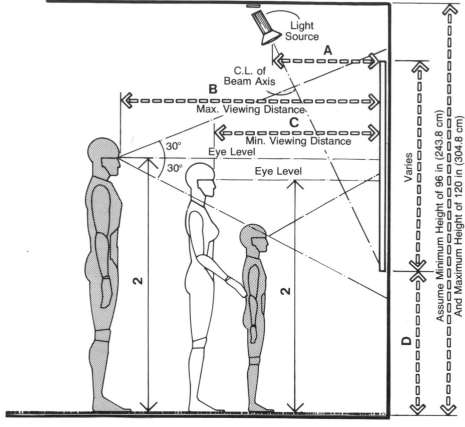

**DISPLAY OF ARTWORK**

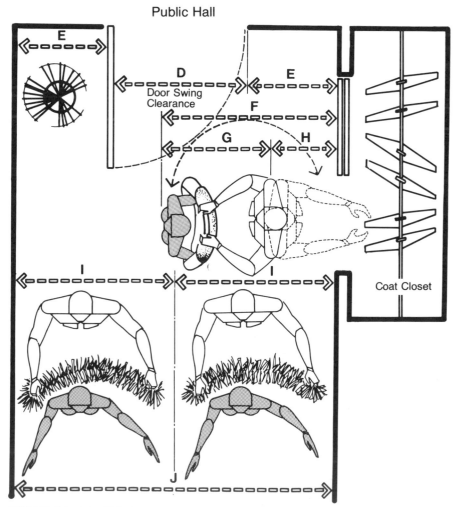

**ENTRANCE FOYER/
REQUIRED CLEARANCES FOR COAT REMOVAL**

| | in | cm |
|---|---|---|
| **A** | 16–24 | 40.6–61.0 |
| **B** | 60–78 | 152.4–198.1 |
| **C** | 30–42 | 76.2–106.7 |
| **D** | 36 | 91.4 |
| **E** | 20–24 | 50.8–61.0 |
| **F** | 51 | 129.5 |
| **G** | 33 | 83.8 |
| **H** | 18 | 45.7 |
| **I** | 40–44 | 101.6–111.8 |
| **J** | 80–88 | 203.2–223.5 |

## 2.2 DINING SPACES

| TABLE | DINING | CIRCULATION | SERVICE | ACTIVITIES | ANTHROPOMETRIC DATA | |
|-------|--------|-------------|---------|------------|---------------------|-|
| 1F,3G | ◑ | | | 6 | EYE HEIGHT SITTING | |
| 1L,2H | ● | | | 12 | THIGH CLEARANCE | |
| 1M,2I | ● | | | 13 | KNEE HEIGHT | |
| 1N,2J | ◑ | | | 14 | POPLITEAL HEIGHT | |
| 1P,2L | ● | | | 16 | BUTTOCK-KNEE LENGTH | |
| 1V,4D | ○ | | | 22 | THUMB TIP REACH | |
| 1W,6B | ● | | ● | 23 | MAXIMUM BODY DEPTH | |
| 1X,6A | ● | ● | ● | 24 | MAXIMUM BODY BREADTH | |

In examining the relationship between human dimension and dining spaces, the areas of most concern to the designer are the clearances around the table and the number of people a table of a particular size can accommodate. The clearance between the edge of the table and the wall or any other physical obstruction must at the very least accommodate two elements: (1) the space occupied by the chair and (2) the maximum body breadth of a person of larger body size as he circulates between the chair and the wall. In dealing with the space occupied by the chair, it should be noted that its position, relative to the edge of the table, will change several times during the course of a meal. Towards the end of a meal, perhaps while the person is engaged in informal conversation or in an effort to change body posture, the chair may be extended farther from the table. As a person leaves the table, the chair may be located even farther away. Comfortable clearance should assume the chair to be at its farthest distance from the table.

Too often in calculating the number of people to be accommodated around the table, the designer relies exclusively on plastic furniture templates or on the application of a 24-in, or 61-cm, center to center chair spacing, instead of considering the maximum body breadth of the person of larger body size, the fact that the elbows may be extended, and, finally, the size of the place setting itself. To ensure a proper interface between the human body and the table during the dining process, not only must the anthropometric considerations discussed above be taken into account, but the human body, the chair, the table, and the place setting must be viewed as a system. It should also be noted that the size of the place setting will determine how much table area will be available for centrally located shared elements, such as beverages or serving dishes. The drawings on the following pages examine all these conditions and should be helpful not only in making preliminary design assumptions, but more importantly in establishing an approach for individual design analysis.

## 2.2 DINING SPACES

To determine table size it is helpful to view the table as consisting of two zones. The place setting zone represents the personal activity space directly in front of the individual diner. Ideally, it should be of adequate size to accommodate the necessary dinnerware, silverware, glassware, etc., both in its original structured form and in its eventual state of disarray during the course of its use. The width of this zone should also accommodate the human dimension and body positions assumed during the eating process. Etiquette aside, it should be generous enough to allow for the inevitable projection of the elbows. Anthropometrically, the maximum body breadth measurement of the larger person should be considered. Accordingly, the optimal width suggested for this zone, allowing for elbow projection, is about 30 in, or 76.2 cm, and the minimal width about 24 in, or 61 cm. To allow for the elements of the setting itself, the optimal and minimal depths suggested for this zone are 18 and 16 in, or 45.7 and 40.6 cm, respectively. The optimal place setting zone can be viewed as a rectangle, 30 by 18 in, or 76.2 by 45.7 cm, and the minimal zone, 24 by 16 in, or 61 by 40.6 cm. The shared access zone represents the table space opposite the place setting zones necessary to accommodate serving dishes and platter, related silverware, glasses, decorative centerpieces, candelabras, etc. The size of this zone varies greatly and is a

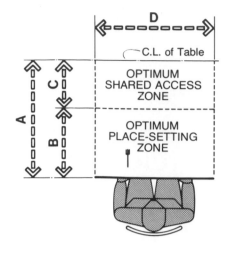

**OPTIMUM PLACE SETTING**

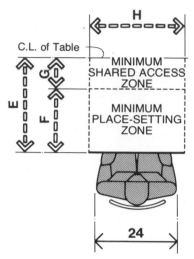

**MINIMUM PLACE SETTING**

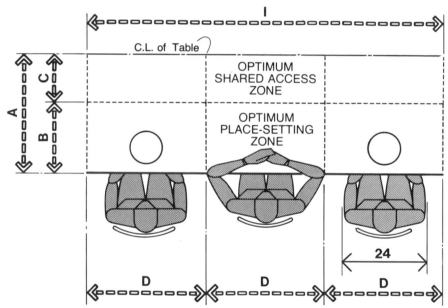

**OPTIMUM PLACE SETTING FOR THREE**

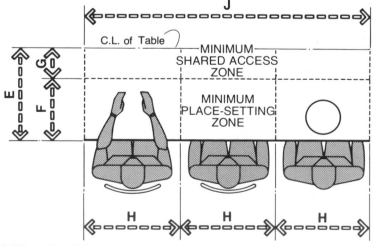

**MINIMUM PLACE SETTING FOR THREE**

|   | in | cm |
|---|----|-----|
| A | 27 | 68.6 |
| B | 18 | 45.7 |
| C | 9 | 22.9 |
| D | 30 | 76.2 |
| E | 21 | 53.3 |
| F | 16 | 40.6 |
| G | 5 | 12.7 |
| H | 24 | 61.0 |
| I | 90 | 228.6 |
| J | 72 | 182.9 |

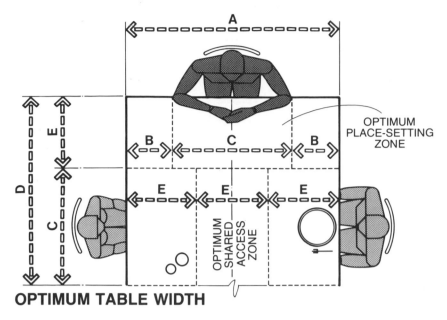

**OPTIMUM TABLE WIDTH**

OPTIMUM PLACE-SETTING ZONE

OPTIMUM SHARED ACCESS ZONE

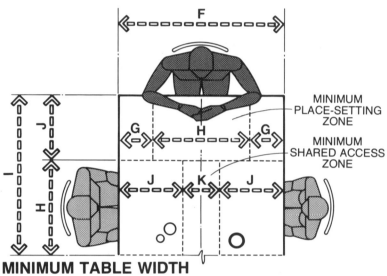

**MINIMUM TABLE WIDTH**

MINIMUM PLACE-SETTING ZONE

MINIMUM SHARED ACCESS ZONE

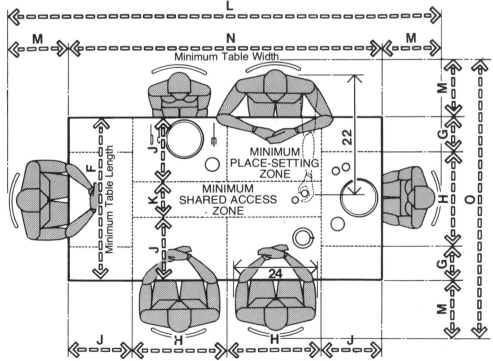

Minimum Table Width

Minimum Table Length

MINIMUM PLACE-SETTING ZONE

MINIMUM SHARED ACCESS ZONE

**RECTANGULAR TABLE / MINIMUM LENGTH AND WIDTH / DINING FOR SIX**

function of lifestyle, type of meal, level of formality and sophistication, serving help available, nature of serving operation, occasion, and number of people. The optimal depth suggested if relatively formal and frequent dinner parties are involved is 18 in, or 45.7 cm. The minimal depth is about 10 in, or 25.4 cm. If half of the depth of this zone is allocated to the individual place setting zone, it is possible to arrive at an optimal and minimal incremental unit of area per diner that can be applied in determining table size to serve any given number of diners. The optimal unit so calculated becomes 30 by 27 in, or 76.2 by 68.6 cm, and the minimal unit 24 by 21 in, or 61 by 53.3 cm, respectively. The drawings on these two pages examine table sizes in terms of their optimal and minimal incremental units. The drawing at the top of the facing page illustrates the basic optimal and minimal units.

The bottom drawing illustrates each of the units arranged three in a row. The drawings at the top of this page illustrate the units arranged around the end of the table, while the bottom drawing illustrates a table for six based on a minimal increment. It should be noted that room size also dictates the size of the table. It is also possible to function with tables of less or certainly greater width. Dining tables of 36 in, or 91.4 cm, for example, are quite common. Much depends, however, on the level of comfort and convenience desired, which, within limits, becomes a matter of personal decision.

| | in | cm |
|---|---|---|
| A | 54 | 137.2 |
| B | 12 | 30.5 |
| C | 30 | 76.2 |
| D | 48 | 121.9 |
| E | 18 | 45.7 |
| F | 42 | 106.7 |
| G | 9 | 22.9 |
| H | 24 | 61.0 |
| I | 40 | 101.6 |
| J | 16 | 40.6 |
| K | 10 | 25.4 |
| L | 116–128 | 294.6–325.1 |
| M | 18–24 | 45.7–61.0 |
| N | 80 | 203.2 |
| O | 78–90 | 198.1–228.6 |

## 2.2 DINING SPACES

The top drawing applies the optimal incremental unit discussed on the preceding page to a rectangular table for formal dining for six. The table size shown is 54 by 96 in, or 137.2 by 243.8 cm. This size will provide each person with an individual place-setting zone of 18 by 30 in, or 45.7 by 76.2 cm, and will allow a shared access zone at the center of the table with a depth of 18 in. The 30-in width provided for each person allows for elbow room.

The bottom drawing, in contrast, shows a minimal, square general purpose table for informal dining. Although the width and depth of the place-setting zones are the same as in the larger rectangular tables, their angular configuration reduces the area significantly as well as the area of the shared access zone. To allow clearance for the chair and head-on circulation behind the chair, a minimum distance of 48 in, or 121.9 cm, must be maintained between the edge of the table and the wall or nearest physical obstruction. A clearance of 36 to 42 in, or 91.4 to 106.7 cm, can be provided to allow restricted circulation. This will require a person to sidestep or the seated person to adjust the chair to allow passage.

| | in | cm |
|---|---|---|
| **A** | 96–102 | 243.8–259.1 |
| **B** | 18–24 | 45.7–61.0 |
| **C** | 12 | 30.5 |
| **D** | 30 | 76.2 |
| **E** | 132–144 | 335.3–365.8 |
| **F** | 96 | 243.8 |
| **G** | 18 | 45.7 |
| **H** | 54 | 137.2 |
| **I** | 36–42 | 91.4–106.7 |
| **J** | 48 min. | 121.9 min. |
| **K** | 18 min. | 45.7 min. |

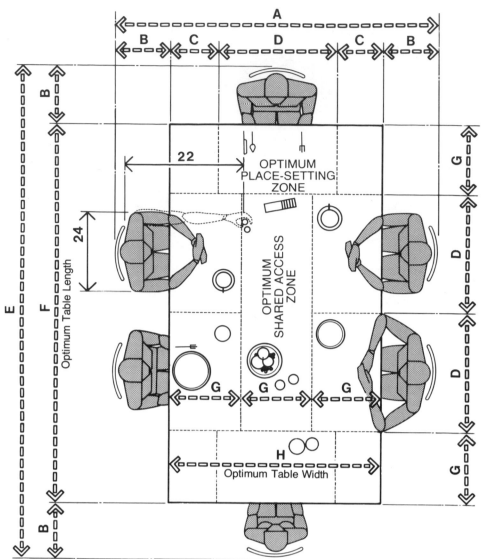

**RECTANGULAR TABLE/OPTIMUM LENGTH AND WIDTH/DINING FOR SIX**

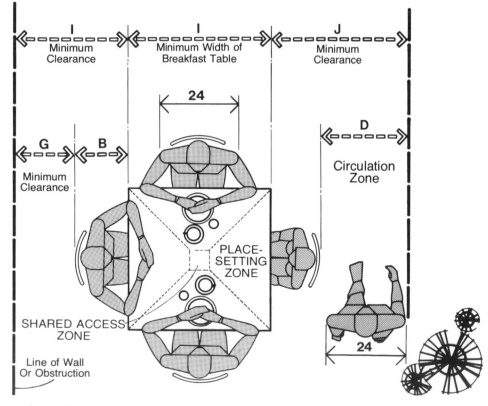

**BREAKFAST / KITCHEN TABLE FOR FOUR**

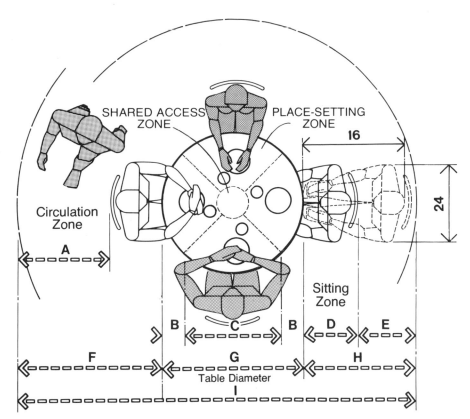

**36-IN (91.4-CM) DIAMETER BREAKFAST/KITCHEN TABLE FOR FOUR**

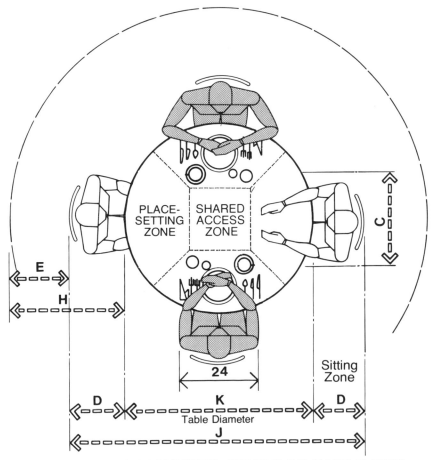

**48-IN (121.9-CM) DIAMETER CIRCULAR TABLE FOR FOUR/MINIMUM SCHEME**

## 2.2 DINING SPACES

The top drawing illustrates a 36-in, or 91.4-cm, diameter round table seating four people and shows the necessary clearances around the perimeter. Four people cannot function comfortably around such a small table for anything but the lightest snacks. The individual place-setting zones are extremely restricted and the shared access zone at the center is too small to accommodate much in the way of serving dishes, platters, or decorative elements. A 48-in, or 121.9-cm, clearance between the perimeter of the table and the wall or nearest physical obstruction is the minimal clearance necessary to allow circulation behind a seated person. A distance of 30 to 36 in, or 76.2 to 91.4 cm, between the table perimeter and the wall is the minimum clearance necessary to permit access to and adjustment of the chair. The 48-in, or 121.9-cm, diameter table shown at the bottom of the page, however, can function adequately for four people. The place-setting zone is reasonably sufficient to accommodate the various place-setting elements and provides generous elbow room as well. Although the central shared access zone is restricted, it provides far more space than the 36-in, or 91.4-cm, diameter table shown above. If used for light snacks or coffee, the table can seat five. The clearances for circulation are the same as for the 36-in table.

| | in | cm |
|---|---|---|
| A | 30 min. | 76.2 min. |
| B | 6 | 15.2 |
| C | 24 | 61.0 |
| D | 18–24 | 45.7–61.0 |
| E | 12 | 30.5 |
| F | 48–54 | 121.9–137.2 |
| G | 36 | 91.4 |
| H | 30–36 | 76.2–91.4 |
| I | 114–126 | 289.6–320.0 |
| J | 84–96 | 213.4–243.8 |
| K | 48 | 121.9 |

## 2.2 DINING SPACES

The optimal place-setting zone at the beginning of this section was established at 18 by 30 in, or 45.7 by 76.2 cm. The 60-in, or 152.4-cm, diameter table shown at the top of the page can easily, if not luxuriously, accommodate four such optimal zones. If perimeter were the only consideration, the table could easily accommodate six and possibly seven people. In the process, however, the area of the individual place-setting zone would fall below optimum size and into the minimal category. The advantage of the round table is its relative flexibility to accommodate additional people. The disadvantage is the floor area consumed. By comparison, a 60- by 66-in, or 152.4- by 167.6-cm, rectangular table, which could effectively occupy about the same floor area, can seat six people and provide each with an optimal place-setting zone of 18 by 30 in. The choice of a 60-in diameter table to seat four people would not be a wise decision. The 72-in, or 182.9-cm, diameter table to seat six people, with optimal place-setting zones, would, on balance, constitute a more sensible choice than a 60-in diameter table to serve four.

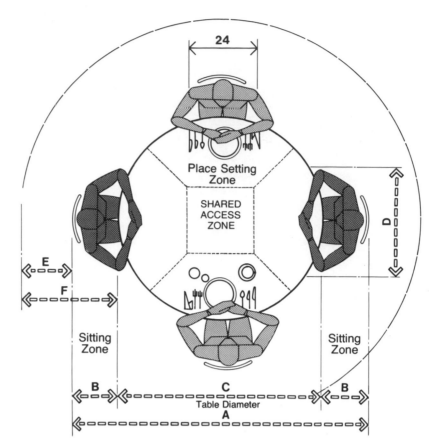

**60-IN (152.4-CM) DIAMETER CIRCULAR TABLE FOR FOUR/OPTIMUM SEATING**

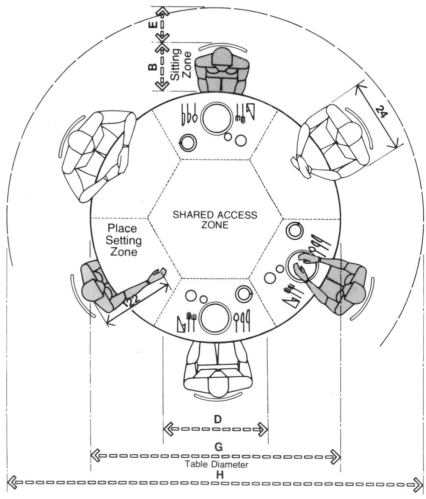

**72-IN (182.9-CM) DIAMETER CIRCULAR TABLE FOR SIX/OPTIMUM SCHEME**

|   | in | cm |
|---|---|---|
| A | 96–108 | 243.8–274.3 |
| B | 18–24 | 45.7–61.0 |
| C | 60 | 152.4 |
| D | 30 | 76.2 |
| E | 12 | 30.5 |
| F | 30–36 | 76.2–91.4 |
| G | 72 | 182.9 |
| H | 132–144 | 335.3–365.8 |

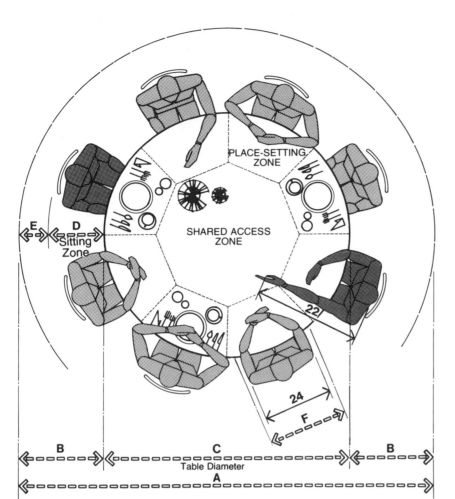

**2.2** DINING SPACES

The top drawing shows a 72-in, or 182.9-cm, diameter table that seats eight people based on a minimal place-setting zone. Although the effective depth of the zone is less than provided in the optimal arrangement shown on the preceding page, the central shared access zone is greater.

The bottom drawing illustrates the clearance suggested for wheelchair access to the dining table and the space required by a person standing, arranging, or otherwise preparing food to be served.

**72-IN (182.9-CM) DIAMETER CIRCULAR TABLE FOR EIGHT/MINIMUM SCHEME**

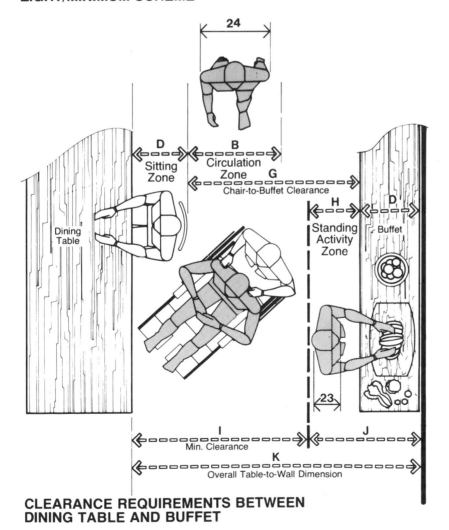

**CLEARANCE REQUIREMENTS BETWEEN DINING TABLE AND BUFFET**

|   | in | cm |
|---|---|---|
| A | 132–144 | 335.3–365.8 |
| B | 30–36 | 76.2–91.4 |
| C | 72 | 182.9 |
| D | 18–24 | 45.7–61.0 |
| E | 12 | 30.5 |
| F | 24 | 61.0 |
| G | 50–54 | 127.0–137.2 |
| H | 50–60 | 127.0–152.4 |
| I | 54 | 137.2 |
| J | 86–102 | 218.4–259.1 |
| K | 90–96 | 228.6–243.8 |

# 2.2 DINING SPACES

The relationship of the chair to the dining table is an important consideration. The top drawing explores two basic aspects of this relationship. The first is the various locations of the chair in relation to the table during the course of the meal and the clearances involved; the chair may be relocated as many as four times during the dining process. At the beginning, it is much closer to the table. Near the end of the meal, perhaps while the person is sipping coffee and attempting to relax by changing body position, the chair may be moved away from the table about 24 in, of 61 cm. Intimate conversation may cause the chair to be brought closer to the table than at the beginning. Finally, as the person rises from the chair at the conclusion of the meal, its final location may be as much as 36 in, or 91.4 cm away. The drawing indicates that the edge of the table should be at least 36 in, or 91.4 cm, away from the wall or nearest obstruction to accommodate all these movements. The height of the seat above the floor should allow the foot to rest firmly on the ground. If the seat height is too great, the foot will dangle and the area of the thigh just behind the knee will become pinched and irritated. A seat height of 16 to 17 in, or 40.6 to 41.3 cm, should be adequate to accommodate most people. Adequate clearance for the thigh should also be provided between the top of the seat and the underside of the table. As indicated on the drawing, 7.5 in, or 19.1 cm, is the minimum required. The backrest of the chair should be properly located to give support to the lumbar region of the back. The height of the table top from the floor should be between 29 and 30 in, or 73.7 to 76.2 cm. The bottom drawing indicates that to allow sufficient clearance for someone to pass or serve, the table should be located between 48 and 60 in, or 121.9 to 152.4 cm, from the wall.

| | in | cm |
|---|---|---|
| A | 30–36 | 76.2–91.4 |
| B | 18–24 | 45.7–61.0 |
| C | 16–17 | 40.6–43.2 |
| D | 7.5 min. | 19.1 min. |
| E | 29–30 | 73.7–76.2 |
| F | 48–60 | 121.9–152.4 |

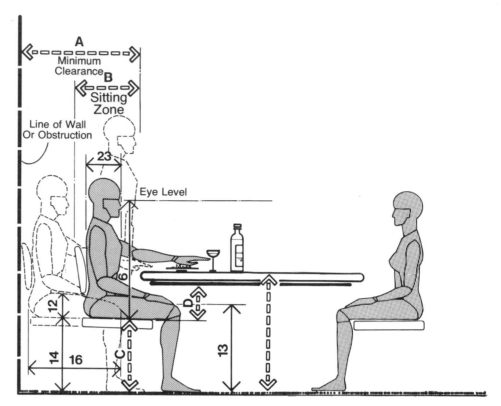

**MINIMUM CHAIR CLEARANCE / NO CIRCULATION**

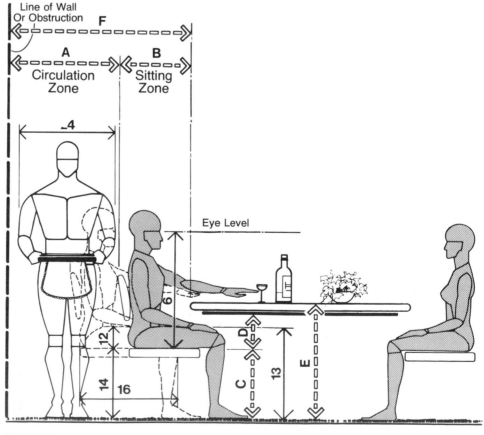

**MINIMUM CLEARANCE BEHIND CHAIR IN PLACE**

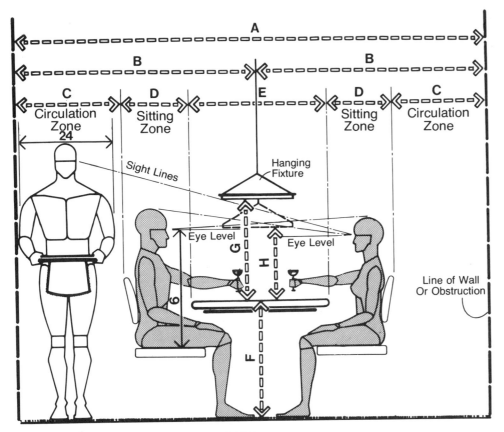

**MINIMUM DINING AREA WIDTH**

The proper height of a chandelier or other type of pendant lighting fixture above a dining table should be based on human dimension to ensure that it does not obstruct vision. The top drawing shows the relationship of fixture height above the table surface to a small and a large person. Eye height sitting is the body measurement to consider anthropometrically. The ideal solution is an adjustable arrangement so that the height of the fixture can be regulated to respond to personal preferences. The information on the drawing is useful in establishing initial height parameters as a basis for preliminary design assumptions. The drawing also indicates a minimal clearance between the table and the wall 48 in, or 121.9 cm, with the chair minimally extended from the table to permit one-lane service circulation behind the seated person.

The bottom drawing provides additional clearance information and suggests a minimum distance of 60 in, or 152.4 cm, between table and wall to accommodate one-lane head-on circulation with the chair extended a maximum distance from the table.

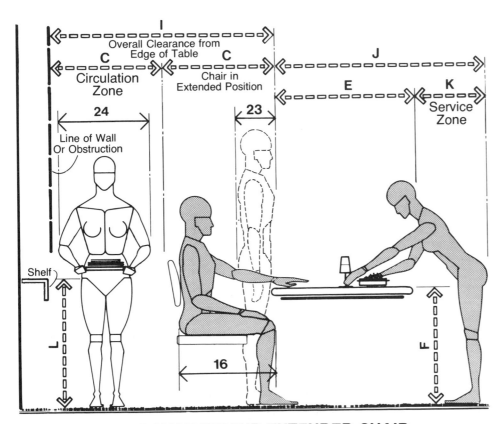

**MINIMUM CLEARANCE BEHIND EXTENDED CHAIR**

|   | in | cm |
|---|---|---|
| A | 132–162 | 335.3–411.5 |
| B | 66–81 | 167.6–205.7 |
| C | 30–36 | 76.2–91.4 |
| D | 18–24 | 45.7–61.0 |
| E | 36–42 | 91.4–106.7 |
| F | 29–30 | 73.7–76.2 |
| G | 27 | 68.6 |
| H | 19 | 48.3 |
| I | 60–72 | 152.4–182.9 |
| J | 54–60 | 137.2–152.4 |
| K | 18 | 45.7 |
| L | 29–36 | 73.7–91.4 |

# 2.2 DINING SPACES

The top drawing shows clearances between the edge of the table and the wall or nearest physical obstruction to allow two-lane service circulation behind the chair, with the chair away from the table. The individual clearances shown require the table to be located 90 to 96 in, or 228.6 to 243.8 cm, from the wall. This clearance is generous for the average residential situation, given minimal room sizes available. It should be noted that in other arrangements illustrated on the preceding pages, a compressed minimal clearance permitting head-on one-lane circulation behind the seated person, with the chair minimally extended from the table, was established at 48 in, or 121.9 cm. The bottom drawing illustrates clearances required in a banquette arrangement where seating is located at one side only. The key body measurements to consider anthropometrically in most clearance situations is the maximum body breadth and maximum body depth of the larger person.

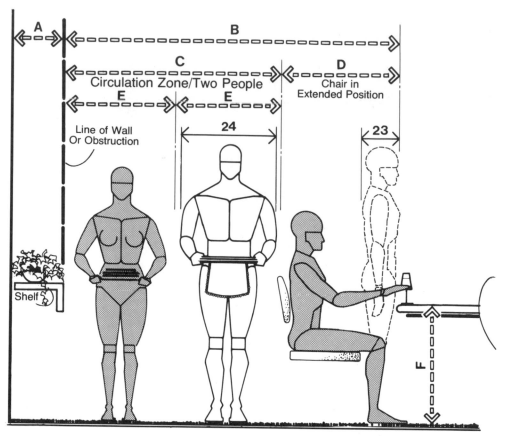

**MINIMUM CLEARANCE FOR TWO BEHIND EXTENDED CHAIR**

|   | in | cm |
|---|---|---|
| A | 12–18 | 30.5–45.7 |
| B | 90–96 | 228.6–243.8 |
| C | 60 | 152.4 |
| D | 30–36 | 76.2–91.4 |
| E | 30 | 76.2 |
| F | 29–30 | 73.7–76.2 |
| G | 101.5–110 | 257.8–279.4 |
| H | 48–54 | 121.9–137.2 |
| I | 17.5–20 | 44.5–50.8 |
| J | 36 | 91.4 |
| K | 18 | 45.7 |
| L | 16–17 | 40.6–43.2 |
| M | 7.5 min. | 19.1 min. |

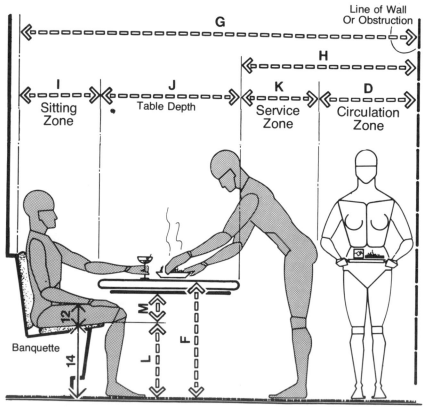

**BANQUETTE SEATING/ SERVICE AND PASSAGE CLEARANCE REQUIREMENTS**

| TABLE | SLEEPING | CIRCULATION | STORAGE | MAKE-UP AND DESK | VISUAL | ACTIVITIES | ANTHROPOMETRIC DATA | |
|---|---|---|---|---|---|---|---|---|
| | | | | | | | **2.3** | **SLEEPING SPACES** |
| 1A,2B | ● | | ◐ | | | | 1 | STATURE |
| 1B,3C | | | ◐ | ● | ◐ | | 2 | EYE HEIGHT |
| 1D,2C | ● | | | | | | 4 | SITTING HEIGHT ERECT |
| 1F,3G | | | | ○ | ◐ | | 6 | EYE HEIGHT SITTING |
| 1L,2H | | | | ● | | | 12 | THIGH CLEARANCE |
| 1M,2I | | | | ● | | | 13 | KNEE HEIGHT |
| 1N,2J | ◐ | | | ◐ | | | 14 | POPLITEAL HEIGHT |
| 1P,2L | | | | ● | | | 16 | BUTTOCK-KNEE LENGTH |
| 1W,6B | | ● | | | | | 23 | MAXIMUM BODY DEPTH |
| 1X,6A | ● | ● | ● | | | | 24 | MAXIMUM BODY BREADTH |

The drawings on the following pages explore the relationship of human dimension to the various components of sleeping spaces, the most obvious being the bed itself, both in its conventional form and in its overhead space-saving design. Often if a designer is preoccupied with glamorizing the sleeping environment, some of the more basic anthropometric considerations are ignored. Is there adequate space around the bed not only to circulate but to make it or vacuum under it? Is there adequate clearance between the bed and a dresser, with a drawer extended for circulation? If a view to the exterior of the space is important, what impact does the sill height have on the sight lines with the human body in a reclining position? In the design of a bunk or loft bed, how much clearance is required from the top of the lower bed to the bottom of the bed above to accommodate the human body in a seated position? How much clearance should be allowed between rows of hanging garments in a walk-in closet for comfortable human access? How high should a storage shelf be located to be within reach? How high should the mirror be over a dressing table for comfortable use?

Templates and rules of thumb as aids in designing the space can often be misleading. What can be equally misleading is for the designer to use himself or herself as a model in an attempt to simulate conditions related to reach and clearance situations, since what may accommodate the designer, may not accommodate the majority of users. The following drawings examine human body size, in relation to the various design situations mentioned, in terms of the anthropometric considerations indicated in the above matrix.

# 2.3 SLEEPING SPACES

The top drawings illustrate standard variations of the typical single and double bed. The figures are shown simply to provide some approximation of the space required by the human body in relationship to the bed area. The drawings should not be taken too literally. The body positions assumed while sleeping may, in fact, take up far more space than shown. The clearances indicated to the edges of the bed are also quite academic and are intended only to provide a better sense of the bed sizes available and the general relationship of body size to bed size.

The relationship between sight lines and the sill or head of a window is critical if a view to the outside is a design consideration. The drawing at the bottom of the page shows the relationships of eye height in sitting, standing, and reclining positions to varying sill heights.

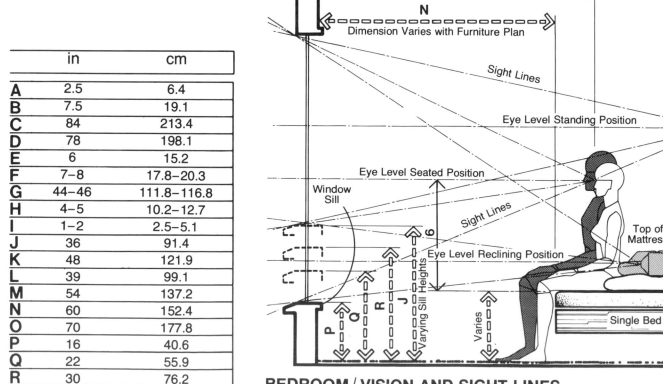

**SINGLE AND DOUBLE BEDS**

**BEDROOM / VISION AND SIGHT LINES**

|   | in | cm |
|---|------|------------|
| A | 2.5 | 6.4 |
| B | 7.5 | 19.1 |
| C | 84 | 213.4 |
| D | 78 | 198.1 |
| E | 6 | 15.2 |
| F | 7–8 | 17.8–20.3 |
| G | 44–46 | 111.8–116.8 |
| H | 4–5 | 10.2–12.7 |
| I | 1–2 | 2.5–5.1 |
| J | 36 | 91.4 |
| K | 48 | 121.9 |
| L | 39 | 99.1 |
| M | 54 | 137.2 |
| N | 60 | 152.4 |
| O | 70 | 177.8 |
| P | 16 | 40.6 |
| Q | 22 | 55.9 |
| R | 30 | 76.2 |

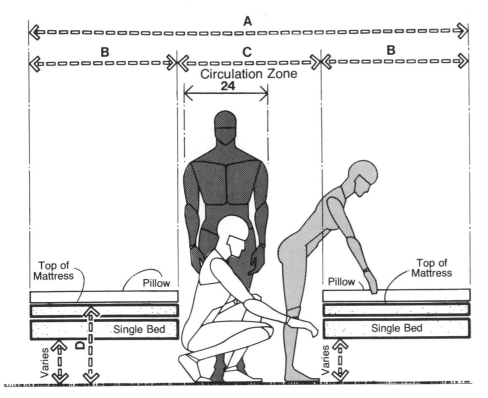

**TWIN BED / CLEARANCES AND DIMENSIONS**

The top drawing illustrates the clearances suggested between single beds to allow for circulation, access, and making up the beds. A minimum of 36 in, or 91.4 cm, is recommended.

To conserve space, underbed storage may be used in many instances. In such situations, it is essential that adequate clearance be provided between the bed and the wall or the nearest physical obstruction to ensure comfortable access.

As indicated in the bottom drawing, a clearance of 46 to 62 in, or 116.8 to 157.5 cm, should be adequate to accommodate the human body in a kneeling position as well as the projection of a partially extended drawer. If it is necessary to provide for circulation that must by-pass the work/activity zone shown, an additional 30 in, or 76.2 cm, should be added.

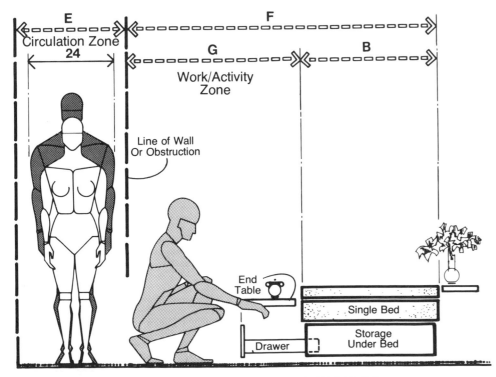

**SINGLE BED / CLEARANCES AND DIMENSIONS**

|   | in | cm |
|---|---|---|
| A | 108–114 | 274.3–289.6 |
| B | 36–39 | 91.4–99.1 |
| C | 36 | 91.4 |
| D | 18–22 | 45.7–55.9 |
| E | 30 | 76.2 |
| F | 82–131 | 208.3–332.7 |
| G | 46–62 | 116.8–157.5 |

# 2.3 SLEEPING SPACES

The three drawings on the page show the clearances involved in various bed-related work activities. The drawing at the top of the page illustrates a kneeling activity which would require a clearance of 37 to 39 in, or 93 to 99 cm, where a bed of low height is involved. Bed making usually results in backache because of the body position required to reach the bed surface. If the height of the bed were located about 24 in, or 61 cm, above the floor, as shown in the center drawing, the strain on the back would be greatly reduced. Such a height, however, does not accommodate the seated user comfortably, as suggested by the rather awkward body position of the seated figure.

In any event, a clearance of 26 to 30 in, or 66 to 76.2 cm, related to the higher bed height, is recommended to accommodate the bed-making activity.

The lower drawing illustrates the clearances involved for vacuuming under the bed. A workzone of 48 to 54 in, or 121.9 to 137.2 cm, is suggested to accommodate this activity. It should be noted that the vacuum cleaner is intentionally shown located outside the workzone merely to stress that the clearance is not overly generous. The cleaner can be located at the side of the user or even a considerable distance away. The configuration of the room and length, type, and flexibility of the cleaning device will all impact on the clearances required.

| | in | cm |
|---|---|---|
| A | 16 | 40.6 |
| B | 36–39 | 91.4–99.1 |
| C | 37–39 | 94.0–99.1 |
| D | 26–30 | 66.0–76.2 |
| E | 24 | 61.0 |
| F | 6–8 | 15.2–20.3 |
| G | 12–16 | 30.5–40.6 |
| H | 18–24 | 45.7–61.0 |
| I | 48–54 | 121.9–137.2 |

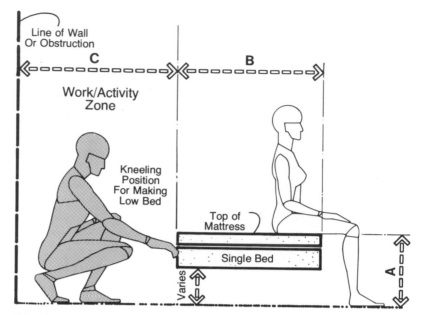

**SINGLE BED / CLEARANCES AND DIMENSIONS**

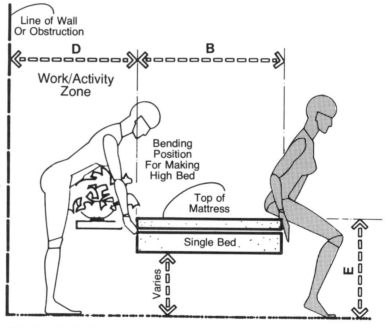

**SINGLE BED / CLEARANCES AND DIMENSIONS**

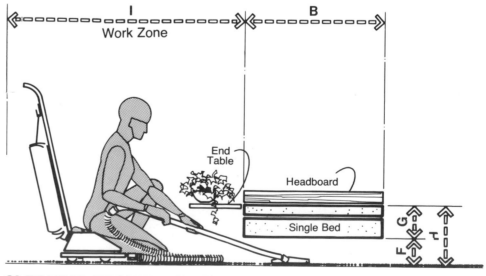

**CLEANING REQUIREMENTS**

## 2.3 SLEEPING SPACES

The drawings at the top and center deal with clearances required by the human body in relation to dressing tables and desks. The drawing at the top shows the minimum clearance suggested between the dressing table and the bed or other physical obstruction to be 24 to 28 in, or 61 to 71.1 cm, if no circulation is required. Such a clearance simply allows for access to the table and for necessary movements and changes in chair position. To accommodate both circulation and dressing table activities, however, requires a clearance between 42 and 46 in, or 106.7 to 116.8 cm.

The center drawings show vertical clearances between the seat surface and the underside of the table and between the seat surface and the floor as well as the distance from the top of the desk to the floor. The clearances between the seat surface and the underside of the table should anthropometrically accommodate the thigh clearance of the person of larger body size and the seat height should accommodate the popliteal height of the larger person. The relationship of seat height to worksurface is a classic one that also applies to dining tables, conference tables, and office desks. Drawing at the bottom of the page shows the clearances required between a dresser and the bed.

**MAKE-UP/DRESSING TABLE**

**DESK OR DRESSING TABLE**

**DRESSER/BED CLEARANCES**

| | in | cm |
|---|---|---|
| **A** | 24–28 | 61.0–71.1 |
| **B** | 12–16 | 30.5–40.6 |
| **C** | 30 | 76.2 |
| **D** | 16–24 | 40.6–61.0 |
| **E** | 42–46 | 106.7–116.8 |
| **F** | 28–40 | 71.1–101.6 |
| **G** | 7 min. | 17.8 min. |
| **H** | 28–30 | 71.1–76.2 |
| **I** | 42–54 | 106.7–137.2 |
| **J** | 18–24 | 45.7–61.0 |
| **K** | 24–30 | 61.0–76.2 |
| **L** | 62–72 | 157.5–182.9 |
| **M** | 20–24 | 50.8–61.0 |
| **N** | 42–48 | 106.7–121.9 |
| **O** | 16–20 | 40.6–50.8 |
| **P** | 18 | 45.7 |
| **Q** | 42 | 106.7 |

# 2.3 SLEEPING SPACES

Overhead sleeping facilities are a common space-saving device, particularly where the number of bedrooms or bedroom size is limited. Although standard bunk beds are available on the market, it is often necessary because of user preference or existing conditions within the interior space to custom design the bed installation. The drawing at the top of the page shows the vertical clearances necessary to accommodate an adult of large body size. The most essential body measurement anthropometrically is sitting height. If vertical space is extremely critical, it would be wise to measure the actual sitting height of the intended user in the hope that a few inches might be saved. It should be noted that 95 percent of men between the ages of 18 and 79 have a sitting height of 38.9 in, or 98.8 cm, or less. The clearance allowed between the top of the mattress and the nearest overhead obstruction is 40 in, or 101.6 cm. Theoretically, if 6 in, or 15.2 cm, is allowed for the depth of the upper bunk and 18 in, or 45.7 cm, is allowed from the floor to the top of the lower bunk, an adult of larger body size could not be accommodated within a conventional 96-in, or 243.8-cm, ceiling height unless the depth of the lower bunk is reduced. The bottom drawing shows that a horizontal clearance of 46 to 52 in, or 116.8 to 157.5 cm, is necessary for comfortable access to the underbed storage.

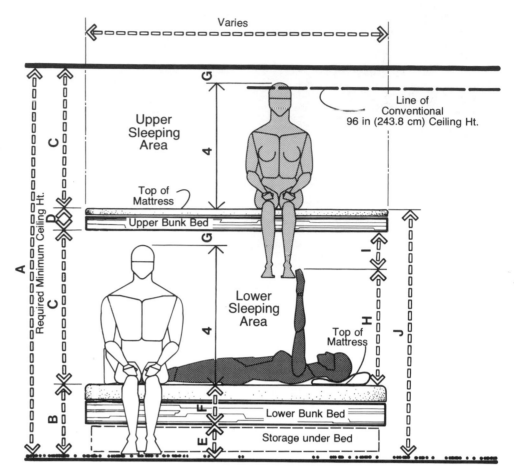

**ADULT BUNK BEDS / FRONT ELEVATION**

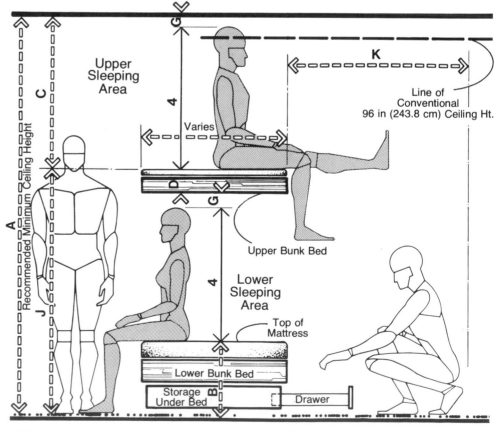

**ADULT BUNK BEDS / END ELEVATION**

|   | in | cm |
|---|------|------------|
| A | 104 | 264.2 |
| B | 18–22 | 45.7–55.9 |
| C | 40–44 | 101.6–111.8 |
| D | 6–8 | 15.2–20.3 |
| E | 8–10 | 20.3–25.4 |
| F | 10–12 | 25.4–30.5 |
| G | 2 | 5.1 |
| H | 28–38 | 71.1–96.5 |
| I | 6–12 | 15.2–30.5 |
| J | 64–74 | 162.6–188.0 |
| K | 46–62 | 116.8–157.5 |

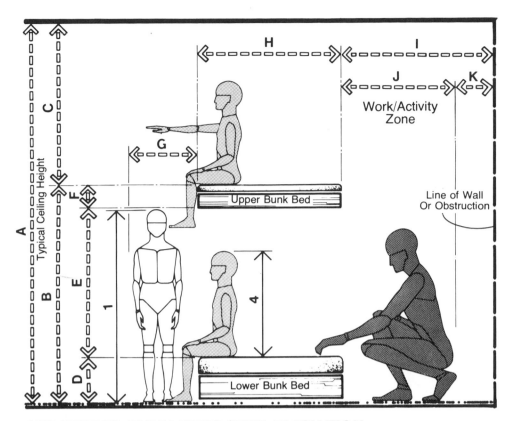

**CHILDREN'S BUNK BEDS / END ELEVATION**

## 2.3 SLEEPING SPACES

The drawing at the top of the page shows the vertical clearances necessary to accommodate children. The critical anthropometric consideration is the sitting height. The drawing shows clearly that a conventional ceiling height of 96 in, or 243.8 cm, will be adequate to accommodate the body size of a seated child on both the lower and upper bunk. The height of the upper bunk should be established as minimally required to accommodate the sitting height of the child so that the ladder climb will not be greater than necessary. The drawing at the bottom of the page illustrates the vertical clearances necessary for a loft bed. To ensure that a person can circulate under the bed without hitting his head, the critical anthropometric dimension is the stature of the person of larger body size. Popliteal height and buttock-toe length are also useful in approximating the degree of intrusion of the leg and the foot of the seated person into the circulation space below.

It should be noted that in design situations where space below the bed is used for a function other than circulation, such as dining or a desk-related activity, the vertical clearances can be reduced accordingly.

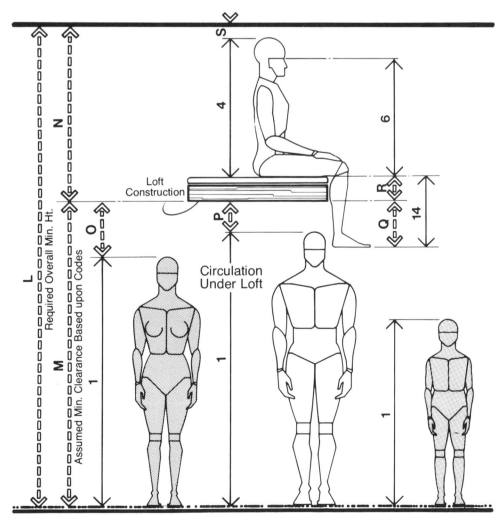

**SLEEPING LOFTS / END ELEVATION**

|   | in | cm |
|---|---|---|
| **A** | 96 | 243.8 |
| **B** | 54.5–62 | 138.4–157.5 |
| **C** | 36.5–39 | 92.7–99.1 |
| **D** | 12–15 | 30.5–38.1 |
| **E** | 36.5–39 | 92.7–99.1 |
| **F** | 6–8 | 15.2–20.3 |
| **G** | 14–18 | 35.6–45.7 |
| **H** | 30–39 | 76.2–99.1 |
| **I** | 37–39 | 94.0–99.1 |
| **J** | 34–36 | 86.4–91.4 |
| **K** | 3 | 7.6 |
| **L** | 130–136 | 330.2–345.4 |
| **M** | 84 | 213.4 |
| **N** | 46–52 | 116.8–132.1 |
| **O** | 17 | 43.2 |
| **P** | 11 | 27.9 |
| **Q** | 5–14 | 12.7–35.6 |
| **R** | 6–8 | 15.2–20.3 |
| **S** | 2 | 5.1 |

# 2.3 SLEEPING SPACES

The two drawings at the top of the page show the vertical clearances related to male and female closet and storage facilities. Wherever possible or practical, the closet shelf should be located within human reach. The height shown for the high shelf has been established based on 5th percentile male and female data in order to place it within reach of individuals of smaller body size. Any shelf located at a greater distance above the floor should be used primarily for storage that requires only infrequent access. The location of the shelf just above the rod is essentially a function of rod height. The clearance between the bottom of the shelf and the top of the rod should allow for easy removal of the hanger.

The bottom drawings illustrate two various types of walk-in storage facilities. Undoubtably, it can be argued that the 36-in, or 91.4-cm, clearance shown between the hanging garment and the storage shelf or between opposite garments could be reduced about 50 percent. The authors contend, however, that in order to achieve any degree of comfort in the selection and removal of the desired garment, a minimum of 36 in should be maintained. The degree to which this dimension can be reduced is a question of the level of comfort the user is prepared to tolerate in exchange for the floor space saved. The two drawings of the plan view of the human figure illustrate clearances required for donning a coat or putting on a pair of stockings.

|   | in | cm |
|---|---|---|
| A | 64–68 | 162.6–172.7 |
| B | 72–76 | 182.9–193.0 |
| C | 12–18 | 30.5–45.7 |
| D | 8–10 | 20.3–25.4 |
| E | 20–28 | 50.8–71.1 |
| F | 34–36 | 86.4–91.4 |
| G | 10–12 | 25.4–30.5 |
| H | 60–70 | 152.4–177.8 |
| I | 69–72 | 175.3–182.9 |
| J | 76 | 193.0 |
| K | 68 | 172.7 |
| L | 42 | 106.7 |
| M | 46 | 116.8 |
| N | 30 | 76.2 |
| O | 18 | 45.7 |

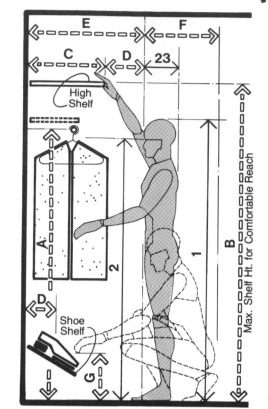

**CLOSET AND STORAGE FACILITIES / MALE**

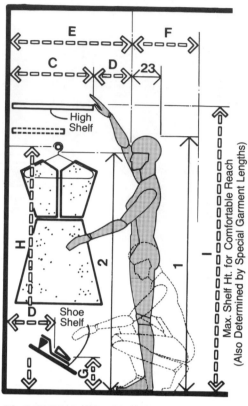

**CLOSET AND STORAGE FACILITIES / FEMALE**

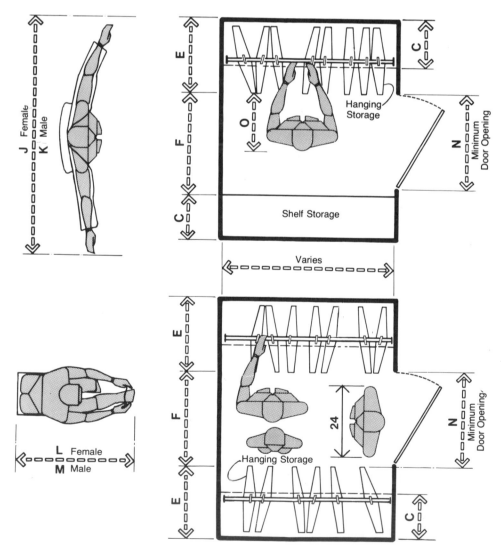

**WALK-IN CLOSET AND STORAGE FACILITIES**

| TABLE | STORAGE | PREPARATION | DINING | SINK | REFRIGERATOR | RANGE/OVEN | ACTIVITIES | ANTHROPOMETRIC DATA |
|---|---|---|---|---|---|---|---|---|
| 1A,2B | ● | | | ● | | | 1 | STATURE |
| 1B,3C | ○ | | | ◐ | ◐ | ● | 2 | EYE HEIGHT |
| 1C,3B | | ◐ | | ◐ | | | 3 | ELBOW HEIGHT |
| 1D,2C | | | ● | | | | 4 | SITTING HEIGHT ERECT |
| 1F,3G | | | ● | | | | 6 | EYE HEIGHT SITTING |
| 1L,2H | | ● | ● | | | | 12 | THIGH CLEARANCE |
| 1P,2L | | ● | ● | | | | 16 | BUTTOCK-KNEE LENGTH |
| 1T,4F | ○ | | | | | | 20 | VERTICAL GRIP REACH |
| 1V,4D | | | | ○ | | | 22 | THUMB TIP REACH |
| 1W,6B | ● | ● | | ● | | ● | 23 | MAXIMUM BODY DEPTH |
| 1X,6A | ● | ● | ● | ● | | ● | 24 | MAXIMUM BODY BREADTH |

# 2.4 COOKING SPACES

The height of a kitchen workcounter, the proper clearance between cabinets or appliances for circulation, the accessibility to overhead or undercounter storage, and proper visibility are among the primary considerations in the design of cooking spaces. All must be responsive to human dimension and body size if the quality of interface between the user and the components of the interior space are to be adequate. In establishing clearances between counters, the maximum body breadth and depth of the user of larger body size must be taken into account as well as the projections of the appliances. Refrigerator doors, cabinet drawers, dishwashing machine doors, and cabinet doors all project to some degree in their open position into the space within which the user must circulate and must be accommodated.

Standard kitchen counter heights manufactured are all about 36 in, or 91.4 cm. But such a height does not necessarily accommodate the body dimension of all users for all tasks. Certain cooking activities, for example, may be more efficiently performed from a standing position, but with a counter height less than 36 in. In overhead cabinets the upper shelves are usually inaccessible to the smaller person, while the lower shelves are usually inaccessible to most without bending or kneeling. The logical answer is the development of kitchen cabinet systems capable of total adjustability to accommodate the human dimension of the individual user. Such a system could accommodate not only those of smaller and larger body size, but also elderly and disabled people. The drawings on the following pages examine the question of human dimension in terms of the anthropometric measurements indicated in the above matrix. It should be noted, however, that the drawings are intended merely to illustrate the relationship of body size to clearances and reach situations and not to suggest an overall functional plan for the kitchen or the ergonomic relationship between workcenters.

# 2.4 COOKING SPACES

The drawings at the top and center of the page illustrate some of the basic horizontal clearances required in a kitchen. The drawing at the top shows clearances between two counters with base cabinets. A total clearance between cabinets of 60 to 66 in, or 152.4 to 167 cm, will accommodate the human body and an extended drawer or hinged cabinet door in the workzone and in the circulation zone the maximum body breadth of a person of larger body size. The B dimension of 48 in, or 121.9 cm, is a recommended minimum clearance between cabinets when the full circulation zone shown is not desired. The center drawing also shows a recommended clearance of 48 in between the face of a cabinet and the nearest physical obstruction.

The drawing at the bottom of the page deals with vertical clearances. The height of the shelf, shown in broken lines, within the overhead cabinets is within reach, allowing for the projection of the base cabinet. The height of the shelf, shown as a solid black line, is slightly greater, but also within reach, since the base cabinet does not interfere. The height of the shelves has been based on 5th percentile female vertical grip reach data to place them within reach of the user with the smaller body size.

|   | in | cm |
|---|---|---|
| A | 60–66 | 152.4–167.6 |
| B | 48 min. | 121.9 min. |
| C | 24–30 | 61.0–76.2 |
| D | 36 | 91.4 |
| E | 48 | 121.9 |
| F | 12–13 | 30.5–33.0 |
| G | 76 max. | 193.0 max. |
| H | 72 max. | 182.9 max. |
| I | 59 | 149.9 |
| J | 25.5 | 64.8 |
| K | 24–26 | 61.0–66.0 |
| L | 15 min. | 38.1 min. |
| M | 18 | 45.7 |
| N | 35–36 | 88.9–91.4 |
| O | 69 max. | 175.3 max. |

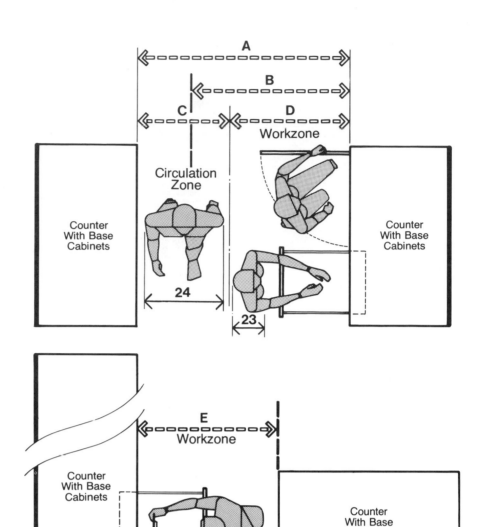

## COUNTER AND BASE CABINETS/ GENERAL CLEARANCE

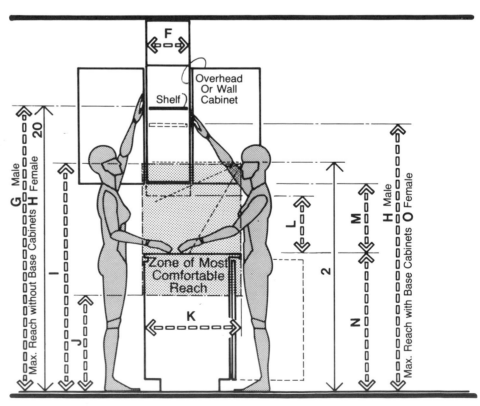

## CABINET REACH COMPARISONS

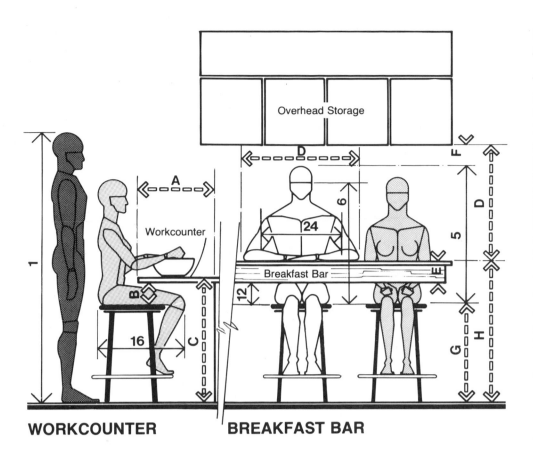

**WORKCOUNTER**　　　**BREAKFAST BAR**

## 2.4 COOKING SPACES

The drawing at the top of the page shows some of the more important horizontal and vertical clearances related to a typical breakfast bar. To ensure comfortable spacing between people, 30 in, or 76.2 cm, should be allocated for the horizontal space required for each person seated at the bar. It should be noted also that a bar height of 36 in, or 91.4 cm, requires that the stool be equipped with a footrest.

The center drawing shows a typical workcounter. Although most kitchen counters have a height of 35 to 36 in, or 88.9 to 91.4 cm, a 32-in, or 81.3-cm, height will accommodate a seated user. Moreover, certain food preparation activities, even if performed from a standing position, are more efficiently and comfortably executed with a lower counter height. This is particularly true for tasks involving some degree of force from the arms and upper back muscles; the rolling of dough would be a good example.

The drawing at the bottom of the page shows the critical counter workzone of a standing user. The outer perimeter is defined by the horizontal thumb tip reach of the user having the smaller body size. The 18-in, or 45.7-cm, dimension indicated was adapted from 5th percentile female data. The critical counter workzone of 18 by 30 in, or 45.7 by 76.2 cm, constitutes the immediate work area directly in front of the user, all of which is comfortably accessible, with little or no side arm reach required. The counter surface beyond this area, which is accessible with some effort, is limited only by the reach capability of the human body, which varies with the size of the individual.

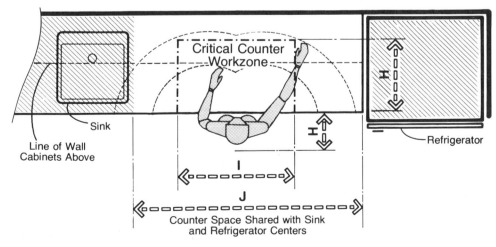

**MIX AND PREPARATION CENTER**

|   | in | cm |
|---|---|---|
| A | 18 min. | 45.7 min. |
| B | 7.5 min. | 19.1 min. |
| C | 32 | 81.3 |
| D | 30 | 76.2 |
| E | 4 max. | 10.2 max. |
| F | 4 | 10.2 |
| G | 22–24.5 | 55.9–62.2 |
| H | 18 | 45.7 |
| I | 36 | 91.4 |
| J | 42 | 106.7 |

# 2.4 COOKING SPACES

The drawing at the top of the page shows the horizontal clearances involved in the vicinity of the dish washing area. While loading or unloading the dishwasher, a clearance of at least 40 in, or 101.6 cm, is recommended to accommodate the human body and the extended dish rack and appliance door. To allow circulation as well, at least another 30 in, or 76.2 cm, should be added.

The drawing at the bottom of the page shows a sectional view through the same area. The recommended counter height is between 35 and 36 in, or 88.9 to 91.4 cm. If no window is provided over the kitchen sink and wall cabinets are to be provided instead, the height between the top of the counter and the bottom of those cabinets should not be less than 22 in, or 55.9 cm.

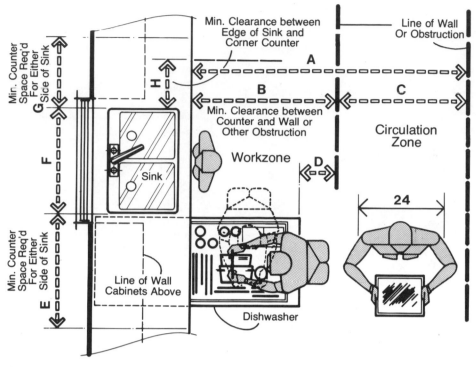

**SINK CENTER**

| | in | cm |
|---|---|---|
| A | 70–76 | 177.8–193.0 |
| B | 40 min. | 101.6 min. |
| C | 30–36 | 76.2–91.4 |
| D | 18 | 45.7 |
| E | 24 min. | 61.0 min. |
| F | 28–42 | 71.1–106.7 |
| G | 18 min. | 45.7 min. |
| H | 12 min. | 30.5 min. |
| I | 24–26 | 61.0–66.0 |
| J | 57 min. | 144.8 min. |
| K | 35–36 | 88.9–91.4 |
| L | 22 min. | 55.9 min. |
| M | 3 | 7.6 |
| N | 4 | 10.2 |

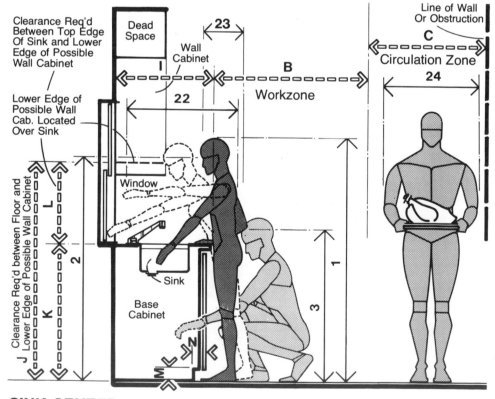

**SINK CENTER**

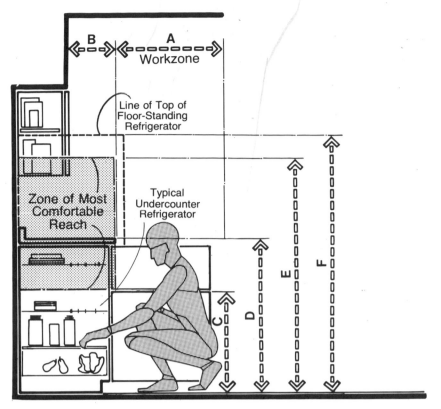

**REFRIGERATOR CENTER/
TYPICAL REFRIGERATOR LOCATIONS**

# 2.4 COOKING SPACES

The two drawings on this page deal primarily with the vertical dimensions related to the refrigerator installation within the kitchen.

The top drawing illustrates a typical floor-standing refrigerator installation as well as a below-counter installation. Superimposed on the sectional view in shaded film is the zone of most comfortable reach. To reach elements located above or below this area requires some additional effort. Below the area, for example, it may be necessary to kneel or stoop. Although, in both the floor-standing and the under-counter situations everything is within physical reach, elements located within the shaded area can be reached almost effortlessly.

The bottom drawing suggests the possibility of a third type of refrigerator that might be wall mounted or located on the top of the counter, so that most of its surface would fall within this shaded area. To allow for proper viewing of the interior, the height of the proposed unit exceeds the upper limits of the shaded zone. Despite its slightly greater height, the unit is just about in line with the height above the floor of the larger-size conventional floor-standing model.

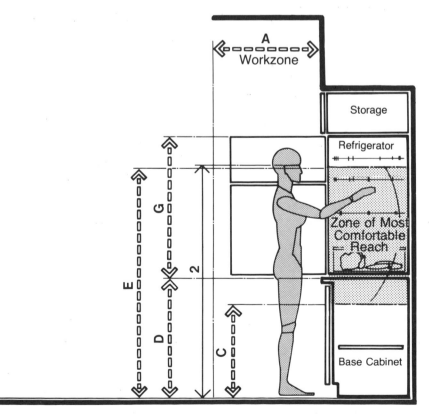

**REFRIGERATOR CENTER/
PROPOSED REFRIGERATOR LOCATION**

|   | in | cm |
|---|---|---|
| **A** | 36 | 91.4 |
| **B** | 11–14 | 27.9–35.6 |
| **C** | 25.5 | 64.8 |
| **D** | 35–36 | 88.9–91.4 |
| **E** | 59 | 149.9 |
| **F** | 55–69.5 | 139.7–176.5 |
| **G** | 30–36 | 76.2–91.4 |

# 2.4 COOKING SPACES

The drawings at the top and bottom of the page illustrate the clearances related to range centers. The top drawing indicates a minimum clearance between appliances of 48 in, 121.9 cm. The anthropometric basis for the clearances are amplified in the drawing below.

The 40-in, or 101.6 cm, wall oven workzone clearance is adequate to accommodate the projected wall oven door, in addition to the maximum body depth dimension of the user. The standing figure shown in broken line, however, indicates both dimensionally and graphically that the 40-in clearance will not permit comfortable circulation when appliances on both sides are in operation at the same time. The range workzone clearance, also 40-in, is adequate to accommodate the open range door and the body size of the kneeling user.

An extremely important, but frequently overlooked, anthropometric consideration in kitchen design is eye height. In this regard, the distance from the top of the range to the underside of the hood should allow the rear burners to be visible to the user.

| | in | cm |
|---|---|---|
| A | 48 min. | 121.9 min. |
| B | 40 | 101.6 |
| C | 15 | 38.1 min. |
| D | 21–30 | 53.3–76.2 |
| E | 1–3 | 2.5–7.6 |
| F | 15 min. | 38.1 min. |
| G | 19.5–46 | 49.5–116.8 |
| H | 12 min. | 30.5 min. |
| I | 17.5 max. | 44.5 max |
| J | 96–101.5 | 243.8–257.8 |
| K | 24–27.5 | 61.0–69.9 |
| L | 24–26 | 61.0–66.0 |
| M | 30 | 76.2 |
| N | 60 min. | 152.4 min. |
| O | 35–36.25 | 88.9–92.1 |
| P | 24 min. | 61.0 min. |
| Q | 35 max. | 88.9 max. |

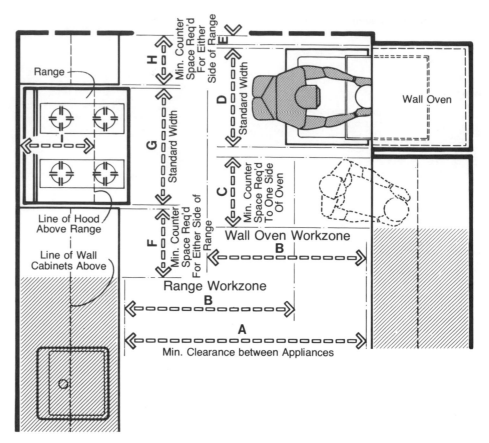

**RANGE CENTER**

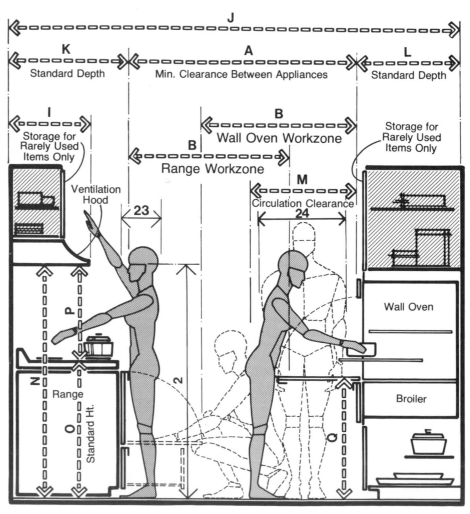

**RANGE CENTER**

| TABLE | LAVATORY | WATER CLOSET | BIDET | SHOWER | BATHTUB | CIRCULATION | ACTIVITIES | ANTHROPOMETRIC DATA | |
|-------|----------|--------------|-------|--------|---------|-------------|------------|---------------------|---|
| 1A,2B |  |  |  | ● |  |  |  | 1 | STATURE |
| 1B,3C | ◐ |  |  |  |  |  |  | 2 | EYE HEIGHT |
| 1C,3B | ◐ |  |  |  |  |  |  | 3 | ELBOW HEIGHT |
| 1J,2F |  |  |  |  | ● |  |  | 10 | HIP BREADTH |
| 1P,2L |  | ● | ● |  |  |  |  | 16 | BUTTOCK-KNEE LENGTH |
| 1R,4B |  |  |  |  | ◐ |  |  | 18 | BUTTOCK-HEEL LENGTH |
| 1S,4C |  |  |  |  | ○ |  |  | 19 | VERTICAL REACH HEIGHT SITTING |
| 1T,4F |  |  |  | ○ |  |  |  | 20 | VERTICAL GRIP REACH |
| 1U,4E |  | ○ |  |  |  |  |  | 21 | SIDE ARM REACH |
| 1V,4D | ○ | ○ |  |  |  |  |  | 22 | THUMB TIP REACH |
| 1W,6B | ● | ● |  |  |  |  |  | 23 | MAXIMUM BODY DEPTH |
| 1X,6A |  |  |  | ● | ● | ● |  | 24 | MAXIMUM BODY BREADTH |

One of the most dramatic examples of a design situation where little consideration is given to the relationship of human dimension and body size to the designed environment can be found in practically every bathroom, private and public. Few designers, builders, and users give any thought to the height above the floor of a lavatory. Hours, if not days, may be spent in the selection of the appropriate color, fixture, model, or trim. The height, however, is rarely specified and is simply left to the contractor in the field, who automatically installs it at the height that it has been installed for years simply because "that's the way it's done." The designer who does specify a height, in either a drawing or written specifications, does nothing more than use the same criteria employed in the field, but gives it more legitimacy by incorporating it into the drawing.

The fact is that it is not natural for the body to assume a stooped posture while washing the hands and face. This posture is necessitated, however, because most basin heights are only about 30 in, or 76.2 cm, above the floor. It is interesting to note that 30 in is also the average height of a desk or dining table, yet if a person were forced to write or eat from a standing position, each of the surfaces would have to be raised at least 6 to 12 in, or 15.2 to 30.5 cm. The drawings on the following pages examine the relationship of body size to the lavatory and other elements of bathroom spaces. The matrix above indicates some of the more important anthropometric measurements that should be considered in the design of bathrooms.

# 2.5 BATHROOMS

The drawing at the top of the page illustrates some of the basic anthropometric considerations related to the lavatory area. Perhaps the most obvious problem concerns the height of the lavatory above the floor. For too long this dimension has been established in the field on so-called trade practice at 31 to 34 in, or 78.7 to 86.3 cm, and has little relationship to the anthropometric requirements involved. Optimum work height for the hands on a counter or work bench situation is established at about 2 to 3 in, or 5 to 7.6 cm, below elbow height. Published data show that only 5 percent of a male sampling measured had an elbow height of 41.3 in, or 104.9 cm, or less, while 5 percent of a female sampling had an elbow height of 38.6 in, or 98 cm. Subtracting 3 in from the female measurement would place a comfortable height for the lavatory at 35.6 in, or 90.4 cm. That is greater than the height at which lavatories are normally installed, presumably to accommodate the majority of the population. Stated another way, more than 95 percent of users are not properly accommodated by the heights at which most lavatories are presently installed. The drawing indicates ranges for adult males, females, and children of lavatory heights suitable to accommodate a greater portion of the respective populations. The bottom drawing indicates horizontal clearances recommended in the lavatory area.

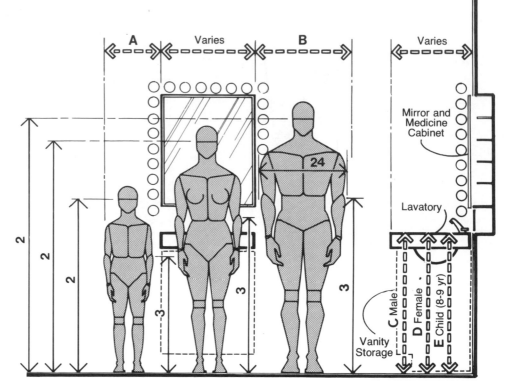

## LAVATORY/GENERAL ANTHROPOMETRIC CONSIDERATIONS

|   | in | cm |
|---|------|-----------|
| A | 15–18 | 38.1–45.7 |
| B | 28–30 | 71.1–76.2 |
| C | 37–43 | 94.0–109.2 |
| D | 32–36 | 81.3–91.4 |
| E | 26–32 | 66.0–81.3 |
| F | 14–16 | 35.6–40.6 |
| G | 30 | 76.2 |
| H | 18 | 45.7 |
| I | 21–26 | 53.3–66.0 |

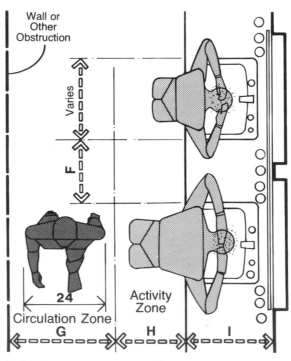

## DOUBLE LAVATORY CLEARANCES

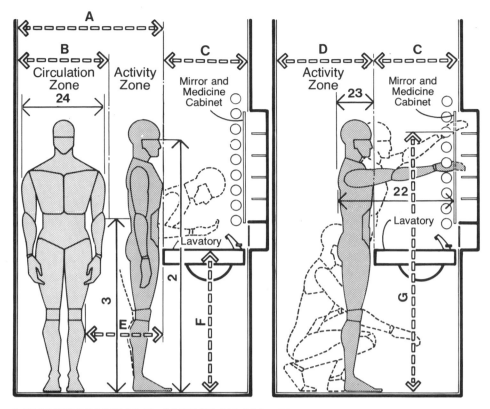

## LAVATORY / MALE ANTHROPOMETRIC CONSIDERATIONS

# 2.5 BATHROOMS

The drawing at the top deals primarily with some of the more critical male anthropometric considerations developed on the preceding page. A lavatory height above the floor of 37 to 43 in, or 94 to 109.2 cm, is suggested to accommodate the majority of users. In order to establish the location of mirrors above the lavatory, eye height should be taken into consideration.

The two drawings at the bottom of the page explore, in much the same manner, the anthropometric considerations related to women and children, respectively. Given the great variability in body sizes to be accommodated within a single family, a strong case can be presented for the development of a height adjustment capability for the lavatory. Until that is developed, there is no reason, on custom installations, why the architect or interior designer cannot take anthropometric measurements of the client to ensure proper interface between the user and the lavatory.

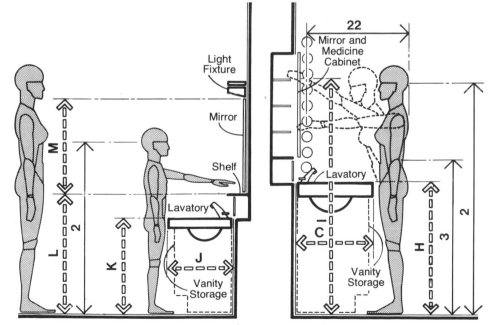

## LAVATORY / FEMALE AND CHILD ANTHROPOMETRIC CONSIDERATIONS

|   | in | cm |
|---|---|---|
| A | 48 | 121.9 |
| B | 30 | 76.2 |
| C | 19–24 | 48.3–61.0 |
| D | 27 min. | 68.6 min. |
| E | 18 | 45.7 |
| F | 37–43 | 94.0–109.2 |
| G | 72 max. | 182.9 max. |
| H | 32–36 | 81.3–91.4 |
| I | 69 max. | 175.3 max. |
| J | 16–18 | 40.6–45.7 |
| K | 26–32 | 66.0–81.3 |
| L | 32 | 81.3 |
| M | 20–24 | 50.8–61.0 |

# 2.5 BATHROOMS

The drawings at the top and center of the page deal with the anthropometric considerations related to the individual water closet and bidet. The drawing at the top left suggests an activity zone or clearance between the face of a water closet to the line of the wall or nearest obstruction of at least 24 in, or 61 cm. Accessories in front or to the side of the user should be within reach. Thumb tip arm reach and side arm reach should both be taken into account in locating these items anthropometrically. A height of about 30 in, or 76.2 cm, from the floor to the center line of the paper dispenser is suggested.

The bottom drawing of the water closet shows some of the horizontal clearances required.

The two drawings of the individual bidet illustrate in a similar manner some of the basic anthropometric requirements and clearances suggested for a typical installation. The bottom drawing indicates some of the clearances involved when the water closet and bidet are located side by side.

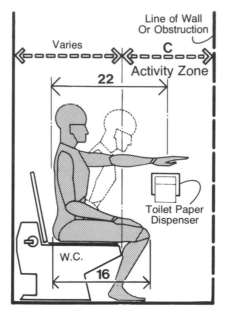

**WATER CLOSET**

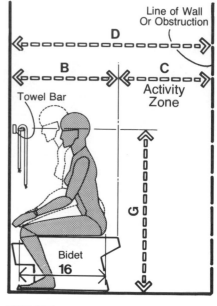

**BIDET**

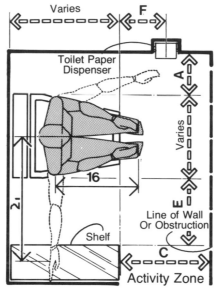

**WATER CLOSET**

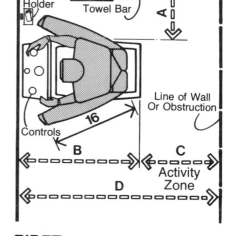

**BIDET**

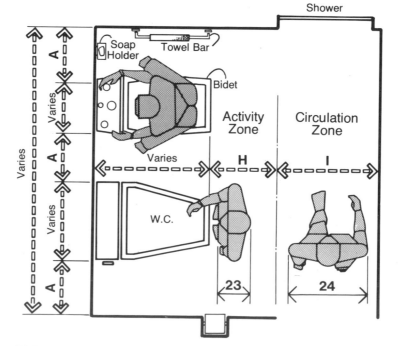

**BIDET AND WATER CLOSET**

| | in | cm |
|---|---|---|
| A | 12 min. | 30.5 min. |
| B | 28 min. | 71.1 min. |
| C | 24 min. | 61.0 min. |
| D | 52 min. | 132.1 min. |
| E | 12–18 | 30.5–45.7 |
| F | 12 | 30.5 |
| G | 40 | 101.6 |
| H | 18 | 45.7 |
| I | 30 | 76.2 |

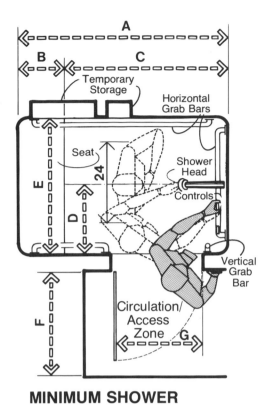

**MINIMUM SHOWER CLEARANCES**

**MINIMUM SHOWER CLEARANCES**

# 2.5 BATHROOMS

The size of a shower stall can vary greatly depending on the level of comfort desired. Safety is also an extremely important consideration. Unless a fairly reliable mixing valve capable of presetting a fixed and desirable water temperature is provided, care should be taken to locate controls within reach but out of direct line of the water path in order to avoid scalding or freezing while operating the controls.

A clearance of 54 in, or 137.2 cm, between walls, as shown in the two drawings at the top, will not only accommodate the variety of body positions shown, but will also allow for a small 12-in, or 30.5-cm, seating surface. The height of the adjustable shower head should be within reach of the adult of smaller body size, but at the same time high enough to clear the head of most people of larger body size. In situations where children use the same facility, an adjustable shower head is suggested in order to place it within reach of the child.

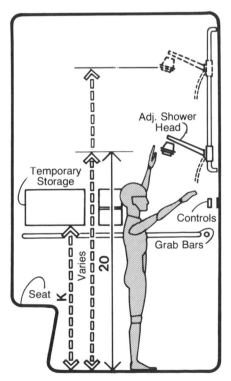

**SHOWER / CHILD ANTHROPOMETRIC CONSIDERATIONS**

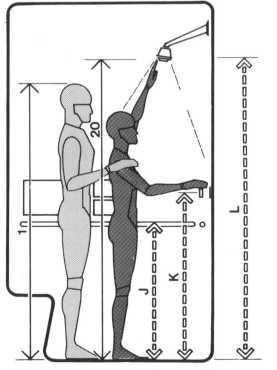

**SHOWER / REACH AND CLEARANCE**

|   | in | cm |
|---|---|---|
| A | 54 | 137.2 |
| B | 12 | 30.5 |
| C | 42 min. | 106.7 min. |
| D | 18 | 45.7 |
| E | 36 min. | 91.4 min. |
| F | 30 | 76.2 |
| G | 24 | 61.0 |
| H | 12 min. | 30.5 min. |
| I | 15 | 38.1 |
| J | 40–48 | 101.6–121.9 |
| K | 40–50 | 101.6–127.0 |
| L | 72 min. | 182.9 min. |

# 2.5 BATHROOMS

The drawing at the top of the page illustrates some of the basic clearances required for a combination shower and tub. Dimensions concerning the shower head are similar to those indicated on the preceding page. The location of the tub controls should be placed within reach of the smaller seated user.

Unless a tub is custom designed, the choice of dimensions is limited to standard available tub models. A knowledge of the anthropometric considerations involved, however, will prove helpful in making the appropriate selection. If the user enjoys reclining and soaking for extended periods, a large-size tub may not necessarily be the wisest selection. The length of the tub at the bottom surface should approximate the buttock-heel length of the smaller user. This will allow the feet to bear against the end of the tub and act as a brace to prevent the body from sliding too far under the water.

The center drawing illustrates that condition. The bottom drawing indicates that a tub width of 40 to 44 in, or 101.6 to 111.8 cm, is necessary to accommodate two people in the tub at the same time.

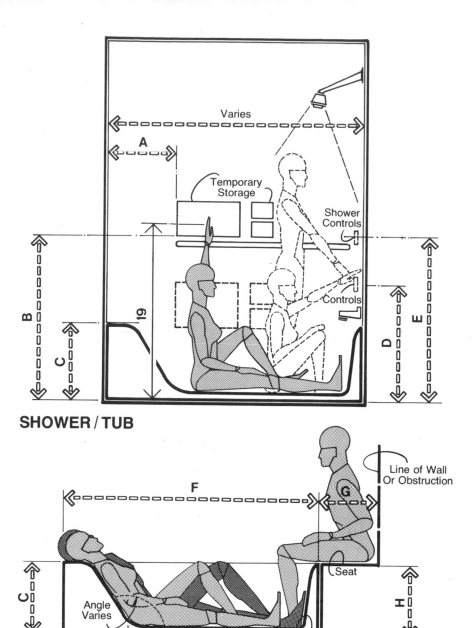

**SHOWER / TUB**

**TUB / RECLINING AND RELAXING**

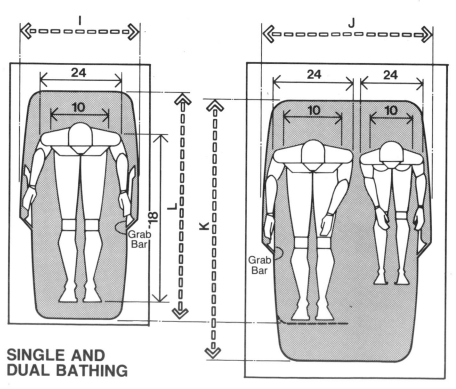

**SINGLE AND DUAL BATHING**

|   | in | cm |
|---|---|---|
| **A** | 18–21 | 45.7–53.3 |
| **B** | 40 | 101.6 |
| **C** | 15–22 | 38.1–55.9 |
| **D** | 30–34 | 76.2–86.4 |
| **E** | 40–50 | 101.6–127.0 |
| **F** | 66 | 167.6 |
| **G** | 12 min. | 30.5 min. |
| **H** | 18 max. | 45.7 max. |
| **I** | 26–27 | 66.0–68.6 |
| **J** | 40–44 | 101.6–111.8 |
| **K** | 66–70 | 167.6–177.8 |
| **L** | 56–60 | 142.2–152.4 |

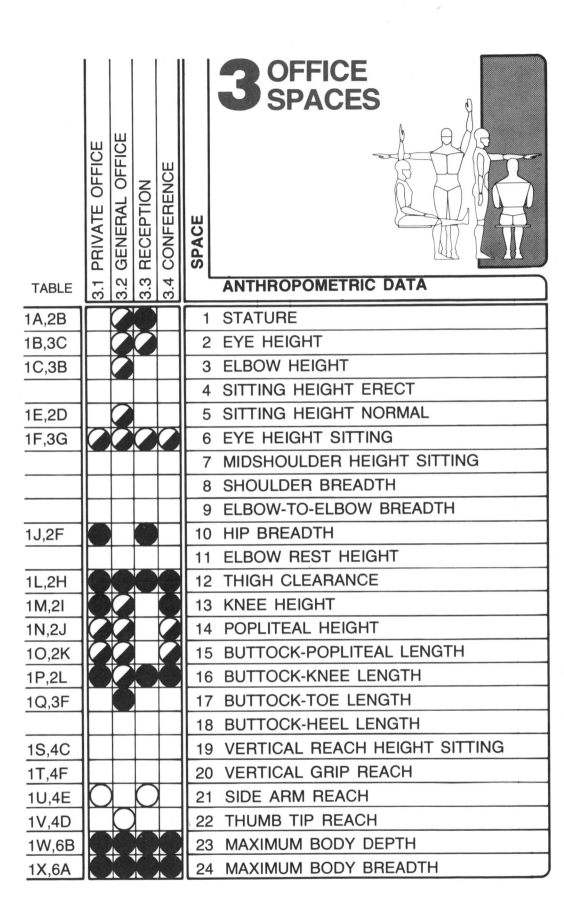

| TABLE | 3.1 PRIVATE OFFICE | 3.2 GENERAL OFFICE | 3.3 RECEPTION | 3.4 CONFERENCE | | ANTHROPOMETRIC DATA |
|---|---|---|---|---|---|---|
| 1A,2B | | ◨ | ◨ | | 1 | STATURE |
| 1B,3C | | ◨ | ◨ | | 2 | EYE HEIGHT |
| 1C,3B | | ◨ | | | 3 | ELBOW HEIGHT |
| | | | | | 4 | SITTING HEIGHT ERECT |
| 1E,2D | | ◨ | | | 5 | SITTING HEIGHT NORMAL |
| 1F,3G | ● | ● | ● | ◨ | 6 | EYE HEIGHT SITTING |
| | | | | | 7 | MIDSHOULDER HEIGHT SITTING |
| | | | | | 8 | SHOULDER BREADTH |
| | | | | | 9 | ELBOW-TO-ELBOW BREADTH |
| 1J,2F | ● | | ● | | 10 | HIP BREADTH |
| | | | | | 11 | ELBOW REST HEIGHT |
| 1L,2H | ● | ● | ● | ● | 12 | THIGH CLEARANCE |
| 1M,2I | ● | ◨ | ◨ | ● | 13 | KNEE HEIGHT |
| 1N,2J | ◨ | ◨ | | ◨ | 14 | POPLITEAL HEIGHT |
| 1O,2K | ◨ | ◨ | | ◨ | 15 | BUTTOCK-POPLITEAL LENGTH |
| 1P,2L | ● | ◨ | ● | ● | 16 | BUTTOCK-KNEE LENGTH |
| 1Q,3F | | ● | | | 17 | BUTTOCK-TOE LENGTH |
| | | | | | 18 | BUTTOCK-HEEL LENGTH |
| 1S,4C | | | | | 19 | VERTICAL REACH HEIGHT SITTING |
| 1T,4F | | | | | 20 | VERTICAL GRIP REACH |
| 1U,4E | ○ | | ○ | | 21 | SIDE ARM REACH |
| 1V,4D | | ○ | | | 22 | THUMB TIP REACH |
| 1W,6B | ● | ● | ● | ● | 23 | MAXIMUM BODY DEPTH |
| 1X,6A | ● | ● | ● | ● | 24 | MAXIMUM BODY BREADTH |

Since the 1950s, office design has become one of the major areas of specialization for the designer. Millions of square feet of office space are designed each year. The proliferation of business and the ensuing demand for large corporation headquarters resulted in the need to plan spaces capable of housing hundreds and even thousands of people within the same space. People spend nearly half their waking hours within an office environment of one type or another. Some may literally spend an entire lifetime in the employ of the same firm. Expanding world markets will create an even greater demand for more space. Moreover, as technology changes, its impact on the methodology of transacting business and the systems involved will necessitate further recycling of existing office spaces to respond to new needs. Concurrently, spiraling costs of construction and land acquisition, increasing scarcity of available urban building sites, and higher production costs will place greater demands on the designer for efficient, cost-conscious, and economical utilization of office space.

The reconciliation of economic imperatives and human factors within the design process will require a greater sensitivity and awareness on the part of the designer to the relationship of human dimension and interior space. Accordingly, the anthropometric implications of people's relationship to various aspects of the office environment, such as conference rooms, private and general offices, and reception areas, are explored in the pages that follow. Clearances between desks, heights of worksurfaces, human reach limitations, human requirements for paths of circulation are all investigated and diagrammed both in plan and section.

## 3.1 THE PRIVATE OFFICE

| TABLE | DESK | LOUNGING | STORAGE | CIRCULATION | ACTIVITIES | | ANTHROPOMETRIC DATA |
|-------|------|----------|---------|-------------|------------|-----|---------------------|
| 1F,3G | ◑ | | | | | 6 | EYE HEIGHT SITTING |
| 1J,2F | ● | ● | | | | 10 | HIP BREADTH |
| 1L,2H | ● | | | | | 12 | THIGH CLEARANCE |
| 1M,2I | ● | | | | | 13 | KNEE HEIGHT |
| 1N,2J | ◑ | | | | | 14 | POPLITEAL HEIGHT |
| 1O,2K | ◑ | | | | | 15 | BUTTOCK-POPLITEAL LENGTH |
| 1P,2L | ● | ● | | | | 16 | BUTTOCK-KNEE LENGTH |
| 1U,4E | | | ○ | | | 21 | SIDE ARM REACH |
| 1W,6B | | ● | | ● | | 23 | MAXIMUM BODY DEPTH |
| 1X,6A | ● | ● | | ● | | 24 | MAXIMUM BODY BREADTH |

The design of certain aspects of private office spaces involves many of the same considerations related to human dimension and body size as were explored in certain aspects of residential spaces. The most important component of the private office space, or any office space for that matter, is the desk itself and related elements. Considering that the user may well spend over half of his waking hours within the immediate workspace, the importance of ensuring a designed environment responsive to human dimension assumes added significance.

The relationship of human dimension to the executive chair was examined in detail in Section 1, while the general anthropometric theory regarding seating was explored in Section 4 of Part A. Although the drawings indicate the importance of certain body dimensions, including popliteal height and buttock-popliteal length related to the chair, it is the relationship of the seated person to the desk itself that is stressed. In this regard, the importance of thigh clearance and knee height in ensuring proper clearance from the top of the seat to the underside of the desk is illustrated and minimum dimensions suggested. Clearances around the desk, the importance of an overhanging desk top for informal desk conferences, the clearances behind the desk so that credenza and file can be within reach are all reflected in the many design situations examined in the drawings on the following pages. The more significant body measurements to be considered are indicated in the matrix above.

# 3.1 THE PRIVATE OFFICE

The drawing at the top illustrates the basic dimensional requirements of an executive workstation with visitor seating for three. While image and scale often dictate the size of the executive desk and the placement of the furniture around it, the generally accepted size suggested is 30 to 45 by 66 to 84 in, or 76.2 to 114.3 by 167.6 to 213.4 cm. The specific work habits of the executive and the nature of his or her business must be considered in determining the appropriate worksurface measurements.

Critical attention must be given to the selection, placement, and clearances provided for seating around the desk. Both drawings indicate the need to carefully consider the buttock-knee length, hip breadth, and maximum body breadth measurements. The dimensions for the various zones and clearances, while predicated on basic anthropometric considerations, are often a function of circulation within the space and the furniture type.

Buttock-toe length as well as body depth determines placement of a visitor's chair in front of the desk, with the distance from the desk often a function of whether the desk has an overhang. Placement of a hanging fixture must relate to an appropriate determination of eye level and sight lines.

| | in | cm |
|---|---|---|
| A | 30–39 | 76.2–99.1 |
| B | 66–84 | 167.6–213.4 |
| C | 21–28 | 53.3–71.1 |
| D | 24–28 | 61.0–71.1 |
| E | 23–29 | 58.4–73.7 |
| F | 42 min. | 106.7 min. |
| G | 105–130 | 266.7–330.2 |
| H | 30–45 | 76.2–114.3 |
| I | 33–43 | 83.8–109.2 |
| J | 10–14 | 25.4–35.6 |
| K | 6–16 | 15.2–40.6 |
| L | 20–26 | 50.8–66.0 |
| M | 12–15 | 30.5–38.1 |
| N | 117–148 | 297.2–375.9 |
| O | 45–61 | 114.3–154.9 |
| P | 30–45 | 76.2–114.3 |
| Q | 12–18 | 30.5–45.7 |
| R | 29–30 | 73.7–76.2 |
| S | 22–32 | 55.9–81.3 |

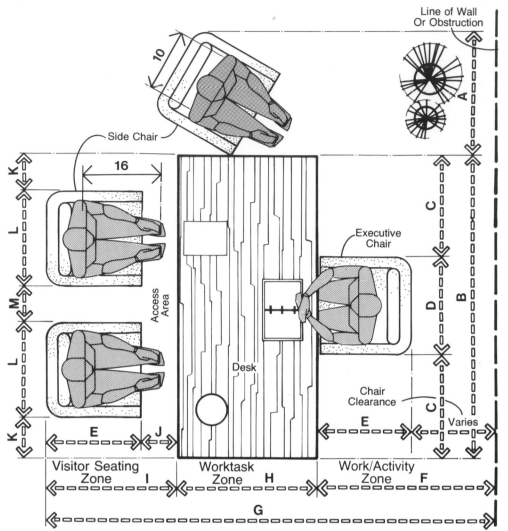

**EXECUTIVE DESK / VISITOR SEATING**

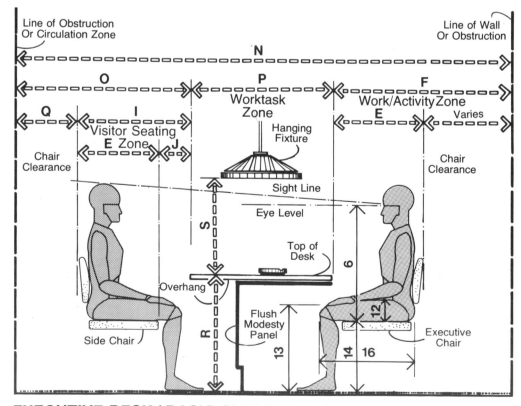

**EXECUTIVE DESK / BASIC CLEARANCES**

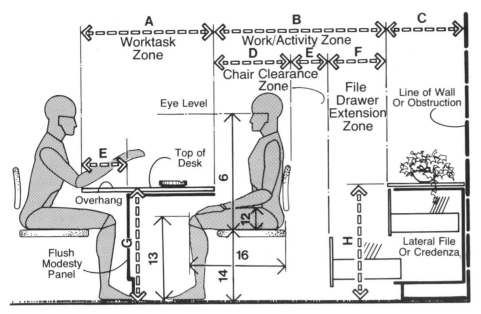

**EXECUTIVE DESK/ BASIC CLEARANCES**

The use of the overhangs, shown on the top drawing, can make a desk suitable for a small conference. As indicated, both knee and toe clearances are a factor. A 42-in, or 106.7-cm, minimum dimension is recommended for the work/activity zone. However, if filing or storage units are provided behind this zone, additional space should be allocated for drawer extension and door swings. In many instances, the work/activity zone distance is also determined by the size of the executive chair, its tilt and swivel mobility, and the work habits of the executive. Side arm reach, as shown in the bottom drawing is often critical in establishing the work/activity zone if specific business equipment, such as calculators, telephones, keyboards, must be within easy reach. The height of the desk as well as that of the credenza behind it will vary from manufacturer to manufacturer. Popliteal height, knee height, and thigh clearance should always be considered in establishing the relationship between seat height and desk height.

Frequently, the executive workstation will be provided with a credenza behind the desk, with vertical storage or shelving above. Assuming that ease of access to the top shelf is of importance, it is recommended that the maximum shelf height to accommodate male reach be no greater than 72 in, or 182.9 cm, and for female reach no greater than 69 in, or 175.3 cm.

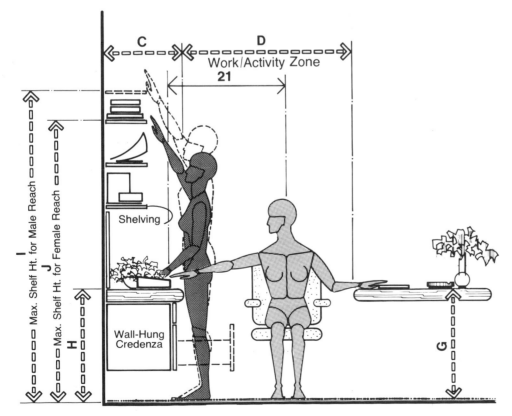

**EXECUTIVE DESK/ CREDENZA CONSIDERATIONS**

| | in | cm |
|---|---|---|
| A | 30–45 | 76.2–114.3 |
| B | 42 min. | 106.7 min. |
| C | 18–24 | 45.7–61.0 |
| D | 23–29 | 58.4–73.7 |
| E | 5–12 | 12.7–30.5 |
| F | 14–22 | 35.6–55.9 |
| G | 29–30 | 73.7–76.2 |
| H | 28–30 | 71.1–76.2 |
| I | 72 max. | 182.9 max. |
| J | 69 max. | 175.3 max. |

# 3.1 THE PRIVATE OFFICE

Many private executive offices are being designed with desks that do not conform with the basic rectangular shape. Such a situation is illustrated in the drawing at the top which shows a circular executive desk. Such a desk is often selected if the executive in question plans to hold conferences within the office and prefers the psychology of having either visitors or employees gather around the worksurface in an egalitarian fashion. While a minimum desk size of 48 in, or 121.9 cm, is shown, this dimension is also influenced by the number of side chairs to be grouped around the desk.

A circular executive desk must be supported by supplementary credenza or file storage within easy reach of the executive chair. Side arm reach relative to the work/activity zone must always be studied carefully.

The drawing at the bottom illustrates a typical circular lounge grouping found within an executive office. Providing for the appropriate leg clearance of 12 to 18 in, or 30.5 to 45.7 cm, is also determined by the sitting zone requirements. Buttock-knee length must also be considered.

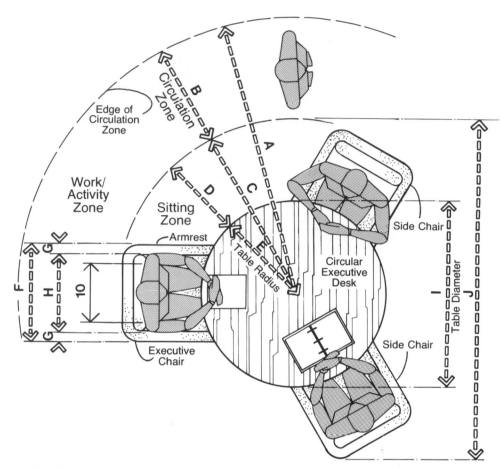

**CIRCULAR EXECUTIVE DESK**

|   | in | cm |
|---|---|---|
| A | 77–88 | 195.6–223.5 |
| B | 30 | 76.2 |
| C | 46–58 | 116.8–147.3 |
| D | 22–28 | 55.9–71.1 |
| E | 24–30 | 61.0–91.4 |
| F | 24–28 | 61.0–71.1 |
| G | 2–3 | 5.1–7.6 |
| H | 20–22 | 50.8–55.9 |
| I | 48–60 | 121.9–152.4 |
| J | 92–116 | 233.7–294.6 |
| K | 36–42 | 91.4–106.7 |
| L | 6–9 | 15.2–22.9 |
| M | 24 | 61.0 |
| N | 42–60 | 106.7–152.4 |
| O | 36–48 | 91.4–121.9 |
| P | 57–78 | 144.8–198.1 |
| Q | 33–48 | 83.8–121.9 |
| R | 12–18 | 30.5–45.7 |
| S | 21–30 | 53.3–76.2 |
| T | 24–32 | 61.0–81.3 |

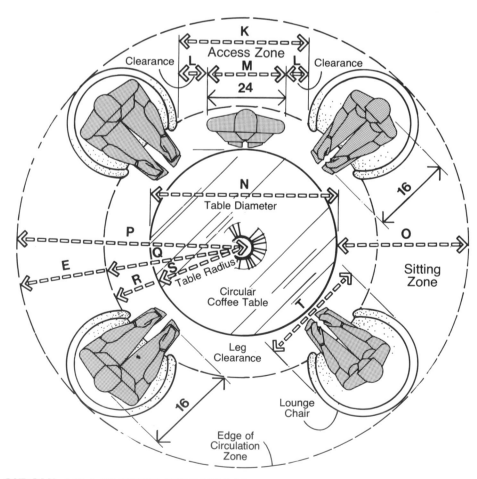

**CIRCULAR LOUNGE GROUPING**

| TABLE | WORKSTATION | FILING | VISUAL | CIRCULATION | ACTIVITIES | | ANTHROPOMETRIC DATA |
|---|---|---|---|---|---|---|---|
| 1A,2B | ◒ | | ◒ | | | 1 | STATURE |
| 1B,3C | ◒ | ◒ | ◒ | | | 2 | EYE HEIGHT |
| 1C,3B | ◒ | ◒ | | | | 3 | ELBOW HEIGHT |
| 1E,2D | ◒ | | ◒ | | | 5 | SITTING HEIGHT NORMAL |
| 1F,3G | ◒ | ◒ | ◒ | | | 6 | EYE HEIGHT SITTING |
| 1L,2H | ● | | | | | 12 | THIGH CLEARANCE |
| 1M,2I | ◒ | | | | | 13 | KNEE HEIGHT |
| 1N,2J | ◒ | | | | | 14 | POPLITEAL HEIGHT |
| 1O,2K | ◒ | | | | | 15 | BUTTOCK-POPLITEAL LENGTH |
| 1P,2L | ◒ | | | | | 16 | BUTTOCK-KNEE LENGTH |
| 1Q,3F | ● | | | | | 17 | BUTTOCK-TOE LENGTH |
| 1V,4D | ○ | | | | | 22 | THUMB TIP REACH |
| 1W,6B | ● | ● | | ● | | 23 | MAXIMUM BODY DEPTH |
| 1X,6A | ● | ● | | ● | | 24 | MAXIMUM BODY BREADTH |

# 3.2 THE GENERAL OFFICE

In the general office as well as the private one, the interface between the seated user and the desk is of central importance. The quality of interface between user and workstation will determine the general comfort and well-being of the office staff and the efficiency of production within the office space.

The proper design of the secretarial chair, its seat height in relation to the popliteal height of the user and the top of the typing return, appropriate backrest design to ensure positive lumbar support, proper height of overhead storage, side arm reach and forward arm reach dimensions of the majority of the users are all extremely critical anthropometric considerations to take into account in the design of general office spaces. Clearance for circulation within general office spaces should accommodate the maximum body breadth and depth of those of larger body size. The relationship of human dimension and body size of the seated person to the filing cabinet is yet another consideration. Eye height of the standing and seated user in relationship to the height of a low partition in an open plan system is one more anthropometric factor to consider. Of importance also is the recognition of the great range in body size between the large and small male, the large and small female, and the large male and small female.

The foregoing considerations are included among the specific design situations examined in the drawings on the following pages, and dimensional data are suggested for use in making preliminary design assumptions. The basic anthropometric measurements to be considered are indicated in the matrix above.

# 3.2 GENERAL OFFICE

The basic workstation, as illustrated in both plan and section on this page, is the fundamental building block in understanding the anthropometric considerations for the planning and design of the general office. The worktask zone must be large enough to accommodate the paperwork, equipment, and other accessories that support the user's function. The work/activity zone dimension, shown on the top drawing, is established by the space requirements needed for use of the typical return. In no case should this distance be less than the 30 in, or 76.2 cm, needed to provide adequate space for the chair clearance zone. The visitor seating zone, ranging in depth from 30 to 42 in, or 76.2 to 106.7 cm, requires the designer to accommodate both the buttock-knee and buttock-toe length body dimensions of the larger user. If an overhang is provided or the desk's modesty panel is recessed, the visitor seating zone can be reduced due to the additional knee and toe clearances provided. The specific type and size of the seating (i.e., if it swivels or if it has casters) also influence these dimensions.

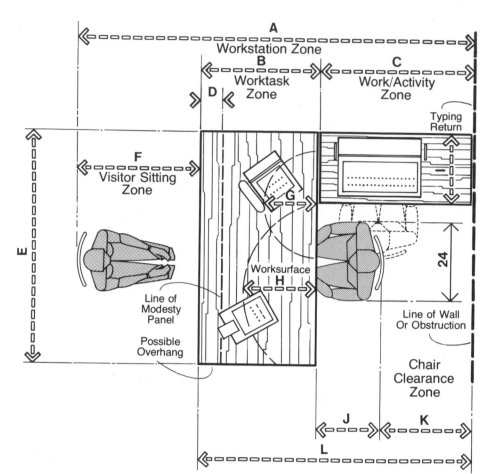

**BASIC WORKSTATION WITH VISITOR SEATING**

| | in | cm |
|---|---|---|
| A | 90–126 | 228.6–320.0 |
| B | 30–36 | 76.2–91.4 |
| C | 30–48 | 76.2–121.9 |
| D | 6–12 | 15.2–30.5 |
| E | 60–72 | 152.4–182.9 |
| F | 30–42 | 76.2–106.7 |
| G | 14–18 | 35.6–45.7 |
| H | 16–20 | 40.6–50.8 |
| I | 18–22 | 45.7–55.9 |
| J | 18–24 | 45.7–61.0 |
| K | 6–24 | 15.2–61.0 |
| L | 60–84 | 152.4–213.4 |
| M | 24–30 | 61.0–76.2 |
| N | 29–30 | 73.7–76.2 |
| O | 15–18 | 38.1–45.7 |

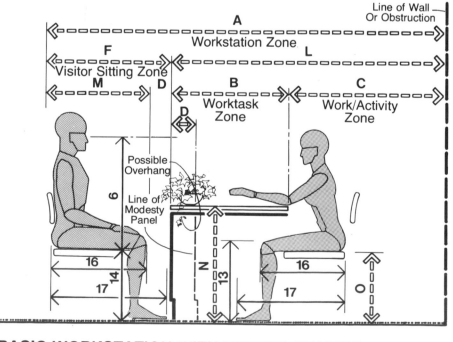

**BASIC WORKSTATION WITH VISITOR SEATING**

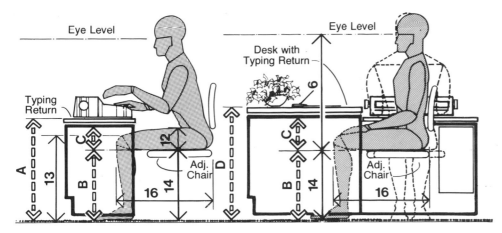

**TYPING RETURN AND DESK / MALE USER**

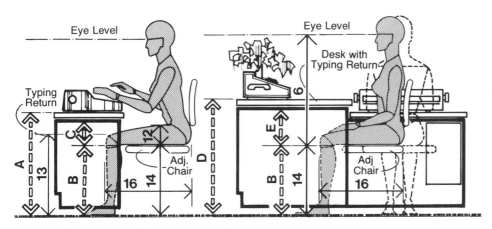

**TYPING RETURN AND DESK / FEMALE USER**

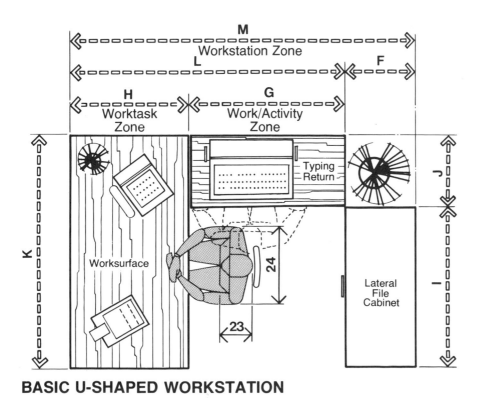

**BASIC U-SHAPED WORKSTATION**

# 3.2 THE GENERAL OFFICE

The two elevations at the top illustrate the major anthropometric considerations for the seated male and female user at both workstation and typing return. What should be noted is the seat height of the chair (a function of popliteal height) and its relationship to the specific task. When the worksurface is lowered to accommodate a specialized function, as in the case of the typing return, special attention must be given to the requirements for thigh clearance. Most standard office typing returns have been geared to the anthropometric requirements of the female user. The popliteal height and thigh clearance requirements of the larger male user may not be readily met.

The plan at the bottom shows the typical workstation expanded into the basic U-shaped configuration. The work/activity zone dimension range is shown as 46 to 58 in, or 116.8 to 147.3 cm; additional space is needed to allow for drawer extension of the lateral file. Not only does it provide more storage, the lateral file unit is generally the same height as that of the worksurface and is often utilized as a supplementary worksurface. The distance between this unit and that of the primary worksurface must be sufficient to allow for movement and rotation of the chair.

|   | in | cm |
|---|-----|-----|
| A | 26–27 | 66.0–68.6 |
| B | 14–20 | 35.6–50.8 |
| C | 7.5 min. | 19.1 min |
| D | 29–30 | 73.7–76.2 |
| E | 7 min. | 17.8 min. |
| F | 18–24 | 45.7–61.0 |
| G | 46–58 | 116.8–147.3 |
| H | 30–36 | 76.2–91.4 |
| I | 42–50 | 106.7–127.0 |
| J | 18–22 | 45.7–55.9 |
| K | 60–72 | 152.4–182.9 |
| L | 76–94 | 193.0–238.8 |
| M | 94–118 | 238.8–299.7 |

# 3.2 THE GENERAL OFFICE

The combined sitting/work zone shown at the top of the page permits the male or female user to rotate 180° for ease of access to a lateral file drawer in the rear. If the minimum clearance shown is not met, access to the file drawer is inhibited, and more awkward body motions or positions for file access are required. A minimum overall dimension to accommodate such a workstation should not be less than 96 in, or 238.8 cm.

In addition to providing appropriate clearance for seat rotation and access to files, it is important to consider the circulation zone requirement for passage behind the seat at the typical workstation. The edge of this zone should take into account the movement of the chair within the chair clearance zone to avoid obstruction of any people circulating behind it. Minimal recommended clearance to allow for that circulation is predicated upon the maximum clothed body breadth of the larger user. Accordingly, this minimum dimension, allowing for the circulation of only one person, should not be less than 30 in, or 76.2 cm. Based upon this minimum dimension and allowing for the requirements of the worktask and chair clearance zones, the overall distance from the front of the worksurface to the line of wall or obstruction should fall between 94 and 114 in, or 238.8 and 289.6 cm.

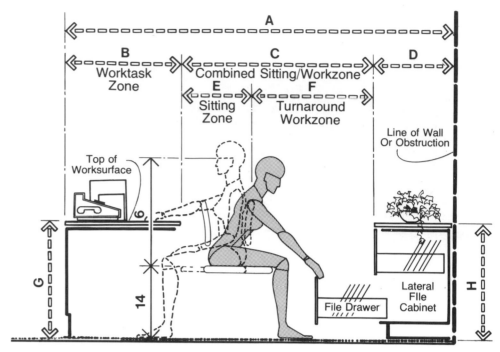

**WORKSTATION WITH BACK LATERAL FILE STORAGE**

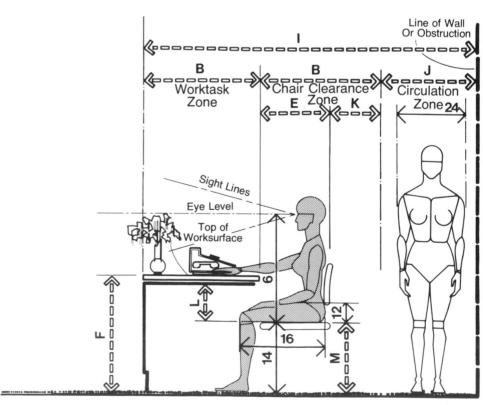

**BASIC WORKSTATION WITH CIRCULATION BEHIND**

|   | in | cm |
|---|---|---|
| A | 96–128 | 243.8–325.1 |
| B | 30–36 | 76.2–91.4 |
| C | 48–68 | 121.9–172.7 |
| D | 18–22 | 45.7–55.8 |
| E | 18–24 | 45.7–61.0 |
| F | 30–44 | 76.2–111.8 |
| G | 29–30 | 73.7–76.2 |
| H | 28–30 | 71.1–76.2 |
| I | 90–102 | 228.6–259.1 |
| J | 30 | 76.2 |
| K | 12 | 30.5 |
| L | 7.5 min. | 19.1 min. |
| M | 15–18 | 38.1–45.7 |

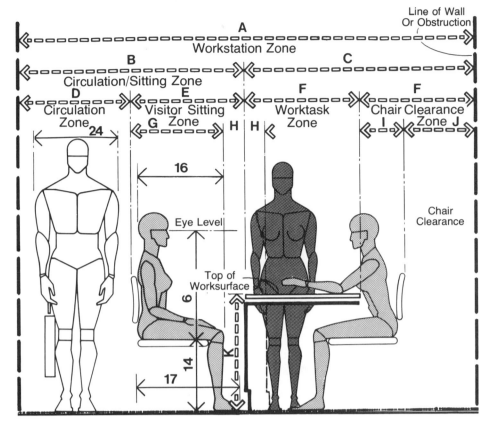

**BASIC WORKSTATION WITH VISITOR SEATING AND CIRCULATION**

## 3.2 THE GENERAL OFFICE

Anthropometrically, the circulation zone and the visitor seating zone must accommodate both maximum body breadth and buttock-toe length measurements of the larger person. Note that in the illustration shown, the visitor seating zone is within an initial range of 24 to 30 in, or 61 to 76.2 cm. Allowing additional clearance from knee to edge of workstation of 6 to 12 in, or 15.2 to 30.4 cm, an overall visitor seating zone ranges from 30 to 42 in, or 76.2 to 106.7 cm. This assumes that the individual in the visitor's chair does not push it back when coming or going, but will stand and then move laterally in the space allocated. It should also be noted that the lack of a desk top overhang does not provide an adequate interface between visitor and desk for close-up conferences. The circulation zone dimension is shown as a minimum of 36 in, or 91.4 cm. In addition to maximum body breadth, the figure in this illustration is shown carrying an attache case in his hand. The attache case is there to suggest that in those circulation zones, where the carrying of objects (documents, trays, files) is required, additional space must be allocated for that function. The elevation at the bottom shows a circulation zone adjacent to the worktask zone that is wide enough to permit clear passage of two people. A minimum dimension of 60 in, or 152.4 cm, is allowed for here, considering once again maximum body breadth constraints.

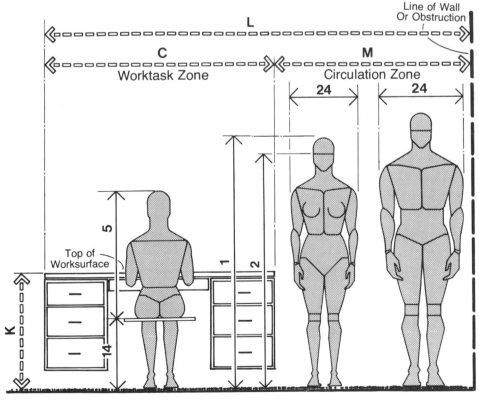

**WORKSTATION AND ADJACENT CIRCULATION**

|   | in | cm |
|---|---|---|
| A | 126–150 | 320.0–381.0 |
| B | 66–78 | 167.6–198.1 |
| C | 60–72 | 152.4–182.9 |
| D | 36 | 91.4 |
| E | 30–42 | 76.2–106.7 |
| F | 30–36 | 76.2–91.4 |
| G | 24–30 | 61.0–76.2 |
| H | 6–12 | 15.2–30.5 |
| I | 12–16 | 30.5–40.6 |
| J | 18–20 | 45.7–50.8 |
| K | 29–30 | 73.7–76.2 |
| L | 120–132 | 304.8–335.3 |
| M | 60 | 152.4 |

# 3.2 THE GENERAL OFFICE

The general office, as it is known today in both conventional and open office planning systems, consists of similar workstations arranged in various configurations. The top drawing shows two such workstations in a typical row arrangement. Basic anthropometric requirements previously established for the individual workstation are used in establishing the dimensions shown. Buttock-knee length and buttock-toe length are the major anthropometric measurements to be considered in establishing the overall dimension shown; they range from 120 to 132 in, or 304.6 to 381 cm. This drawing also involves two other anthropometric measurements: eye height sitting and eye height standing. The importance of these dimensions is addressed later in this section.

Grouping the typical workstation in a U-shaped configuration is illustrated in the plan at the bottom of this page. Such a grouping is often used when the people assigned to the paired workstation share common responsibilities or work together on joint tasks or where the sharing of the combined workstation zone results in saving floor space. When such space is shared, the notion of territory is sometimes obscured due to the lack of any clear lines of demarcation. Clearly, the U-shaped configuration, in comparison with the row arrangement at the top, is less restrictive and less confining to the user.

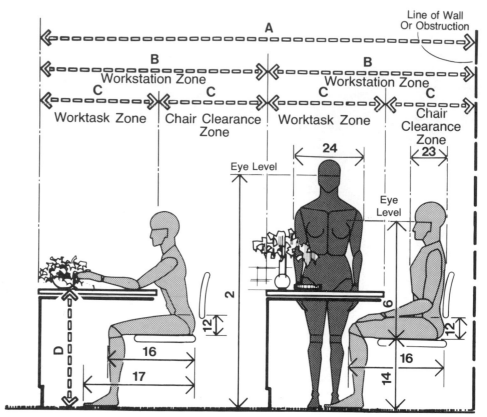

**ADJACENT WORKSTATIONS / ROW ARRANGEMENT**

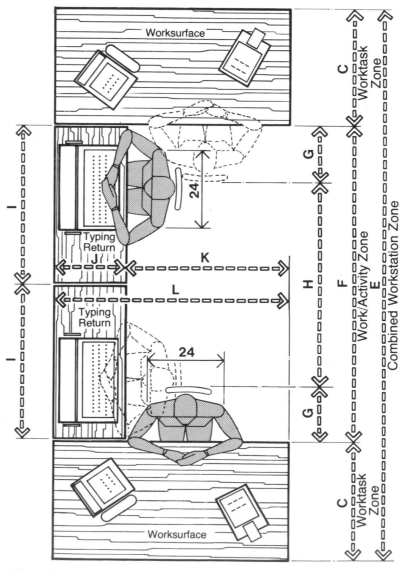

**ADJACENT WORKSTATIONS/U-SHAPE**

|   | in | cm |
|---|---|---|
| A | 120–144 | 304.8–365.8 |
| B | 60–72 | 152.4–182.9 |
| C | 30–36 | 76.2–91.4 |
| D | 29–30 | 73.7–76.2 |
| E | 120–168 | 304.8–426.7 |
| F | 60–96 | 152.4–243.8 |
| G | 18–24 | 45.7–61.0 |
| H | 24–48 | 61.0–121.9 |
| I | 30–48 | 76.2–121.9 |
| J | 18–22 | 45.7–55.9 |
| K | 42–50 | 106.7–127.0 |
| L | 60–72 | 152.4–182.9 |

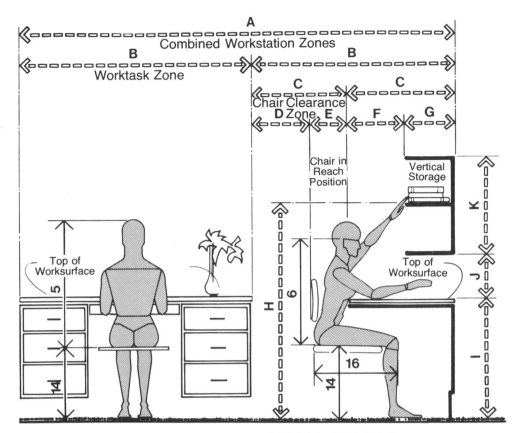

**BASIC WORKSTATION WITH VERTICAL STORAGE**

# 3.2 THE GENERAL OFFICE

With office space becoming more expensive to construct and lease, it has become necessary for designers of the office environment to develop ways in which to utilize space more efficiently. The illustrations on this page focus on vertical storage over the horizontal worksurface plane.

The drawing at the top shows the basic workstation with storage located above the top of the worksurface. With the chair placed in the reach position for the user, the height of the upper shelf above the floor should fall between 53 and 58 in, or 134.6 and 147.3 cm. The vertical storage unit above the plane of the horizontal worksurface serves an additional purpose, as demonstrated by the bottom drawing. At the height shown on this drawing, the 95th percentile eye height standing is approximately the same elevation as that of the storage element. The subdivision of space, thereby providing some degree of visual privacy, is accomplished without constructing more permanent floor-to-ceiling partitions.

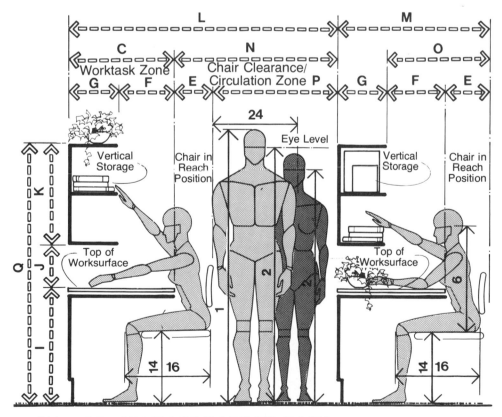

**BASIC WORKSTATIONS BACK TO BACK WITH VERTICAL STORAGE**

|   | in | cm |
|---|---|---|
| A | 120–144 | 304.8–365.8 |
| B | 60–72 | 152.4–182.9 |
| C | 30–36 | 76.2–91.4 |
| D | 18–20 | 45.7–50.8 |
| E | 12–16 | 30.5–40.6 |
| F | 18–24 | 45.7–61.0 |
| G | 12 | 30.5 |
| H | 53–58 | 134.6–147.3 |
| I | 29–30 | 73.7–76.2 |
| J | 15 min. | 38.1 min. |
| K | 25–31 | 63.5–78.7 |
| L | 78–94 | 198.1–258.8 |
| M | 42–52 | 106.7–132.1 |
| N | 48–58 | 121.9–147.3 |
| O | 30–40 | 76.2–101.6 |
| P | 36–42 | 91.4–106.7 |
| Q | 69–76 | 175.3–193.0 |

# 3.2 THE GENERAL OFFICE

A typical situation that occurs in planning the general office is the relationship of the basic desk or workstation to filing and storage. The drawing at the top of the page shows a sitting zone of 18 to 24 in, or 45.7 to 61 cm. Reflected within this range are buttock-knee length and buttock-toe length measurements. Circulation behind the desk is obstructed when the drawer of the lateral file cabinet is in an extended position. When the file drawer is in the closed position, a 30-in, or 76.2-cm, circulation zone is provided.

The drawing shown on the bottom of the page demonstrates the relationship of the workstation with a circulation zone behind it, as well as an allowance for full extension of the file drawer. The distance the extended file drawer projects is a function of the type of file storage unit. An overall dimension range of 48 and 56 in, or 121.9 and 142.2 cm, is provided to accommodate a circulation zone and the file drawer in its extended position. It should be noted, however, that if constant access to the file cabinets is necessary, the circulation zone will be violated, in which case a different plan arrangement should be considered.

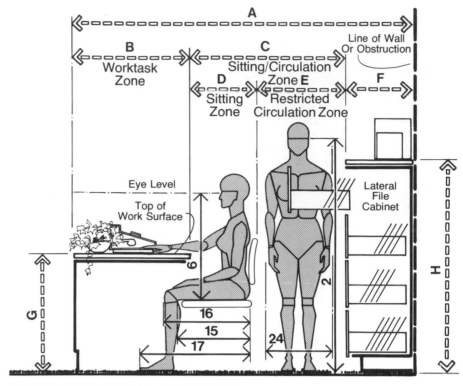

**DESK WITH FILING, STORAGE, AND RESTRICTED CIRCULATION**

|   | in | cm |
|---|---|---|
| **A** | 96–112 | 243.8–284.5 |
| **B** | 30–36 | 76.2–91.4 |
| **C** | 48–54 | 121.9–137.2 |
| **D** | 18–24 | 45.7–61.0 |
| **E** | 30 | 76.2 |
| **F** | 18–22 | 45.7–55.9 |
| **G** | 29–30 | 73.7–76.2 |
| **H** | 54–58 | 137.2–147.3 |
| **I** | 110–136 | 279.4–345.4 |
| **J** | 42–52 | 106.7–132.1 |
| **K** | 48–56 | 121.9–142.2 |
| **L** | 20–28 | 50.8–71.1 |
| **M** | 12–16 | 30.5–40.6 |
| **N** | 18–26 | 45.7–66.0 |

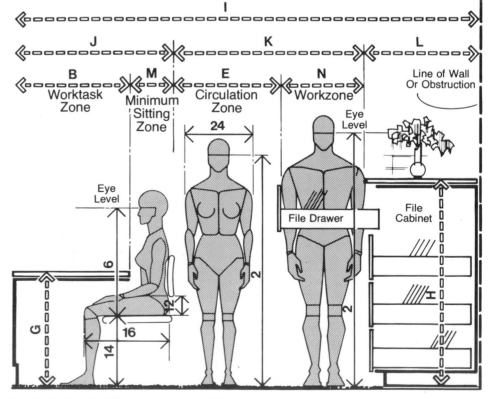

**DESK WITH FILING AND STORAGE**

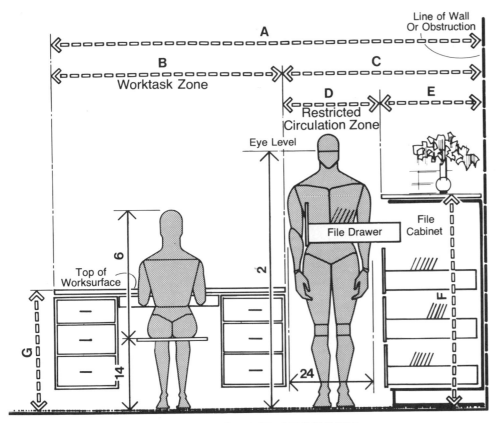

**WORKSTATION WITH FILING AND STORAGE**

## 3.2 THE GENERAL OFFICE

As the drawing at the top clearly demonstrates, an obstructed circulation zone results if appropriate consideration is not given to the extension of the file drawer. Such a situation must be avoided at all costs, unless the file cabinet in question is clearly used for dead files or the circulation zone is one of limited usage. The drawing at bottom, however, shows proper filing and access clearances. Access to the extended drawer has been provided both from the side and from the front. The work zone, specifically provided for filing, accommodates the anthropometric dimension of body depth, in addition to allowing for the extended file drawer. Immediately contiguous to the file work zone is a semiactive circulation zone of 36 in, or 91.4 cm, based upon maximum body breadth of the larger person. A 36-in, or 91.4-cm, dimension should be utilized instead of 30 in, or 76.2 cm, if the person using that path of circulation is also carrying files, folders, and so forth.

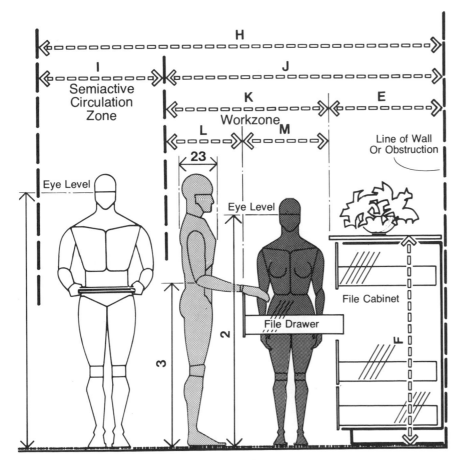

**FILING/ACCESS CLEARANCES**

|   | in | cm |
|---|---|---|
| A | 110–130 | 279.4–330.2 |
| B | 60–72 | 152.4–182.9 |
| C | 50–58 | 127.0–147.3 |
| D | 30 | 76.2 |
| E | 20–28 | 50.8–71.1 |
| F | 54–58 | 137.2–147.3 |
| G | 29–30 | 73.7–76.2 |
| H | 92–108 | 233.7–274.3 |
| I | 36 | 91.4 |
| J | 56–72 | 142.2–182.9 |
| K | 36–44 | 91.4–111.8 |
| L | 18 | 45.7 |
| M | 18–26 | 45.7–66.0 |

# 3.2 THE GENERAL OFFICE

In many offices, file storage can be found lining the edges of a circulation zone. The combined work/circulation zone illustrated at the top of the page shows clearance required for a larger person to circulate between two extended file drawers. With opposing drawers fully extended, unobstructed circulation is clearly limited. If, however, the file drawers are separated by several feet along the path of circulation and access to the drawer is from the side, it is possible to provide circulation for two people.

The drawing at the bottom shows the space required within a typical file storage room where through circulation is not a major consideration. Depending upon the height of the file drawer, the human body must assume different positions to gain free and clear access. The male figure shown kneeling requires a space of 36 in, or 91.4 cm, for clearance. At the same time, the minimum work area needed for a person standing in front of a file has been established at 18 in, or 45.7 cm.

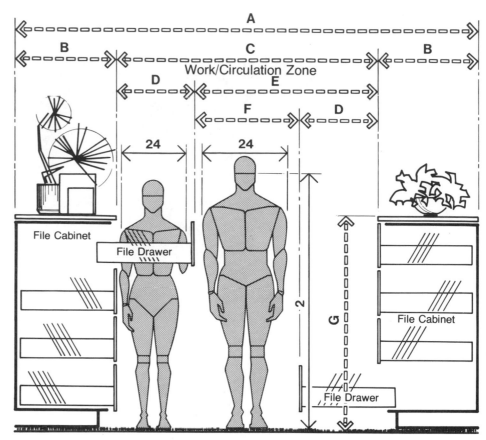

**FILING/ACCESS CLEARANCES**

|   | in | cm |
|---|---|---|
| A | 106–138 | 269.2–350.5 |
| B | 20–28 | 50.8–71.1 |
| C | 66–82 | 167.6–208.3 |
| D | 18–26 | 45.7–66.0 |
| E | 48–56 | 121.9–142.2 |
| F | 30 | 76.2 |
| G | 54–58 | 137.2–147.3 |
| H | 122–138 | 309.9–350.5 |
| I | 34–42 | 86.4–106.7 |
| J | 40–54 | 101.6–137.2 |
| K | 18–22 | 45.7–55.9 |
| L | 16–20 | 40.6–50.8 |
| M | 18 | 45.7 |
| N | 22–36 | 55.9–91.4 |

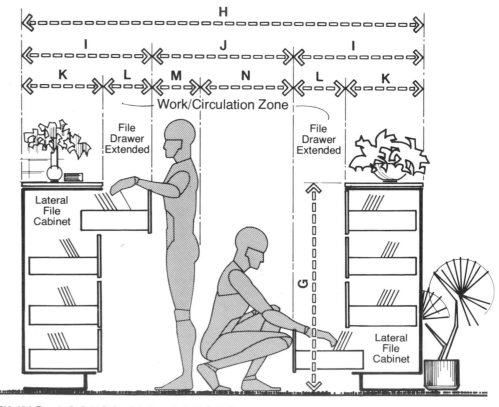

**FILING ACCESS CLEARANCES**

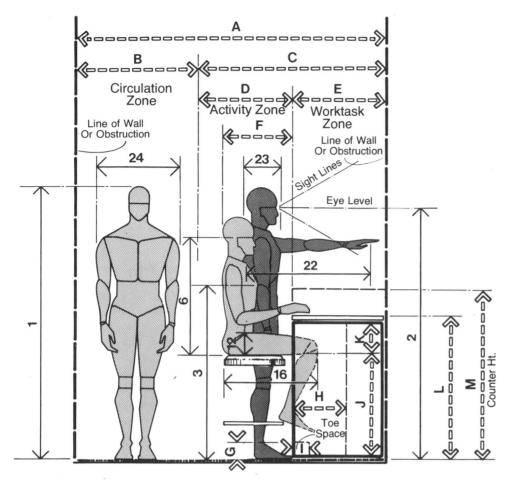

**WORK COUNTER / MALE USER**

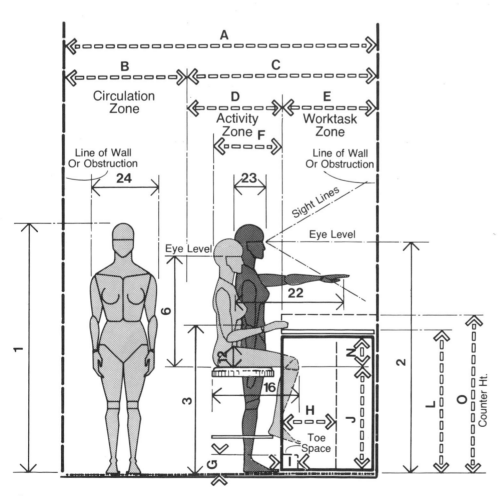

**WORKCOUNTER / FEMALE USER**

# 3.2 THE GENERAL OFFICE

Within the general office, worktasks must be performed on horizontal counter-type worksurfaces. These tasks are performed while the male or female user is standing or sitting on a stool or perch-type seat. Many factors influence the design of this type of workstation, including the specific nature of the work being performed. Of critical importance in anthropometrically establishing the appropriate counter height is the elbow height measurement. A range of 34 to 39 in, or 86.4 to 99.1 cm, is recommended for counter height to accommodate a stool and of 40 to 44 in, or 101.6 to 111.8 cm, to accommodate a male or female user in a standing position.

Eye height must be considered if the counter height task relates to visual displays or controls. To the extent that ease of access to these displays or controls is of importance anthropometrically, the thumb tip reach measurement of the smaller person is critical in establishing proper counter depth. The designer must also be concerned with thigh clearance and buttock-knee length in finalizing any design. (For additional discussion, see Section 7.3, Work and Crafts Centers, and Section 9.2, Workstation Displays.)

| | in | cm |
|---|---|---|
| A | 68–96 | 172.7–243.8 |
| B | 30–36 | 76.2–91.4 |
| C | 38–60 | 96.5–152.4 |
| D | 20–24 | 50.8–61.0 |
| E | 18–36 | 45.7–91.4 |
| F | 18 | 45.7 |
| G | 3 | 7.6 |
| H | 14–18 | 35.6–45.7 |
| I | 4 | 10.2 |
| J | 22–24.5 | 55.9–62.2 |
| K | 7.5 min. | 19.1 min. |
| L | 34–39 | 86.4–99.1 |
| M | 42–44 | 106.7–111.8 |
| N | 7 min. | 17.8 min. |
| O | 40–42 | 101.6–106.7 |

# 3.2 THE GENERAL OFFICE

The growth and development of open office planning and office landscape systems have spurred the design and manufacture of numerous free-standing low partitions or privacy screens. These partitions are used to subdivide office space, providing various degrees of acoustic and visual privacy, and to define territory and circulation paths. A basic decision always confronting the designer concerns the height of the partition system. The information provided on this page represents a survey of privacy screens manufactured by some of the largest producers of office systems furniture and equipment. All are shown in relation to the large and small male and female user in both a sitting and standing position.

In considering the selection of the appropriate partition or screen height, the anthropometric dimensions of critical importance are those of eye height standing and eye height sitting. It should be understood, however, that sight lines are also important in establishing visual privacy. What should be considered too is the nature of the visual privacy desired. Is the seated person on one side of the screen to be shielded from the view of a standing or seated person on the other side of the screen? Is the seated person to be permitted to look over the screen? The purpose of the privacy screen will determine if seated or standing eye level data should be used and if that data should be 5th or 95th percentile data. (More detailed information on vision and sight lines can be found in Section 9.1.)

| | in | cm |
|---|---|---|
| A | 40–44 | 101.6–111.8 |
| B | 47–50 | 119.4–127.0 |
| C | 60–64 | 152.4–162.6 |
| D | 78–80 | 198.1–203.2 |
| E | 96 | 243.8 |

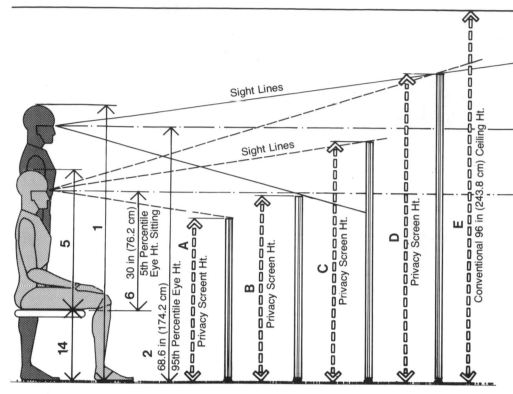

**LANDSCAPE PARTITIONS/MALE ANTHROPOMETRIC CONSIDERATIONS**

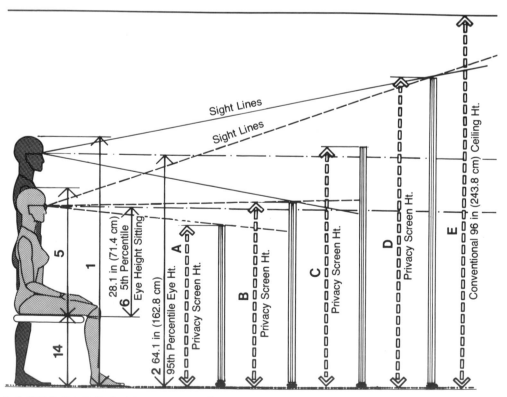

**LANDSCAPE PARTITIONS/FEMALE ANTHROPOMETRIC CONSIDERATIONS**

| TABLE | VISUAL | WORKSTATION | SEATING | CIRCULATION | ACTIVITIES | ANTHROPOMETRIC DATA | |
|---|---|---|---|---|---|---|---|
| 1A,2B | | ● | | | | 1 | STATURE |
| 1B,3C | ◐ | ◐ | | | | 2 | EYE HEIGHT |
| 1F,3G | ◐ | ◐ | | | | 6 | EYE HEIGHT SITTING |
| 1J,2F | | | ● | | | 10 | HIP BREADTH |
| 1L,2H | | ● | | | | 12 | THIGH CLEARANCE |
| 1P,2L | | ● | ● | | | 16 | BUTTOCK-KNEE LENGTH |
| 1U,4E | | ○ | | | | 21 | SIDE ARM REACH |
| 1W,6B | | ● | ● | ● | | 23 | MAXIMUM BODY DEPTH |
| 1X,6A | | ● | ● | ● | | 24 | MAXIMUM BODY BREADTH |

# 3.3 RECEPTION SPACES

The drawings on the following pages examine the relationship of human dimension to the design of reception spaces. The three key areas of concern include visitor seating, the reception desk, and location of graphics or corporate identification. In regard to seating, the clearances around the seating elements to accommodate circulation are stressed more than the design of the individual seating unit itself, which is examined in more detail in Section 4 of Part A and Section 1 of Part C. Of particular importance is the design of the reception desk in terms of its responsiveness to the anthropometric requirements of the seated receptionist and the standing visitor within the context of a high counter-type arrangement and a conventional desk arrangement.

The depth of the worksurface should accommodate the thumb tip reach measurements of the user of smaller body size so that packages and correspondence can be exchanged. Of equal importance is eye height sitting to ensure visibility over the counter and eye contact with the standing visitor. Eye height of both the seated and standing person is also essential in establishing the height and location of corporate signage or other graphic material to ensure its visibility. Details of such elements of reception spaces are included in this section as well as suggested clearances and other dimensions for use in preliminary design assumptions. The key anthropometric measurements are indicated in the above matrix.

# 3.3 RECEPTION SPACES

The corporate logo is often displayed within the reception room. Since it is used to graphically identify the tenant, it must be placed in a visually prominent location. The drawing at the top of the page indicates the critical anthropometric measurements to be considered. The eye height of the smaller and larger seated and standing viewer defines the visual ranges to be considered. The specific vertical and horizontal dimensions of the company identification or display should vary with the distance of the viewer from the display as well as the design intent of the graphics. (Section 9 in Part C should be consulted for additional information on sight lines.)

Illustrated at the bottom of the page is the circular workstation sometimes used in relatively large reception spaces. Two major factors that influence the ultimate size of this element are the minimum radius to accommodate the receptionist within the inner circular area and the circumference of the outer perimeter available to accommodate visitors.

The key anthropometric body dimensions required to accommodate the receptionist are that of buttock-knee length and body depth, permitting the movement and clearance of the chair. The minimum recommended diameter is shown as 44 in, or 111.8 cm. The depth of the worksurface, anthropometrically, should accommodate the side arm reach and thumb tip reach dimensions of the smaller person. A dimension in the range of 24 to 30 in, or 61 to 76.2 cm, is recommended.

|   | in | cm |
|---|------|------|
| A | 22 | 55.9 |
| B | 46–52 | 116.8–132.1 |
| C | 18–22 | 45.7–55.9 |
| D | 24–30 | 61.0–76.2 |
| E | 44 | 111.8 |
| F | 76 | 193.0 |
| G | 92–104 | 233.7–264.2 |

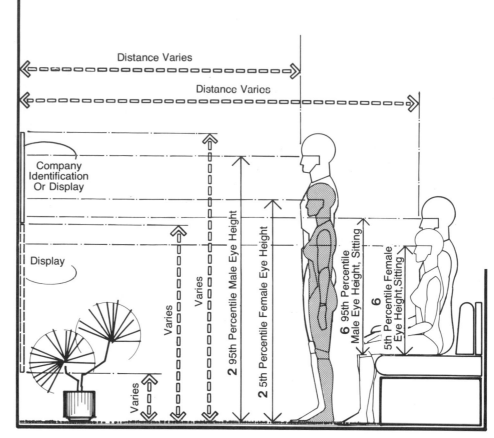

**DISPLAY / VISUAL RELATIONSHIPS**

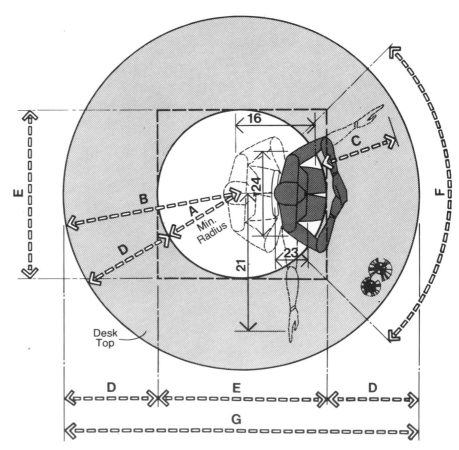

**CIRCULAR RECEPTIONIST'S WORKSTATION**

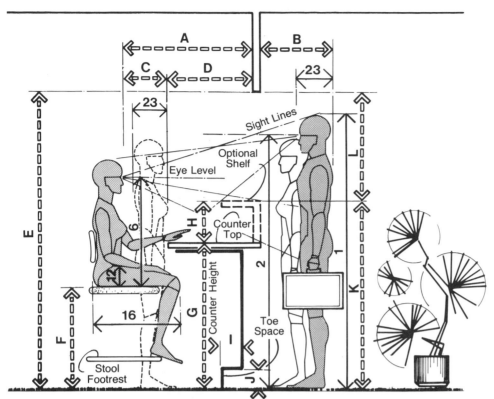

**RECEPTIONIST'S WORKSTATION / COUNTER HEIGHT**

# 3.3 RECEPTION SPACES

For the purpose of privacy or security, the receptionist's workstation is often an area physically separated by built-in furniture and/or partitions. The drawing at the top of the page shows a counter height receptionist's workstation. While the relationship of worksurface to seat height is key, other anthropometric considerations are eye height and sitting height normal. The minimum height of the opening above the floor has been established at 78 in, or 198.1 cm. Sitting height and eye height are significant in providing unobstructed vision. The drawing at the bottom depicts a desk height receptionist's workstation. The depth of the worksurface ranges from 26 to 30 in, or 66 to 76.2 cm, allowing for thumb tip reach required for the exchange of papers and packages. Both drawings show in broken line an added counter top element often provided for security or as a visual screen of the worksurface top.

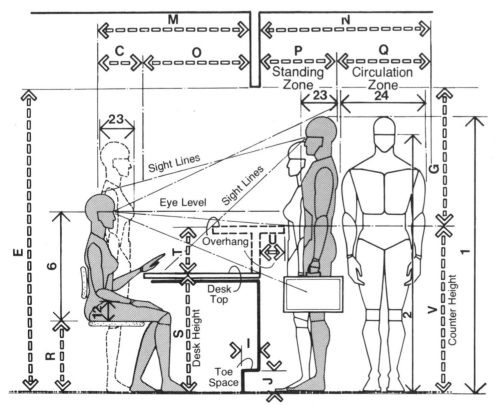

**RECEPTIONIST'S WORKSTATION / DESK HEIGHT**

|   | in | cm |
|---|---|---|
| A | 40–48 | 101.6–121.9 |
| B | 24 min. | 61.0 min. |
| C | 18 | 45.7 |
| D | 22–30 | 55.9–76.2 |
| E | 78 min. | 198.1 min. |
| F | 24–27 | 61.0–68.6 |
| G | 36–39 | 91.4–99.1 |
| H | 8–9 | 20.3–22.9 |
| I | 2–4 | 5.1–10.2 |
| J | 4 | 10.2 |
| K | 44–48 | 111.8–121.9 |
| L | 34 min. | 86.4 min. |
| M | 44–48 | 111.8–121.9 |
| N | 54 | 137.2 |
| O | 26–30 | 66.0–76.2 |
| P | 24 | 61.0 |
| Q | 30 | 76.2 |
| R | 15–18 | 38.1–45.7 |
| S | 29–30 | 73.7–76.2 |
| T | 10–12 | 25.4–30.5 |
| U | 6–9 | 15.2–22.9 |
| V | 39–42 | 99.1–106.7 |

# 3.3 RECEPTION SPACES

Typical reception room visitor seating arrangements are shown on this page, with emphasis on the individual seating unit instead of sofa-type seating. While the width of the individual seating unit varies, certain key anthropometric dimensions influence the placement of the unit as well as the overall dimensions. The primary anthropometric dimension determining seat width is that of hip breadth. Seat depth is determined by the buttock-popliteal length measurement. For a more detailed discussion of seating design criteria, Section 4 in Part A and Section 1 in Part C should be consulted. Location of the armchair in relation to a coffee table must take into account two conflicting requirements: clearance for circulation between chair and table and placement of the table to accommodate the reach limitations of the smaller person. There is no perfect solution. A distance between 15 and 18 in, or 38.1 and 45.7 cm, however, allows for the leg projection of the seated person and also accommodates the maximum body depth of the larger person so that he may sidestep, if necessary, to pass. Some body contact and/or adjustment of body position or posture of both seated and standing person may be required.

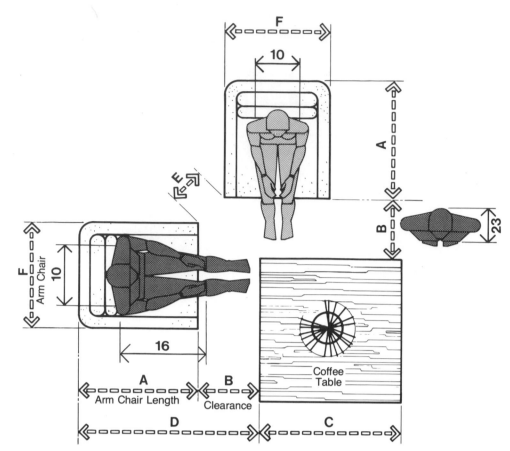

**RECEPTION ROOM SEATING**

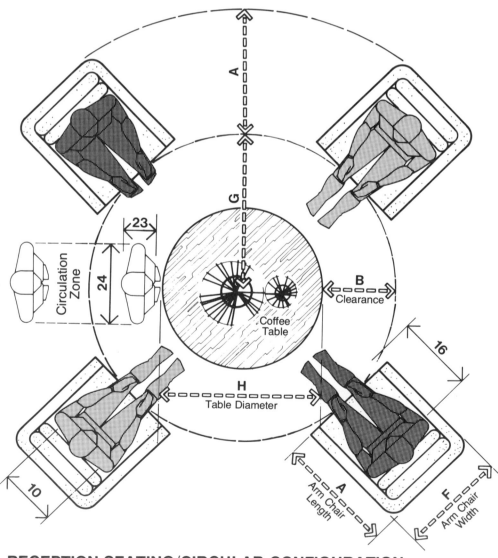

**RECEPTION SEATING/CIRCULAR CONFIGURATION**

|   | in | cm |
|---|---|---|
| A | 28–32 | 71.1–81.3 |
| B | 15–18 | 38.1–45.7 |
| C | 30–48 | 76.2–121.9 |
| D | 43–50 | 109.2–127.0 |
| E | 9–12 | 22.9–30.5 |
| F | 28–36 | 71.1–91.4 |
| G | 33–42 | 83.8–106.7 |
| H | 36–48 | 91.4–121.9 |

## 3.4 CONFERENCE ROOMS

| TABLE | TABLE | AUDIOVISUAL | CIRCULATION | ACTIVITIES | ANTHROPOMETRIC DATA | |
|---|---|---|---|---|---|---|
| 1F,3G | ◑ | ◑ | | | 6 | EYE HEIGHT SITTING |
| 1L,2H | ● | | | | 12 | THIGH CLEARANCE |
| 1M,2I | ● | | | | 13 | KNEE HEIGHT |
| 1N,2J | ◑ | | | | 14 | POPLITEAL HEIGHT |
| 1O,2K | ◑ | | | | 15 | BUTTOCK-POPLITEAL LENGTH |
| 1P,2L | ● | | | | 16 | BUTTOCK-KNEE LENGTH |
| 1W,6B | ● | ● | ● | | 23 | MAXIMUM BODY DEPTH |
| 1X,6A | ● | ● | ● | | 24 | MAXIMUM BODY BREADTH |

The general approach in establishing conference table sizes is much the same as that used for dining tables. Instead of the place setting used with dining tables, a workzone to accommodate documents, papers, and other reference materials should be taken into consideration. The amount of material to be accommodated, however, may vary greatly depending on the nature of the organization involved and the type of meeting. The amount of perimeter space allocated to each individual should at the very least be adequate to accommodate the maximum body breadth, allow for the extension of the elbows away from the body, and provide for documents and other material. If public hearings or meetings involving a large degree of formality and protocol are involved, allowances around the table may be increased so significantly as to make the accommodation of human dimension academic. The other factor to be considered in conjunction with seat spacing is its effect on sight lines directed at either end of the table. Clearances around the table for circulation should accommodate the maximum body breadth of the user of larger body size and allow for the space taken up by the chair itself. The drawings on the following pages illustrate various table configurations and include dimensional data suggested for use in making preliminary design assumptions. The key anthropometric data to be considered is indicated in the above matrix.

# 3.4 CONFERENCE ROOMS

The two drawings at the top of the page illustrate a square and a circular conference arrangement for four people. Such a minimal-size table might be found within a small room or, more commonly, interspersed within the framework of a larger space or open office plan. A recommended distance of 18 to 24 in, or 45.7 to 61 cm, is shown for the distance required from the edge of the table to the back of the chair, with the chair in a normal position. Anthropometric considerations determining this dimension are buttock-knee length and maximum body depth measurements of people of larger body size.

The drawing at the bottom of the page shows the typical relationship of two people sitting across from each other at a conference table. The distance across the table becomes an important factor if papers are to be exchanged. A width of 36 to 54 in, or 91.4 to 137.2 cm, is recommended. Table height should also be analyzed for its relationship to popliteal height, knee height, and thigh clearance. A range of 29 to 30 in, or 73.7 to 76.2 cm, is preferred, with the smaller dimension favored where writing tasks are emphasized.

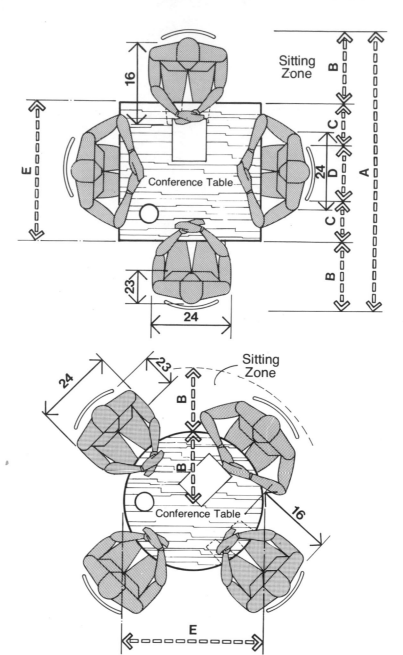

**CONFERENCE TABLES / SQUARE AND CIRCULAR**

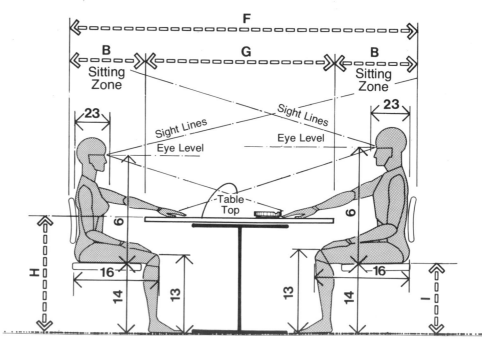

**CONFERENCE TABLES / GENERAL MALE AND FEMALE CONSIDERATIONS**

|   | in | cm |
|---|---|---|
| A | 72–96 | 182.9–243.8 |
| B | 18–24 | 45.7–61.0 |
| C | 8–12 | 20.3–30.5 |
| D | 20–24 | 50.8–61.0 |
| E | 36–48 | 91.4–121.9 |
| F | 72–102 | 182.9–259.1 |
| G | 36–54 | 91.4–137.2 |
| H | 29–30 | 73.7–76.2 |
| I | 16–17 | 40.6–43.2 |

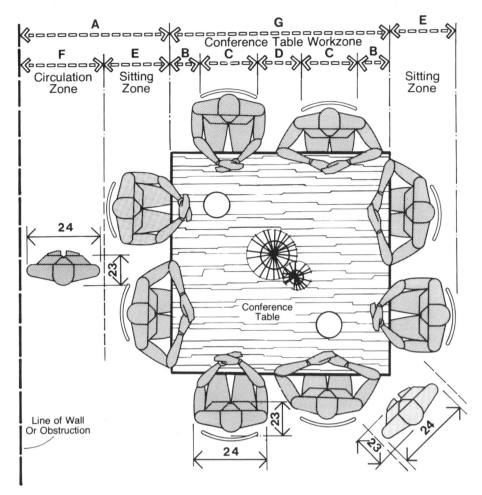

**SQUARE CONFERENCE TABLE**

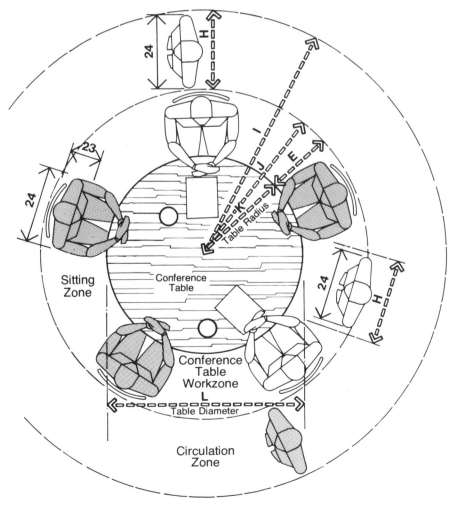

**CIRCULAR CONFERENCE TABLE**

# 3.4 CONFERENCE ROOMS

Consideration must be given to clearances and circulation around the larger conference table, as indicated on the drawings. A minimum of 48 in, or 121.9 cm, is suggested from the edge of the table to the wall or nearest obstruction. This dimension under ordinary circumstance allows for a circulation zone beyond the sitting zone of 30 to 36 in, or 76.2 to 91.4 cm, based upon a maximum body breadth measurement of the larger person. The greater dimension is recommended to allow for the chair in a pulled-out position.

The actual dimensions of the conference table are a function of the number of people to be seated. The square table illustrated provides for eight people, with each side ranging from 54 to 60 in, or 137.2 to 152.4 cm. The larger dimension is more appropriate to accommodate people of larger body size and to allow for a more generous work zone for each person. This translates into 30 in, or 76.2 cm, per person, which constitutes a comfortable perimeter allocation. The circular table at the bottom comfortably accommodates five people while allowing for a 30-in, or 76.2-cm, access zone between chairs. To accommodate both sitting zone and circulation zone, a space with a radius ranging from 72 to 81 in, or 182.9 to 205.7 cm, must be provided.

|   | in | cm |
|---|-----|-----|
| A | 48–60 | 121.9–152.4 |
| B | 4–6 | 10.2–15.2 |
| C | 20–24 | 50.8–61.0 |
| D | 6–10 | 15.2–25.4 |
| E | 18–24 | 45.7–61.0 |
| F | 30–36 | 76.2–91.4 |
| G | 54–60 | 137.2–152.4 |
| H | 30 | 76.2 |
| I | 72–81 | 182.9–205.7 |
| J | 42–51 | 106.7–129.5 |
| K | 24–27 | 61.0–68.6 |
| L | 48–54 | 121.9–137.2 |

# 3.4 CONFERENCE ROOMS

The drawing at the top of the page represents a U-shaped conference table that might ordinarily be associated with a large-scale corporate board meeting or a public hearing. Such an arrangement, in addition to the basic anthropometric considerations mentioned on the previous pages, must also accommodate access and circulation. In the situation shown, the conference table work zone includes an internal circulation zone for two people, with maximum body breadth the controlling factor in establishing the 54- to 60-in, or 137.2- to 152.4-cm, clearance.

The spacing of chairs is not only important in terms of defining appropriate work zones at the table, but essential in providing optimal sight lines where the room must also incorporate an audiovisual wall. As indicated in the two plans at the bottom of the page, a minimal clearance between chairs creates an unnecessarily large obstructed vision area, compared with the limited obstructed vision area when the chair spacing is increased. Sight lines and angles of vision are also a function of the distance of the table edge to the audiovisual wall. A minimum of 72 in, or 182.8 cm, is recommended. (Section 9, Audiovisual Spaces, in Part C should be consulted for more specific information.)

| | in | cm |
|---|---|---|
| A | 138–180 | 350.5–457.2 |
| B | 18–24 | 45.7–61.0 |
| C | 12–21 | 30.5–53.3 |
| D | 32–36 | 81.3–91.4 |
| E | 14–18 | 35.6–45.7 |
| F | 108–132 | 274.3–335.3 |
| G | 24–36 | 61.0–91.4 |
| H | 60 | 152.4 |
| I | 30 | 76.2 |
| J | 72 | 182.9 |
| K | 24–28 | 61.0–71.1 |
| L | 3–6 | 7.6–15.2 |
| M | 12–16 | 30.5–40.6 |

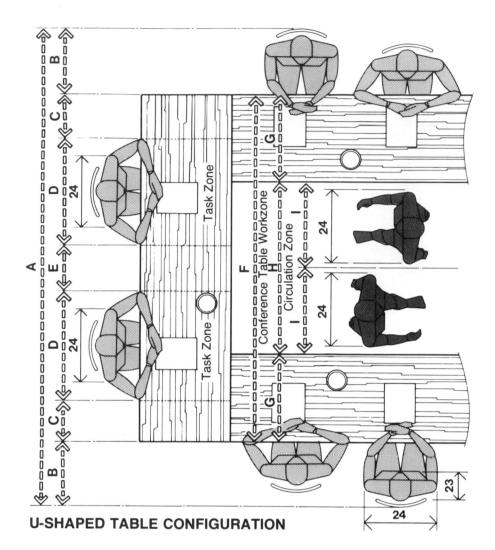

**U-SHAPED TABLE CONFIGURATION**

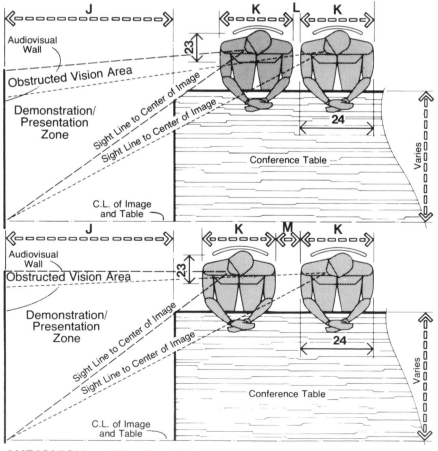

**AUDIOVISUAL CONFERENCE TABLE CONFIGURATION AND VISION LINES**

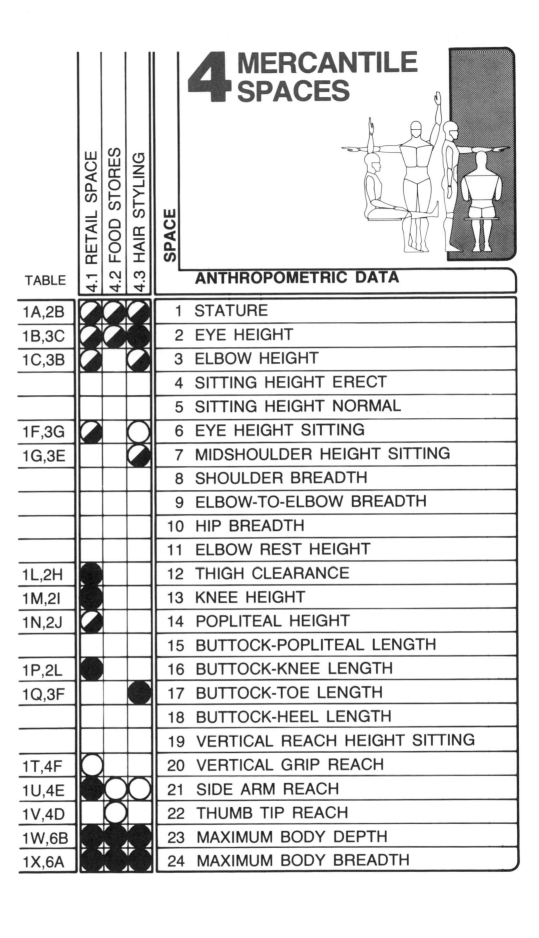

# 4 MERCANTILE SPACES

| TABLE | 4.1 RETAIL SPACE | 4.2 FOOD STORES | 4.3 HAIR STYLING | SPACE ANTHROPOMETRIC DATA | |
|---|---|---|---|---|---|
| 1A,2B | ◐ | ◐ | ◐ | 1 | STATURE |
| 1B,3C | ◐ | ◐ | ○ | 2 | EYE HEIGHT |
| 1C,3B | ◑ | | ◐ | 3 | ELBOW HEIGHT |
| | | | | 4 | SITTING HEIGHT ERECT |
| | | | | 5 | SITTING HEIGHT NORMAL |
| 1F,3G | ◑ | | ○ | 6 | EYE HEIGHT SITTING |
| 1G,3E | | | ◐ | 7 | MIDSHOULDER HEIGHT SITTING |
| | | | | 8 | SHOULDER BREADTH |
| | | | | 9 | ELBOW-TO-ELBOW BREADTH |
| | | | | 10 | HIP BREADTH |
| | | | | 11 | ELBOW REST HEIGHT |
| 1L,2H | ● | | | 12 | THIGH CLEARANCE |
| 1M,2I | ● | | | 13 | KNEE HEIGHT |
| 1N,2J | ◑ | | | 14 | POPLITEAL HEIGHT |
| | | | | 15 | BUTTOCK-POPLITEAL LENGTH |
| 1P,2L | ● | | | 16 | BUTTOCK-KNEE LENGTH |
| 1Q,3F | | | ● | 17 | BUTTOCK-TOE LENGTH |
| | | | | 18 | BUTTOCK-HEEL LENGTH |
| | | | | 19 | VERTICAL REACH HEIGHT SITTING |
| 1T,4F | ○ | | | 20 | VERTICAL GRIP REACH |
| 1U,4E | ● | ○ | ○ | 21 | SIDE ARM REACH |
| 1V,4D | | ○ | | 22 | THUMB TIP REACH |
| 1W,6B | ● | ● | ● | 23 | MAXIMUM BODY DEPTH |
| 1X,6A | ● | ● | ● | 24 | MAXIMUM BODY BREADTH |

The first stores in this country were simply incorporated into the homes of the craftsmen who produced and sold their wares on the premises. The shop was usually located in a front room, with quarters for the family and apprentices at the rear or on another floor. By the 19th century, however, a new breed of enterprising merchants emerged who were primarily interested, not in the production of the product, but in its purchase and resale to others. At first, they too operated from their homes, but the storage requirements for their inventory soon compelled them to take over the entire house for business purposes. Eventually, they outgrew the house as a place of operation and had to relocate in buildings that could be used for warehousing as well as sales. Although sales was essential to their operation, the building's interior still looked and functioned as a warehouse, not the store as it is perceived today. Ambiance, user comfort, store image, display systems, and adjacency planning were not considered. Customer convenience, in terms of building location and design, was traded off for storage space and proximity to transportation arteries. By the turn of the century, some thought was given to the display of merchandise, and stores begn to lose some of the warehouse look. After World War II, as large chain store operations were created, as shopping centers and malls evolved as a new prototype for mercantile space, and as new stores were constructed throughout the country, emphasis was placed on the design of store interiors, based on market research, buying habits, merchandising theory, and customer convenience.

Today the essential function of mercantile spaces, small or large, is to display and sell merchandise. If the quality of the interface between the customer and the interior space is poor, the purpose of that space is defeated. Likewise, if the quality of the interface between the store personnel and that space is not adequate, the effectiveness of the store will be diminished. The points of interface are too numerous to examine thoroughly here, yet among the most obvious are the interface between the customer and the display and between customer, display, and sales personnel. Human dimension and its impact on the quality of that interface will be examined in the drawings on the following pages. The relationship, for example, among fields of vision, eye height, and display is extremely important; the most creative display is worthless if it can only be seen by a small percentage of customers. The height of the counter so that it will accommodate the body sizes of the majority of customers is equally important. The location of shelving within reach of those of both small and large size is another consideration. Clearance adequate to allow comfortable circulation is yet another factor. To be responsive to these considerations requires an understanding of the anthropometric requirements involved.

| TABLE | DISPLAY | SHOPPING | SELLING | STORAGE | FITTING | WRAPPING | ACTIVITIES | ANTHROPOMETRIC DATA | |
|---|---|---|---|---|---|---|---|---|---|
| 1A,2B | ◑ | | ◑ | | ● | ● | 1 | STATURE |
| 1B,3C | ◑ | ◑ | | ◑ | | | 2 | EYE HEIGHT |
| 1C,3B | | ◑ | ◑ | | | ◑ | 3 | ELBOW HEIGHT |
| 1F,3G | ◑ | ◑ | | | | | 6 | EYE HEIGHT SITTING |
| 1L,2H | | ● | | | | | 12 | THIGH CLEARANCE |
| 1M,2I | | ● | | | | | 13 | KNEE HEIGHT |
| 1N,2J | | ◑ | | | | | 14 | POPLITEAL HEIGHT |
| 1P,2L | | ● | | | | | 16 | BUTTOCK-KNEE LENGTH |
| 1T,4F | | | ● | ○ | | ● | 20 | VERTICAL GRIP REACH |
| 1U,4E | | | | | ● | | 21 | SIDE ARM REACH |
| 1W,6B | | ● | ● | | | ● | 23 | MAXIMUM BODY DEPTH |
| 1X,6A | | ● | ● | | | ● | 24 | MAXIMUM BODY BREADTH |

In an interior environment such as a retail space, where customer convenience and comfort are a matter of corporate policy, the responsiveness of the design to human dimension and body size is extremely critical. The interface between the user and the various types of sales counters and shelf displays, for example, must be of the highest quality. Included among the drawings on the following pages are illustrations of various counter types for use from both seated and standing positions, indicating the anthropometric considerations involved and suggested dimensional clearances for use in making preliminary design assumptions.

Proper visibility of displays both from within and from without is also crucial to the successful design of a retail space. In this regard, the eye height of the small and large viewer and the geometric implications of human vision must be accommodated. The height of a wrapping counter, the size of a dressing cubicle, the critical dimensions of a shoe department, and circulation around and between merchandise displays must all accommodate users of varying body size. Illustrations of these aspects of retail spaces are also among the drawings included in this section, together with suggested clearances. The anthropometric measurements of significant importance are indicated in the above matrix.

# 4.1 RETAIL SPACES

The drawing at the top of the page shows the optimum height of viewing planes located at 12-in, or 30.5-cm, intervals, with the viewer stationed 12 in away from the show window. Two sets of data are presented: one concerns the viewing planes related to a viewer of small body size, and the other, planes related to a viewer of larger body size. The eye level of the former was based on 5th percentile female data and the latter on 95th percentile male data. As in other situations, the diagram should not be taken too literally, since it does not take into account head movement or the scanning capability of the eye, each of which can significantly increase the area that the eye can see. By using the geometric approach implied in the diagram, the size of optimum viewing planes can be established with the viewer in different locations.

The drawing at the bottom explores visual relationships related to interior displays. For further information on visual displays, refer to Section 9.

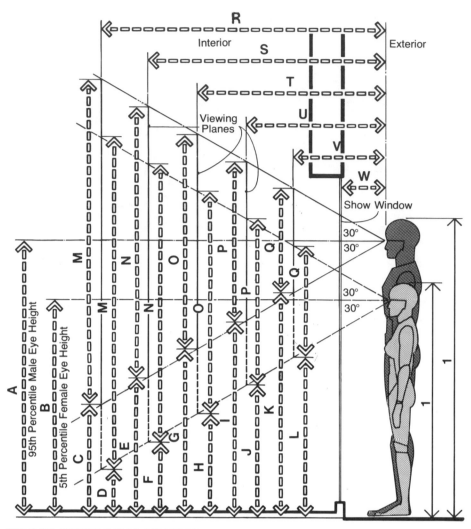

**SHOW WINDOW / OPTIMUM VIEWING PLANES**

| | in | cm |
|---|---|---|
| A | 68.6 | 174.2 |
| B | 56.3 | 143.0 |
| C | 27.0 | 68.7 |
| D | 14.7 | 37.4 |
| E | 28.0 | 71.2 |
| F | 28.3 | 72.0 |
| G | 41.5 | 105.4 |
| H | 28.6 | 72.6 |
| I | 47.8 | 121.5 |
| J | 36.3 | 92.2 |
| K | 54.8 | 139.1 |
| L | 42.5 | 107.8 |
| M | 83.1 | 211.1 |
| N | 69.3 | 175.9 |
| O | 55.4 | 140.8 |
| P | 41.6 | 105.6 |
| Q | 27.7 | 70.4 |
| R | 72 | 182.9 |
| S | 60 | 152.4 |
| T | 48 | 121.9 |
| U | 36 | 91.4 |
| V | 24 | 61.0 |
| W | 12 | 30.5 |
| X | 84 | 213.4 |

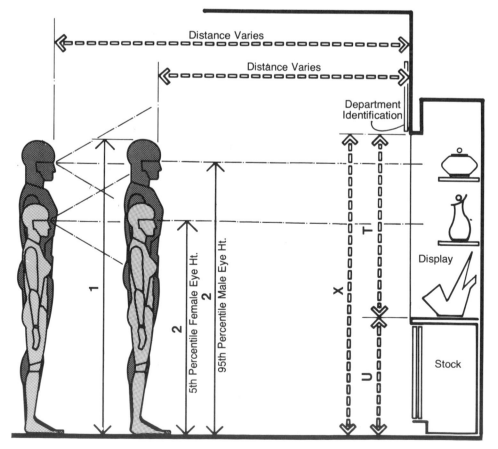

**DISPLAY / VISUAL RELATIONSHIPS**

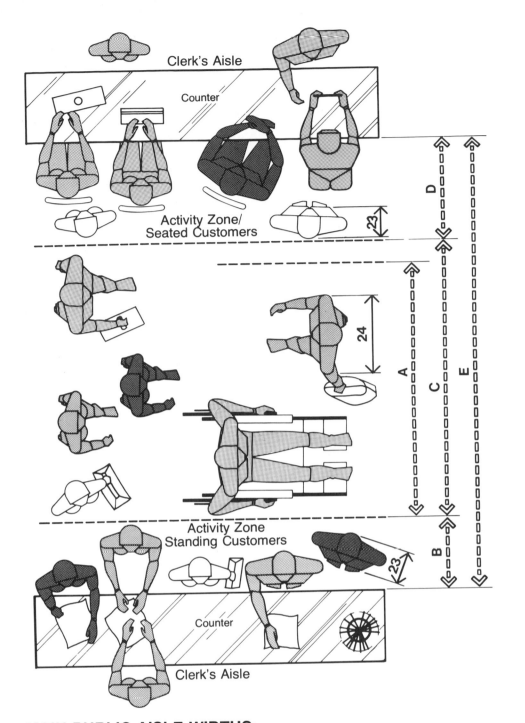

Clerk's Aisle

Counter

Activity Zone/
Seated Customers

23

24

Activity Zone
Standing Customers

23

Counter

Clerk's Aisle

A C E

D

B

**MAIN PUBLIC AISLE WIDTHS**

The top drawing illustrates the clearances suggested between counters on opposite sides of a main aisle. The total clearance suggested is between 117 and 120 in, or 297.2 and 304.8 cm. This allows an activity zone for standing customers facing the lower counter and a larger activity zone for standing and/or seated customers facing the upper counter, as well as a generous through circulation lane between the two.

The drawing at the bottom of the page illustrates the clearances suggested for a secondary aisle. The clearance in front of the merchandise case at the left takes into consideration a kneeling figure removing merchandise from a low shelf, while the clearance in front of the case on the right is only a minimum of 18 in, or 45.7 cm, which accommodates a person standing parallel to the case, either looking or handling merchandise displayed on the top surface. Although the maximum clearance between cases could be as much as 90 in, or 228.6 cm, a restricted minimum clearance of 51 in, or 129.5 cm, could be used if one is willing to accept some body contact or sidestepping required by a third person to pass between people engaged in activities on either side.

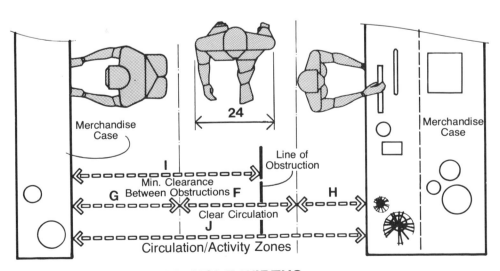

Merchandise Case

24

Line of Obstruction

Merchandise Case

Min. Clearance Between Obstructions F

I

G

Clear Circulation

H

J

Circulation/Activity Zones

**SECONDARY PUBLIC AISLE WIDTHS**

| | in | cm |
|---|---|---|
| A | 66 min. | 167.6 min. |
| B | 18 | 45.7 |
| C | 72 | 182.9 |
| D | 26–30 | 66.0–76.2 |
| E | 116–120 | 294.6–304.8 |
| F | 30–36 | 76.2–91.4 |
| G | 18–36 | 45.7–91.4 |
| H | 18 min. | 45.7 min. |
| I | 51 min. | 129.5 min. |
| J | 66–90 | 167.6–228.6 |

# 4.1 RETAIL SPACES

The drawing at the top of the page shows the clearances required for a medium height display counter. The suggested seat height of 21 to 22 in, or 53.3 to 55.8 cm, requires a footrest for the seated customer. The counter height shown will allow the display to be viewed by both the seated customer and the standing sales clerk. The customer activity zone allows adequate space for the chair. Knee height, buttock-knee length, popliteal height, and eye height sitting are all significant human dimensions to consider in the design of counters to be used by a seated customer.

The drawing at the bottom of the page is of a low 30-in, or 76.2-cm, display counter also for use by a seated customer. The anthropometric considerations are the same. Although the counter height is responsive to the anthropometric requirements of the seated customer, it is less than ideal for the standing clerk. For the standing user's optimum comfort, the counter height should be about 2 or 3 in, or 5 to 7.6 cm, below elbow height. This will allow a person to handle objects comfortably on the counter surface or use the counter as support for his or her arms. The 30-in height is too low to permit such use.

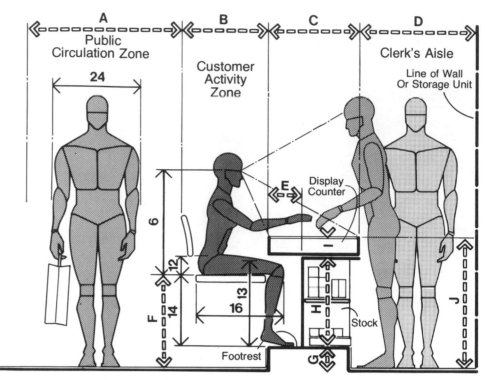

**SEATED CUSTOMER / DESIRABLE COUNTER HEIGHT**

| | in | cm |
|---|---|---|
| A | 36 | 91.4 |
| B | 26–30 | 66.0–76.2 |
| C | 18–24 | 45.7–61.0 |
| D | 30 min. | 76.2 min. |
| E | 10 | 25.4 |
| F | 21–22 | 53.3–55.9 |
| G | 5 | 12.7 |
| H | 23–25 | 58.4–63.5 |
| I | 4–6 | 10.2–15.2 |
| J | 34–36 | 86.4–91.4 |
| K | 30 | 76.2 |
| L | 16–17 | 40.6–43.2 |

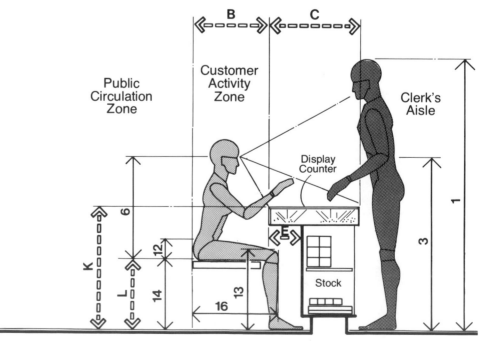

**SEATED CUSTOMER / LOW COUNTER HEIGHT**

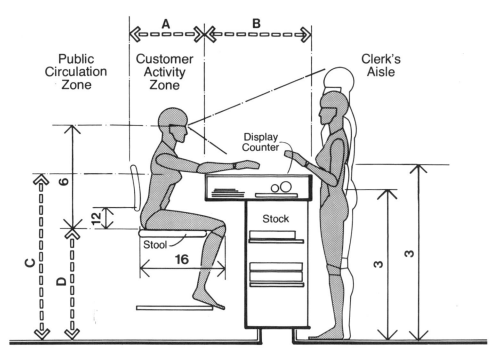

**SEATED CUSTOMER / HIGH COUNTER HEIGHT**

Labels in drawing: Public Circulation Zone, Customer Activity Zone, Clerk's Aisle, Display Counter, Stock, Stool, A, B, C, D, 6, 12, 16, 3, 3

The top drawing shows the clearances involved for a 42-in, or 106.7-cm, high counter to service a seated user. By filling the recess with an additional display, however, the counter can also be used exclusively as a typical sales counter. It should be noted, however, that although sometimes used for special display situations, such a counter height is not recommended. Both the customer and the sales clerk of smaller body size would find coping with such a height uncomfortable anthropometrically, particularly when one considers that the counter would be higher than the elbow height of slightly over 5 percent of the population. From a merchandising viewpoint, where customer convenience is of paramount importance, it would be unwise to exceed 39 to 40 in, or 99 to 101.6 cm, as a counter height. In addition, the smaller sales clerk forced to tend such a counter for extended periods of time could be subjected to severe backaches and pains. Getting on and off a high stool for elderly and disabled people or those of smaller body size can be not only difficult, but hazardous. The bottom drawing illustrates the clearances for a typical sales counter.

**TYPICAL SALES AREA / STANDING CUSTOMER**

Labels in drawing: Circulation Zone, Customer Activity Zone, Clerk's Aisle With Circulation, Display, Display Counter, Stock, Stock, E, F, G, H, I, J, K Max. Shelf Ht., 23, 24, 2, 3, 3

| | in | cm |
|---|---|---|
| A | 26–30 | 66.0–76.2 |
| B | 18–24 | 45.7–61.0 |
| C | 42 | 106.7 |
| D | 28 | 71.1 |
| E | 84–112 | 213.4–284.5 |
| F | 18 | 45.7 |
| G | 18–24 | 45.7–61.0 |
| H | 30–48 | 76.2–121.9 |
| I | 18–22 | 45.7–55.9 |
| J | 35–38 | 88.9–96.5 |
| K | 72 | 182.9 |

# 4.1 RETAIL SPACES

Shelving is probably used more than any other single interior component for the storage and/or display of merchandise. Not only must the merchandise be within reach anthropometrically, but it must be fairly visible as well. The heights established must therefore be responsive to vertical grip reach dimensions as well as to eye height. In establishing height limits, the body size data of the smaller person should be used. Since in retail spaces, departments may cater exclusively to members of one sex or the other, two sets of data are presented. One is based on the body size of the smaller female and the other on the body size of the smaller male. The suggested heights reflect a compromise between reach requirements and visibility requirements.

The drawing at the bottom of the page illustrates the clearances involved in hanging-type merchandise cases. Rod heights should be related not only to human reach limitations, but in certain cases to the sizes of the merchandise displayed. There is usually no conflict in respect to garments.

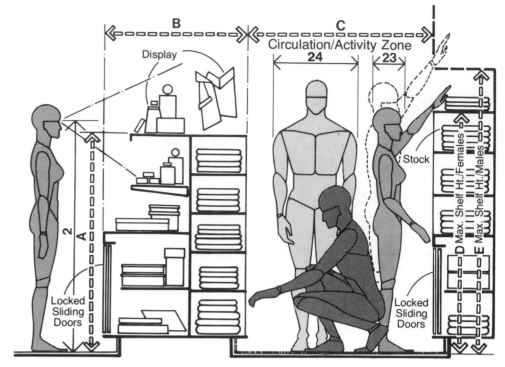

**TYPICAL MERCHANDISE CASES**

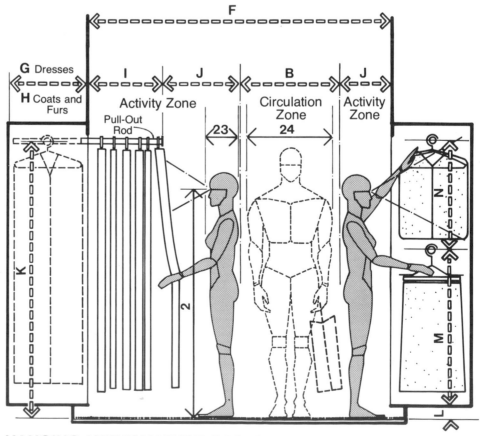

**HANGING MERCHANDISE CASES**

|   | in | cm |
|---|---|---|
| A | 48 max. | 121.9 max. |
| B | 30–36 | 76.2–91.4 |
| C | 51 min. | 129.5 min. |
| D | 66 | 167.6 |
| E | 72 | 182.9 |
| F | 84–96 | 213.4–243.8 |
| G | 20–26 | 50.8–66.0 |
| H | 28–30 | 71.1–76.2 |
| I | 18–24 | 45.7–61.0 |
| J | 18 min. | 45.7 min. |
| K | 72 max. | 182.9 max. |
| L | 4 | 10.2 |
| M | 42 | 106.7 |
| N | 26 min. | 66.0 min. |

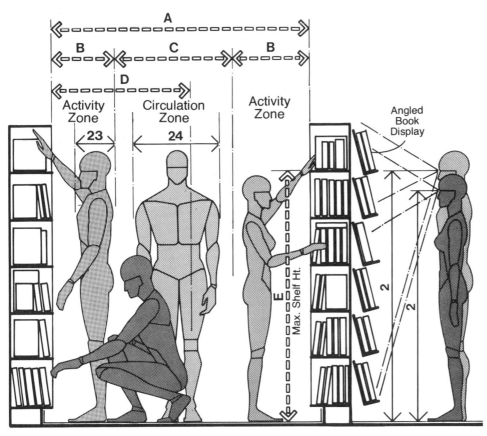

**BOOK STORE / DISPLAY AREA**

The drawing at the top of the page concerns book and magazine displays and suggests the anthropometric considerations involved. The rationale is essentially the same as that indicated for the general merchandise shelving on the preceding page. In regard to books, however, the question of visibility is even more critical. To perceive the basic form, shape, and color of general merchandise may be sufficient, but for books and magazines, the legibility of printed matter must be taken into account. The distance between the customer and the display, lighting, and angle of sight should all be considered. It is suggested that to supplement the information shown on the drawing, Sections 9.1 and 9.2 also be consulted.

The drawing at the bottom of the page deals with human dimension and the fitting area of a shoe store. The fitting zone clearance should accommodate the body size of the seated customer and that of the sales clerk. The 60 to 66 in, or 152.4 to 167.6 cm, clearance should be viewed as a minimum. The buttock-heel length of the larger person was considered in anthropometrically establishing the clearance dimension. In regard to the workzone, vertical grip reach measurements of the smaller male and female should be used in establishing shelf heights, while maximum body breadth and maximum body depth of the larger person should be considered in establishing clearances.

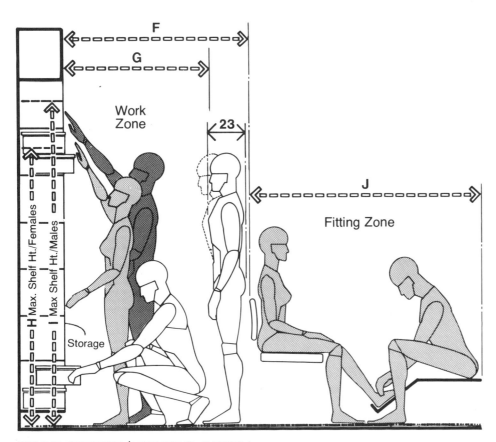

**SHOE STORE / FITTING AREA**

|   | in | cm |
|---|---|---|
| A | 66 min. | 167.6 min. |
| B | 18 min. | 45.7 min. |
| C | 30 min. | 76.2 min. |
| D | 36 | 91.4 |
| E | 68 | 172.7 |
| F | 48 | 121.9 |
| G | 36 min. | 91.4 min. |
| H | 66 | 167.6 |
| I | 72 | 182.9 |
| J | 60–66 | 152.4–167.6 |

# 4.1 RETAIL SPACES

Dressing rooms should accommodate the human body in the various positions a person assumes while in the process of dressing and disrobing. The drawing at the top of the page suggests a room size of 54 to 60 in, or 137.2 to 152.4 cm, by a minimum width of 36 in, or 91.4 cm. Stature, maximum body breadth, minimum body depth, and side arm reach of the larger person should all be considered in determining dressing room size.

The drawing at the bottom of the page illustrates some of the clearances required for a wrapping counter. Given the nature of the activity involved, a counter height of 35 to 36 in, or 88.9 to 91.4 cm, would accommodate the majority of people. Horizontal clearances must accommodate the maximum body depth of the larger person within the activity zone, and the maximum body breadth of the larger person in the circulation zone. Depending on the intensity of the operation and the number of clerks, the circulation and the activity zone can be combined and the clearance between the front and rear counter reduced to 30 in, or 76.2 cm.

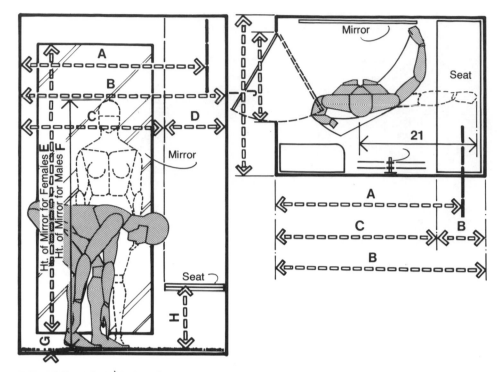

**DRESSING ROOMS**

|   | in | cm |
|---|---|---|
| A | 48 min. | 121.9 min. |
| B | 54–58 | 137.2–147.3 |
| C | 42 | 106.7 |
| D | 12–16 | 30.5–40.6 |
| E | 68 min. | 172.7 min. |
| F | 75 min. | 190.5 min. |
| G | 4 | 10.2 |
| H | 16 | 40.6 |
| I | 36 min. | 91.4 min. |
| J | 24 | 61.0 |
| K | 29–32 | 73.7–81.3 |
| L | 48 | 121.9 |
| M | 26 | 66.0 |
| N | 18 | 45.7 |
| O | 30 | 76.2 |
| P | 18–24 | 45.7–61.0 |
| Q | 6–10 | 15.2–25.4 |
| R | 35–36 | 88.9–91.4 |
| S | 35 | 88.9 |

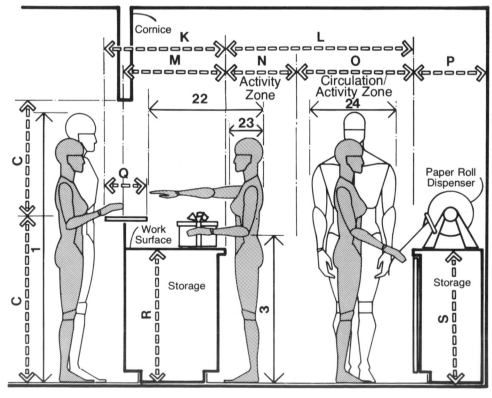

**WRAPPING COUNTER**

# 4.2 FOOD STORES

| TABLE | DISPLAY | SHOPPING | CHECKOUT | ACTIVITIES | ANTHROPOMETRIC DATA | |
|-------|---------|----------|----------|------------|---------------------|--|
| 1A,2B | ◒ | ◒ | | 1 | STATURE | |
| 1B,3C | ◒ | ◒ | | 2 | EYE HEIGHT | |
| 1U,4E | | ○ | ○ | 21 | SIDE ARM REACH | |
| 1V,4D | | ○ | ○ | 22 | THUMB TIP REACH | |
| 1W,6B | | ● | | 23 | MAXIMUM BODY DEPTH | |
| 1X,6A | | ● | ● | 24 | MAXIMUM BODY BREADTH | |

When considering the implication of human dimensions in relation to the design of self-service food stores, the shopping cart should be viewed as an extension of the human figure and the combined measurements as a unit to be accommodated for purposes of establishing necessary clearances. This is more critical in terms of overall length than width considerations, since the maximum body breadth dimension, particularly of those of larger body size, is also sufficient to accommodate the width of the cart itself. Height of shelving for display of merchandise should be responsive to the reach limitations of the smaller shopper, and the display of merchandise should relate to the eye height of the majority of users. Depending on store size and economics, width of aisles should include an activity zone directly adjacent to the merchandise display unit adequate to accommodate a standing or kneeling user, who is scanning shelves, selecting goods, or loading a cart, as well as a circulation zone that could accommodate two lanes of shoppers with carts. Clearances between checkout booths should be adequate to accommodate a wheelchair-bound shopper. The situations discussed are included among the illustrations found on the following pages together with dimensional suggestions for use in making preliminary design assumptions. The anthropometric measurements of major consideration are indicated in the above matrix.

# 4.2 FOOD STORES

The drawing at the top left shows the overall clearance required by a customer and shopping cart to be about 42 in, or 106.7 cm. The clearance required to accommodate a man and woman abreast is illustrated in the drawing at top right and shown to be 60 in, or 52.4 cm. To allow for a small child, an additional 18 in, or 45.7 cm, should be added. Maximum body breadth is the key body measurement to consider anthropometrically.

The drawing at the bottom of the page illustrates the clearances necessary between typical checkout counters. A clearance of a minimum of 36 in, or 91.4 cm, will accommodate not only the able-bodied customer, but also the wheelchair shopper. The overall dimensions of the wheelchair itself are 25 by 42 in, or 63.5 by 106.7 cm.

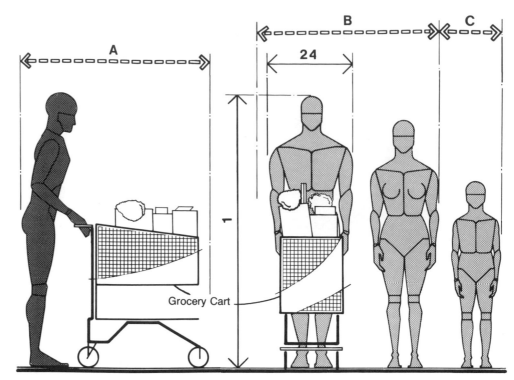

**CUSTOMER CLEARANCES**

**CHECKOUT AREA / WHEELCHAIR CLEARANCE**

|   | in | cm |
|---|---|---|
| A | 42 | 106.7 |
| B | 60 | 152.4 |
| C | 18 | 45.7 |
| D | 25 | 63.5 |
| E | 36 min. | 91.4 min. |

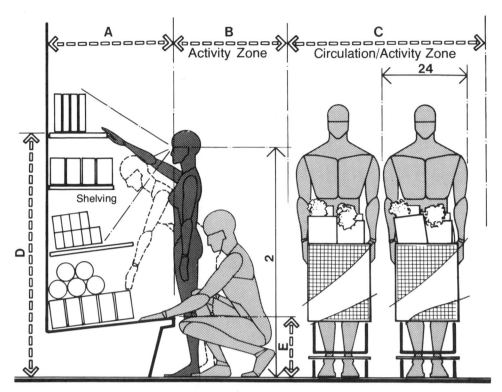

**SUPER-SHELVING WITH CIRCULATION**

The drawing at the top of the page illustrates the clearances related to a supermarket shelving display. An allowance of a minimum of 36 in, or 91.4 cm, in front of the shelving should be provided to accommodate the kneeling figure. An additional 60 in, or 152.4 cm, will accommodate two shoppers walking abreast.

The drawing at the bottom of the page provides information on clearances required for an island display. A space of 30 in, or 76.2 cm, on either side of the counter should be adequate for shopper activity related to the handling of merchandise on display. Maximum body breadth or cart width, whichever is greater, should be the key dimension. The 30-in dimension accommodates both. It should be noted that this clearance is for the activity zone exclusively. It is assumed in the drawing that circulation will be accommodated outside this zone.

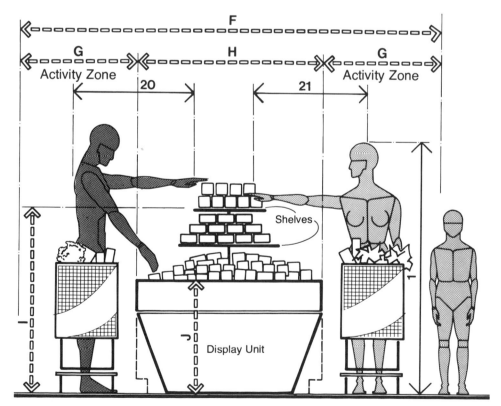

**ISLAND DISPLAY**

|   | in | cm |
|---|---|---|
| A | 32 | 81.3 |
| B | 36 max. | 91.4 max. |
| C | 60 | 152.4 |
| D | 63 max. | 160.0 max. |
| E | 15 max. | 38.1 max. |
| F | 108 | 274.3 |
| G | 30 | 76.2 |
| H | 48 | 121.9 |
| I | 48 max. | 121.9 max. |
| J | 30–32 | 76.2–81.3 |

# 4.2 FOOD STORES

The comprehensive drawing here incorporates some of the isolated pieces of information shown on the preceding pages. It also provides minimum clearances between shelving and island displays. As suggested, the 72-in, or 189.9-cm, clearances between food displays are minimum. Although a 72-in clearance accommodates a shopper and cart adjacent to each of the opposing food displays, circulation for a third shopper to pass between them would be restricted. One of the two shoppers on either side would be obligated to move out of the way to permit passage. To accommodate clear central circulation, an additional 30 in, or 76.3 cm, should be added to the 72-in minimum clearance, providing a total clearance between food displays of at least 102 in, or 259 cm.

Super Shelving

Activity Zone

Note That 30 in (76.2 cm) Should Be Added for Clear Central Circulation

Activity Zone

Island Display

Activity Zone

Activity Zone

Super Shelving

| | in | cm |
|---|---|---|
| **A** | 72 min. | 182.9 min. |
| **B** | 36 | 91.4 |
| **C** | 30 min. | 76.2 min. |
| **D** | 48 | 121.9 |
| **E** | 192 | 487.7 |

**AISLE CLEARANCES**

| TABLE | STYLING | SHAMPOOING | DRYING | WAITING | CIRCULATION | ACTIVITIES | | ANTHROPOMETRIC DATA |
|---|---|---|---|---|---|---|---|---|
| 1A,2B | ● | ◐ | | | | | 1 | STATURE |
| 1B,3C | ● | | | | | | 2 | EYE HEIGHT |
| 1C,3B | | ◐ | | | | | 3 | ELBOW HEIGHT |
| 1F,3G | ○ | | | | | | 6 | EYE HEIGHT SITTING |
| 1G,3E | | ◐ | | | | | 7 | SHOULDER HEIGHT SITTING |
| 1Q,3F | | | ● | ● | | | 17 | BUTTOCK-TOE LENGTH |
| 1U,4E | ○ | | | | | | 21 | SIDE ARM REACH |
| 1W,6B | ● | | | | ● | | 23 | MAXIMUM BODY DEPTH |
| 1X,6A | | ● | | | ● | | 24 | MAXIMUM BODY BREADTH |

# 4.3 HAIR STYLING

One of the most important considerations in making hair styling spaces responsive to human dimension is that of adjustability. Given the tremendous variability in body size, both in terms of the customer and the stylist and the nature of the activity involved, it is virtually impossible to accommodate the majority of people without some degree of adjustability to compensate for the great variability in body size. The range of adjustment possible in most standard chairs on the market is not great enough. The styling operation, for example, requires the operator to style the hair of the seated customer about the lower head, neck, and shoulder areas. Not only is it essential that the stylist have a clear view of the work area, but in many instances he or she must be able to step back and check for smoothness and level of cut. Even with the chair elevated to its maximum position, the taller stylist must still stoop to perform his work. Until such time that more chairs with a greater range of adjustability become available, the interior designer or architect should explore other ways to make the operation more responsive to the limitations imposed by human dimension and body size.

Another area where much improvement is needed is the interface among customer, chair, wash basin, and operator in the typical shampoo station. Since most facilities do not permit comfortable neck flexion, the most critical phase of the interface involves the head and wash basin. Moreover, the hard, although rounded, edge of the basin in direct contact with the back of the neck adds to the discomfort. The quality of the interface could perhaps be improved by building adjustment capability into the chair so that the body may be placed in a more horizontal position. Within the limitations imposed by existing equipment, the drawings on the following pages illustrate some of the typical situations encountered in the design of hair styling spaces. The anthropometric measurements of major concern are indicated in the above matrix.

# 4.3 HAIR STYLING

A plan view showing two styling stations and required clearances is shown in the drawing at the top of the page. To accommodate the seated customer and provide for circulation and appropriate movement of the hair stylist, a space of 95 to 105 in, or 241.3 to 266.7 cm, deep and 83 to 87 in, or 210.8 to 221 cm, wide is required for each station. To conserve floor space, however, it is suggested that the spaces required for the individual styling stations overlap each other by 24 in, or 61 cm. The area of overlap is used as a shared activity zone.

The bottom drawing shows the styling station in elevation. It should be noted that despite the adjustability of the chair, the range of movement does not allow the chair to be elevated high enough to permit the stylist to work around the lower head and neck area without stooping.

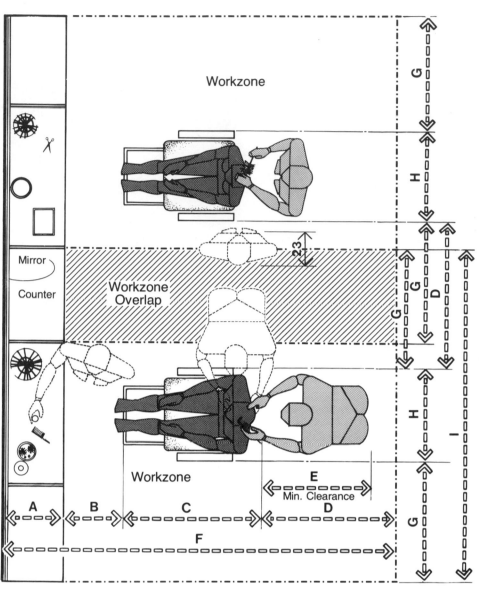

**STYLING STATIONS**

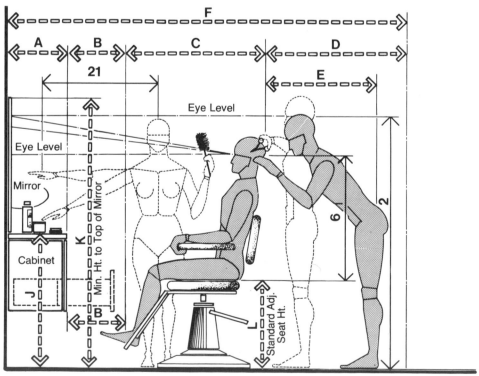

**STYLING STATION/
STANDARD ADJUSTABLE CHAIR HEIGHTS**

|   | in | cm |
|---|---|---|
| A | 16–18 | 40.6–45.7 |
| B | 15 min. | 38.1 min. |
| C | 29–36 | 73.7–91.4 |
| D | 36 | 91.4 |
| E | 30 min. | 76.2 min. |
| F | 96–105 | 243.8–266.7 |
| G | 30 | 76.2 |
| H | 23–27 | 58.4–68.6 |
| I | 83–87 | 210.8–221.0 |
| J | 34–36 | 86.4–91.4 |
| K | 68 min. | 172.7 min. |
| L | 19.5–25 | 49.5–63.5 |

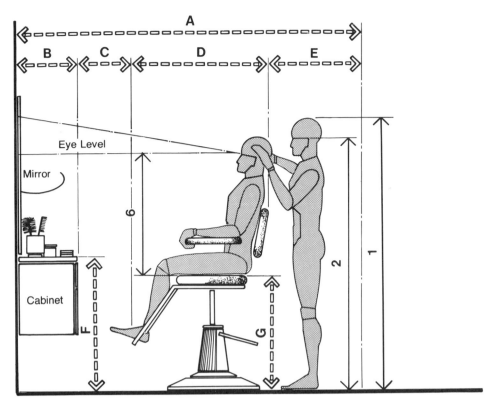

**STYLING STATION/
OPTIMUM ADJUSTABLE CHAIR HEIGHTS**

# 4.3 HAIR STYLING

The drawing at the top of the page illustrates a proposed styling chair with an adjustability range of 24 to 36 in, or 61 to 91.4 cm. Such a range, not presently available, would enable the stylist, especially one having a large stature, to trim the back of the head comfortably without having to stoop.

The drawing at the left on the bottom of the page illustrates the clearances required for the waiting area. A minimum clearance of 37 in, or 94 cm, from the wall will accommodate the seated customer. This dimension includes an allowance of 12 in, or 30.5 cm, to accommodate leg projection beyond the edge of the front of the seat. A space of 36 in, or 91.4 cm, is adequate for one-lane circulation in front of the seating. For one person to pass another within the 36-in circulation zone will, however, require one or the other to step aside.

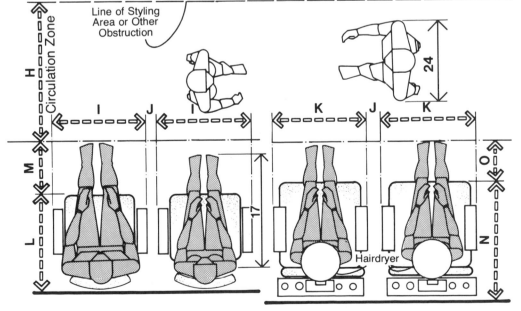

**WAITING AREA AND
CIRCULATION/
CLEARANCES**

**DRYING AREA AND
CIRCULATION/
CLEARANCES**

|   | in | cm |
|---|---|---|
| A | 84–93 | 213.4–236.2 |
| B | 16–18 | 40.6–45.7 |
| C | 15 min. | 38.1 min. |
| D | 29–36 | 73.7–91.4 |
| E | 24 | 61.0 |
| F | 34–36 | 86.4–91.4 |
| G | 24–36 | 61.0–91.4 |
| H | 36 | 91.4 |
| I | 23–27 | 58.4–68.6 |
| J | 4 min. | 10.2 min. |
| K | 24–27 | 61.0–68.6 |
| L | 25–28 | 63.5–71.1 |
| M | 12 | 30.5 |
| N | 31–36 | 78.7–91.4 |
| O | 10 | 25.4 |

# 4.3 HAIR STYLING

The drawing at the top of the page shows a plan view of a shampoo station. A minimum of 82 in, or 208.3 cm, from the wall is required to accommodate the basin and the seated user with feet extended. A space of 24 in, or 61 cm, between chairs is adequate to accommodate a person while engaged in the shampooing activity.

The drawings at the center and the bottom of the page show the shampoo station in elevation. The center drawing illustrates the chair in use by a male customer, while the bottom drawing illustrates the chair in use by a female customer. The clearances shown in each drawing are about the same. It should be noted, however, that since the body size of the larger female is smaller than the body size of the larger male, the clearance from the wall required in the shampoo station exclusively catering to women could be a few inches smaller. Since the difference is minimal, it would be more practical to allow sufficient clearance to accommodate the male customer of larger body size. However, in situations where space may be extremely tight, the small clearance required for the female could be helpful in conserving space. Of greatest importance anthropometrically is that the chair have maximum flexibility in terms of both seat height and backrest angle to ensure a comfortable body fit or interface between the back of the neck and the basin.

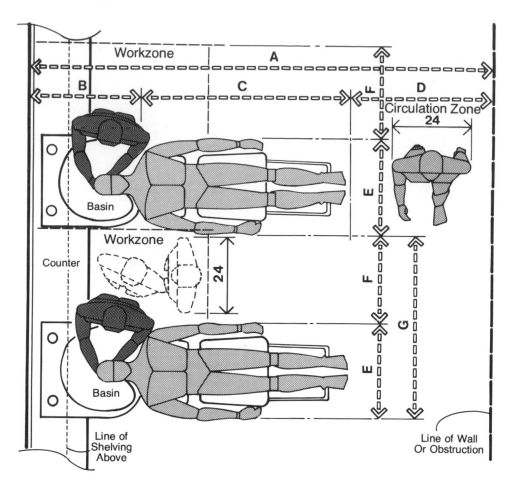

**SHAMPOO STATIONS**

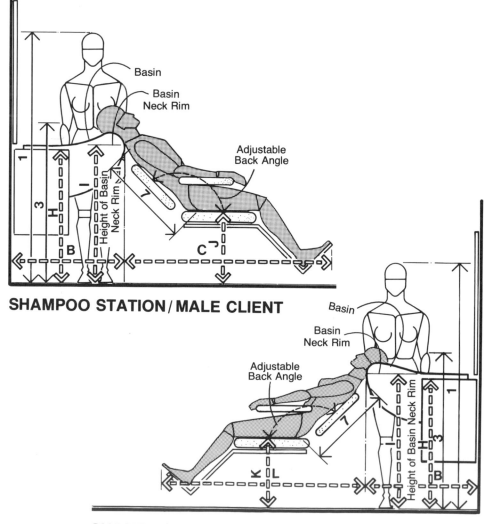

**SHAMPOO STATION / MALE CLIENT**

**SHAMPOO STATION / FEMALE CLIENT**

|   | in | cm |
|---|---|---|
| A | 118–126 | 299.7–320.0 |
| B | 28–30 | 71.1–76.2 |
| C | 54–60 | 137.2–152.4 |
| D | 36 | 91.4 |
| E | 24–28 | 61.0–71.1 |
| F | 24 | 61.0 |
| G | 48–52 | 121.9–132.1 |
| H | 34 | 86.4 |
| I | 35 | 88.9 |
| J | 17–18 | 43.2–45.7 |
| K | 18–19 | 45.7–48.3 |
| L | 52–58 | 132.1–147.3 |

# 5 EATING AND DRINKING SPACES

| TABLE | 5.1 BARS | 5.2 FOOD COUNTERS | 5.3 DINING SPACES | SPACE | ANTHROPOMETRIC DATA |
|---|---|---|---|---|---|
| 1A,2B | ◖ | | | 1 | STATURE |
| 1B,3C | ◖ | | | 2 | EYE HEIGHT |
| | | | | 3 | ELBOW HEIGHT |
| 1D,2C | | | ● | 4 | SITTING HEIGHT ERECT |
| | | | | 5 | SITTING HEIGHT NORMAL |
| 1F,3G | | | ● | 6 | EYE HEIGHT SITTING |
| | | | | 7 | MIDSHOULDER HEIGHT SITTING |
| | | | | 8 | SHOULDER BREADTH |
| | | | | 9 | ELBOW-TO-ELBOW BREADTH |
| | | | | 10 | HIP BREADTH |
| | | | | 11 | ELBOW REST HEIGHT |
| 1L,2H | ● | ● | ● | 12 | THIGH CLEARANCE |
| 1M,2I | ● | ● | ● | 13 | KNEE HEIGHT |
| 1N,2J | ◖ | ◖ | ◕ | 14 | POPLITEAL HEIGHT |
| 1O,2K | | ◖ | | 15 | BUTTOCK-POPLITEAL LENGTH |
| 1P,2L | ● | ● | ● | 16 | BUTTOCK-KNEE LENGTH |
| | | | | 17 | BUTTOCK-TOE LENGTH |
| | | | | 18 | BUTTOCK-HEEL LENGTH |
| | | | | 19 | VERTICAL REACH HEIGHT SITTING |
| | | | | 20 | VERTICAL GRIP REACH |
| 1U,4E | | ○ | | 21 | SIDE ARM REACH |
| 1V,4D | ○ | | ○ | 22 | THUMB TIP REACH |
| 1W,6B | ● | ● | ● | 23 | MAXIMUM BODY DEPTH |
| 1X,6A | ● | ● | ● | 24 | MAXIMUM BODY BREADTH |

It has been estimated that somewhere in the vicinity of 46 million people in the U.S. eat out daily, with a median per capita expenditure of more than $3.50. As leisure time increases and the emerging so-called leisure ethic becomes more firmly entrenched as a way of life, as the number of single men and women continues to increase, as more women return to the labor market, and as family incomes increase, the amount of time and money spent eating outside the home will become even greater.

The eating and drinking establishment is a necessity for some, a luxury for others, and to many, perhaps, a brief escape from boredom or loneliness. However, despite its raison d'etre or the contrasts in ambiance that may exist among the neighborhood tavern, the singles bar, and the elegant gourmet restaurant, the anthropometric requirements of the user remain the one constant in the design equation. The quality of the interface between the customer and the various elements of the interior space determine the level of user comfort and, in many cases, the eventual success or failure of the establishment.

The diagrams and text on the following pages deal with those human dimensions that relate to the design of bars, food counters, dining areas, and other elements that constitute typical eating and drinking spaces. The anthropometric requirements of those who work in these spaces are also explored. In addition, the problems of the wheelchair-bound patron are examined, particularly in terms of general accessibility and interface with the table.

# 5.1 BARS

| TABLE | SERVICE | DRINKING | CIRCULATION | ACTIVITIES | ANTHROPOMETRIC DATA | |
|-------|---------|----------|-------------|------------|-----|---|
| 1A,2B | | ◐ | | | 1 | STATURE |
| 1B,3C | | ◐ | | | 2 | EYE HEIGHT |
| 1L,2H | | ● | | | 12 | THIGH CLEARANCE |
| 1M,2I | | ● | | | 13 | KNEE HEIGHT |
| 1N,2J | | ◐ | | | 14 | POPLITEAL HEIGHT |
| 1P,2L | | ● | | | 16 | BUTTOCK-KNEE LENGTH |
| 1V,4D | ○ | | | | 22 | THUMB TIP REACH |
| 1W,6B | ● | ● | ● | | 23 | MAXIMUM BODY DEPTH |
| 1X,6A | ● | ● | ● | | 24 | MAXIMUM BODY BREADTH |

The drawings on the following pages illustrate in plan and section the considerations that should make the design of bars more sensitive to human body size. Clearances and other dimensional data for use in making preliminary design assumptions are also indicated. The anthropometric measurements of major concern are indicated in the matrix above.

In earlier sections of the book, it was stated that anthropometry can serve as an extremely helpful tool in the design process if used within the larger perspective of all the other human factors that impact on that process, such as the many psychological, sociological, and cultural factors that the designer must also take into account. It seems particularly appropriate while dealing with the subject of bar design to relterate the concept that in fitting the designed environment to the body, clearances and space also have more sophisticated and subtle implications. The clearances allowed for seating at the bar, for example, could in many instances ensure an ideal body fit between patron and bar and at the same time negate the very reason for the particular drinking place or tavern. The greater the seating density and the closer the seats, the greater the degree of social interaction. A singles bar, for example, whose seating arrangement was overly conservative and tended to insulate patrons from each other would obviously not be very successful. However, there are many situations where intense social interaction between patrons is, as a matter of policy or personal preference, not a desirable objective, nor would the patrons frequenting such places necessarily feel at ease under such conditions.

# 5.1 BARS

The distance between bar and back-bar should allow adequate workspace. A minimum of 36 in, or 90 cm, should provide space for one bartender to serve and another to circulate behind him. Maximum body depth and maximum body breadth are the primary anthropometric considerations in establishing clearance. A one-bartender operation would require a 30-in, or 75-cm, clearance.

In regard to bar stools, clearance between the stool seats is more critical than center line spacing, and it should allow patrons of larger body size a comfortable side approach and departure from the stool without body contact with the next person. A 12-in, or 30-cm, wide stool on 24-in, or 61-cm, centers, which is quite common, will allow only less than 5 percent of male users access to the stool without disturbing the next patron, while a 30-in, or 75-cm, spacing will accommodate 95 percent of the users. The tradeoff, however, would be the loss of two seats for every 120 in, or 300 cm, of bar length. A spacing of 12-in stools on 28-in, or 70 cm, centers is suggested as a compromise. The ultimate decision is an individual one and must reconcile human factors with economic viability.

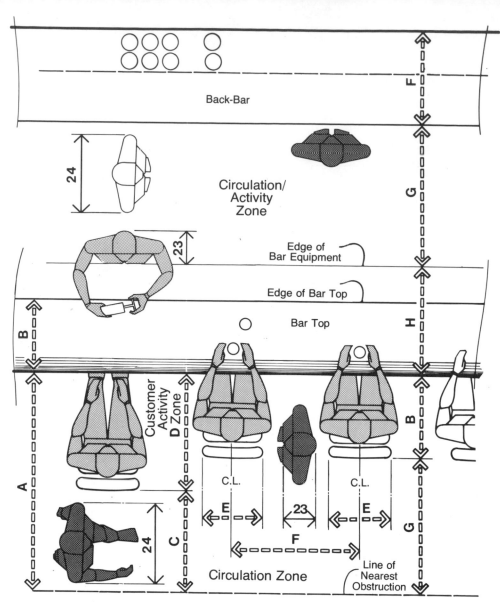

**BAR AND BACK-BAR**

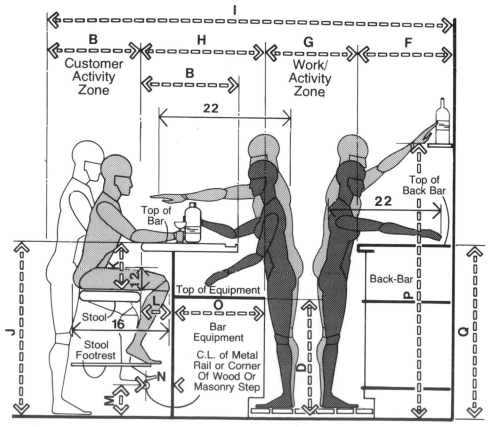

**BAR / SECTION**

|   | in | cm |
|---|------|-----------|
| A | 54 | 137.2 |
| B | 18–24 | 45.7–61.0 |
| C | 24 | 61.0 |
| D | 30 | 76.2 |
| E | 16–18 | 40.6–45.7 |
| F | 24–30 | 61.0–76.2 |
| G | 30–36 | 76.2–91.4 |
| H | 28–38 | 71.1–96.5 |
| I | 100–128 | 254.0–325.1 |
| J | 42–45 | 106.7–114.3 |
| K | 11–12 | 27.9–30.5 |
| L | 6–7 | 15.2–17.8 |
| M | 7–9 | 17.8–22.9 |
| N | 6–9 | 15.2–22.9 |
| O | 22–26 | 55.9–66.0 |
| P | 60–69 | 152.4–175.3 |
| Q | 36–42 | 91.4–106.7 |

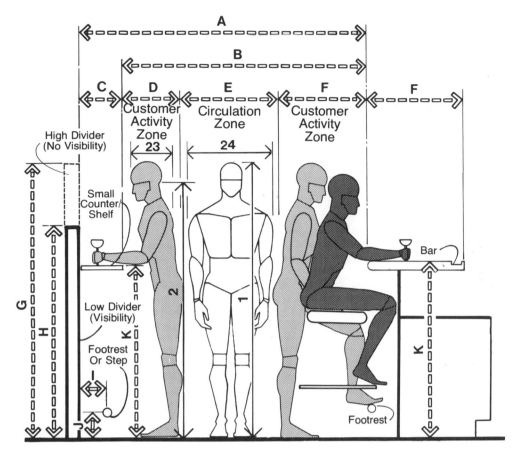

**BAR / CLEARANCES PUBLIC SIDE**

# 5.1 BARS

To ensure proper circulation and interface, adequate clearances in front of the bar are illustrated in the top drawing. A customer activity zone of 18 to 24 in, or 45.7 to 61.0 cm, should be provided to allow for seating, standing, and access, in addition to a general circulation zone of at least 30 in, or 76.2 cm. If a supplementary drinking surface or shelf is provided, a smaller activity zone of 18 in is suggested in front of the shelf. The shelf can be 10 to 12 in, or 25.4 to 30.5 cm, deep. The bottom drawing shows suggested clearances for 18 or 24 in cocktail tables.

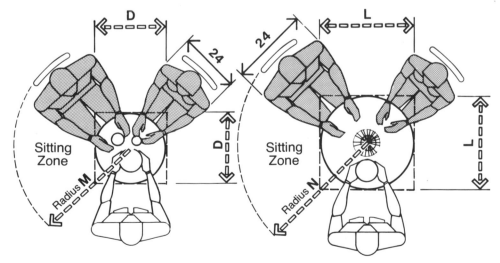

**COCKTAIL TABLES / SEATING FOR TWO**

|   | in | cm |
|---|---|---|
| A | 76–84 | 193.0–213.4 |
| B | 66–72 | 167.6–182.9 |
| C | 10–12 | 25.4–30.5 |
| D | 18 | 45.7 |
| E | 30 | 76.2 |
| F | 18–24 | 45.7–61.0 |
| G | 76 | 193.0 |
| H | 54–56 | 137.2–142.2 |
| I | 6–9 | 15.2–22.9 |
| J | 7–9 | 17.8–22.9 |
| K | 42–45 | 106.7–114.3 |
| L | 24 | 61.0 |
| M | 29–33 | 73.7–83.8 |
| N | 32–36 | 81.3–91.4 |

# 5.1 BARS

Bar seating is a classic example where hidden dimensions, as well as anthropometric factors, must be considered in determining seat spacing. Cultural differences, for example, may dictate proximity between patrons. In one instance closeness may cause discomfort for patrons, and in another case it may be desirable. The density of people and the spacing of seats also impact on social interaction; the greater the density, the greater the probability of such interaction. The drawings, however, deal essentially with the anthropometrics involved and the possible density models. The top drawing illustrates a low-density situation, based on one seated or standing patron per 30 in, or 76.2 cm, of bar length. Such a density model would preclude body contact, allow comfortable changes in body position, and ensure relative privacy.

The center drawing illustrates a medium density model, based on 24-in, or 61-cm, spacing; takes occasional pairing into account, as shown by the dotted figure; and allows for occasional body contact and territorial intrusion. The bottom drawing illustrates a high-density model, with patrons standing two to three deep and a density factor of over 1.5 patrons per 12 in, or 30 cm, of bar length.

| | in | cm |
|---|---|---|
| A | 30 | 76–2 |
| B | 24–30 | 61.0–76.2 |
| C | 28–38 | 71.1–96.5 |
| D | 24 | 61.0 |
| E | 120 | 304.8 |
| F | 18–30 | 45.7–76.2 |
| G | 36–54 | 91.4–137.2 |

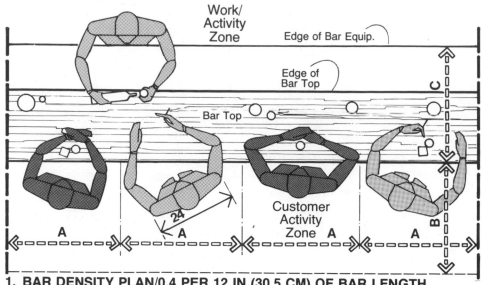

**1. BAR DENSITY PLAN/0.4 PER 12 IN (30.5 CM) OF BAR LENGTH ONE DEEP AT BAR**

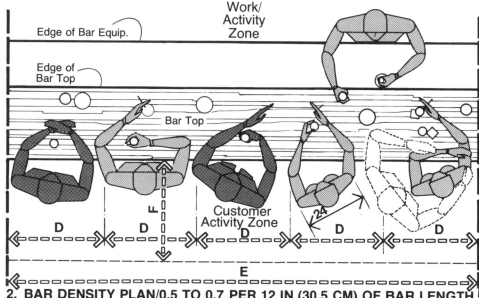

**2. BAR DENSITY PLAN/0.5 TO 0.7 PER 12 IN (30.5 CM) OF BAR LENGTH ONE DEEP AT BAR**

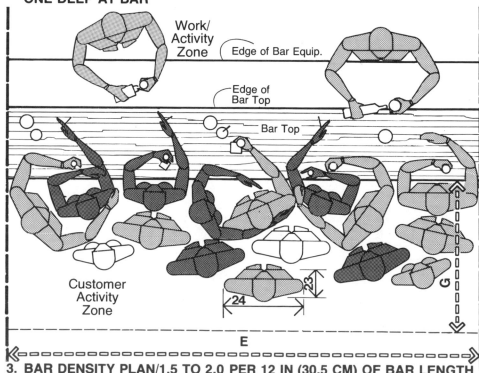

**3. BAR DENSITY PLAN/1.5 TO 2.0 PER 12 IN (30.5 CM) OF BAR LENGTH TWO TO THREE DEEP AT BAR**

**BAR DENSITY PLANS**

| TABLE | SERVICE | EATING | CIRCULATION | ACTIVITIES | ANTHROPOMETRIC DATA | |
|---|---|---|---|---|---|---|
| 1L,2H | | ● | | | 12 | THIGH CLEARANCE |
| 1M,2I | | ● | | | 13 | KNEE HEIGHT |
| 1N,2J | | ◑ | | | 14 | POPLITEAL HEIGHT |
| 1P,2L | | ● | | | 16 | BUTTOCK-KNEE LENGTH |
| 1U,4E | | | | ○ | 21 | SIDE ARM REACH |
| 1W,6B | ● | | | ● | 23 | MAXIMUM BODY DEPTH |
| 1X,6A | ● | ● | | ● | 24 | MAXIMUM BODY BREADTH |

## 5.2 FOOD COUNTERS

The basic approach to ensuring a proper interface between customer and food counter is similar to that used for a bar. Maximum body breadth and depth should be taken into account in establishing clearances for workspace behind the counter. The height of the shelves and depth of the counters should accommodate the human reach limitations of those of smaller body size, for such clearances will also accommodate those of larger body size.

With respect to the public side of the counter, the relationship between seat height and top of the counter should also accommodate the human body properly. One common error is in the relationship of seat height to footrest in relation to a high counter. In many instances, the footrest is too low to accommodate the feet. The result is that the customer's feet simply dangle above the footrest without coming into contact with its surface. This lack of contact does not provide the body with the stability it requires, so muscular forces must take over in order to maintain equilibrium, causing general discomfort, aches, and pains. As if this were not bad enough, the weight of the dangling foot causes pressure on the underside of the thigh just behind the knee, resulting not only in irritation to the skin but obstruction of the circulation of blood.

These conditions are included among the drawings on the following pages, and suggested clearances and other dimensional data for use in making preliminary design assumptions are indicated. The basic anthropometric body measurements most frequently considered in the design of food counters are indicated in the matrix above.

# 5.2 FOOD COUNTERS

The top drawing shows some of the basic clearances required for a typical counter: 36 in, or 91.4 cm, for workspace behind the counter; 18- to 24-in, or 45.7 to 61 cm, for the counter top; and 60 to 66 in, or 152.4 to 167.6 cm, between the front face of the counter and the nearest obstruction. The bottom drawing shows a section through the counter and back counter. Most counters are about 42 in, or 106.7 cm, in height. The clearance from the top of the seat to the underside of the counter top and the depth of the counter top overhang are extremely important. Buttock-knee length and thigh clearance are the key anthropometric measurements to consider for proper body fit. Footrest heights should take into consideration popliteal height. In most cases this is ignored, and 42-in counters are provided with 7-in, or 17.8-cm, footrests that are 23 in, or 58.4 cm, below the seat surface, which cannot work. The popliteal height of the larger user, based on 99th percentile data, is only about 20 in, or 50.8 cm. Therefore, the feet dangle unsupported several inches above the footrest and the body is deprived of any stability. The footrest shown on the drawing, although higher, only serves a portion of the seated users and is intended primarily for standing patrons. The most logical solution is a separate footrest, integral with the stool.

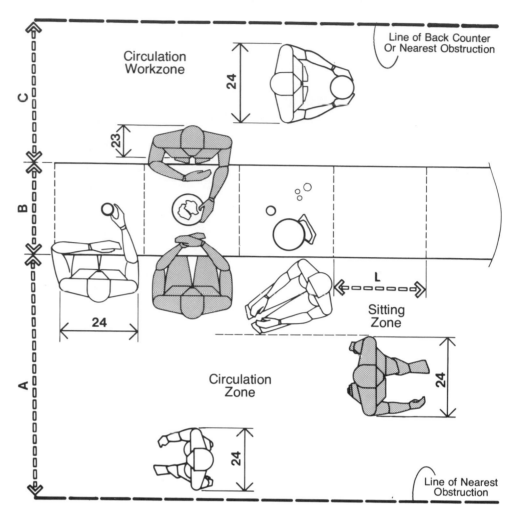

**LUNCH COUNTER**

| | in | cm |
|---|---|---|
| A | 60–66 | 152.4–167.6 |
| B | 18–24 | 45.7–61.0 |
| C | 36 | 91.4 |
| D | 24 | 61.0 |
| E | 12–18 | 30.5–45.7 |
| F | 35–36 | 88.9–91.4 |
| G | 42 | 106.7 |
| H | 30–31 | 76.2–78.7 |
| I | 11–12 | 27.9–30.5 |
| J | 10 | 25.4 |
| K | 12–13 | 30.5–33.0 |

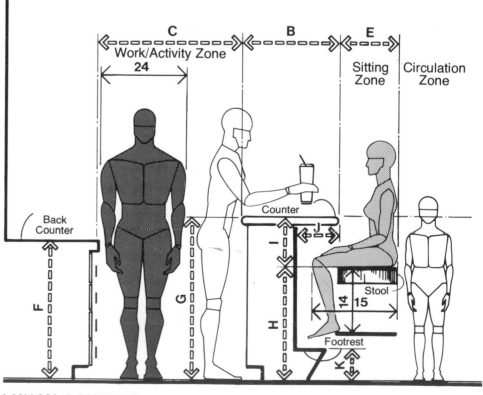

**LUNCH COUNTER**

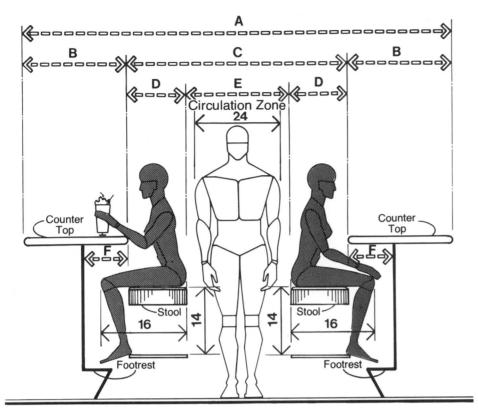

**LUNCH COUNTERS/CLEARANCE BETWEEN STOOLS**

# 5.2 FOOD COUNTERS

The top drawing illustrates in section clearances required between counters when arranged parallel to each other. This is a rather common situation, with counter layouts in a repetitive U configuration. The overall clearance measured from the front edge of one counter to the other is 60 to 72 in, or 152.4 to 182.9 cm. The clearance between counters allows an activity zone for the seated patron at each counter, in addition to a public circulation zone between stools of 36 in, or 91.4 cm. Maximum body breadth is the anthropometric measurement used in establishing the clearance for circulation. Refer to the drawings on the preceding page for additional information regarding the relationship and body fit of the user to the stool, counter, and footrest, and the anthropometric measurements involved. The drawing at the bottom of the page shows in section the clearances required between a counter and a row of tables—another frequently used arrangement. A minimum clearance of 48 in, or 121.9 cm, between the outside edge of the counter stool and the edge of the table allows for a combined circulation and service zone.

**LUNCH COUNTER | TABLE CLEARANCES**

|   | in | cm |
|---|---|---|
| A | 96–120 | 243.8–304.8 |
| B | 18–24 | 45.7–61.0 |
| C | 60–72 | 152.4–182.9 |
| D | 12–18 | 30.5–45.7 |
| E | 36 min. | 91.4 min. |
| F | 10 | 25.4 |
| G | 60–66 | 152.4–167.6 |
| H | 48 min. | 121.9 min. |
| I | 42 | 106.7 |
| J | 12–13 | 30.5–33.0 |
| K | 30–31 | 76.2–78.7 |
| L | 11–12 | 27.9–30.5 |
| M | 16–17 | 40.6–43.2 |
| N | 29–30 | 73.7–76.2 |

# 5.2 FOOD COUNTERS

The top drawing shows a section through a typical soda fountain and indicates some of the basic dimensions and clearances involved. A critical consideration in terms of anthropometrics is reach. The counter here, as for a bar, is essentially a partial enclosure, or "skin," for the fountain equipment. It is the depth of this equipment that establishes the location of the counterperson relative to the customer and the counter surface. The depth of the equipment varies with type and manufacture, but is usually about 30 to 32 in, or 76.2 to 81.3 cm. The counter top itself is normally about 18 in, or 45.9 cm, deep. Limiting the overall dimension from the face of the equipment to the customer's side of the counter top, as shown, will keep the counter-top surface within reach of the counterperson. If the counter top is located further away than suggested in the drawing, the designer should verify that reach is not impaired. The bottom drawing shows clearances necessary to make self-service food counters accessible to the wheelchair user. The service lane must be a minimum of 34 in, or 86.4 cm, to accommodate the wheelchair and the food within a 20-in, or 50.8-cm, maximum reach.

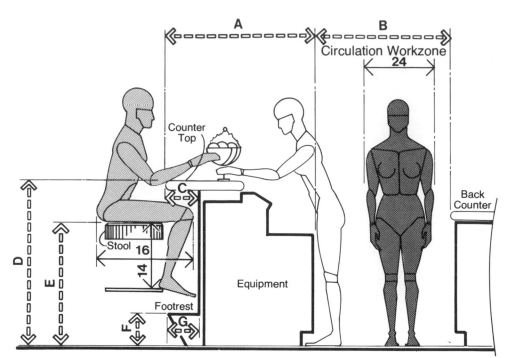

**SODA FOUNTAIN**

|   | in | cm |
|---|---|---|
| A | 41–43 | 104.1–109.2 |
| B | 30–36 | 76.2–91.4 |
| C | 10 | 25.4 |
| D | 42 | 106.7 |
| E | 31–32 | 78.7–81.3 |
| F | 12–13 | 30.5–33.0 |
| G | 9 | 22.9 |
| H | 20 max. | 50.8 max. |
| I | 34 min. | 86.4 min. |
| J | 34 max. | 86.4 max. |

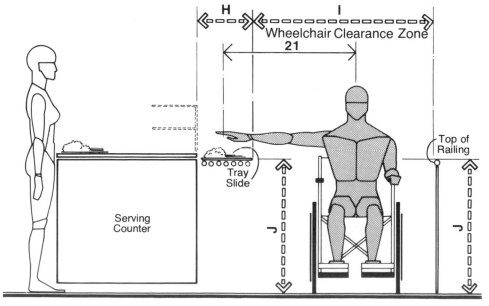

**FOOD SERVICE COUNTERS/WHEELCHAIR ACCESS**

## 5.3 DINING SPACES

| TABLE | SERVICE | DINING | CIRCULATION | ACTIVITIES | ANTHROPOMETRIC DATA | |
|-------|---------|--------|-------------|------------|---------------------|-|
| 1D,2C | | ● | | | 4 | SITTING HEIGHT ERECT |
| 1F,3G | | ◐ | | | 6 | EYE HEIGHT SITTING |
| 1L,2H | | ● | | | 12 | THIGH CLEARANCE |
| 1M,2I | | ● | | | 13 | KNEE HEIGHT |
| 1N,2J | | ◐ | | | 14 | POPLITEAL HEIGHT |
| 1O,2K | | ◐ | | | 15 | BUTTOCK-POPLITEAL LENGTH |
| 1P,2L | | ● | | | 16 | BUTTOCK-KNEE LENGTH |
| 1V,4D | | ○ | | | 22 | THUMB TIP REACH |
| 1W,6B | ● | ● | ● | | 23 | MAXIMUM BODY DEPTH |
| 1X,6A | ● | ● | ● | | 24 | MAXIMUM BODY BREADTH |

Proper clearances for circulation and service aisles, adequate knee and thigh space between the top of the seat and the underside of the table, accessibility for the wheelchair-bound person, and adequate clearance around the perimeter of the table are the basic factors to take into account to ensure the proper relationship between human dimension and dining space. These considerations, all fairly straightforward, can be accommodated fairly simply. The proper allowance per individual seated diner along the table perimeter and, by extension, the table size do require additional thought and in some instances individual research.

All too often, however, the standard table size is simply accepted without question as being adequate to accommodate the designated number of seated diners. The design problem is then viewed exclusively in terms of the number of such tables that can be located within the given space. The fact is that most standard tables used in public dining spaces are not adequate to comfortably accommodate the user. In most instances the only factor taken into account in selecting the size of the table is whether its length can accommodate the width of the chair placed in front of it. The space necessary to accommodate the individual diner should take into account several factors: (1) the width of the chair, (2) the maximum body breadth of a diner of larger body size, plus an allowance for the extension of the elbows away from the body, and (3) the size of the place setting.

Among other considerations examined in the drawings on the following pages is the development of an incremental unit to be used in allocating the proper space per diner. Various table sizes are then established, based on optimal and minimal variations of this individual place-setting zone.

# 5.3 DINING SPACES

The place setting is made up of a studied arrangement of dinnerware and related accessories. During the dining process, it is transformed into a state of disarray, covering a larger zone of the table than at the beginning. This expanded zone occupies a minimum area of 14 by 24 in, or 35.6 by 61 cm. The first group of drawings figuratively labeled shows these zones in relation to tables of varying depth, but of constant minimal width of 24 in, or 61 cm. The center strips represent the surface available for serving dishes, flowers, etc. If we allow for the intrusion of these elements into contiguous zones, a depth of only 40 in, or 101.6 cm, is adequate for their comfortable placement.

In the lower group of drawings these same zones are applied to a 30-in, or 76.2-cm, width. This is related to the maximum body movement involved in the dining activity. Etiquette aside, a 24-in width will allow the arms of the larger user to project beyond the table into circulation lanes. The authors contend that a 30 by 40 in, or 76.2 by 101.6 cm, table is the optimum size to comfortably accommodate two people. The 30-in dimension corresponds to human body breadth. The 40-in dimension allows sufficient room for place setting and accommodates horizontal reach.

| | in | cm |
|---|---|---|
| **A** | 66–78 | 167.6–198.1 |
| **B** | 18–24 | 45.7–61.0 |
| **C** | 30 | 76.2 |
| **D** | 14 | 35.6 |
| **E** | 2 | 5.1 |
| **F** | 24 | 61.0 |
| **G** | 72–84 | 182.9–213.4 |
| **H** | 36 | 91.4 |
| **I** | 16 | 40.6 |
| **J** | 4 | 10.2 |
| **K** | 76–88 | 193.0–223.5 |
| **L** | 40 | 101.6 |
| **M** | 8 | 20.3 |

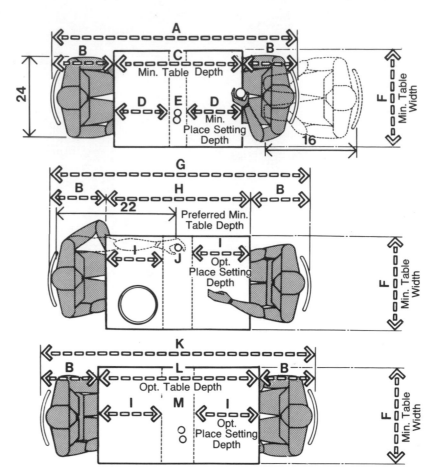

**TABLE SIZES/MINIMUM TABLE WIDTH WITH MINIMUM, PREFERRED MINIMUM, AND OPTIMUM TABLE DEPTHS**

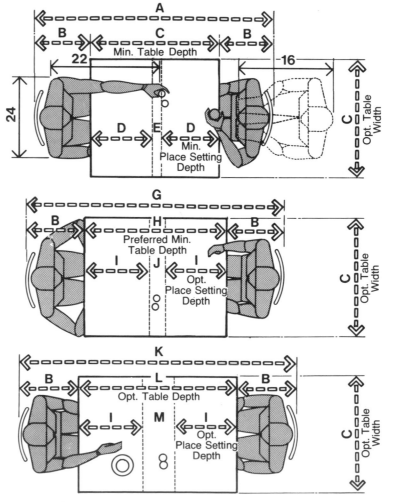

**TABLE SIZES/OPTIMUM TABLE WIDTH WITH MINIMUM, PREFERRED MINIMUM, AND OPTIMUM TABLE DEPTHS**

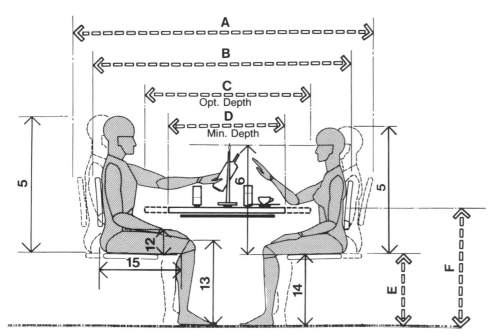

**TABLES/MINIMUM AND OPTIMUM DEPTHS/
VERTICAL CLEARANCES**

Both drawings deal with the height and clearance of dining tables. The top drawing relates to the plans on the preceding page and illustrates a 30- and a 40-in, or a 76.2- and a 101.6-cm, table. The portions of the drawing shown in dotted line reflect the 40-in table. The bottom drawing deals with wheelchair access to a dining table. Clearance from the floor to the underside of the table is critical if the wheelchair-bound diner is to be accommodated. Unfortunately, conflicting requirements, depending on the source consulted, show this dimension to be 29 or 30 in, or 72.5 or 75 cm. The American National Standards Institute (ANSI) indicates the required height of the armrest from the floor to be 29 in, or 72.5 cm. Some state legislation requires 30 in, or 75 cm, to the underside of the table. Unfortunately, a 30-in dimension would place the top of the table surface at about 31 in, or 78.7 cm. Such a height would not comfortably accommodate able-bodied diners of smaller size. To raise the seat height would cause the feet of the smaller user to dangle unsupported, and footrests would be somewhat impractical in a public space. Since armrest heights of many wheelchairs do not, in fact, exceed 29 in, or 72.5 cm, and since most models have removable or adjustable arms, the authors recommend a 29-in clearance, instead of 30 in. Such a dimension will accommodate both handicapped and able-bodied users.

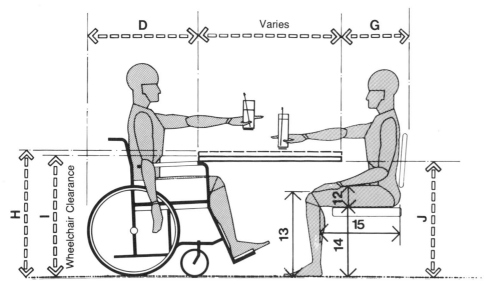

**TABLES / WHEELCHAIR CLEARANCE**

|   | in | cm |
|---|---|---|
| A | 76–88 | 193.0–223.5 |
| B | 66–78 | 167.6–198.1 |
| C | 40 | 101.6 |
| D | 30 | 76.2 |
| E | 16–17 | 40.6–43.2 |
| F | 29–30 | 73.7–76.2 |
| G | 18–24 | 45.7–61.0 |
| H | 31 | 78.7 |
| I | 30 min. | 76.2 min. |
| J | 29 min. | 73.7 min. |

# 5.3 DINING SPACES

The top drawing shows minimal clearance for a combined service and circulation aisle in a low-volume operation. It should be noted that the width indicated will not accommodate two lanes. Either the waiter or customer would have to step aside to avoid body contact. In a high-volume operation, with long aisle lengths, such a clearance would be inadequate. The bottom drawing illustrates a situation where chairs abut a service aisle. The drawing is not intended to serve as a standard for aisle clearance, but merely to indicate all factors involved in establishing that clearance, including intrusions of the chairs into the aisle space. The chair may be relocated as many as four times during the course of the meal. At the beginning, it is much closer to the table. Near the end of the meal in an attempt to relax, one may move the chair away from the table about 24 in, or 61 cm. During intimate conversation it may be brought even closer to the table. Finally, in rising from the chair at the conclusion of the meal, its final location may be as much as 36 in, or 91.4 cm, away. If all intrusions are considered, the clearance between tables could total as much as 108 in, or 274.3 cm, which may prove uneconomical. Yet, to ignore the intrusions would be unrealistic. The authors suggest that, as a reasonable compromise, a clearance between tables of 84 in, or 213.4 cm, be used for preliminary design assumptions.

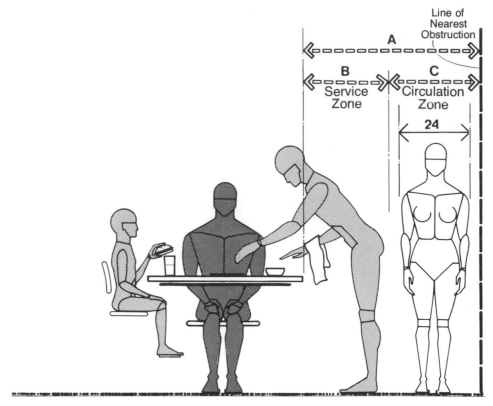

## TABLES / CLEARANCE FOR WAITER SERVICE AND CIRCULATION

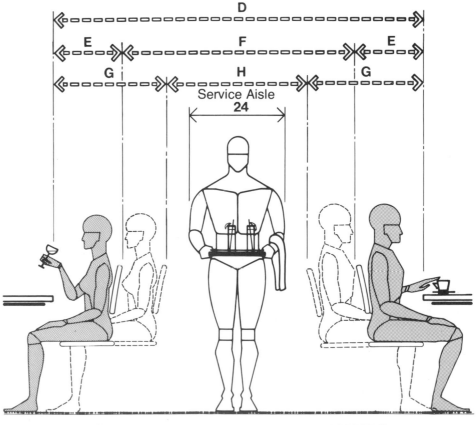

## SERVICE AISLE / CLEARANCE BETWEEN CHAIRS

|   | in | cm |
|---|---|---|
| A | 48 | 121.9 |
| B | 18 | 45.7 |
| C | 30 | 76.2 |
| D | 96–108 | 243.8–274.3 |
| E | 18–24 | 45.7–61.0 |
| F | 60 | 152.4 |
| G | 30–36 | 76.2–91.4 |
| H | 36 | 91.4 |

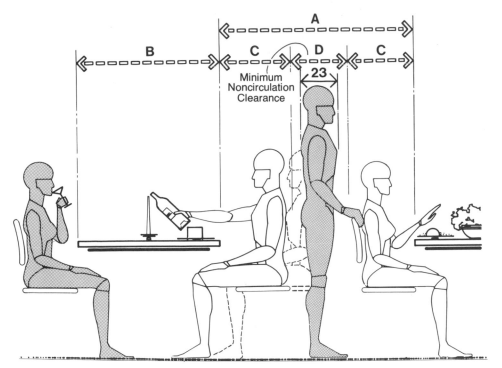

## TABLES / MINIMUM CLEARANCE AND NONCIRCULATION ZONES

In certain table arrangements, chairs of two adjacent tables may be located back to back and some clearance between them must be provided. This clearance would not be for purposes of public circulation or service, but simply to allow access to the chair. A minimum clearance of 18 in, or 45 cm, from chair to chair, as indicated in the top drawing, or a minimum clearance of 54 in, or 137.2 cm, between tables would be adequate. A 66-in, or 167.7-cm, clearance between tables is preferred. The minimum recommended clearance for a service lane is 36 in, or 91.4 cm, as illustrated in the drawings at the center and bottom. Should the diagonal arrangement in the bottom drawing involve smaller tables, the chairs may project beyond the corners of the table. However, the integrity of the 36-in clearance should be maintained. If the chairs do project, the clearance should be measured between the chairs and not the table corners.

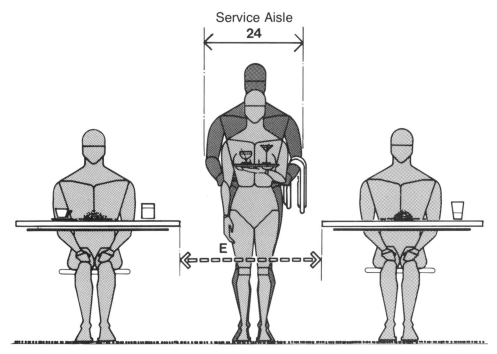

## SERVICE AISLE / CLEARANCE BETWEEN TABLES

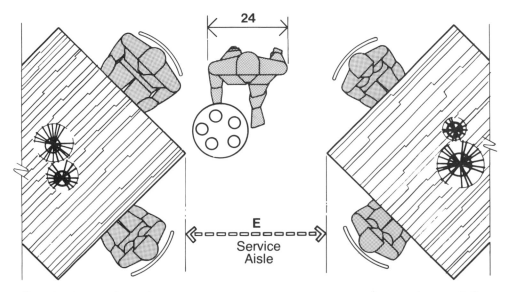

## SERVICE AISLE / CLEARANCE BETWEEN TABLE CORNERS

|   | in | cm |
|---|---|---|
| A | 54–66 | 137.2–167.6 |
| B | 30–40 | 76.2–101.6 |
| C | 18–24 | 45.7–61.0 |
| D | 18 | 45.7 |
| E | 36 | 91.4 |

# 5.3 DINING SPACES

In planning for wheelchair access, the portion of the chair projecting beyond the table will be between 24 and 30 in, or 61 and 76.2 cm. It is suggested that the larger figure be used for preliminary design assumptions. What is not indicated on the drawing are the clearances required for wheelchair maneuvering to and from the table. Turning radii and other information relating to the maneuverability of the wheelchair are provided elsewhere in this book. The drawing at the bottom of the page indicates the clearances required for chair movement in connection with a round table. It should also be noted that the lane width needed to accommodate a wheelchair should be a minimum of 36 in, or 91.4 cm.

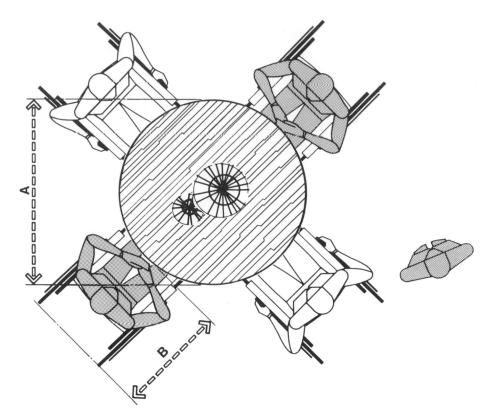

## TABLES / WHEELCHAIR SEATING

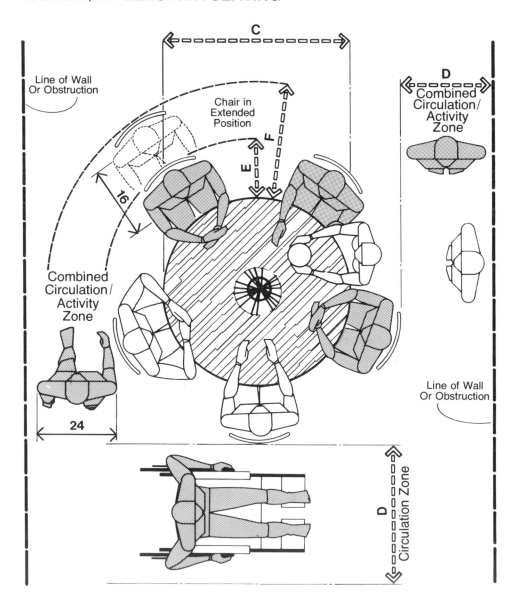

| | in | cm |
|---|---|---|
| A | 48–54 | 121.9–137.2 |
| B | 24–30 | 61.0–76.2 |
| C | 48 | 121.9 |
| D | 36 | 91.4 |
| E | 18–24 | 45.7–61.0 |
| F | 30–36 | 76.2–91.4 |

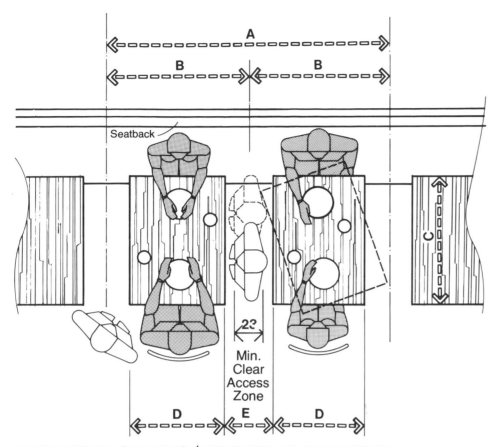

Seatback

23
Min.
Clear
Access
Zone

A

B                    B

C

D          E          D

**BANQUETTE SEATING / MINIMUM CLEARANCES**

Both drawings illustrate the clearances involved for banquette dining arrangements. One of the more critical considerations is access to the banquette seat. The top drawing indicates a minimum clearance between tables. The maximum body depth of the larger person, based on the 99th percentile data, is 13 in, or 33 cm. Allowing for clothing and body movement in addition to the basic body dimension, it becomes apparent that access to the banquette seat for the larger person may require moving the table. The bottom drawing suggests a 24-in, or 61-cm, clearance between tables, which will permit access without disturbing the table location. That spacing will also provide more privacy for the patrons.

F

G                    G

Seatback

24

Clear
Access
Zone

C          H          C

**BANQUETTE SEATING / RECOMMENDED CLEARANCES FOR ACOUSTIC AND VISUAL PRIVACY**

|   | in | cm |
|---|---|---|
| A | 72–76 | 182.9–193.0 |
| B | 36–38 | 91.4–96.5 |
| C | 30 | 76.2 |
| D | 24 | 61.0 |
| E | 12–14 | 30.5–35.6 |
| F | 108 | 274.3 |
| G | 54 | 137.2 |
| H | 24 | 61.0 |

# 5.3 DINING SPACES

Booths, particularly in situations where both the seating and the table are fixed, provide no margin for individual adjustment. This lack of flexibility makes it essential that the anthropometric aspects of the design be considered closely. The height of the compressed seat should reflect popliteal height data; the depth of the seat, buttock-popliteal length data; the distance from the top of the seat to the underside of the table, thigh clearance data; the height of the booth or that of a hanging light fixture above the table top, eye-height sitting data; and the width of the seat, maximum body breadth data.

Equally important is the relation of human dimensions to the aisle for clearance of public and service circulation. The two drawings illustrate in both plan and section some of the basic anthropometric considerations involved.

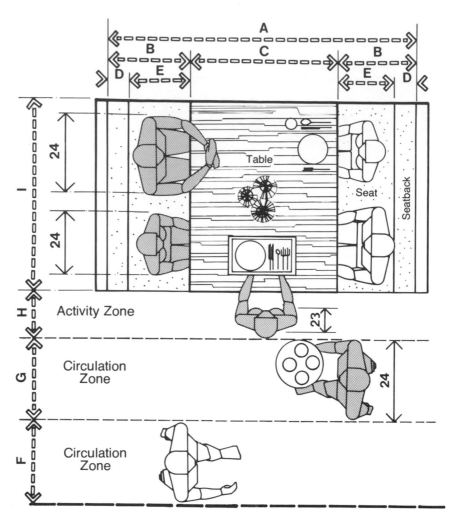

**BOOTH SEATING AND CIRCULATION CLEARANCES**

| | in | cm |
|---|---|---|
| A | 65–80 | 165.1–203.2 |
| B | 17.5–20 | 44.5–50.8 |
| C | 30–40 | 76.2–101.6 |
| D | 2–4 | 5.1–10.2 |
| E | 15.5–16 | 39.4–40.6 |
| F | 30 | 76.2 |
| G | 36 | 91.4 |
| H | 18 | 45.7 |
| I | 48–54 | 121.9–137.2 |
| J | 16–17 | 40.6–43.2 |
| K | 29–30 | 73.7–76.2 |

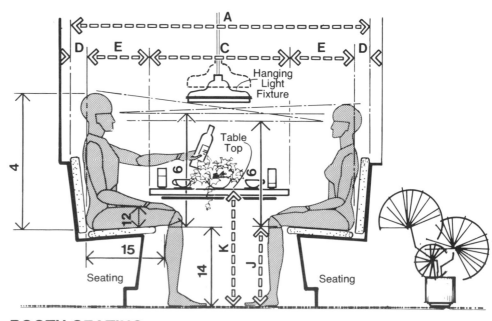

**BOOTH SEATING**

# 6 HEALTH CARE SPACES

| TABLE | 6.1 MEDICAL TREATMENT | 6.2 DENTAL TREATMENT | 6.3 HOSPITAL ROOMS | SPACE — ANTHROPOMETRIC DATA |
|---|---|---|---|---|
| 1A,2B | ◐ | ◐ | | 1 STATURE |
| 1B,3C | ◐ | ◐ | ◐ | 2 EYE HEIGHT |
| 1C,3B | ◐ | | | 3 ELBOW HEIGHT |
| | | | | 4 SITTING HEIGHT ERECT |
| | | | | 5 SITTING HEIGHT NORMAL |
| 1F,3G | ◐ | ◐ | ◐ | 6 EYE HEIGHT SITTING |
| | | | | 7 MIDSHOULDER HEIGHT SITTING |
| | | | | 8 SHOULDER BREADTH |
| | | | | 9 ELBOW-TO-ELBOW BREADTH |
| | | | | 10 HIP BREADTH |
| | | | | 11 ELBOW REST HEIGHT |
| 1L,2H | | ● | | 12 THIGH CLEARANCE |
| | | | | 13 KNEE HEIGHT |
| | | | | 14 POPLITEAL HEIGHT |
| | | | | 15 BUTTOCK-POPLITEAL LENGTH |
| 1P,2L | | ● | ● | 16 BUTTOCK-KNEE LENGTH |
| | | | | 17 BUTTOCK-TOE LENGTH |
| | | | | 18 BUTTOCK-HEEL LENGTH |
| 1S,4C | | | | 19 VERTICAL REACH HEIGHT SITTING |
| 1T,4F | | | | 20 VERTICAL GRIP REACH |
| 1U,4E | ○ | | | 21 SIDE ARM REACH |
| 1V,4D | ○ | ○ | ○ | 22 THUMB TIP REACH |
| 1W,6B | ● | ● | ● | 23 MAXIMUM BODY DEPTH |
| 1X,6A | ● | ● | ● | 24 MAXIMUM BODY BREADTH |

Health care facilities range in sophistication and scope from a modest doctor's or dentist's office to a large hospital complex. Facilities may also include nursing homes, group practices, mental health complexes, drug rehabilitation centers, and medical or dental schools. Demand for health facilities continues to grow, in terms not only of new structures, but also of modernization of existing buildings. Facilities are constantly being retrofitted and added to; and most recently, the recycling and adaptation of buildings, originally intended for other uses, to house health care functions is yet another option taken to meet the growing needs for space.

As in other building types, the anthropometric considerations in the design of health-related interior spaces are extremely important. When the nature of the circumstances surrounding one's brief or extended stay in one of these facilities, whether as patient or visitor, is considered, the quality of the interface between the user and the space takes on greater significance. It is essential also that in terms of the professional and paraprofessional staff, the level of their interface with the work environment be of the highest quality.

All the following situations involve an understanding of human dimension and its impact on the design of interior space: adequate space around a bed for visitor seating and circulation; proper heights and clearances for a nurse's station so that it is responsive to the anthropometric requirements of nurse, patient, and visitor; the placement of the viewing systems so they can accommodate the eye height of the tall and short, seated and standing, male or female viewer; the height of a laboratory or utility table so that it is accessible to those of large or small body size; and clearances necessary to make these spaces accessible to those confined in wheelchairs. The drawings and related text on the following pages examine some of these typical situations and provide the dimensional information necessary for preliminary design assumptions.

| TABLE | EXAMINING | STORAGE | SINK | X-RAY VIEWING | LABORATORY | CIRCULATION | ACTIVITIES | ANTHROPOMETRIC DATA | |
|---|---|---|---|---|---|---|---|---|---|
| 1A,2B | | | ◗ | | | | | 1 | STATURE |
| 1B,3C | | ◗ | ◗ | ◗ | | | | 2 | EYE HEIGHT |
| 1C,3B | ◗ | | ◗ | | | | | 3 | ELBOW HEIGHT |
| 1F,3G | | | | ◗ | ◗ | | | 6 | EYE HEIGHT SITTING |
| 1U,4E | ○ | | | | | | | 21 | SIDE ARM REACH |
| 1V,4D | | | | ○ | | | | 22 | THUMB TIP REACH |
| 1W,6B | | ● | | | | ● | | 23 | MAXIMUM BODY DEPTH |
| 1X,6A | | | | | | ● | | 24 | MAXIMUM BODY BREADTH |

# 6.1 MEDICAL TREATMENT ROOMS

The drawings on the following pages explore various elements of the medical treatment room, including the examination tables, laboratory tables, wash basins, and film viewing systems, in terms of the clearances and other dimensional requirements necessary to ensure their responsiveness to human body size. The heights of tables and counters and their relationship to the heights of the seats used with them are illustrated, and appropriate clearances and other dimensional data to ensure a proper body fit are indicated. The drawings also illustrate comparative relationships between the body size of the female and male user in terms of the various interior elements involved. The major anthropometric measurements to be considered are indicated in the matrix above. Perhaps the most interesting element, in terms of the anthropometric considerations, is the wall-mounted film viewing system. In all probability the design approach will also prove applicable to various other medical equipment not included in the drawings. Of particular concern in any kind of viewing system is the eye height of the seated and standing male and female viewer of large and small body size. These data are extremely useful, if not absolutely essential, in establishing the proper height above the floor at which the unit must be located. The critical problem is to establish a height that will accommodate the majority of users, taking into account the significant difference in eye height between people of small and large body size. Of the drawings that follow is a series concerned exclusively with this aspect of human dimension. One interesting observation is that the difference in eye height between that of a viewer of very small body size and that of one of very large body size is almost twice as much when both people are standing than when both are in a seated position.

# 6.1 MEDICAL TREATMENT ROOMS

The principal anthropometric considerations with film viewing systems involve eye height and human reach capability. The two drawings at the top of the page illustrate reach considerations for the tall and the short user. The drawing at the left shows a small female with 5th percentile reach measurements in contrast with a male of larger body size, reaching over a 24-in, or 61-cm, counter top to make contact with the system surface. The 24-in obstruction reduces the effective reach of the smaller user. The drawing at the right shows that reducing the counter depth below the viewing system to 18 in, or 45.7 cm, enables the smaller user to more comfortably reach the system surface.

The two drawings at the center of the page illustrate the viewing relationship of the small and large male and female standing viewers to the system. It should be noted that the female of smaller body size has the least comfortable viewing position.

The two drawings at the bottom of the page compare the same pairs of viewers in a seated position with the top of the system located 52.5 in, or 133.4 cm, above the floor. Note how the difference in eye heights between viewers of small and large body size is much less when the viewers are seated than when they are standing.

The seated arrangement accommodates the majority of viewers with maximum comfort. For standing viewers a dimension of 72 in, or 182.9 cm, from the top of the system to the floor accommodates most people, but at varying levels of comfort. The smaller viewer may have to rely more heavily on eye and head movement to scan the display.

| | in | cm |
|---|---|---|
| A | 5–6 | 12.7–15.2 |
| B | 18 | 45.7 |
| C | 24 | 61.0 |
| D | 36 | 91.4 |
| E | 72 | 182.9 |
| F | 30 | 76.2 |
| G | 52.5 | 133.4 |

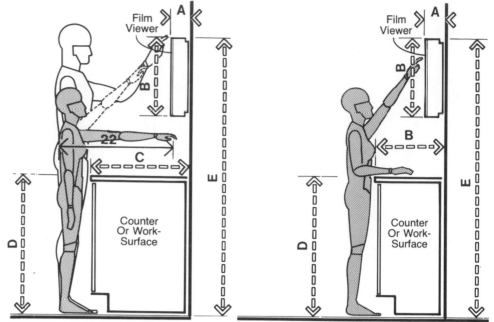

**REACH/TALL AND SHORT STANDING MALE AND FEMALE VIEWERS**

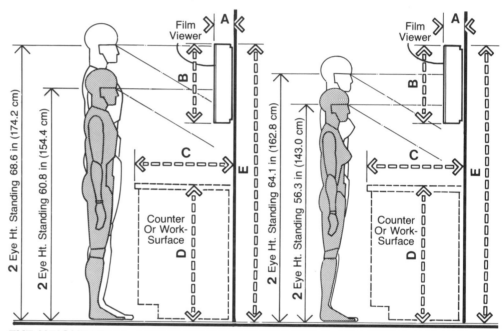

**EYE HEIGHT/TALL AND SHORT STANDING MALE AND FEMALE VIEWERS**

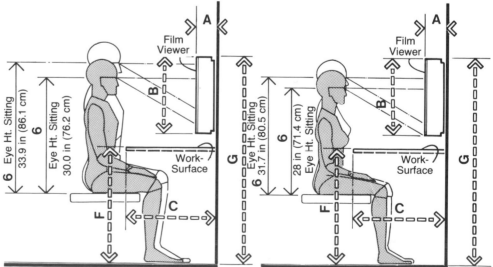

**EYE HEIGHT/TALL AND SHORT SEATED MALE AND FEMALE VIEWERS**

**FILM-VIEWING SYSTEMS (FVS)/ANTHROPOMETRIC CONSIDERATIONS**

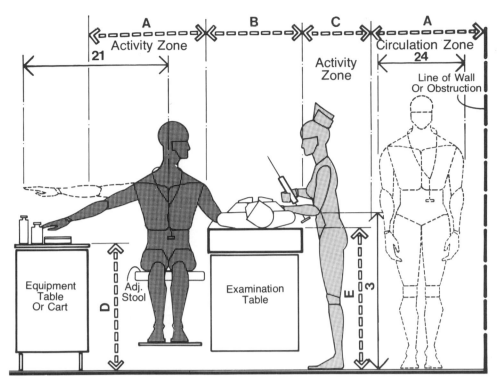

**EXAM AREA/REACH AND CLEARANCE**

# 6.1 MEDICAL TREATMENT ROOMS

The top drawing illustrates recommended clearances around an examination table. A space of at least 30 in, or 76.2 cm, should be allowed for the doctor to function. If the procedure requires instruments or other nearby apparatus, side arm reach data should be used to establish the additional clearance required for the table or cart involved.

The two drawings at the bottom of the page illustrate the anthropometric considerations involved when planning a small laboratory area. The drawing at the left shows the relationship of a female of smaller body size to the table and the wall cabinet above. The shelf should be anthropometrically within the reach of the smaller person in a seated position. Eye height sitting is also a useful measurement to consider, in relation not only to the microscope, but to the visibility of any displays that might be tacked on the facing wall surface. Within certain limits, the adjustability of the seat can be used to raise and lower the eye level as required to accommodate the height of the microscope above the table surface. The drawing on the right illustrates the same relationships for a male of smaller body size.

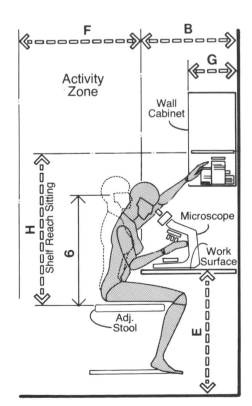

**LAB AREA/ FEMALE CONSIDERATIONS**

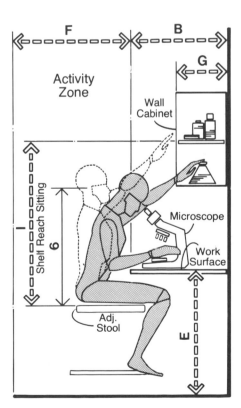

**LAB AREA/ MALE CONSIDERATIONS**

| | in | cm |
|---|---|---|
| **A** | 30 | 76.2 |
| **B** | 24 | 61.0 |
| **C** | 18 | 45.7 |
| **D** | 30–36 | 76.2–91.4 |
| **E** | 34–38 | 86.4–96.5 |
| **F** | 27 | 68.6 |
| **G** | 12–15 | 30.5–38.1 |
| **H** | 39 max. | 99.1 max. |
| **I** | 42 max. | 106.7 max. |

# 6.1 MEDICAL TREATMENT ROOMS

The drawing at the top of the page illustrates the relationship of a male user to an instrument and supply cabinet and a wash-up sink. With respect to the former, eye height and reach are the key anthropometric considerations. The material on the shelves should be accessible to the person of smaller body size. Therefore, 5th percentile reach data should be used to establish the height of the shelf above the floor. It is also important that the depth of the wall cabinet and the distance of the bottom of the cabinet from the top of the counter not obstruct the user's vision of the full counter surface. The overall height of the wall cabinet should allow the user, with a minimum degree of eye and head movement, to visually scan the contents of the cabinet with the least amount of discomfort. For the wash-up sink, the anthropometric measurements of greatest significance are eye height, to establish the location of the mirror, and elbow height, to establish the height of the sink. Research has shown that 2 to 3 in, or 5 to 7.6 cm, below the elbow is a comfortable height for the top of the sink. Generally, sinks are located too low, causing the user discomfort and back pain.

| | in | cm |
|---|---|---|
| A | 18–22 | 45.7–55.9 |
| B | 36–40 | 91.4–101.6 |
| C | 12–18 | 30.5–45.7 |
| D | 18–21 | 45.7–53.3 |
| E | 18 | 45.7 |
| F | 60 max. | 152.4 max. |
| G | 35–36 | 88.9–91.4 |
| H | 72 max. | 182.9 max. |
| I | 21 | 53.3 |
| J | 18–24 | 45.7–61.0 |
| K | 37–43 | 94.0–109.2 |
| L | 54 max. | 137.2 max. |
| M | 24 | 61.0 |
| N | 30–36 | 76.2–91.4 |
| O | 56 max. | 142.2 max. |
| P | 69 max. | 175.3 max. |
| Q | 32–36 | 81.3–91.4 |
| R | 48 max. | 121.9 max. |

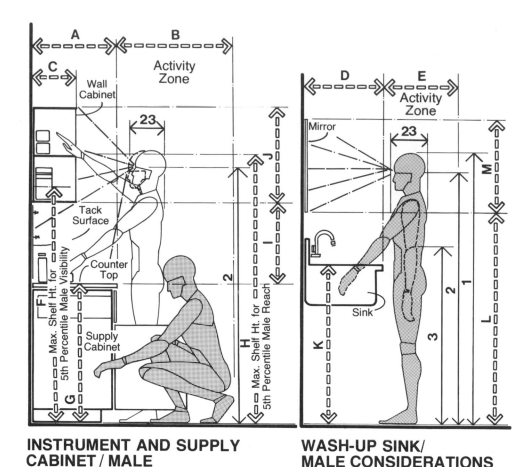

**INSTRUMENT AND SUPPLY CABINET / MALE CONSIDERATIONS**

**WASH-UP SINK/ MALE CONSIDERATIONS**

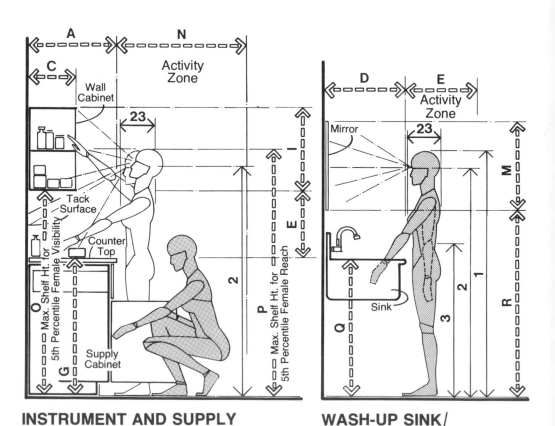

**INSTRUMENT AND SUPPLY CABINET / FEMALE CONSIDERATIONS**

**WASH-UP SINK/ FEMALE CONSIDERATIONS**

| TABLE | TREATMENT | LABORATORY | X-RAY VIEWING | CIRCULATION | ACTIVITIES | ANTHROPOMETRIC DATA |
|---|---|---|---|---|---|---|
| 1A,2B | ● | ◐ | | | 1 | STATURE |
| 1B,3C | ◐ | ◐ | | | 2 | EYE HEIGHT |
| 1F,3G | ◐ | | ◐ | | 6 | EYE HEIGHT SITTING |
| 1L,2H | | ● | ● | | 12 | THIGH CLEARANCE |
| 1P,2L | ● | | ● | | 16 | BUTTOCK-KNEE LENGTH |
| 1V,4D | ○ | | | | 22 | THUMB TIP REACH |
| 1W,6B | ● | ● | | ● | 23 | MAXIMUM BODY DEPTH |
| 1X,6A | ● | | | ● | 24 | MAXIMUM BODY BREADTH |

# 6.2 DENTAL TREATMENT ROOMS

Clearances and other dimensional data related to the typical dental treatment room are shown in the drawings on the pages that follow. Included among the drawings are illustrations in both plan and section of laboratory and x-ray spaces as well as the chair area. Of greatest interest anthropometricly is the almost complete range of adjustability in the design of the patient's chair and the dentist's stool, providing the possibility of creating an almost endless number of interface options. The level of sophistication involved demonstrates clearly that the technological capability necessary to apply the concept of adjustability to other interior systems is available. The basic anthropometric considerations of concern to the designer are not the interface between the seated or standing dentist and the seated or standing patient, but between the dentist and/or the paraprofessional and the various support facilities in the dental treatment room. Counters must be of proper height for comfortable and efficient use. If used from a seated position, the distance from the top of the seat to the underside of the counter must be sufficient to accommodate thigh clearance and knee height. The depth of the counter and the location of shelves either above or below should be related to the limitations of reach of the user of smaller body size. Clearance between the dentist's chair and the wall or nearest physical obstruction, should be sufficient to accommodate at the very least the maximum body breadth of the person of large body size.

# 6.2 DENTAL TREATMENT ROOMS

Rapid technological advances in design and fabrication of dental equipment systems have resulted in dental treatment rooms of great compactness and efficiency. In many instances, anthropometric considerations must be reinterpreted to permit a closer interface among dentist, dental assistant, and the dental equipment systems. Shown on this page are the basic anthropometric and dimensional considerations that should prove helpful to the designer in making certain initial design and planning assumptions. In both drawings, the clearance provided between the dental chair and workcounter, referred to as the "dentist's workzone," is of critical importance in terms of optimizing time/motion efficiency. A dimensional range of 18 to 24 in, or 45.7 to 61.0 cm, is recommended; this overrides ordinary circulation zone requirements. Most dentists have their own preferences for the location and type of instrument delivery systems and other related backup components. In addition, the rapidly evolving dental equipment technology mandates that the designer research the latest systems available.

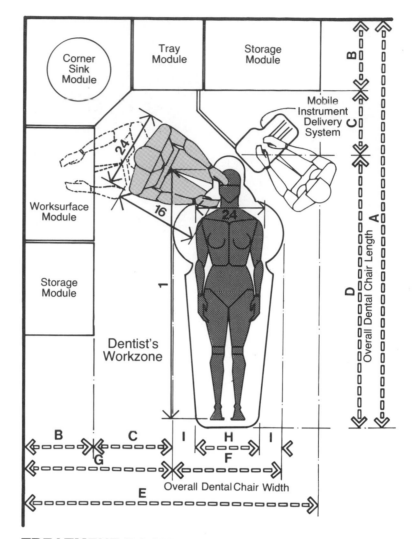

**TREATMENT ROOM**

| | in | cm |
|---|---|---|
| A | 104–118 | 264.2–299.7 |
| B | 18–22 | 45.7–55.9 |
| C | 18–24 | 45.7–61.0 |
| D | 68–72 | 172.7–182.9 |
| E | 66–84 | 167.6–213.4 |
| F | 20–26 | 50.8–66.0 |
| G | 36–46 | 91.4–116.8 |
| H | 16–18 | 40.6–45.7 |
| I | 2–4 | 5.1–10.2 |
| J | 74–86 | 188.0–218.4 |
| K | 10–12 | 25.4–30.5 |
| L | 8–10 | 20.3–25.4 |
| M | 36 min. | 91.4 min. |
| N | 56–70 | 142.2–177.8 |
| O | 28–30 | 71.1–76.2 |
| P | 12–16 | 30.5–40.6 |
| Q | 16–24 | 40.6–61.0 |

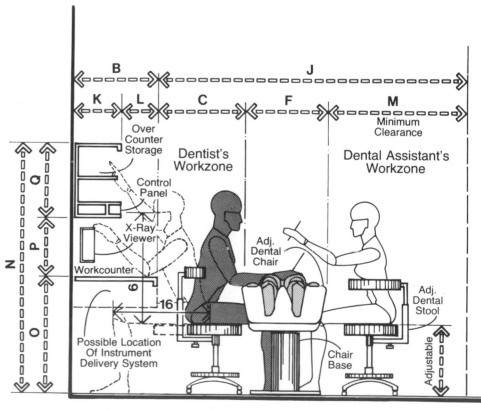

**TREATMENT ROOM / VERTICAL CONSIDERATIONS**

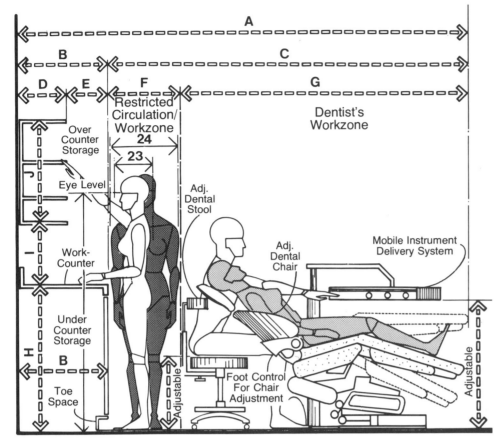

## TREATMENT ROOM / VERTICAL CONSIDERATIONS

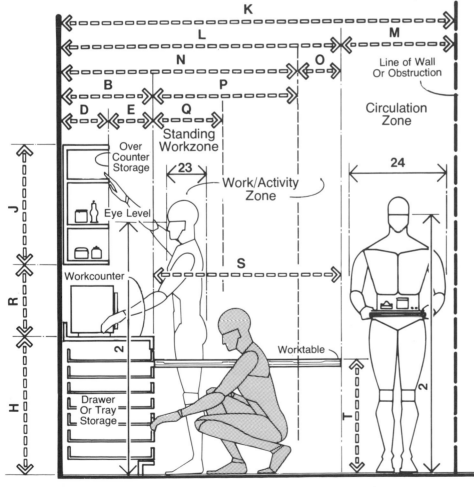

## LABORATORY

Dental equipment and delivery systems clearly demonstrate the concept of adjustability that might just as readily be applied to other interior systems. In the dental treatment room, the total adjustability of the patient's chair, the dentist's stool, and the mobile delivery system all serve as reinforcement of the primary anthropometric needs. In many instances, the dentist may elect to treat a patient while standing. For that position, it is important to understand the vertical clearances related to wall and cabinet storage. Ease of access in performing the various medical procedures, especially those related to patient treatment, must be of the highest priority. The dental laboratory, as illustrated in the bottom drawing, is one of several basic work environments that must be incorporated into a comprehensive dental work area. While the laboratory can vary in size, depending on the dentist's specialty, prime concern must be for those tasks performed in a standing position. Workcounter, worktable, and overcounter storage height must be closely reviewed. A workcounter height of 36 in, or 91.4 cm, is recommended, while the height of the worktable might fall in the dimensional range of 28 to 30 in, or 71.7 to 76.2 cm.

|   | in | cm |
|---|---|---|
| A | 104–118 | 264.2–299.7 |
| B | 18–22 | 45.7–55.9 |
| C | 86–96 | 218.4–243.8 |
| D | 10–12 | 25.4–30.5 |
| E | 8–10 | 20.3–25.4 |
| F | 18–24 | 45.7–61.0 |
| G | 68–72 | 172.7–182.9 |
| H | 36 | 91.4 |
| I | 12–16 | 30.5–40.6 |
| J | 16–28 | 40.6–71.1 |
| K | 94–102 | 238.8–259.1 |
| L | 64–72 | 162.6–182.9 |
| M | 30 | 76.2 |
| N | 52–60 | 132.1–152.4 |
| O | 12 | 30.5 |
| P | 34–38 | 86.4–96.5 |
| Q | 18 | 45.7 |
| R | 16–18 | 40.6–45.7 |
| S | 46–54 | 116.8–137.2 |
| T | 28–30 | 71.1–76.2 |

# 6.2 DENTAL TREATMENT ROOMS

The development of dental x-ray negatives has evolved in recent years from the traditional manual-type sink/ developer to more sophisticated automatic counter top developers. In the examples of both of these methods illustrated at the top of the page, the height of the worksurface must be considered. The desired sink/developer worksurface should be 35 to 36 in, or 88.9 to 91.4 cm. The height of the worksurface for an automatic counter top developer should be the same, unless the specific piece of equipment dictates otherwise. In both instances the standing workzone, as determined by maximum body depth, is established at an absolute minimum of 18 in, or 45.7 cm.

The drawing at the bottom of the page provides information on alternate methods of viewing x-rays. X-rays may be reviewed either by one or two people at a time or by a larger group of people. The height of the table surface required to accommodate an x-ray viewer should assume a dimensional range from 29 to 31 in, or 73.7 to 78.7 cm. Special attention should be paid to clearance if the user is wheelchair-bound. If the x-ray viewer were placed on a vertical wallsurface to accommodate group viewing, eye height sitting would be the operative anthropometric consideration.

|   | in | cm |
|---|---|---|
| A | 52–56 | 132.1–142.2 |
| B | 52–60 | 132.1–152.4 |
| C | 34–38 | 86.4–96.5 |
| D | 18 | 45.7 |
| E | 22–24 | 55.9–61.0 |
| F | 12–18 | 30.5–45.7 |
| G | 24–28 | 61.0–71.1 |
| H | 48 min. | 121.9 min. |
| I | 35–36 | 88.9–91.4 |
| J | 84–100 | 213.–254.0 |
| K | 18–22 | 45.7–55.9 |
| L | 36–48 | 91.4–121.9 |
| M | 30 | 76.2 |
| N | 10–12 | 25.4–30.5 |
| O | 8–10 | 20.3–25.4 |
| P | 18–24 | 45.7–61.0 |
| Q | 29–31 | 73.7–78.7 |
| R | 16–24 | 40.6–61.0 |
| S | 30 | 76.2 |

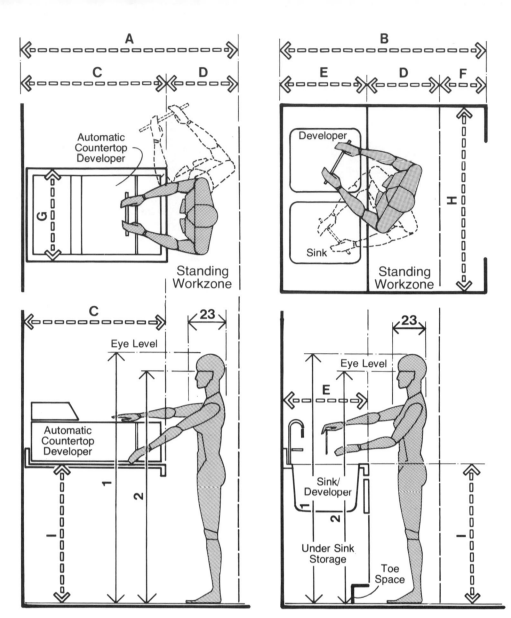

**DARKROOM AND AUTOMATIC DEVELOPING EQUIPMENT**

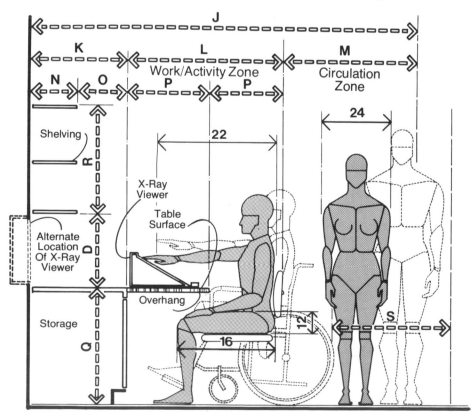

**X-RAY VIEWING**

| TABLE | NURSING STATION | PATIENT BEDROOM | BEDROOM LAVATORY | CIRCULATION | ACTIVITIES | | ANTHROPOMETRIC DATA |
|-------|-----------------|-----------------|------------------|-------------|------------|----|---------------------|
| 1B,3C | | ◑ | | | | 2 | EYE HEIGHT |
| 1F,3G | ◑ | | | | | 6 | EYE HEIGHT SITTING |
| 1P,2L | | ● | | | | 16 | BUTTOCK-KNEE LENGTH |
| 1V,4D | | | ○ | | | 22 | THUMB TIP REACH |
| 1W,6B | ● | ● | | ● | | 23 | MAXIMUM BODY DEPTH |
| 1X,6A | ● | ● | | ● | | 24 | MAXIMUM BODY BREADTH |

# 6.3 HOSPITAL ROOMS

The diagrams that follow illustrate some of the more obvious anthropometric concepts to be taken into account in the design of patients' rooms and nurses' stations. Of the basic considerations, one that has significant emotional impact on both patient and visitor is seating visitors comfortably around the hospital bed. Unfortunately, in many instances the clear overall depth of the room is not sufficient for such accommodation. The design of nurses' stations must also respond to human dimension and body size. The height of the station on the public side should relate to elbow height. The worksurface on the nurses' side should be desk height. The distance from the top of the seat to the underside of the desk should allow sufficient room for thigh clearance. Files should ideally be within reach of the person of smaller body size. The room must also meet the needs of the person confined to a wheelchair. For this, there should be sufficient space to maneuver the chair and adequate clearance under a lavatory to allow the arms of the chair to pass under the rim of the fixture.

# 6.3 HOSPITAL ROOMS

The drawing at the top of the page shows a plan view of a typical nurses' station and the clearances necessary to accommodate the human dimensions involved. A space of 36 in, or 91.4 cm, is a preferred minimum clearance between the desk and back counter. This will allow access to the back counter by a second person while the nurse is engaged at the desk; it also makes the files accessible to the nurse who swivels her chair.

The bottom drawing shows a section through the same station. Anthropometrically, several considerations become apparent. The surface of the rear face of the counter should be sloped slightly. The more the sight line approaches a 90° angle with the display, the clearer the visibility will be. The height of the counter should be comfortable for the visitor and yet not obstruct the vision of the nurse. To ensure the former, 2 to 3 in, or 5 to 7.6 cm, below elbow height should provide a comfortable counter height. For the latter, eye height sitting should be taken into account.

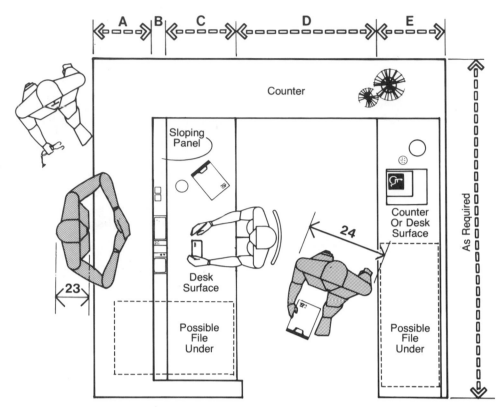

**NURSE'S STATION**

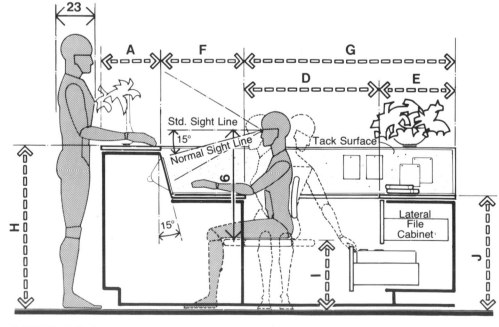

**NURSE'S STATION**

| | in | cm |
|---|---|---|
| A | 15–18 | 38.1–45.7 |
| B | 3–3.5 | 7.6–8.9 |
| C | 18 | 45.7 |
| D | 36 min. | 91.4 min. |
| E | 20 | 50.8 |
| F | 21–21.5 | 53.3–54.6 |
| G | 56 min. | 142.2 min. |
| H | 42–43 | 106.7–109.2 |
| I | 15–18 | 38.1–45.7 |
| J | 30 | 76.2 |

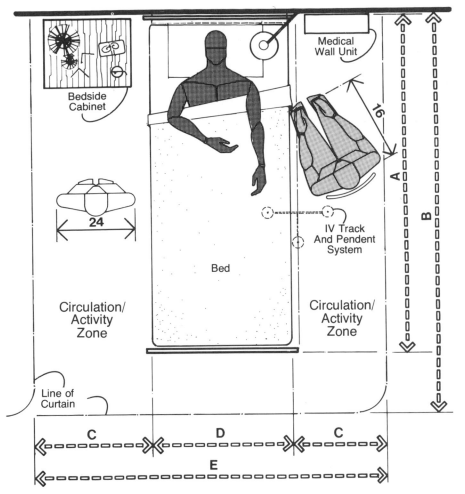

**PATIENT BED CUBICLE WITH CURTAINS**

## 6.3 HOSPITAL ROOMS

The drawing at the top of the page shows recommended clearances around an individual hospital bed. A space of 30 in, or 76.2 cm, will allow for circulation and visitor seating around the bed. This clearance will also be adequate to accommodate a standard medical wall unit on one side and a night table on the other.

The drawing at the bottom shows the cubicle in elevation. The maximum body breadth of the larger user is the principal human dimension to be accommodated anthropometrically for proper clearance between the edge of the bed and the curtain. Since 95 percent of the sample population measured showed a maximum body breadth of 22.8 in, or 57.9 cm, or less, the 30-in clearance should be adequate. To ensure privacy, eye height or stature of the larger person would be the anthropometric measurement to consider in establishing curtain height.

**PATIENT BED CUBICLE WITH CURTAINS**

|   | in | cm |
|---|---|---|
| A | 87 | 221.0 |
| B | 96 | 243.8 |
| C | 30 min. | 76.2 min. |
| D | 39 | 99.1 |
| E | 99 min. | 251.5 min. |
| F | 2–3 | 5.1–7.6 |
| G | 15 | 38.1 |
| H | 54 min. | 137.2 min. |

# 6.3 HOSPITAL ROOMS

The top drawing is based on a double room having a depth of 15 ft, or 4.57 m, which although not very desirable, is frequently found in existing hospital spaces. Half the depth would allow 90 in, or 228.6 cm, for each bed position. The drawing illustrates that an adequate circulation/activity zone of 30 in, or 76.2 cm, can only be provided on one side of the bed. It should be noted that the seated figures to the right of the bed project into the space allocated for the adjacent bed position, suggesting the need for a shared circulation/activity zone between beds. A preferred minimum clearance depth for a double room should be 16.5 ft, or 5 m, to ensure separate circulation/activity zones on both sides of the bed, as indicated in the drawing on the following page. The bottom drawing indicates the clearance required by a wheelchair user to circulate. Using the right wheel as a pivot point, the wheelchair can change directions within 54 in, or 137.2 cm.

|   | in | cm |
|---|---|---|
| **A** | 30 min. | 76.2 min. |
| **B** | 39 | 99.1 |
| **C** | 21 | 53.3 |
| **D** | 90 | 228.6 |
| **E** | 54 | 137.2 |
| **F** | 87 | 221.0 |
| **G** | 140 | 355.6 |
| **H** | 54 min. | 137.2 min. |

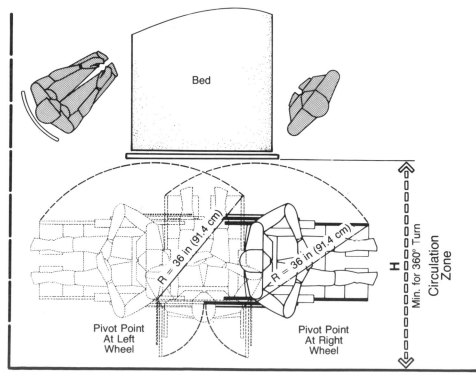

**PATIENT BEDROOM**

**PATIENT BEDROOM / WHEELCHAIR MANEUVERING SPACE**

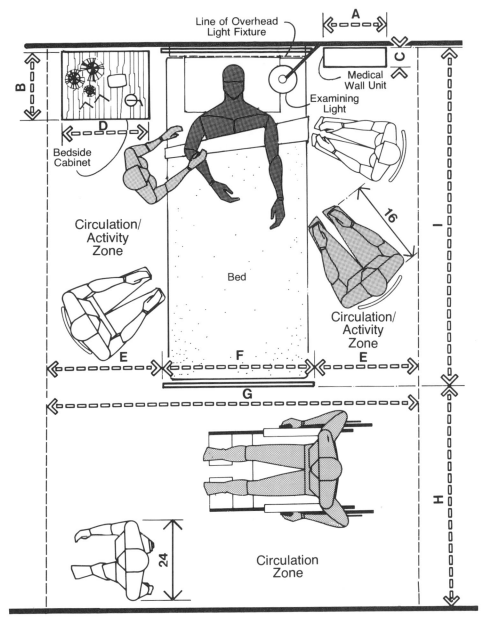

**PERSONAL AREA / DOUBLE OR FOUR BEDROOM**

The drawing at the top of the page shows the personal area around an individual bed in a double or four-bed arrangement. A preferred depth of 99 in, or 251.5 cm, will allow for a 30-in, or 76.2-cm, circulation/activity zone on both sides of the bed. A space of 96 in, or 243.8 cm, would be the absolute minimum and would require that a few inches of zone space be shared with the personal area of the adjacent bed position.

The drawing at the bottom of the page illustrates the relationship of the wheelchair user to a wall-hung hospital lavatory. It is essential that sufficient clearance be provided to allow the wheelchair to slide partially under the bottom edge of the fixture. For proper access to controls anthropometrically, thumb tip reach should be taken into account. For this, 5th percentile data should be used. If the controls are within reach of the person of small body size, they will also be within reach of those having a larger body size. For further information concerning the interface between the wheelchair user and the lavatory, refer to Section 8.3, Public Bathrooms.

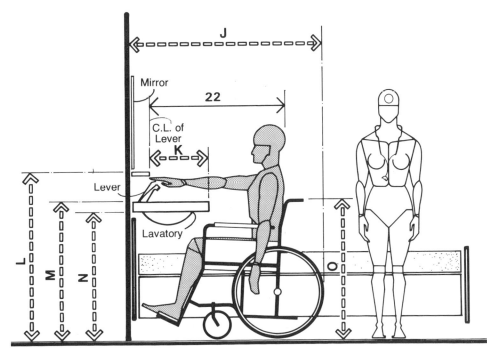

**BEDROOM LAVATORY**

|   | in | cm |
|---|---|---|
| **A** | 17–18 | 43.2–45.7 |
| **B** | 18 | 45.7 |
| **C** | 5–6 | 12.7–15.2 |
| **D** | 20 | 50.8 |
| **E** | 28.5–30 | 72.4–76.2 |
| **F** | 39 | 99.1 |
| **G** | 96–99 | 243.8–251.5 |
| **H** | 48–66 | 121.9–167.6 |
| **I** | 87 | 221.0 |
| **J** | 48 | 121.9 |
| **K** | 18 max. | 45.7 max. |
| **L** | 40 max. | 101.6 max. |
| **M** | 34 max. | 86.4 max. |
| **N** | 30 min. | 76.2 min. |
| **O** | 36 | 91.4 |

# 6.3 HOSPITAL ROOMS

The drawing at the top of the page shows the clearances required in front of a hospital room door to accommodate a wheelchair user. An area of 60 by 60 in, or 152.4 by 152.4 cm, is preferred to allow the disabled user to maneuver the wheelchair into an appropriate approach position, open the door, and exit. A wheelchair can also be maneuvered within a 48- by 48-in, or 121.9- by 121.9-cm, area, but such a space allocation is extremely tight and should be viewed as an absolute minimum. Since door openings to hospital rooms are large enough to allow the passage of beds and other relatively wide equipment, the standard door widths are more than adequate to accommodate the wheelchair.

The drawing at the bottom of the page illustrates the door clearance necessary to allow the passage of a standard bed. In broken line, the drawing also indicates the outline of a wheelchair, showing that a door width appropriate for the passage of a bed is more than adequate to accommodate the passage of a wheelchair.

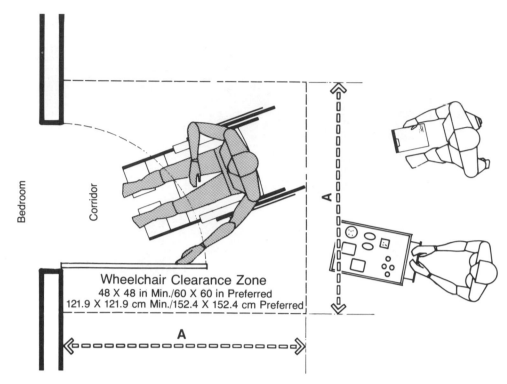

Wheelchair Clearance Zone
48 X 48 in Min./60 X 60 in Preferred
121.9 X 121.9 cm Min./152.4 X 152.4 cm Preferred

**BEDROOM ENTRANCE DOOR**

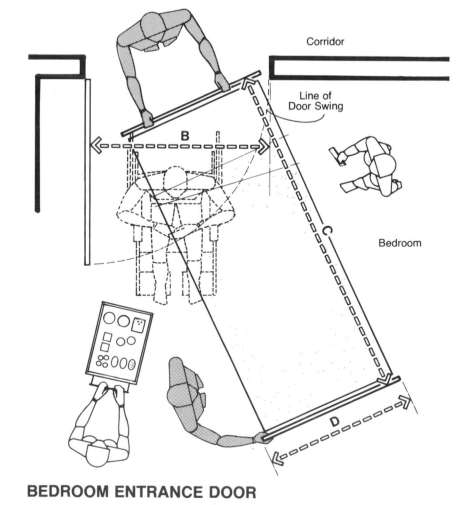

**BEDROOM ENTRANCE DOOR**

|   | in | cm |
|---|-----|------|
| **A** | 60 | 152.4 |
| **B** | 46–48 | 116.8–121.9 |
| **C** | 87 | 221.0 |
| **D** | 39 | 99.1 |

| TABLE | 7.1 EXERCISE ROOMS | 7.2 SPORTS AND GAMES | 7.3 WORK AND CRAFT | SPACE — ANTHROPOMETRIC DATA |
|---|---|---|---|---|
| 1A,2B,7B | ● | ◐ | ◐ | 1 STATURE |
| 1B,3C | | | ◐ | 2 EYE HEIGHT |
| 1C,3B | | ◐ | ◐ | 3 ELBOW HEIGHT |
| 1D,2C | ● | | | 4 SITTING HEIGHT ERECT |
| 1E,2D | | | ◐ | 5 SITTING HEIGHT NORMAL |
| | | | | 6 EYE HEIGHT SITTING |
| 1G,3E | ◐ | | | 7 MIDSHOULDER HEIGHT SITTING |
| | | | | 8 SHOULDER BREADTH |
| | | | | 9 ELBOW-TO-ELBOW BREADTH |
| | | | | 10 HIP BREADTH |
| 1K,2G | | | ◐ | 11 ELBOW REST HEIGHT |
| 1L,2H,7F | | | ● | 12 THIGH CLEARANCE |
| | | | | 13 KNEE HEIGHT |
| 1N,2J,7H | ● | | ◐ | 14 POPLITEAL HEIGHT |
| 1O,2K,7I | ● | | ◐ | 15 BUTTOCK-POPLITEAL LENGTH |
| 1P,2L | ● | | | 16 BUTTOCK-KNEE LENGTH |
| | | | | 17 BUTTOCK-TOE LENGTH |
| 1R,4B | ● | | | 18 BUTTOCK-HEEL LENGTH |
| | | | | 19 VERTICAL REACH HEIGHT SITTING |
| 1T,4F | | ● | | 20 VERTICAL GRIP REACH |
| 1U,4E | ● | ● | ○ | 21 SIDE ARM REACH |
| 1V,4D | ◐ | ● | ○ | 22 THUMB TIP REACH |
| 1W,6B | ● | | ● | 23 MAXIMUM BODY DEPTH |
| 1X,6A | ● | ● | ● | 24 MAXIMUM BODY BREADTH |

Rising incomes, shorter work weeks, longer vacations, more holidays, earlier retirement, increased longevity, smaller families, greater affluence, and a host of other socioeconomic factors have resulted in a change in lifestyle and value systems. For many, the so-called work ethic has given way to the emerging leisure ethic. By the year 2000, for example, it has been estimated that over 2 billion people will be traveling and that tourism may well rank among the world's largest industries. Some $160 billion were spent in 1977 on leisure and recreation, and some sources contend that measured by people's spending, leisure time activities have become the nation's number one industry.

This leisure and recreation boom will increase the demand for the design of private and commercial interior spaces to house the various facilities and/or systems. These may range from traditional sports and games to sophisticated exercise and body building equipment and thermally controlled environments. Some may involve intensely vigorous participation, while others may be relatively passive. Other facilities may include arts and crafts and do-it-yourself activities. Some pursuits of the future may be similar to those with which we are familiar today. Many may not. For certain, all will involve human dimension and interior space and the interface between people and the components of that space. The height of a workbench or drawing table for comfortable and practical use, the nature of the exercise equipment, and the anthropometric requirements for the user's interface with that equipment are just a few of the factors that must be considered.

Human body size and dimension are a particularly significant factor in the more physical and active sports. The avid sports fan need not refer to published anthropometric data to tell you that the size of the professional athlete has undergone a dramatic increase over the last forty years. The 176-lb, or 80-kilo, defensive football player, once considered large, is now thought by many to be too small to play as a wide receiver. The tall 73-in, or 185-cm, basketball center of the 1930s is now too short to play the guard position. The Olympic track records of forty and fifty years ago are now being easily broken by women. The size, physical strength, speed skills, training methods, and diet of today's athlete have improved to such an extent that dimensional standards and space requirements that once were adequate must be recalculated.

# 7.1 EXERCISE AREAS

| TABLE | EXERCISE | SAUNA | LOCKER ROOM | ACTIVITIES | | ANTHROPOMETRIC DATA |
|---|---|---|---|---|---|---|
| 1A,2B | ● | ● | | | 1 | STATURE |
| 1D,2C | ● | | | | 4 | SITTING HEIGHT ERECT |
| 1G,3E | ◑ | | | | 7 | MIDSHOULDER HEIGHT SITTING |
| 1N,2J | | ◑ | ◑ | | 14 | POPLITEAL HEIGHT |
| 1O,2K | | ◑ | | | 15 | BUTTOCK-POPLITEAL LENGTH |
| 1P,2L | ● | ● | ● | | 16 | BUTTOCK-KNEE LENGTH |
| 1R,4B | ● | | | | 18 | BUTTOCK-HEEL LENGTH |
| 1U,4E | ● | | | | 21 | SIDE ARM REACH |
| 1V,4D | ● | | ○ | | 22 | THUMB TIP REACH |
| 1W,6B | ● | | ● | | 23 | MAXIMUM BODY DEPTH |
| 1X,6A | ● | ● | ● | | 24 | MAXIMUM BODY BREADTH |

The drive for health and physical fitness has made exercise activities a popular pastime for many and a major business enterprise for others. Some activities require no equipment, while others involve equipment ranging in levels of sophistication and cost from a simple set of fixed-weight dumbbells to precision-engineered nine-station exercise machines costing thousands of dollars. In all situations, however, the spaces designated to house these activities must respond to human dimension. The drawings on the following pages illustrate some of the more fundamental exercise activities and suggest clearances and other dimensional data for use in making preliminary design assumptions. The major anthropometric measurements to consider are indicated in the above matrix.

Saunas and hydrotherapeutic whirlpool equipment are also frequently provided within exercise spaces. A few representative models illustrating the relationship of the human body to the equipment are also included in the drawings in this section.

Most exercise spaces also include locker facilities of one type or another and their design must respond to human dimension and body size as well. The height of the benches must conform to the general anthropometric requirements for seating. Of principal concern is the popliteal height of the user. Buttock-heel length and/or buttock-toe length data of the user having a larger body size are useful in determining the extent to which the body of the seated user will project into the space between the edge of the bench and the face of the locker. This dimension plus the maximum body breadth of a larger person can then be used in establishing a comfortable overall clearance between bench and locker for circulation as well as accommodation of the person seated on the bench.

# 7.1 EXERCISE AREAS

The top drawing indicates in side and front view the clearances required by the human body while engaged in sit-up exercises. Although it is recommended that in establishing clearances, the person of larger body size be used as a model, the ranges shown reflect small and large male and female data. The 5th and 95th percentile vertical grip reach measurements were used as the basis of the dimensions, with an allowance to compensate for the fact that the anthropometric measurement does not quite extend to the tip of the fingers. The authors suggest that even if the design is intended for a particular population of smaller body size, the larger measurements be used. The largest clearance required would be for the large male, and is shown as 91.5 in or 232.4 cm.

The center drawing provides the designer with the dimensional information necessary to establish basic spacing for an exercise class.

The bottom drawing shows the clearance required for push-up exercises. Stature would be the most useful anthropometric measurement to consider.

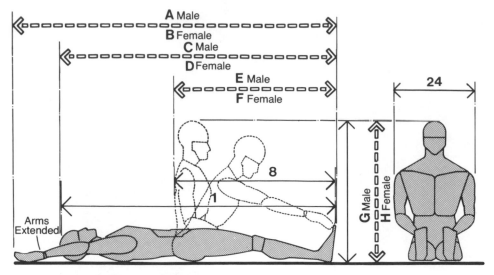

**SIT-UP FLOOR EXERCISE**

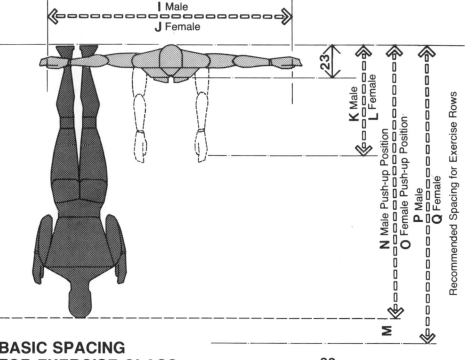

**BASIC SPACING FOR EXERCISE CLASS**

|   | in | cm |
|---|---|---|
| A | 80–91.5 | 203.2–232.4 |
| B | 75–87 | 190.5–221.0 |
| C | 65–74 | 165.1–188.0 |
| D | 60–69 | 152.4–175.3 |
| E | 32–37 | 81.3–94.0 |
| F | 27–37 | 68.6–94.0 |
| G | 33.2–38.0 | 84.3–96.5 |
| H | 30.9–35.7 | 78.5–90.7 |
| I | 58–68 | 147.3–172.7 |
| J | 54–76 | 137.2–193.0 |
| K | 29.7–35.0 | 75.4–88.9 |
| L | 26.6–31.7 | 67.6–80.5 |
| M | 6–12 | 15.2–30.5 |
| N | 63–73 | 160.0–185.4 |
| O | 61–67 | 154.9–170.2 |
| P | 79–85 | 200.7–215.9 |
| Q | 73–79 | 185.4–200.7 |
| R | 23–38 | 58.4–96.5 |
| S | 10–16 | 25.4–40.6 |

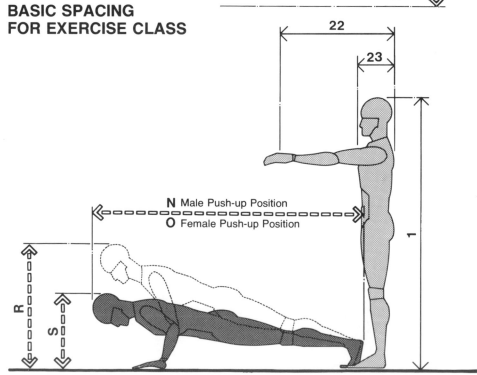

**SPACE REQUIREMENTS FOR BASIC PUSH-UP POSITION**

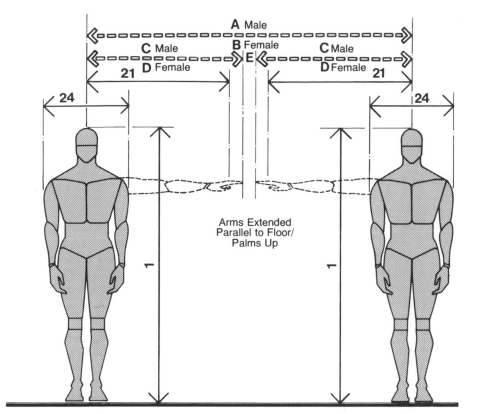

## MINIMUM EXERCISE CLEARANCE REQUIREMENTS

Arms Extended
Parallel to Floor/
Palms Up

The top drawing should be helpful in establishing minimum center spacing for standing exercises in place. The drawing is not intended as a standard, but rather as a base of reference for preliminary design assumptions. The nature of the particular exercise and the intensity of body movements involved should all be taken into consideration.

Certain exercises require significant head room. Dance and similar activities, for example, require considerable clearance to avoid accidents. The bottom drawing shows only two such possibilities. There are, obviously, many variations. The tables in Part B should provide the necessary data with which to establish clearances appropriate to those variations.

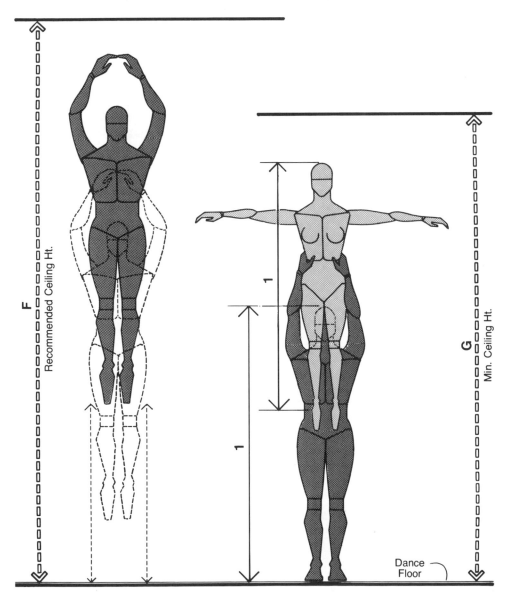

## DANCE AND EXERCISE PRACTICE ROOMS/ CEILING HEIGHT REQUIREMENTS

Dance Floor

|   | in | cm |
|---|-----|-----|
| A | 65–80 | 165.1–203.2 |
| B | 61–88 | 154.9–223.5 |
| C | 31–37 | 78.7–94.0 |
| D | 29–41 | 73.7–104.1 |
| E | 3–6 | 7.6–15.2 |
| F | 144 | 365.8 |
| G | 120 | 304.8 |

# 7.1 EXERCISE AREAS

The two corresponding drawings show typical exercise equipment available on the market. The top drawing typifies the classic exercise bicycle and shows some of the clearances required in a commercial installation. The bottom drawing is representative of the many weight-lifting devices presently in use. The front and side views indicate some of the overall dimensions as well as the relationship of the human body to the equipment. Dimensions and general configuration vary with model and manufacturer, but the information shown can be used for making preliminary design assumptions.

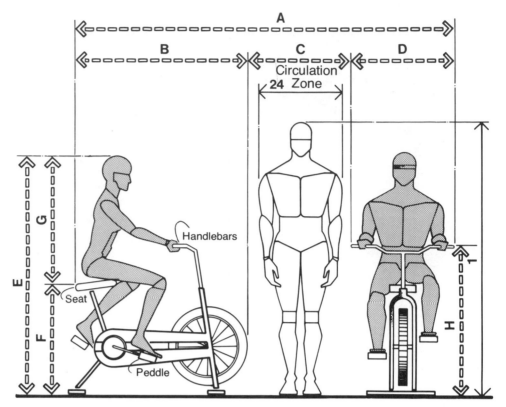

**EXERCISE BICYCLE**

| | in | cm |
|---|---|---|
| A | 83–104 | 210.8–264.2 |
| B | 35–48 | 88.9–121.9 |
| C | 30 | 76.2 |
| D | 18–26 | 45.7–66.0 |
| E | 55–68 | 139.7–172.7 |
| F | 25–30 | 63.5–76.2 |
| G | 30–38 | 76.2–96.5 |
| H | 46 | 116.8 |
| I | 36–48 | 91.4–121.9 |
| J | 58–76 | 147.3–193.0 |
| K | 12–18 | 30.5–45.7 |
| L | 12 | 30.5 |
| M | 6–12 | 15.2–30.5 |
| N | 4–10 | 10.2–25.4 |
| O | 48–54 | 121.9–137.2 |
| P | 9–14 | 22.9–35.6 |
| Q | 18–20 | 45.7–50.8 |

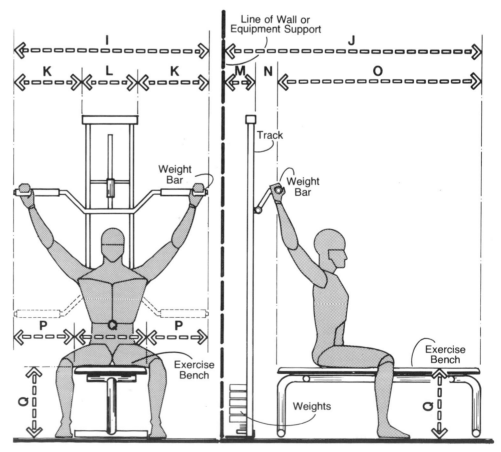

**WALL-MOUNTED LATISSIMUS POWER LIFT UNIT**

**ANTHROPOMETRICALLY CONTOURED
HYDROTHERAPY POOL**

Most hydrotherapy pools provide turbulent hot water massage. Some models, such as the ones shown on this page, have been anthropometrically contoured to provide proper support for the back, particularly in the lumbar region. The pools are manufactured in a variety of profiles to accommodate different body positions. The height of the pools is between 33 and 38 in, or 83.8 and 96.5 cm. The lengths and widths vary with the model.

**ANTHROPOMETRICALLY CONTOURED
HYDROTHERAPY POOL**

|   | in | cm |
|---|------|-----------|
| A | 33–38 | 83.8–96.5 |
| B | 9–12 | 22.9–30.5 |
| C | 38–44 | 96.5–111.8 |
| D | 13–16 | 33.0–40.6 |
| E | 12–15 | 30.5–38.1 |
| F | 11–14 | 27.9–35.6 |
| G | 8–11 | 20.3–27.9 |

# 7.1 EXERCISE AREAS

The sauna is essentially a thermal bath using dry heat, unlike the low heat and high humidity of the steam bath. Although there are many complete prefabricated models on the market, the heater units can be purchased separately. It is therefore relatively simple to custom design an individual installation.

The top drawing illustrates some of the critical dimensions involved. Two possible ceiling heights are indicated. The alternate height will allow more comfortable access to the second tier bench, while the normal height will permit installation within the conventional 96-in, or 243.8-cm, ceiling limitations of most residential interior spaces.

The bottom drawing shows a section through a typical locker room. The restricted circulation zone shown at the right would require either the seated or the standing person to move out of the way to avoid body contact. The circulation zone at the left would allow more comfortable passage without body contact.

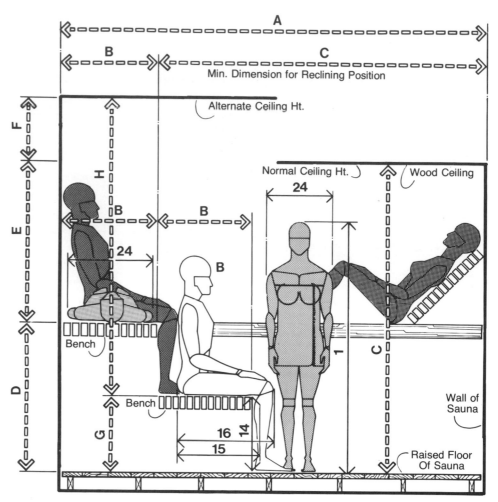

**SECTION THROUGH SAUNA ROOM**

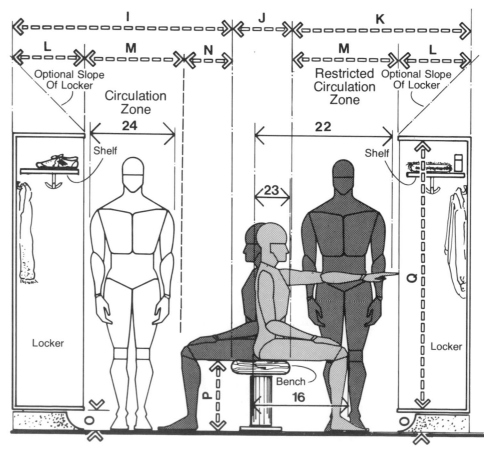

**LOCKER ROOM**

|   | in | cm |
|---|---|---|
| **A** | 108 | 274.3 |
| **B** | 24 | 61.0 |
| **C** | 84 | 213.4 |
| **D** | 36–40 | 91.4–101.6 |
| **E** | 44–48 | 111.8–121.9 |
| **F** | 12–14 | 30.5–35.6 |
| **G** | 18–20 | 45.7–50.8 |
| **H** | 78 min. | 198.1 min. |
| **I** | 56–64 | 142.2–162.6 |
| **J** | 12–15 | 30.5–38.1 |
| **K** | 42–48 | 106.7–121.9 |
| **L** | 12–18 | 30.5–45.7 |
| **M** | 30 | 76.2 |
| **N** | 14–16 | 35.6–40.6 |
| **O** | 4–6 | 10.2–15.2 |
| **P** | 14–17 | 35.6–43.2 |
| **Q** | 60–72 | 152.4–182.9 |

| | | | **7.2** SPORTS AND GAMES | |
|---|---|---|---|---|

| TABLE | TABLE TENNIS | POOL TABLE | BASKETBALL | ACTIVITIES | ANTHROPOMETRIC DATA |
|---|---|---|---|---|---|
| 1A,2B | | | ◗ | 1 | STATURE |
| 1C,3B | ◗ | ◗ | | 3 | ELBOW HEIGHT |
| 1T,4F | | | ◗ | 20 | VERTICAL GRIP REACH |
| 1U,4E | ● | | | 21 | SIDE ARM REACH |
| 1X,6A | | ● | | 24 | MAXIMUM BODY BREADTH |

Aside from the basic anthropometric considerations involved to accommodate most sports and game activities, certain of these activities present some unique problems. Can basketball, for example, be truly considered a "sport" if most players must have a 99th percentile stature to participate? A player with a 90th or 95th percentile stature, although possessing skills and agility, would be at an obvious disadvantage for no reason but the body size of his opponent. A tall player may use a stuff shot, since his tremendous height enables him to jump high in the air. With both hand and ball positioned slightly above the rim of the basket, he is then able in one swift downward thrust to literally stuff the ball through the basket. A proposal is presently under consideration to raise the height of the rim to deny the tall player the use of this shot. It is doubtful that Dr. James Naismath, when he conceived the game in 1891, envisioned an 84-in, or 214-cm center, with the ability to forcefully stuff a round ball into a wooden basket. This condition is one of the many explored in the text and the drawings on the following pages. Perhaps the relationships between human dimension and the degree to which it impacts on the intended spirit of competitive sports should be studied across the board in all areas of athletics—surely a novel and interesting investigation for designer and anthropometrist alike.

The present lack of enforceable building code regulations to ensure that the design of interior spaces housing active sports corresponds to human dimension and the dynamics of people in motion constitutes a potential threat to the safety of the participant. There are, for example, no code regulations that establish the minimum space needed between the basketball court boundary lines and the nearest obstruction to allow a player running off the court to reduce his rate of speed to avoid crashing head-on into a wall or other obstacle. Similarly, there are no code requirements establishing minimum clearances between a diving board and any overhead obstruction or between a tennis court baseline and back fence. Nor do minimum ceiling height requirements exist for spaces where a gymnast practices or performs.

The absence of regulations of the type mentioned not only poses a serious threat to the safety of the users, but it makes both client and designer legally responsible in the event of injury or death if it can be demonstrated that reasonable clearances were not provided. Moreover, in cases where extra-legal guidelines, recommended standards, or simple rules of thumb are the only criteria available, the designer should seriously question and reevaluate them in terms of current published anthropometric data and the nature and character of the materials and physical arrangement of the equipment involved. Included among the drawings on the pages that follow are examples of some of the problems mentioned. The matrix above indicates some of the more relevant anthropometric measurements applicable to spaces used for sports and game activities.

# 7.2 SPORTS AND GAMES

The top drawing indicates side clearance requirements for a table tennis installation within a residential environment: 48 in, or 121.9 cm, is the absolute minimum, while 72 in, or 182.9 cm, is preferred. The bottom drawing indicates the clearances required at either end of the table. In a close-up position, the player usually functions within 24 to 36 in, or 61 to 91.4 cm, of the edge of the table. An overall clearance between the edge of the table and the wall or nearest physical obstruction—between 84 and 120 in, or 213.4 to 304.8 cm—is suggested. The smaller figure should be regarded as an absolute minimum, and the larger figure as the preferred clearance. The latter, however, may be difficult to provide in terms of the room size required. The extent of clearance is a function of the size of the players and the intensity and skill with which the game is played. What must be considered is not only the space required for low-key volleying but the space required, for example, to chase a strategically placed ball, return it, decelerate, and ultimately stop, all in enough time to avoid colliding into the wall at the rear or side of the playing area.

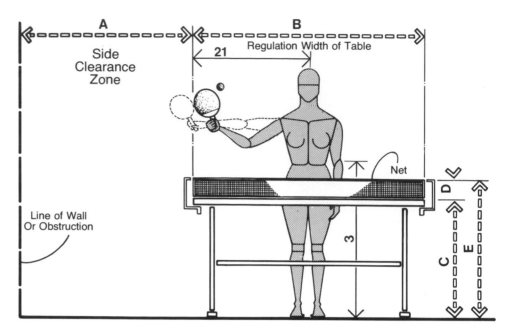

**RESIDENTIAL TABLE TENNIS REQUIREMENTS**

|   | in | cm |
|---|---|---|
| A | 48–72 | 121.9–182.9 |
| B | 60 | 152.4 |
| C | 30 | 76.2 |
| D | 6 | 15.2 |
| E | 36 | 91.4 |
| F | 84–132 | 213.4–335.3 |
| G | 54 | 137.2 |
| H | 60–96 | 152.4–243.8 |
| I | 24–36 | 61.0–91.4 |

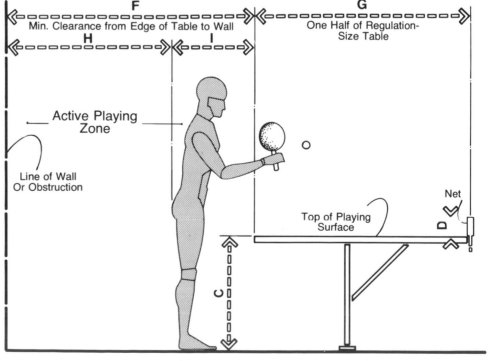

**RESIDENTIAL TABLE TENNIS REQUIREMENTS/ REAR CLEARANCE ZONE**

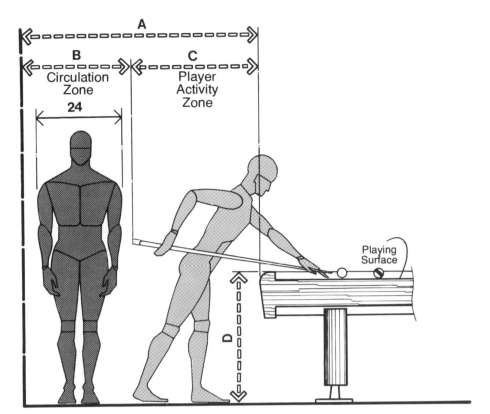

**BILLIARD AND POOL TABLE REQUIREMENTS**

The top drawing indicates the clearance required from the edge of a pool or billiard table to the wall or nearest physical obstruction. A clearance of 60 to 72 in, or 152.4 to 182.9 cm, is suggested to allow the possibility for some circulation behind the active player. The activity zone shown applies for most shots. In some instances, due to the nature of the play, the stance of the player, and the length of the cue stick, there may be some intrusion into the circulation zone.

Safety zones and clearances around the perimeter of a basketball court are not included in codes and ordinances that presumably deal with the public safety. In relatively passive sports and games, the problem is not serious. In sports where the action is more intense, such as basketball, the lack of adequate safety zone clearances may cause injuries to the players and may even prove fatal.

The drawing below suggests minimum clearances to allow the player, running and/or dribbling the ball at full speed, sufficient time and space to decelerate and stop before colliding with the wall.

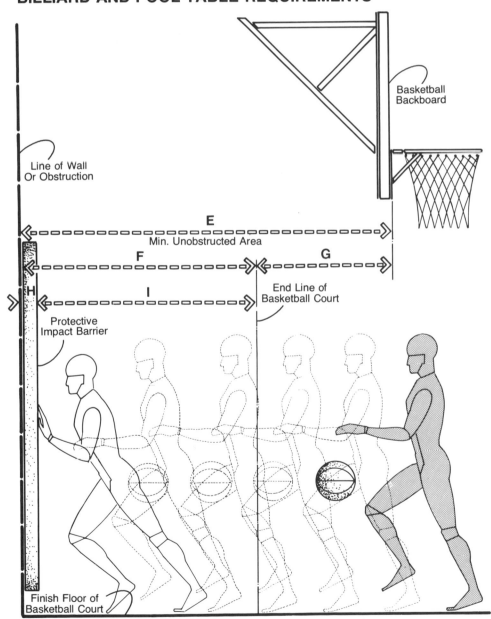

**BASKETBALL COURT / SAFETY AREA CLEARANCES**

|   | in | cm |
|---|---|---|
| A | 60–72 | 152.4–182.9 |
| B | 30 | 76.2 |
| C | 30–42 | 76.2–106.7 |
| D | 33–34 | 83.8–86.4 |
| E | 142–172 | 360.7–436.9 |
| F | 94–124 | 238.8–315.0 |
| G | 48 | 121.9 |
| H | 4–8 | 10.2–20.3 |
| I | 90–116 | 228.6–294.6 |

## 7.2 SPORTS AND GAMES

The drawing here provides some useful information about human dimension and the sport of basketball. Aside from the dimensional data indicated, the subject serves as an excellent example of how anthropometric considerations relate to almost every facet of our daily life and, in fact, to most human activity. Many of the top professional basketball players have 99th percentile stature and reach dimensions. The extraordinary height and reach of some of these athletes, as well as jumping ability, enable them to do a so-called stuff shot. The player leaps high into the air, slightly above the rim of the basket, and literally stuffs the ball through. Such a player has a distinct advantage, totally unrelated to skill. To compensate for this, a proposal to raise the height of the rim on AAU and NCAA basketball courts is presently under consideration. The drawing shows the present rim height of 120 in, or 304.8 cm, and the proposed rim height of 144 in, or 365.8 cm. It is interesting to note that the top of the head of a player with a stature of 88 in, or 223.5 cm, is only 32 in, or 81.3 cm, below the rim.

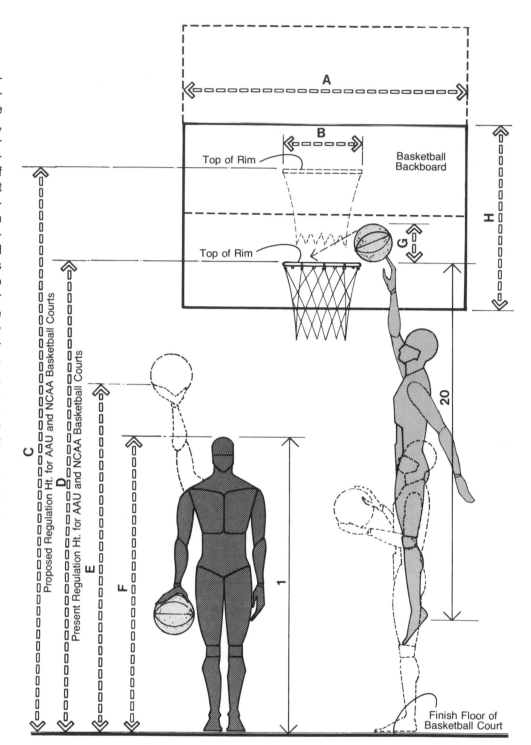

**BASKETBALL BACKBOARD AND RIM MODIFICATIONS**

|   | in | cm |
|---|---|---|
| **A** | 72 | 182.9 |
| **B** | 18 | 45.7 |
| **C** | 144 | 365.8 |
| **D** | 120 | 304.8 |
| **E** | 91–115 | 231.1–292.1 |
| **F** | 72–88 | 1829–223.5 |
| **G** | 9.6 | 24.4 |
| **H** | 48 | 121.9 |

# 7.3 WORK AND CRAFT CENTERS

| TABLE | PAINTING | DRAFTING | WORKSHOP | ART | ACTIVITIES | | ANTHROPOMETRIC DATA |
|---|---|---|---|---|---|---|---|
| 1A,2B,7B | | | | ◑ | | 1 | STATURE |
| 1B,3C | ◑ | | | ◑ | | 2 | EYE HEIGHT |
| 1C,3B | | | ◑ | ◑ | | 3 | ELBOW HEIGHT |
| 1E,2D | | ◑ | | ◑ | | 5 | SITTING HEIGHT NORMAL |
| 1F,3G | ◑ | | | | | 6 | EYE HEIGHT SITTING |
| 1K,2G | | | | ◑ | | 11 | ELBOW REST HEIGHT |
| 1L,2H | | ● | ● | ● | | 12 | THIGH CLEARANCE |
| 1N,2J,7H | | ◑ | ◑ | ◑ | | 14 | POPLITEAL HEIGHT |
| 1O,2K,7I | | ◑ | ◑ | ◑ | | 15 | BUTTOCK-POPLITEAL LENGTH |
| 1U,4E | | ○ | | | | 21 | SIDE ARM REACH |
| 1V,4D | | ○ | | | | 22 | THUMB TIP REACH |
| 1W,6B | | | ● | | | 23 | MAXIMUM BODY DEPTH |
| 1X,6A | | | ● | ● | | 24 | MAXIMUM BODY BREADTH |

The drawings on the following pages illustrate the clearances suggested for use in making preliminary design assumptions about various types of work and craft spaces. The types involved are areas designed for painting, drafting, children's arts and crafts, and general workbench activities. It should be noted, however, that the drawings are not necessarily intended to show all the work and craft space types possible, nor in the spaces illustrated are all the tools or equipment normally associated with the activities necessarily indicated. To do so would require an entire volume of drawings dealing exclusively with work and craft spaces. The spaces included, however, were selected as representative of certain types of activities in order to illustrate some typical interface situations and the anthropometric considerations involved. One interesting anthropometric problem that applies to any child-oriented work and craft space is the obvious, radical difference in body size between the child and the instructor or teacher. If worksurfaces are designed exclusively to accommodate the body dimensions of the child, the height of the worksurface will be too low to accommodate the adult during any instructional activity or individual demonstration that involves the use of that surface. The approach, therefore, is a design that will reconcile the differences in body size and accommodate the needs of each. The problem is a difficult one and perhaps there is no perfect solution. A higher worksurface height and adjustable seat are one approach. Another may be of a more architectural nature and involves changes in floor levels within the space.

# 7.3 WORK AND CRAFT CENTERS

Most artists have individual preferences regarding the arrangement of their particular studio or workplace. In regard to human dimension and the artist's interface with his or her space, the factors to consider also vary greatly. Techniques, media, style, process all impact on the anthropometric requirements. The top drawing, therefore, should not be taken too literally. It is not intended to illustrate in detail a specific plan that will necessarily be responsive to the personal needs of all artists. It is intended simply to illustrate some of the components of the space. The anthropometric considerations involved must be examined with respect to the individual artist and the specific activities involved.

There are, however, some basic considerations that apply in most situations. Vertical reach from a standing and sitting position is helpful in locating shelving for art supplies. Side and forward arm reach measurements can be useful in locating various components of the space, relative to each other and the artist, in the most efficient manner possible. The eye height of a seated and standing person can be used to determine the location of visual displays and reference materials above the floor. Elbow height can be extremely helpful in establishing the height of a utility table. The text related to workbenches on the following pages of this section is also applicable to the artist's utility or prep table.

| | in | cm |
|---|---|---|
| A | 108 | 274.3 |
| B | 84 | 213.4 |
| C | 24 | 61.0 |
| D | 42 | 106.7 |
| E | 36 | 91.4 |
| F | 48 | 121.9 |
| G | 72 | 182.9 |
| H | 72–86 | 182.9–218.4 |
| I | 30–36 | 76.2–91.4 |
| J | 18 | 45.7 |

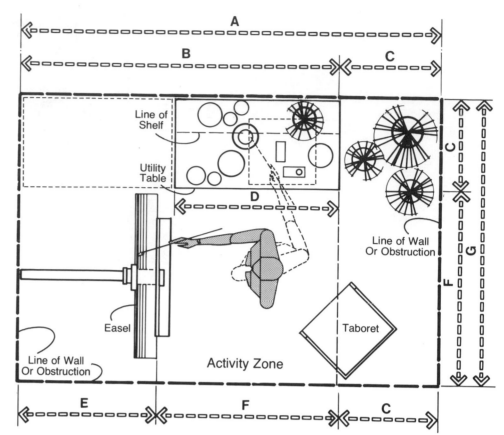

**PAINTING FACILITIES**

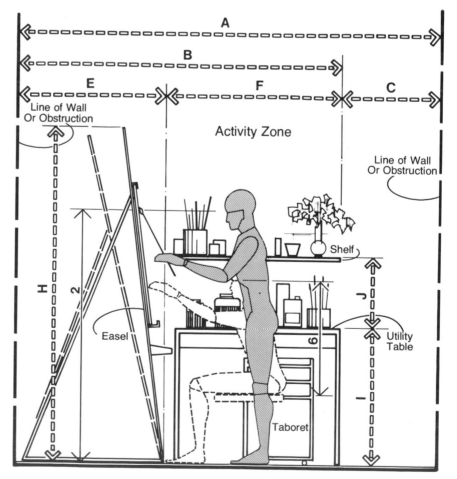

**PAINTING FACILITIES**

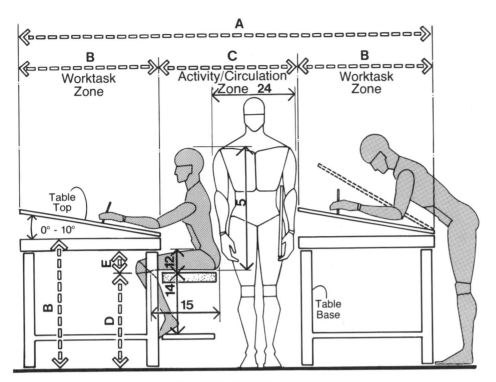

**DRAFTING TABLES/CLEARANCE BETWEEN**

Workplaces for drafting and related types of activities for general group use or instructional purposes can be arranged on the basis of individual drafting tables, as shown in the top drawing, or as cubicles or workstations, as indicated in the bottom drawing. The top drawing shows the clearances involved between tables as well as the clearances necessary for proper interface between the seated and standing person and the table. A table height of 36 in, or 91.4 cm, as opposed to regular desk height, will permit use of the table from both a seated and a standing position. Proper minimum clearance between the top of the seat surface and the underside of the table, as shown, is essential. An adjustable stool can be extremely helpful in compensating for variability in body size. Provisions for a footrest are also a critical consideration. Because of the height of the table, the distance of the seat above the floor will invariably be higher than normal and exceed the popliteal height of most, if not all, intended users. This will cause the feet to dangle above the floor, resulting not only in a lack of proper body stability but pressure on the underside of the thigh just behind the knee. This pressure will cause irritation of the tissue involved and impede blood circulation, resulting in considerable discomfort. The lack of body stability will require compensatory muscular force to maintain equilibrium, resulting in additional discomfort and pain.

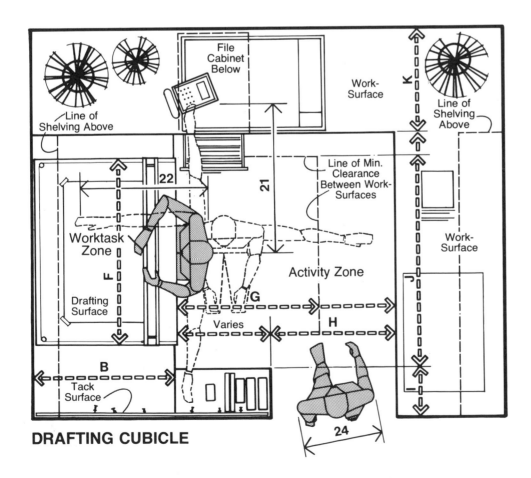

**DRAFTING CUBICLE**

|   | in | cm |
|---|---|---|
| A | 108–120 | 274.3–304.8 |
| B | 36 | 91.4 |
| C | 36–48 | 91.4–121.9 |
| D | 21–27.5 | 53.3–69.9 |
| E | 7.5 | 19.1 |
| F | 48–60 | 121.9–152.4 |
| G | 36–60 | 91.4–152.4 |
| H | 30 | 76.2 |
| I | 12 | 30.5 |
| J | 54–60 | 137.2–152.4 |
| K | 27–30 | 68.6–76.2 |

# 7.3 WORK AND CRAFTS CENTER

For standing work height, the height of the elbows above the floor (elbow height) should be considered. If considerable muscular force is required, the distance from the elbow to the top of the bench should be clearly greater. If minimal physical force is involved, a distance between the elbow and the bench top of between 3.5 and 6 in, or 8.9 and 15.2 cm, should be adequate. For preliminary design assumptions, a height of 34 to 36 in, or 86.4 to 91.4 cm, would be reasonable. In regard to bench heights for seated work, 24 to 29 in, or 60.9 to 73.6 cm, can be used for preliminary design assumptions. The limitations of human reach must also be taken into account in locating overhead tool storage. The bottom drawing indicates some of the critical dimensions related to an arts and crafts center for children ranging in age from 6 to 11 years. The critical anthropometric consideration is in making the design responsive to the body size of the child as well as the adult. A teacher forced to bend to the surface of tables scaled down to the body size of a child would suffer fatigue and backache in a short time. Adjustability in both chair and table, however, can reconcile the needs of differing requirements.

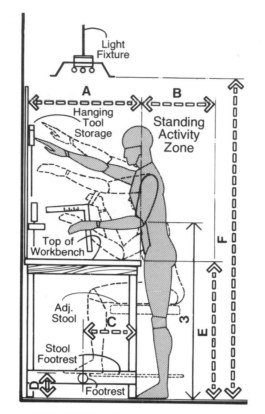

**HIGH WORKBENCH**

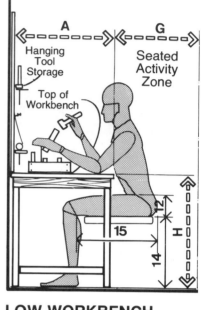

**LOW WORKBENCH**

| | in | cm |
|---|---|---|
| A | 18–36 | 45.7–91.4 |
| B | 18 | 45.7 |
| C | 6–9 | 15.2–22.9 |
| D | 7–9 | 17.8–22.9 |
| E | 34–36 | 86.4–91.4 |
| F | 84 | 213.4 |
| G | 18–24 | 45.7–61.0 |
| H | 29–30 | 73.7–76.2 |
| I | 65 | 165.1 |
| J | 36 | 91.4 |
| K | 30 | 76.2 |
| L | 15 | 38.1 |
| M | 21 | 53.3 |
| N | 24 | 61.0 |
| O | 22–27 | 55.9–68.6 |
| P | 29 | 73.7 |
| Q | 34 | 86.4 |
| R | 33 | 83.8 |
| S | 26 | 66.0 |
| T | 16 | 40.6 |

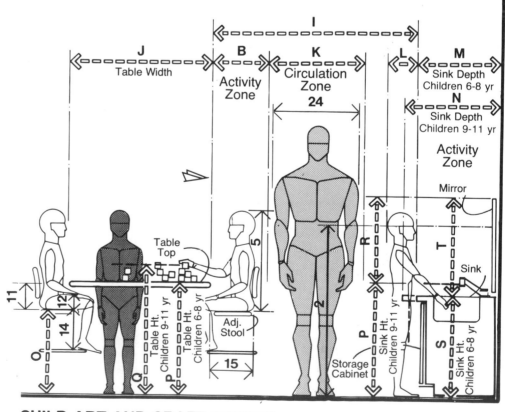

**CHILD ART AND CRAFT CENTER**

# 8 PUBLIC SPACES

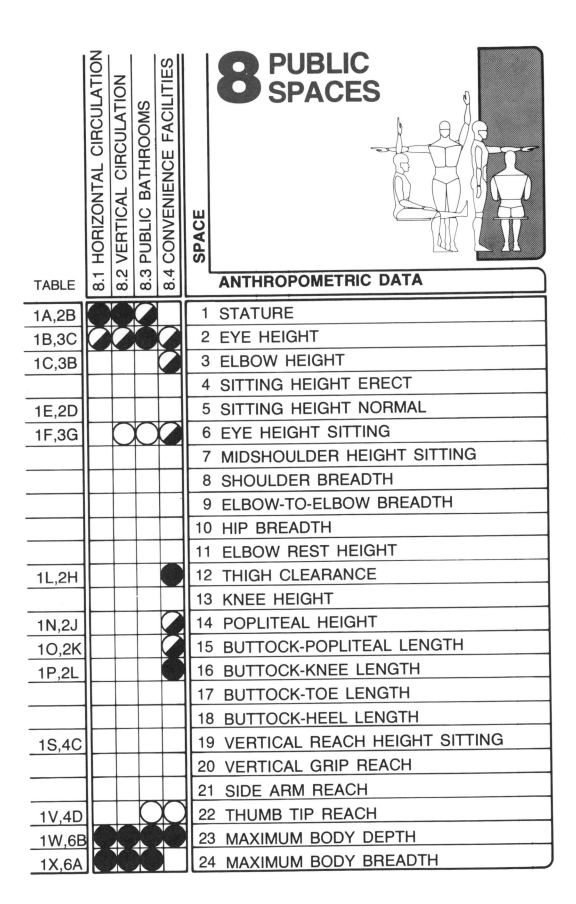

| TABLE | 8.1 HORIZONTAL CIRCULATION | 8.2 VERTICAL CIRCULATION | 8.3 PUBLIC BATHROOMS | 8.4 CONVENIENCE FACILITIES | ANTHROPOMETRIC DATA |
|---|---|---|---|---|---|
| 1A,2B | ● | ● | ◐ |  | 1 STATURE |
| 1B,3C | ◐ | ◐ | ● | ◐ | 2 EYE HEIGHT |
| 1C,3B |  |  |  | ◐ | 3 ELBOW HEIGHT |
|  |  |  |  |  | 4 SITTING HEIGHT ERECT |
| 1E,2D |  |  |  |  | 5 SITTING HEIGHT NORMAL |
| 1F,3G |  | ○ | ○ | ◐ | 6 EYE HEIGHT SITTING |
|  |  |  |  |  | 7 MIDSHOULDER HEIGHT SITTING |
|  |  |  |  |  | 8 SHOULDER BREADTH |
|  |  |  |  |  | 9 ELBOW-TO-ELBOW BREADTH |
|  |  |  |  |  | 10 HIP BREADTH |
|  |  |  |  |  | 11 ELBOW REST HEIGHT |
| 1L,2H |  |  |  | ● | 12 THIGH CLEARANCE |
|  |  |  |  |  | 13 KNEE HEIGHT |
| 1N,2J |  |  |  | ◐ | 14 POPLITEAL HEIGHT |
| 1O,2K |  |  |  | ◑ | 15 BUTTOCK-POPLITEAL LENGTH |
| 1P,2L |  |  |  | ● | 16 BUTTOCK-KNEE LENGTH |
|  |  |  |  |  | 17 BUTTOCK-TOE LENGTH |
|  |  |  |  |  | 18 BUTTOCK-HEEL LENGTH |
| 1S,4C |  |  |  |  | 19 VERTICAL REACH HEIGHT SITTING |
|  |  |  |  |  | 20 VERTICAL GRIP REACH |
|  |  |  |  |  | 21 SIDE ARM REACH |
| 1V,4D |  |  | ○ | ○ | 22 THUMB TIP REACH |
| 1W,6B | ● | ● | ● | ● | 23 MAXIMUM BODY DEPTH |
| 1X,6A | ● | ● | ● |  | 24 MAXIMUM BODY BREADTH |

Public spaces, such as corridors, lobbies, and concourses, are subject to a tremendous intensity of usage involving fluctuating peaks of activity and human occupancy loads. In office buildings, peaks relate to working hours. In transportation facilities patterns of usage are dictated by arrival and departure activities. In theater, convention centers, or sports centers, scheduling of events determines the periods of occupancy. Adequate provisions for human locomotion through these public spaces, as well as provisions for related convenience facilities are important design considerations.

The quality of the interface between the human body and the interior space impacts not only on the level of user comfort involved, but on the public safety. To determine door widths, corridor widths, and stair dimensions, body size must be the ultimate yardstick. Caution should be exercised in accepting prevailing standards or rules of thumb to establish critical clearances without questioning their anthropometric validity, even though these standards may be incorporated into existing codes or ordinances. It serves no purpose to conform to the language and not the intent of these codes, which is to ensure the public safety. The unit or increment of measurement that must be applied to establish proper width clearances must reflect current published maximum body breadth dimensions. The data selected must accommodate the majority of users. This is too critical a factor to be based on antiquated rules of thumb. The design of public rest rooms must also reflect this unit of measurement if they are to function properly. It is absurd, for example, to provide the number of fixtures that may be required by codes if the spacing selected will only allow half of them to be used simultaneously. In addition, public spaces should be responsive to the needs of the disabled user. Controls should be within reach of chair-bound people, stair design should accommodate elderly people, and human locomotion for ambulant disabled people should be barrier free. The drawings on the following pages are intended to call attention to some of the anthropometric factors to be considered in the design of public spaces. The first of these drawings deals with the basic unit of measurement: the maximum body breadth and depth of the human body.

| TABLE | CORRIDOR | QUEUING | ACTIVITIES | **8.1** HORIZONTAL CIRCULATION SPACES |
|-------|----------|---------|------------|---|
| | | | | **ANTHROPOMETRIC DATA** |
| 1A,2B | | ● | 1 | STATURE |
| 1B,3C | | ◐ | 2 | EYE HEIGHT |
| 1W,6B | ● | ● | 23 | MAXIMUM BODY DEPTH |
| 1X,6A | ● | ● | 24 | MAXIMUM BODY BREADTH |

Horizontal circulation spaces may include typical corridors found in public buildings ranging from 60- to 144-in, or 152.4- to 365.8-cm wide, lobbies, pedestrian promenades, plazas in enclosed shopping malls, and large circulation and concourse areas in transportation terminals. Planning these spaces can be a fairly sophisticated and complicated matter, involving such factors as flow volume (usually expressed as pedestrians per foot width of walkway per minute), time and distance headways, walking speeds, queue lengths. The services of a traffic engineer or pedestrian planning specialist are usually required to properly design the larger spaces. Part of the process, no matter how sophisticated, is consideration of the human factor of body size and dimension. In addition some insight into physiological and psychological factors is also required. The intent here is to focus primarily on the anthropometric aspects, with the knowledge that this constitutes but a small part of the entire design process. The drawings on the following pages deal primarily with the human body and its maximum body depth and breadth as the basic increment of measurement. This incremental unit is then applied within the context of queuing situations and corridors.

# 8.1 HORIZONTAL CIRCULATION SPACES

In dealing with pedestrian locomotion, the human body must serve as the basic increment of measure and the larger-size person as the model in establishing clearance dimensions. If such clearances accommodate larger people, they obviously can accommodate those of smaller body size. The top diagram shows three views of the human figure, including critical 95th percentile dimensions of the three anthropometric measurements. In establishing breadth and depth dimensions, an allowance of 3 in, or 7.6 cm, for garments, including heavy outer winter clothing, was used. The breadth dimension assumes that the clothing consists of six layers. Accordingly, the aggregate allowance of 3 in is assumed to be equally distributed: one layer on the inside and outside surface of both arms and one layer on each side of the torso. The overall dimension so calculated is 28.8 in, or 65.5 cm. Heretofore, the generally accepted measurement was 22 in, or 55.9 cm, presumably based on the shoulder breadth of an average person. The authors contend that this is not a valid figure, since the critical anthropometric measurement to be utilized should be body breadth, not shoulder breadth and "average" data do not accommodate the majority of the population.

The diagram and chart below should also prove useful in the design of circulation spaces. They have been adapted from a study of pedestrian movement and queuing by Dr. John Fruin to establish relative levels of service based on pedestrian density. The basic unit is the human body, which is envisioned as a so-called body ellipse of 18 by 24 in, or 45.6 by 61 cm.

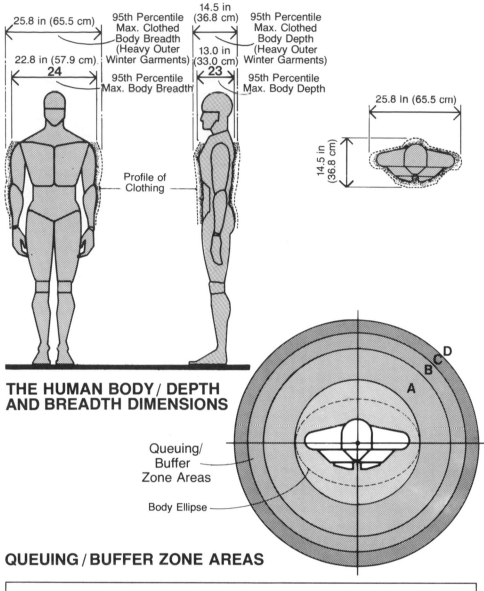

## THE HUMAN BODY/DEPTH AND BREADTH DIMENSIONS

Queuing/Buffer Zone Areas

Body Ellipse

## QUEUING/BUFFER ZONE AREAS

| QUEUING DENSITY ANALYSIS* | | RADIUS | | AREA | |
|---|---|---|---|---|---|
| DESIGNATION | DESCRIPTION | in | cm | sq ft | sq cm |
| A. Touch Zone | Below this area of occupancy, frequent unavoidable contact between people likely. No possibility of circulation within this zone. Movement restricted to shuffling. Occupancy similar to slightly crowded elevator. | 12 | 30.5 | 3 | .28 |
| B. No-Touch Zone | Contact between people can be avoided as long as movement within area is not necessary. Movement possible as a group. | 18 | 45.7 | 7 | .65 |
| C. Personal Zone | At this spacing a full body depth separates standees. Limited lateral circulation between people possible by moving sideways between them. Within range of spatial occupancy that has been selected in experiments emphasizing comfort standards. | 21 | 53.3 | 10 | .95 |
| D. Circulation Zone | Circulation within queuing area possible without disturbing others. | 24 | 61 | 13 | 1.4 |

*Chart adapted from John J. Fruin, *Pedestrian Planning and Design* (New York: Metropolitan Association of Urban Designers and Environmental Planners, 1971).

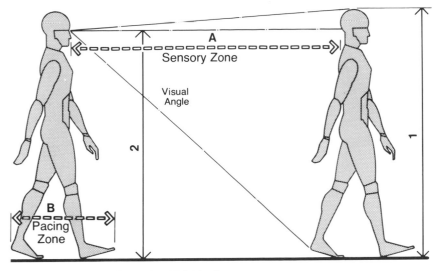

**LOCOMOTION SPACE ZONES**

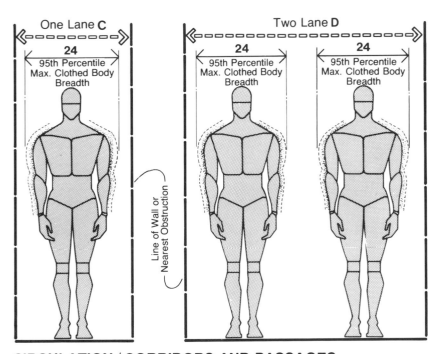

**CIRCULATION / CORRIDORS AND PASSAGES**

The top drawing illustrates the two zones involved in walking. The pacing zone is the distance required to place one foot in front of the other. This distance varies with the individual due to the many psychological, physiological, and cultural factors involved, as well as sex, age, and physical condition. Most adults, however, have a pacing distance of between 24 and 36 in, or 61 and 91.4 cm. The sensory zone is the distance required for perception, evaluation, and reaction in sufficient time to avoid danger, all while the body is in motion. The multitude of human factors involved makes measurement of this distance extremely difficult. One indicator, however, might be the distance one person has to be behind the other to observe him from head to toe. This is approximated to be about 84 in, or 213.4 cm, in a normal walking situation. In single- and double-lane corridors and passageways, clearances of 36 and 68 in, or 91.4 and 172.7 cm, respectively, are suggested. A 30-in, or 76.2-cm, minimum is suggested for a single lane with no physical obstructions on either side. If carrying items or pushing a small cart is involved, the 36-in minimum should still be used. The double-lane clearance allows for two people abreast to circulate comfortably without body contact. The drawing at the bottom of the page suggests the amount of space occupied by people carrying various types of hand luggage.

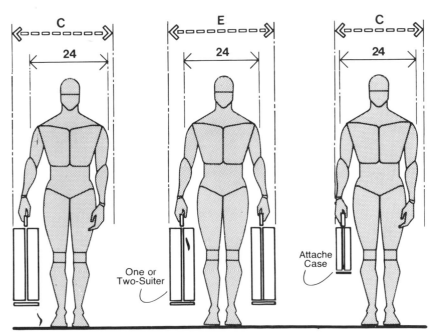

**BODY BREADTH CLEARANCES WITH LUGGAGE**

|   | in | cm |
|---|---|---|
| **A** | 84 | 213.4 |
| **B** | 22–36 | 55.9–91.4 |
| **C** | 30–36 | 76.2–91.4 |
| **D** | 68 | 172.7 |
| **E** | 36–42 | 91.4–106.7 |

# 8.1 HORIZONTAL CIRCULATION SPACES

The purpose of the drawing at the top is to provide some idea of the physical relationship between human dimension and corridor width in terms of the number of lanes that can be accommodated. The row with three persons abreast is based on 95th percentile maximum clothed body breadth, while the row with four abreast is based on 5th percentile data. The corridor width was arbitrarily selected as 96 in, or 243.8 cm. The drawing should not be taken literally. The statistical likelihood of having the lineup of body sizes shown, at any single point in time, would be remote unless the space was originally intended to serve a specific user population of larger or smaller body size. Moreover, the 24-in, or 61-cm, lane with a 1.6-in clearance is obviously not intended as a standard.

The bottom drawing is intended to provide some insight into relative densities possible within a 120-in, or 308.4-cm, queue. Lane A shows as many people lined up as possible, with no regard for comfort or body contact. When an allowance for clothing is added to the maximum body breadth, the people in lane A would be pressed tightly together, violating all notions of personal space and comfort. Lanes B and C show the number of people that could be lined up, based on the densities of 3 and 7 sq ft, or .28 and .65 sq m per person, respectively.

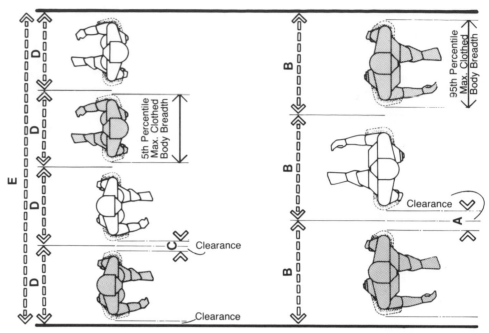

**ACCOMMODATION OF SMALL AND LARGE USERS ABREAST IN A 96-IN (243.8-CM) CORRIDOR OR PASSAGE WIDTH**

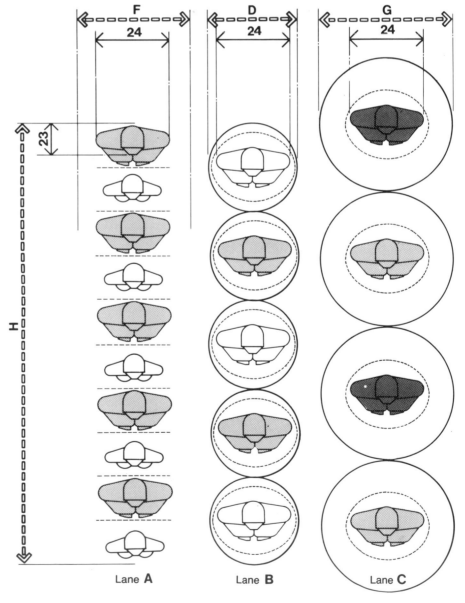

Lane **A**      Lane **B**      Lane **C**

**QUEUE LINES / COMPARATIVE DENSITIES**

|   | in | cm |
|---|---|---|
| **A** | 4.5 | 11.4 |
| **B** | 32 | 81.3 |
| **C** | 1.6 | 4.1 |
| **D** | 24 | 61.0 |
| **E** | 96 | 243.8 |
| **F** | 30 | 76.2 |
| **G** | 36 | 91.4 |
| **H** | 120 | 304.8 |

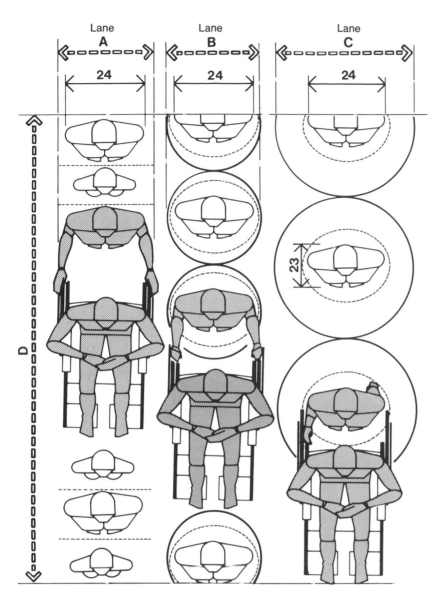

The drawing at the top indicates the impact of a wheelchair-bound person on the same queue shown on the preceding page. The bottom drawing indicates corridor width clearances necessary to accommodate wheelchair circulation. Full two-way passage requires 60 in, or 152.4 cm, to allow two wheelchairs to pass side by side. Clearance for a single wheelchair is 36 in, or 91.4 cm. A 54-in, or 137.2-cm, corridor will allow an able-bodied individual to walk along side or pass a wheelchair-bound person. Ideally, rest stops should be provided where corridor lengths are particularly long. These may be in the form of properly designed alcoves along the circulation path; rest room lounges or reception areas may be substituted if reasonably located. Maximum distance between rest room stops should be about 100 ft, or 30.5 m. Provisions for wheelchair turning should also be considered. A full 360° turn can be negotiated within a 60-in, or 152.4-cm, diameter circle.

**QUEUE LINES / COMPARATIVE DENSITIES INCLUDING WHEELCHAIR-BOUND**

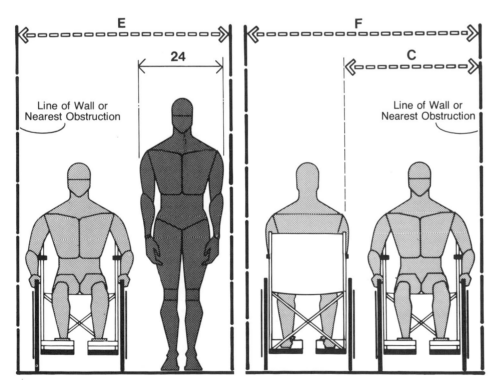

**PARTIAL 2-WAY CIRCULATION**   **FULL 2-WAY CIRCULATION**

**WHEELCHAIR CIRCULATION / CORRIDORS AND PASSAGES**

|   | in | cm |
|---|----|----|
| A | 30 | 76.2 |
| B | 24 | 61.0 |
| C | 36 | 91.4 |
| D | 120 | 304.8 |
| E | 54 | 137.2 |
| F | 60 | 152.4 |

# 8.1 HORIZONTAL CIRCULATION SPACES

The top drawing indicates that a 60-in, or 152.4-cm, clearance is necessary for a person on crutches to walk along side or pass a person in a wheelchair. A 42-in, or 106.7-cm, clearance is needed to accommodate a person standing sideways, while allowing a wheelchair-bound person to pass. The other two drawings indicate the clearances necessary to accommodate a wheelchair in spaces where a series of two doors are involved. One drawing illustrates a situation where the two doors are in a row and the other where the doors are at right angles. A clearance of 84 in, or 213.4 cm, is necessary to allow the wheelchair to clear the first door as it swings shut. Since the length of the wheelchair is 42 in, or 106.7 cm, the 84-in dimension would allow for a door as wide as 36 in, or 91.4 cm, and an additional clearance of 6 in, or 15.2 cm, to spare. The 12-in, or 30.5-cm, minimum clearance on either side of the door allows enough maneuvering room for the wheelchair to approach the door at a slight angle and a person to grasp the door knob or pull and then back away. This is helpful when approaching the door from the in-swing side. When the doors are located at right angles to each other, it is essential that adequate space be provided to avoid interference between the two doors.

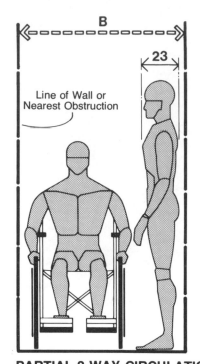

**PARTIAL 2-WAY CIRCULATION**

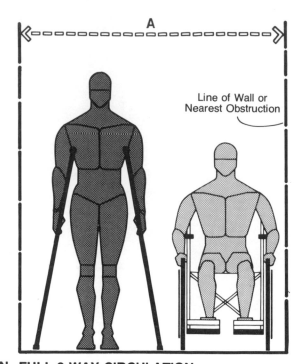

**FULL 2-WAY CIRCULATION**

## WHEELCHAIR CIRCULATION/CORRIDORS AND PASSAGES

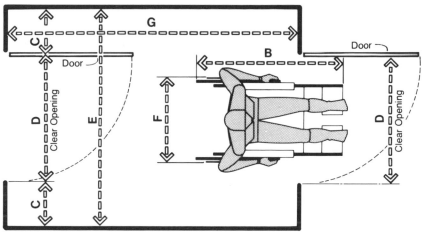

## WHEELCHAIR CIRCULATION / DOORS IN ALIGNMENT

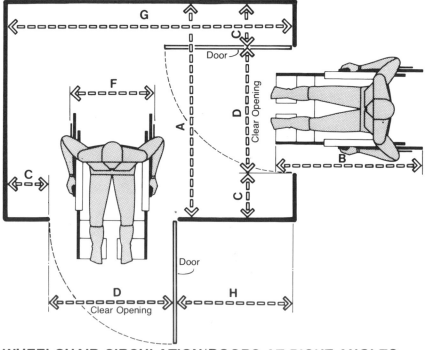

## WHEELCHAIR CIRCULATION/DOORS AT RIGHT ANGLES

|   | in | cm |
|---|---|---|
| A | 60 | 152.4 |
| B | 42 | 106.7 |
| C | 12 min. | 30.5 min. |
| D | 32 | 81.3 |
| E | 56 min. | 142.2 min. |
| F | 25 | 63.5 |
| G | 84 | 213.4 |
| H | 36 min. | 91.4 min. |

# 8.2 VERTICAL CIRCULATION SPACES

| TABLE | ESCALATOR | STAIR | RAMP | ELEVATOR | ACTIVITIES | ANTHROPOMETRIC DATA | |
|---|---|---|---|---|---|---|---|
| 1A,2B | ● | | | | 1 | STATURE | |
| 1B,3C | ◐ | | | ◐ | 2 | EYE HEIGHT | |
| 1F,3G | | | | ○ | 6 | EYE HEIGHT SITTING | |
| 1W,6B | | | | ● | 23 | MAXIMUM BODY DEPTH | |
| 1X,6A | ● | ● | ● | ● | 24 | MAXIMUM BODY BREADTH | |

No public space can function without adequate vertical circulation systems. If these systems are not designed with human body size in mind, however, the efficiency and use of these systems are diminished. Moreover, the personal safety of the user is endangered. Nowhere is this more critical than in stair design. Both the width of the stair and the tread/riser relationship must reflect the human dimension. For stair width, most prevailing standards and guidelines directly or indirectly employ a unit of measurement of 22 in, or 55.9 cm, which purportedly represents the width of a so-called average person, a basic contention with which the authors disagree and which will be explored in the drawings and text on the following pages. This 22-in increment, however, is used as a basis for establishing lane width and has been in use and unchallenged for at least 25 years.

Tread/riser relationships are also based on assorted rules of thumb and formulas, many of which are in conflict with each other. One such formula, over 400 years old, is incorporated into the building code of the city of New York. That these formulas produce some kind of generally reasonable design is not disputed. What should be questioned is the quality of that design. How does a 9.5-in, or 24.1-cm, tread, for example, accommodate a maximum shod foot length of 14 in, or 35.6 cm? How much contact surface does the design provide? How much human energy is consumed in ascending the stair? What percentage of the user population is accommodated? If the stair is to be used to evacuate the building in the event of fire, can we afford to accommodate any less than 100 percent of the users? Does the tread/riser relationship reflect the needs of elderly people? These questions must be answered if designers are to be responsive to the human factors involved. There is also no doubt that proper tread/riser proportion involves other considerations as well, such as human gait, sensory perception, age, sex. A "perfect" solution may not be possible in view of the nature of the problem, but something more than a rule of thumb is needed. The drawings on the following pages examine some of these conditions and suggest clearances and other dimensional data responsive to human dimension and body size and useful in establishing preliminary design assumptions. The matrix above indicates some of the more relevant anthropometric measurements to consider.

# 8.2 VERTICAL CIRCULATION SPACES

The drawing of the 48-in, or 121.9-cm, two-lane escalator is intended to illustrate that 48 in is inadequate to comfortably accommodate larger-sized people on the same tread. Moreover, the 40-in, or 101.6-cm, clearance at the bottom limits the user's stance, thereby reducing body stability. Stair motion, body contact, and lack of stability, taken together, present a safety hazard. This may account for the fact that the presence of two people on the same tread is not a very frequent occurrence.

The authors contend that the standard 44-in, or 117.7-cm, stair width, based on two 22-in, or 55.9-cm, body increments, will not accommodate those of larger body size. The argument against the 22-in increment is presented in the text related to the first drawing in Section 8.1.

Rail clearance should accommodate the hand thickness of the larger user and handrail size, the inside grip diameter of the smaller user. Adding glove thickness to the data shown in the drawing, a 2-in, or 5.1-cm, clearance and a 1.5-in, or 3.8-cm, rail diameter will accommodate most people.

|   | in | cm |
|---|---|---|
| A | 48 | 121.9 |
| B | 25.8 | 65.5 |
| C | 7.1 | 18.0 |
| D | 12.9 | 32.8 |
| E | 40 | 101.6 |
| F | 68 | 172.7 |
| G | 44 | 111.8 |
| H | 4.2 | 10.7 |
| I | 4.9 | 12.4 |
| J | 2 min. | 5.1 min. |
| K | 1.5 | 3.8 |
| L | 3.5 max. | 8.9 max. |
| M | 30–34 | 76.2–86.4 |
| N | 1.5 min. | 3.8 min. |

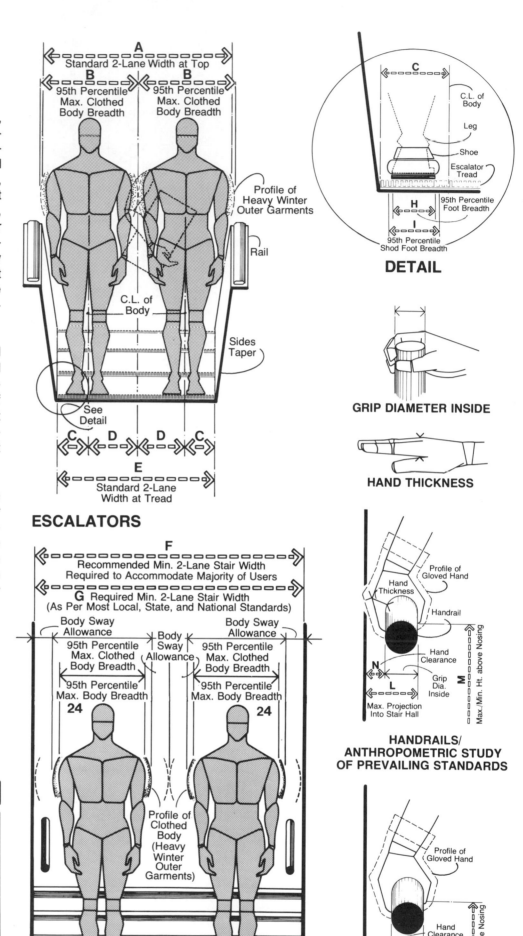

**ESCALATORS**

**STAIRS/EXISTING AND RECOMMENDED 2-LANE WIDTH**

**DETAIL**

**GRIP DIAMETER INSIDE**

**HAND THICKNESS**

**HANDRAILS/ ANTHROPOMETRIC STUDY OF PREVAILING STANDARDS**

**HANDRAILS/ RECOMMENDED DESIGN BY AUTHORS**

## STAIRS

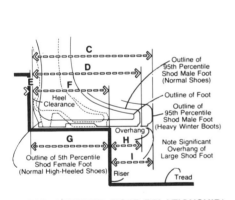

Handrail

B

A

T = Tread

R = Riser

See Details For Riser-Tread Relationship

99th Percentile Clothed Stature Including Shoes and Hat

1

2

The top drawing shows some basic dimensional data and suggests the viewing zones involved. Although the stair is nearly as old as the architectural discipline itself, relatively little research has been done and most code requirements are based on rules of thumb, some dating back to the 17th century. The tread-riser relationship is the most important consideration here.

The bottom drawings show the anthropometric relationship between shod foot length and tread depth. Ninety-five percent of users with heavy winter boots have a shod foot length of about 9 in, or 22.9 cm, or less. The 9.5-in, or 24.1-cm, tread presently in common use allows comfortable tread contact for only 5 percent of the users, while the foot of the larger user overhangs the tread by more than 5 in, or 12.7 cm—certainly a cause for concern, especially for old and physically disabled people.

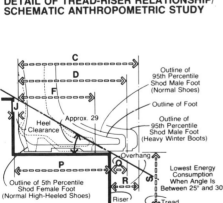

**DETAIL OF TREAD-RISER RELATIONSHIP/ SCHEMATIC ANTHROPOMETRIC STUDY**

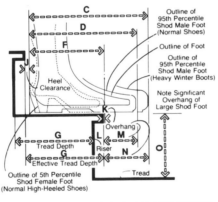

**DETAIL OF TREAD-RISER RELATIONSHIP/ TYPICAL DESIGN IN COMMON USE**

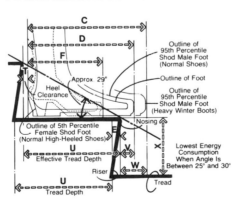

**TREAD-RISER RELATIONSHIP/ RECOMMENDED PROPORTIONS (LEHMAN, 1962)**

**DETAIL OF TREAD-RISER RELATIONSHIP/ RECOMMENDED PROPORTIONS BY AUTHORS WHERE STRUCTURAL AND SPACE CONDITIONS PERMIT**

## DETAILS OF TREAD-RISER RELATIONSHIP

|   | in | cm |
|---|---|---|
| A | 30–34 | 76.2–86.4 |
| B | 84 min. | 213.4 min. |
| C | 14.3 | 36.3 |
| D | 12.9 | 32.8 |
| E | 0.3 | 0.6 |
| F | 9.1 | 23.1 |
| G | 9.5 | 24.1 |
| H | 3.7 | 9.3 |
| I | 5 | 12.7 |
| J | 0.5 | 1.3 |
| K | 0.1 | 0.3 |
| L | 1.3 | 3.2 |
| M | 3.9 | 9.9 |
| N | 5.3 | 13.5 |
| O | 7.5 | 19.1 |
| P | 11.4 | 29.0 |
| Q | 2 | 5.1 |
| R | 3.4 | 8.6 |
| S | 6.7 | 17.0 |
| T | 0.5–1 | 1.3–2.5 |
| U | 11.8 | 29.8 |
| V | 1.6–2.1 | 4.1–5.3 |
| W | 3–3.5 | 7.6–8.9 |
| X | 6.8 | 17.1 |

# 8.2 VERTICAL CIRCULATION SPACES

Vertical circulation systems must be responsive to the needs of people confined to wheelchairs as well as to those of able-bodied people. Corridor and lobby call buttons should be located 54 in, or 137.2 cm, above the floor. Emergency controls should be arranged so that the lowest button is a minimum of 30 in, or 76.2 cm, above the cab floor and the highest button a maximum of 48 in, or 121.9 cm, above the cab floor. Emergency buttons should be grouped together at the bottom of the panel. The center line of a telephone should be a maximum of 48 in above the cab floor and the height at the top of the handrail should be located between 32 and 34 in, or 81.3 and 86.4 cm, above the cab floor.

Ramps are also an important factor in providing accessibility of buildings to handicapped people. Most regulations and guidelines insist on a maximum gradient of one unit of height for every twelve units of length and a maximum horizontal distance of 30 ft, or 9 m, without a horizontal landing of at least 42 in, or 106.7 cm. Landings should be provided at all changes in ramp direction and at entrances and exits. Platform lengths should provide at least 42-in clearance from any door swing into the ramp. Where the door does not swing into the ramp, the platform should extend a minimum of 24 in, or 61 cm, past the latch side of the door.

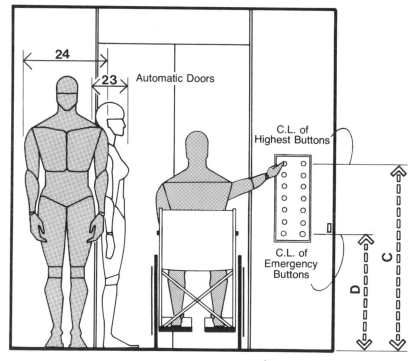

**ELEVATORS / LOBBY**

**ELEVATORS / CAB INTERIOR**

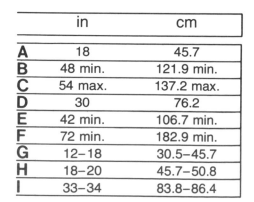

|   | in | cm |
|---|---|---|
| **A** | 18 | 45.7 |
| **B** | 48 min. | 121.9 min. |
| **C** | 54 max. | 137.2 max. |
| **D** | 30 | 76.2 |
| **E** | 42 min. | 106.7 min. |
| **F** | 72 min. | 182.9 min. |
| **G** | 12–18 | 30.5–45.7 |
| **H** | 18–20 | 45.7–50.8 |
| **I** | 33–34 | 83.8–86.4 |

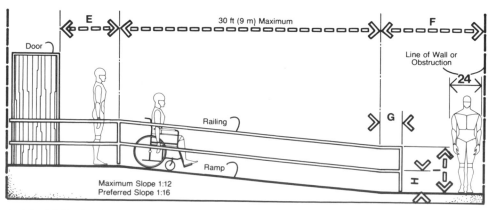

**ACCESS RAMP**

| TABLE | LAVATORY | URINAL | WATERCLOSET | CIRCULATION | ACTIVITIES | ANTHROPOMETRIC DATA | |
|---|---|---|---|---|---|---|---|
| 1A,2B | ◑ | | | | | 1 | STATURE |
| 1B,3C | ● | | ● | ● | | 2 | EYE HEIGHT |
| 1F,3G | ○ | | | | | 6 | EYE HEIGHT SITTING |
| 1V,4D | ○ | | | | | 22 | THUMB TIP REACH |
| 1W,6B | ● | ● | | | | 23 | MAXIMUM BODY DEPTH |
| 1X,6A | ● | ● | | ● | | 24 | MAXIMUM BODY BREADTH |

The term "public" toilet facility is to a large degree generic since it is quite possible and proper to create subclassifications depending on the user population it is intended to serve. A public facility located in an air, bus, or rail terminal, for example, would serve a transient user as opposed to a similar facility provided for the convenience of the workers in a large midtown office building. These facilities may have much and at the same time very little in common. To varying degrees they both have peak periods of use. The anthropometric considerations, particularly during these peak periods, are also quite similar. Since the intent is to focus on human dimension as it relates to interior space, no attempt has been made to establish a classification system or to comment on the inherent design of the fixtures themselves.

What is painfully obvious in the drawings on the following pages is that most public toilet facility designs appear to be totally insensitive to human dimension and body size. Most designs crowd the designated number of fixtures required by local agencies in the least amount of floor space possible. The fact is that the spacing of fixtures, particularly urinals (19 and 21 in, or 48.3 and 53.6 cm, on center is not uncommon), does not accommodate the majority of users. Published anthropometric data, for example, indicates that only 5 percent of a sample population measured has a maximum body breadth dimension of 18.8 in, or 47. 8 cm, or less. When a clothing allowance is added, it becomes obvious that a 19- or a 21-in, or a 48.3- or a 53.6-cm, spacing would make it almost impossible for people to use the urinals without coming into body contact with each other. The same type of situation exists with regard to lavatory fixtures. When one considers the hidden dimensions, body buffer zones, privacy factor, such spacing becomes totally unacceptable. For this reason it is not uncommon in public bathrooms to observe situations of extreme crowding and congestion with people queued up waiting to use the facilities while at the same time every other fixture may be unoccupied. The drawings on the following pages examine these conditions and such clearances and other dimensional data more responsive to human body size and dimension, while the matrix above suggests some of the more important anthropometric measurements to consider in the design of public bathrooms.

# 8.3 PUBLIC BATHROOMS

Stall urinals are available for battery installations on 21-in, or 53.3-cm, centers. The authors contend that such spacing will not properly accommodate the majority of users. The larger-sized person has a maximum clothed body breadth dimension of almost 26 in, or 66 cm. Postures assumed while urinating, in addition to the space taken up by partially opened garments, will increase this dimension even more. Given the anthropometric realities and consideration of personal space, a 32-in, or 81.3-cm, spacing is more responsive to human factors. The stall partition should extend 8 to 10 in, or 20.3 to 25.4 cm, beyond the face of the urinal, and an activity zone of 18 in, or 45.7 cm, in front of the fixture should be assumed. A circulation zone of 54 in, or 137.2 cm, will allow for pedestrian and wheelchair traffic. Urinal stalls for wheelchair users should be a minimum of 36 in, or 91.4 cm, wide for proper access. Minimum toilet stall dimensions required for a front transfer approach by the wheelchair user are 42 by 72 in, or 106.7 by 182.9 cm. A wheelchair clearance zone should be provided in front of the stall.

|   | in | cm |
|---|------|------|
| A | 32 | 81.3 |
| B | 54 | 137.2 |
| C | 18 | 45.7 |
| D | 8–10 | 20.3–25.4 |
| E | 14 min. | 35.6 min. |
| F | 36 min. | 91.4 min. |
| G | 42 | 106.7 |
| H | 25 | 63.5 |
| I | 19 | 48.3 |
| J | 17 max. | 43.2 max. |
| K | 12 min. | 30.5 min. |
| L | 14 max. | 35.6 max. |
| M | 48 | 121.9 |
| N | 18 min. | 45.7 min. |
| O | 12 | 30.5 |
| P | 42 min. | 106.7 min. |
| Q | 1.5 min. | 3.8 min. |
| R | 72 min. | 182.9 min. |

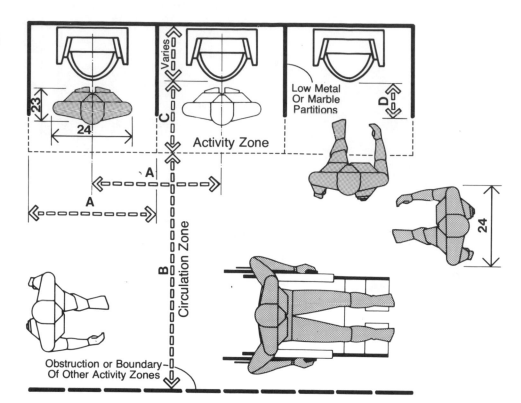

**URINAL LAYOUT**

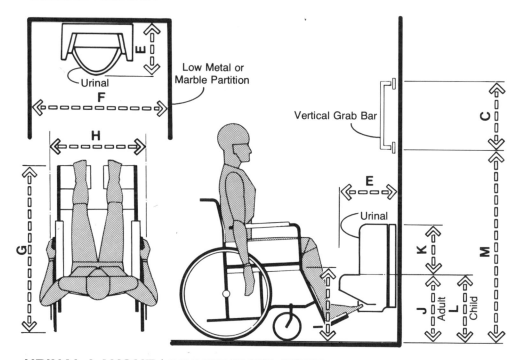

**URINAL LAYOUT / CHAIRBOUND USER**

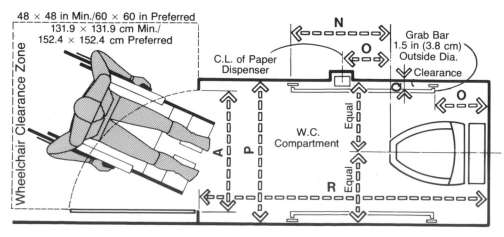

**W.C. COMPARTMENT / FRONT TRANSFER APPROACH**

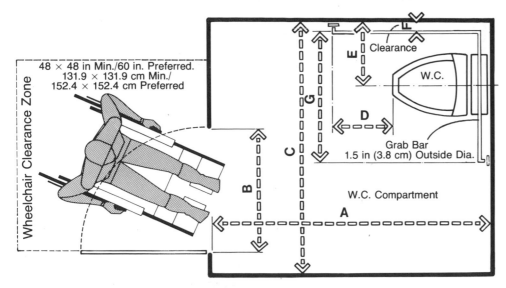

48 × 48 in Min./60 in. Preferred.
131.9 × 131.9 cm Min./
152.4 × 152.4 cm Preferred

Wheelchair Clearance Zone

Clearance

W.C.

Grab Bar
1.5 in (3.8 cm) Outside Dia.

W.C. Compartment

## WATER CLOSET COMPARTMENT/ SIDE APPROACH TRANSFER

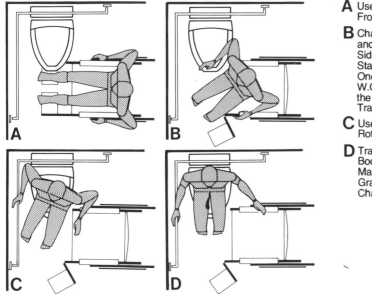

**A** User Approaches W.C. From the Side

**B** Chair Armrest Is Removed and Footrest Is Swung to Side for Clearance. For Stability and Leverage, One Hand Is Placed on W.C. Seat or Grab Bar and the Other on Chair. Transfer Movement Begins

**C** User Lifts, Slides, and Rotates onto W.C. Seat

**D** Transfer Is Complete. Body Stability Is Maintained by Grasping Grab Bar and Seat of Chair

## TECHNIQUE FOR SIDE APPROACH TRANSFER

# 8.3 PUBLIC BATHROOMS

Rather than the front transfer approach discussed on the preceding page, a more comfortable access to the W.C. for the wheelchair user is the side approach transfer. The top drawing shows the minimum compartment dimensions for such a transfer: 66 by 72 in, or 167.6 by 182.9 cm. To appreciate the problems faced by those confined to a wheelchair in gaining access to rest room facilities, it is necessary to understand something of the transfer process. The center drawing attempts to break down that process into four basic movements; techniques will vary from user to user, but the process is essentially as illustrated. The bottom drawing shows some of the basic heights and clearances to be considered in a conventional W.C. compartment. Note that different heights for the W.C. are suggested in response to the anthropometric requirements of elderly people and children.

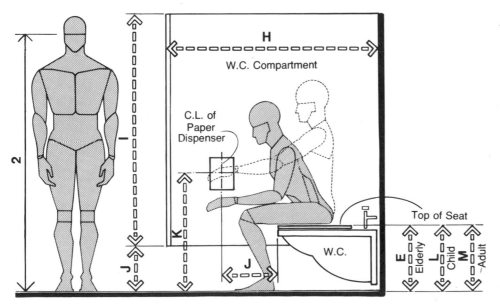

W.C. Compartment

C.L. of Paper Dispenser

Top of Seat

W.C.

Elderly
Child
Adult

## WATER CLOSET

|   | in | cm |
|---|---|---|
| **A** | 72 min. | 182.9 min. |
| **B** | 32 | 81.3 |
| **C** | 66 min. | 167.6 min. |
| **D** | 18 min. | 45.7 min. |
| **E** | 18 | 45.7 |
| **F** | 1.5 min. | 3.8 min. |
| **G** | 36 | 91.4 |
| **H** | 54 min. | 137.2 min. |
| **I** | 58 | 147.3 |
| **J** | 12 | 30.5 |
| **K** | 30 max. | 76.2 max. |
| **L** | 10 | 25.4 |
| **M** | 14–15 | 35.6–38.1 |

# 8.3 PUBLIC BATHROOMS

Lavatories, like urinals, are all too often located too close to each other. The result is an installation that may save floor space and may conform to the code in terms of quantity of fixtures, but simply does not permit the user comfortable access. It has been stated elsewhere that the larger-sized person has a maximum clothed body breadth dimension of almost 26 in, or 66 cm, which already exceeds the width of most lavatory models usually specified for public rest rooms. The body movements involved in the washing and grooming process increase the space occupied by the user even more. Unless adequate space is provided, body contact with the adjacent user will occur. A 32-in, or 81.3-cm, spacing as shown should provide for comfortable use of the fixtures. An activity zone of 18 in, or 45.7 cm, in front of the fixtures should be assumed. A circulation zone of 54 in, or 137.2 cm, is the minimum dimension that will allow for both wheelchair and pedestrian traffic. The drawing at the bottom indicates some of the basic clearances and heights required to make the lavatory accessible to the wheelchair user.

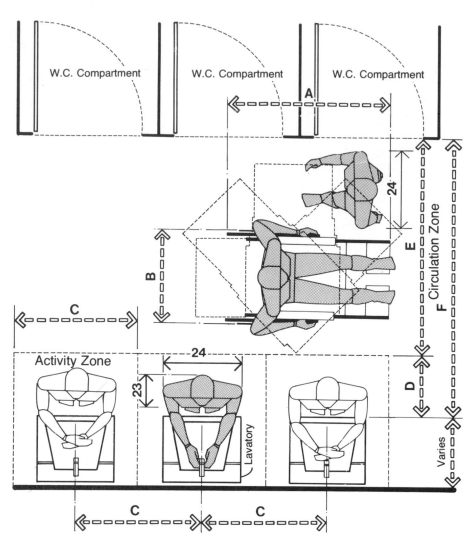

**LAVATORY LAYOUT**

| | in | cm |
|---|---|---|
| A | 42 | 106.7 |
| B | 25 | 63.5 |
| C | 32 | 81.3 |
| D | 18 | 45.7 |
| E | 54 | 137.2 |
| F | 72 | 182.9 |
| G | 30 min. | 76.2 min. |
| H | 48 | 121.9 |
| I | 18 max. | 45.7 max. |
| J | 36 | 91.4 |
| K | 19 | 48.3 |
| L | 30 min. | 76.2 min. |
| M | 34 max. | 86.4 max. |
| N | 40 max. | 101.6 max. |

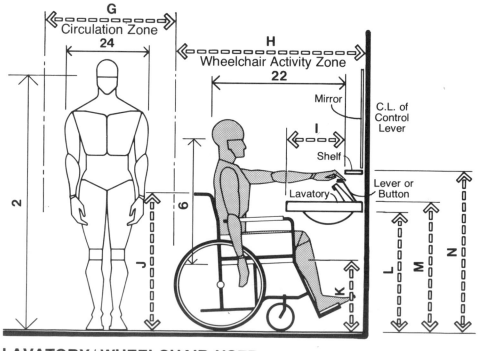

**LAVATORY / WHEELCHAIR USER**

| TABLE | TELEPHONE | DRINKING FOUNTAIN | VENDING MACHINE | REFUSE RECEPTACLE | ACTIVITIES | ANTHROPOMETRIC DATA |
|---|---|---|---|---|---|---|
| 1B,3C | ◑ | | | | 2 | EYE HEIGHT |
| 1C,3B | | | | ◑ | 3 | ELBOW HEIGHT |
| 1F,3G | ◑ | | ◑ | | 6 | EYE HEIGHT SITTING |
| 1L,2H | ● | | | | 12 | THIGH CLEARANCE |
| 1N,2J | ◑ | | | | 14 | POPLITEAL HEIGHT |
| 1O,2K | ◑ | | | | 15 | BUTTOCK-POPLITEAL LENGTH |
| 1P,2L | ● | | | | 16 | BUTTOCK-KNEE LENGTH |
| 1V,4D | | | | ○ | 22 | THUMB TIP REACH |
| 1W,6B | ● | | | | 23 | MAXIMUM BODY DEPTH |

# 8.4 PUBLIC CONVENIENCE FACILITIES

Public convenience facilities must be provided in the design of public spaces. The type and quantity of such facilities will vary depending on the size and nature of the public space involved. They may range from a modest but strategically placed ash urn to a battery of public telephones. It is essential that these facilities be accessible to able-bodied people as well as to semiambulant, elderly, and chair-bound people. The quality of interface between the user and these facilities requires a knowledge of human dimension. A public phone, for example, does a chair-bound user no good if he can't reach the coin slot. The drawings on the following pages illustrate some typical situations showing the human body in relation to a range of some basic public convenience facilities encountered in public spaces. The anthropometric measurements of major concern in the design and placement of these facilities are indicated in the matrix above.

# 8.4 PUBLIC CONVENIENCE FACILITIES

For public telephones to be accessible to wheelchair users, dial, coin slot, and head set should not be more than 48 in, or 121.9 cm, above the floor. It is also desirable that adjustable volume control be provided with the headset to assist those with hearing disabilities. Tactile and visual instructions should be provided for those users with sight disabilities. Wall-mounted units should have adequate space for wheelchair approach parallel to the front face of the equipment. Where shelves are provided below the telephone unit, a clearance of at least 29 in, or 73.7 cm, from the floor to the underside of the lowest part of the shelf should be provided.

If booths are provided for the chairbound, at least 42 in, or 106.7 cm, of clear floor space should be provided between walls. The telephone unit should be mounted on the side wall and a 32-in, or 81.3-cm, clear door opening should be provided.

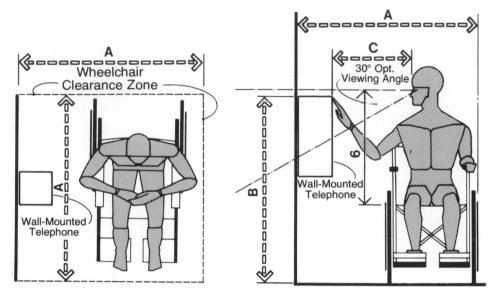

**PUBLIC TELEPHONES / DISABLED USERS**

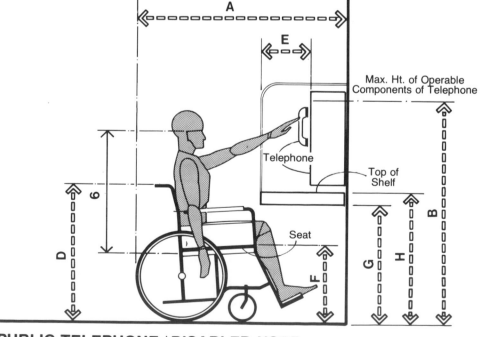

**PUBLIC TELEPHONE / DISABLED USER**

|   | in | cm |
|---|---|---|
| A | 48 | 121.9 |
| B | 48 max. | 121.9 max. |
| C | 13–20 | 33.0–50.8 |
| D | 36 | 91.4 |
| E | 8–12 | 20.3–30.5 |
| F | 19 | 48.3 |
| G | 29 min. | 73.7 min. |
| H | 32 max. | 81.3 max. |

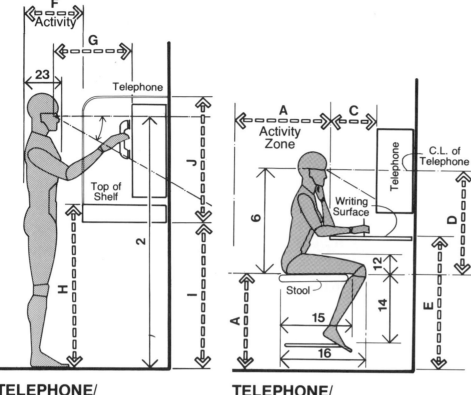

**TELEPHONE/ STANDING USER**

**TELEPHONE/ SEATED USER**

# 8.4 PUBLIC CONVENIENCE FACILITIES

The top drawings indicate some of the key dimensions for a wall-mounted public telephone. The installation intended to serve the seated user should comfortably serve a large number of standing users as well.

The drawing at the bottom shows the critical measurements necessary so that a drinking fountain can be accessible to both handicapped and able-bodied people. A distance of 30 in, or 76.2 cm, from the rim to the floor will make the fountain accessible to both wheelchair users and children. Some codes allow the use of a conventional drinking fountain to serve the wheelchair user if it does not exceed 36 in, or 91.4 cm, in height. The authors suggest that the 30-in height be used and, if necessary, a maximum height of 34 in, or 86.4 cm, not be exceeded. It is recommended also that hand-operated controls or combined hand-and-foot controls be used.

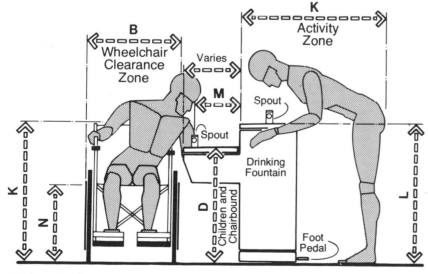

**DRINKING FOUNTAIN HEIGHTS**

| | in | cm |
|---|---|---|
| A | 24 | 61.0 |
| B | 25 | 63.5 |
| C | 12 | 30.5 |
| D | 30 | 76.2 |
| E | 34 | 86.4 |
| F | 18 | 45.7 |
| G | 13–20 | 33.0–50.8 |
| H | 43 | 109.2 |
| I | 37 | 94.0 |
| J | 32.5 | 82.6 |
| K | 36 | 91.4 |
| L | 36 max. | 91.4 max. |
| M | 8 min. | 20.3 min. |
| N | 19 | 48.3 |

# 8.4 PUBLIC CONVENIENCE FACILITIES

The top drawings indicate recommended heights for refuse receptacles to serve chairbound and semiambulant users. Provisions for a support can be extremely helpful.

The drawings at the bottom show a floor-type and wall-hung or shelf-type vending machine installation. Proper location of operating controls and coin slots is essential if the machines are to serve handicapped as well as able-bodied people. To be accessible to the chairbound user, the controls should be no less than 24 in, or 61.0 cm, nor more than 48 in, or 121.9 cm, above the floor. An activity zone of 42 in, or 106.7 cm, should be assumed in front of the machine for a person in a wheelchair. Where purely mechanical pull devices are used, they should require a minimal amount of force for operation.

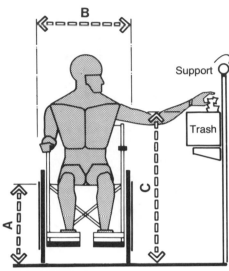

**REFUSE RECEPTACLE/ CHAIRBOUND**

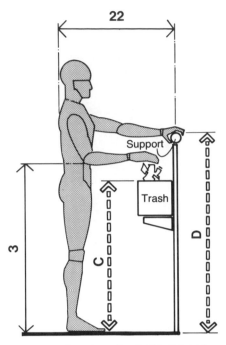

**REFUSE RECEPTACLE/ SEMIAMBULANT**

|   | in | cm |
|---|---|---|
| A | 19 | 48.3 |
| B | 25 | 63.5 |
| C | 40 | 101.6 |
| D | 48–54 | 121.9–137.2 |
| E | 30 | 76.2 |
| F | 24 min. | 61.0 min. |
| G | 48 max. | 121.9 max. |
| H | 48 | 121.9 |
| I | 36 max. | 91.4 max. |

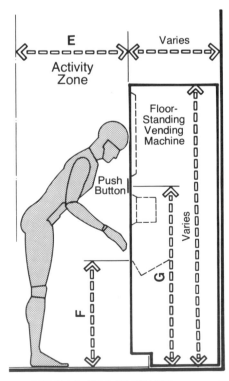

**VENDING MACHINES**

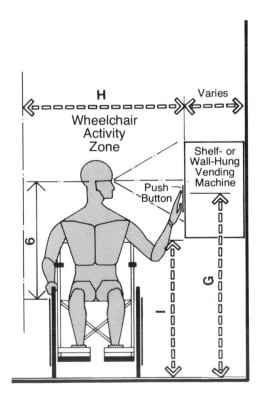

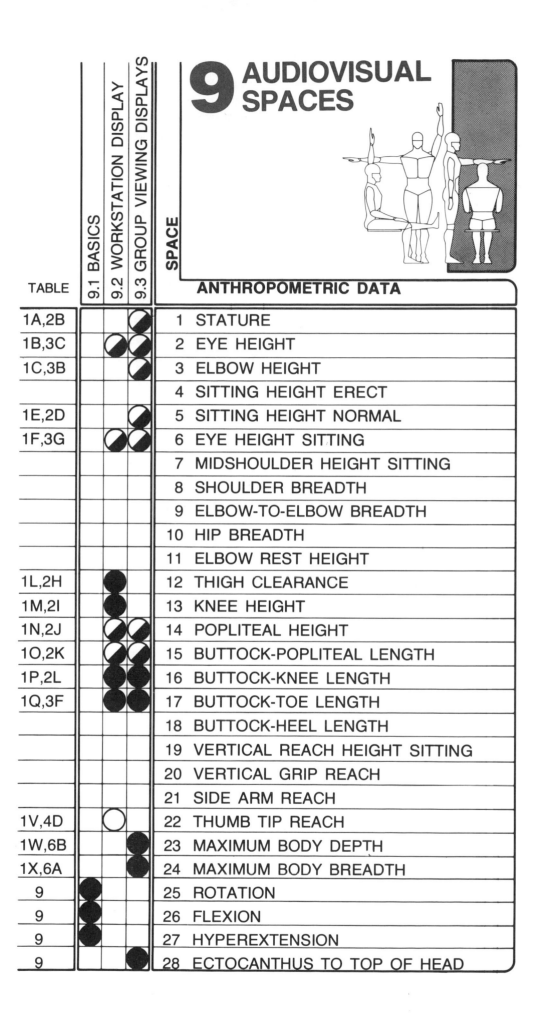

# 9 AUDIOVISUAL SPACES

| TABLE | 9.1 BASICS | 9.2 WORKSTATION DISPLAY | 9.3 GROUP VIEWING DISPLAYS | SPACE — ANTHROPOMETRIC DATA | |
|---|---|---|---|---|---|
| 1A,2B | | | ◐ | 1 | STATURE |
| 1B,3C | | ◐ | ◐ | 2 | EYE HEIGHT |
| 1C,3B | | | ◐ | 3 | ELBOW HEIGHT |
| | | | | 4 | SITTING HEIGHT ERECT |
| 1E,2D | | | ◐ | 5 | SITTING HEIGHT NORMAL |
| 1F,3G | | ◐ | ◐ | 6 | EYE HEIGHT SITTING |
| | | | | 7 | MIDSHOULDER HEIGHT SITTING |
| | | | | 8 | SHOULDER BREADTH |
| | | | | 9 | ELBOW-TO-ELBOW BREADTH |
| | | | | 10 | HIP BREADTH |
| | | | | 11 | ELBOW REST HEIGHT |
| 1L,2H | | ● | | 12 | THIGH CLEARANCE |
| 1M,2I | | ● | | 13 | KNEE HEIGHT |
| 1N,2J | | ◐ | ◐ | 14 | POPLITEAL HEIGHT |
| 1O,2K | | ◐ | ● | 15 | BUTTOCK-POPLITEAL LENGTH |
| 1P,2L | | ● | ● | 16 | BUTTOCK-KNEE LENGTH |
| 1Q,3F | | ● | ● | 17 | BUTTOCK-TOE LENGTH |
| | | | | 18 | BUTTOCK-HEEL LENGTH |
| | | | | 19 | VERTICAL REACH HEIGHT SITTING |
| | | | | 20 | VERTICAL GRIP REACH |
| | | | | 21 | SIDE ARM REACH |
| 1V,4D | | ○ | | 22 | THUMB TIP REACH |
| 1W,6B | | | ● | 23 | MAXIMUM BODY DEPTH |
| 1X,6A | | | ● | 24 | MAXIMUM BODY BREADTH |
| 9 | ● | | | 25 | ROTATION |
| 9 | ● | | | 26 | FLEXION |
| 9 | ● | | | 27 | HYPEREXTENSION |
| 9 | | | ● | 28 | ECTOCANTHUS TO TOP OF HEAD |

In recent years, the information explosion has given rise to a wide variety of audiovisual systems required to transmit that information. Applications can be found in almost every sector of the business and educational community. Trading rooms in brokerage houses, screening rooms in advertising agencies, conference rooms in corporate offices, libraries, auditoriums, and lecture halls in educational institutions are only a few of the many interior spaces for which visual communications systems must be planned. The systems range in complexity from a simple television readout to serve a single viewer at a workstation to multiscreen audiovisual presentations in an auditorium seating several hundred people.

Projections for the future include the use of closed circuit television for international conferences via satellite/sight transmission. Conferences between personnel of branch offices of large business corporations via closed circuit television, already a reality, may become routine. The use of audiovisual communications systems in the educational field is increasing rapidly, and some speculate that students soon will receive a greater portion of their education through film, slides, television, and computers than through live instruction. In terms of residential applications, the advent of CB radios, home computers, video tape cassettes, sophisticated stereophonic sound systems, home sound movies all clearly indicate that sophisticated audiovisual communications systems will become as much a part of tomorrow's home as was the radio in the thirties and forties and the TV in the fifties, sixties, and seventies. The design of audiovisual spaces requires some knowledge of acoustics, audition, and human vision. It is with respect to vision, however, that anthropometrics are particularly significant. Accordingly, the human eye and visual field serve as the basis for the drawings and data on the following pages. The eye height of short people compared with that of tall people in standing and seated positions, the difference in eye heights between males and females, the extent of a person's visual field, comfortable viewing zones, and the degree to which head movement and eye rotation can increase viewing capability are all essential factors in ensuring the proper interface between viewer and visual communication system.

The quality of the interface between any visual communication system and the viewer is, to a very large degree, a function of the extent to which the design of that system and the interior space in which it is housed responds to certain fundamental human capabilities and constraints. The more important factors for the architect or interior designer to consider involve the biomechanics of the human body and the geometry of the visual field. A third factor, the eye heights of seated and standing viewers, will also be discussed in the following section. In regard to biomechanics, the area of particular concern centers on the limits of the range of head movement. The degree to which the viewer may rotate the head in the vertical and horizontal planes will quite obviously widen or restrict his or her field of vision. The geometry of the visual field is equally significant since this aspect of the eye establishes the viewer's cones of vision and related viewing angles. It should be noted that in addition to head movement, the eyes themselves are capable of rotation. The range of eye movement up or down or from side to side adds to the viewer's ability to scan visual displays. The drawings on the following pages deal with the basics: the range of head movement in the horizontal and vertical planes and the visual field in the horizontal and vertical planes.

# 9.1 BASICS

Joint motions and positions are usually recorded in three basic planes—sagittal, frontal or coronal, and transverse—or in planes parallel to them. The sagittal plane is a vertical plane taken through the center of the body and perpendicular to body breadth. The frontal or coronal plane is also a vertical plane and is assumed to be taken through the body and perpendicular to the sagittal plane. The transverse plane is a horizontal plane perpendicular to the other two planes. For purposes of biokinematic research, these three planes are viewed as an orthogonal axis system centered on the pelvis.

The top drawing illustrates the range of head movement in the transverse or horizontal plane. Anthropometrically, the motion is referred to as "neck rotation" and a range of 45° to the left or right can be achieved without strain or discomfort by most people. A simple trial rotation by the reader will demonstrate the tremendous increase in the area that can be scanned from a single fixed location. The lower drawing illustrates the range of head movement in the vertical or sagittal plane. A range from 0° to 30° in either direction is possible without discomfort. Anthropometrically, the movement is termed "neck flexion." If measured downward, it is described as "ventral," and if measured toward the back or upward, it is described as "dorsal." International Standard Orthopaedic Measurements (ISOM), however, refer to the downward motion as "flexion" and the upward motion as "extension." Again, a simple experiment by the reader illustrates the tremendous increase in the field that can be scanned as a result of head movement, even if that movement is only a few degrees in magnitude.

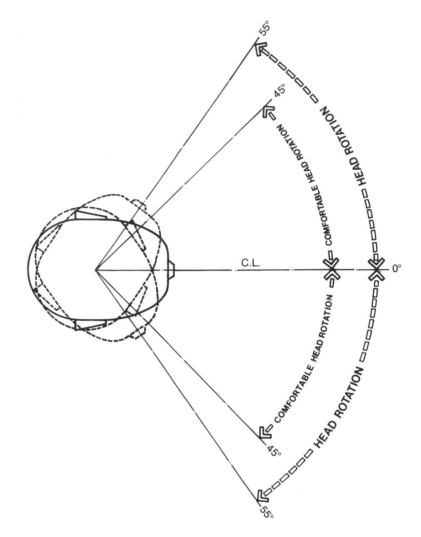

**HEAD MOVEMENT IN HORIZONTAL PLANE**

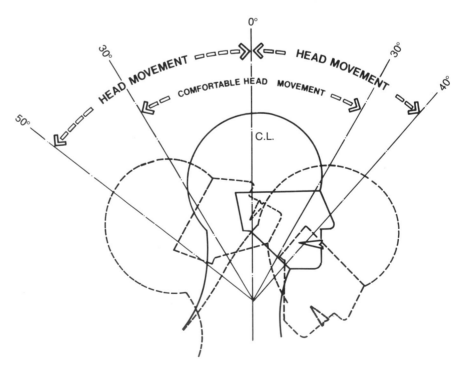

**HEAD MOVEMENT IN VERTICAL PLANE**

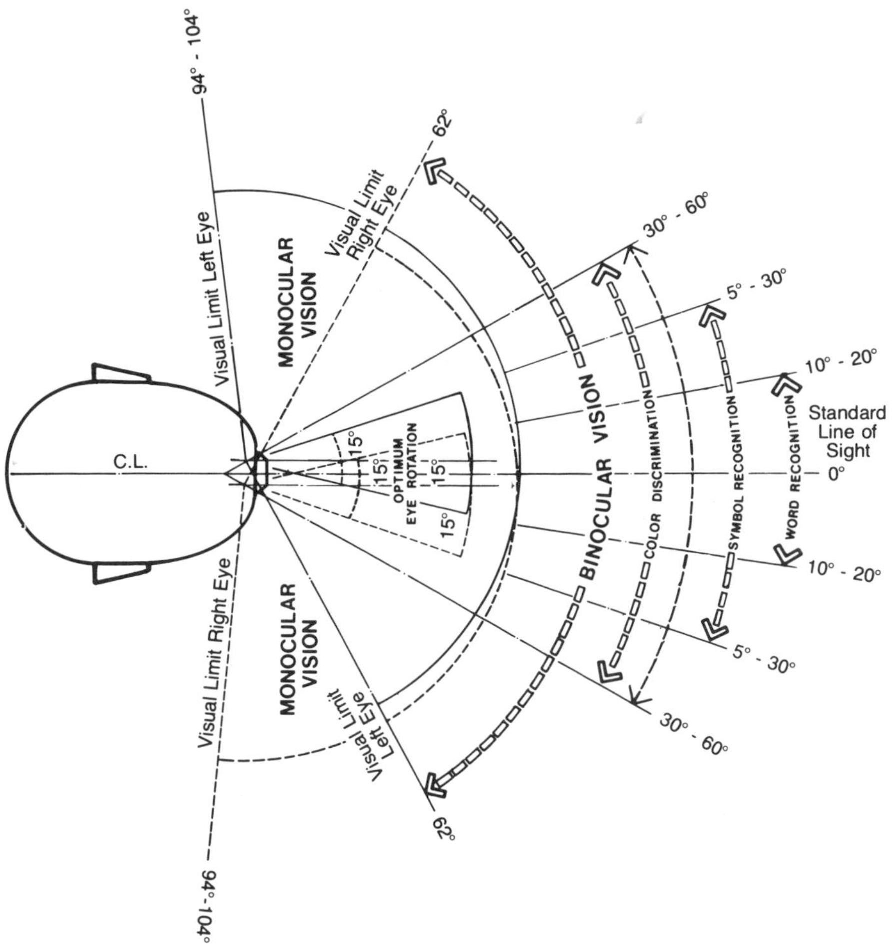
94° - 104°
Visual Limit Left Eye
Visual Limit Right Eye
MONOCULAR VISION
MONOCULAR VISION
Visual Limit Right Eye
Visual Limit Left Eye
62°
30° - 60°
5° - 30°
10° - 20°
Standard Line of Sight
0°
10° - 20°
5° - 30°
30° - 60°
62°
94° - 104°
C.L.
15°
15°
15°
15°
OPTIMUM EYE ROTATION
BINOCULAR VISION
COLOR DISCRIMINATION
SYMBOL RECOGNITION
WORD RECOGNITION

**VISUAL FIELD IN HORIZONTAL PLANE**

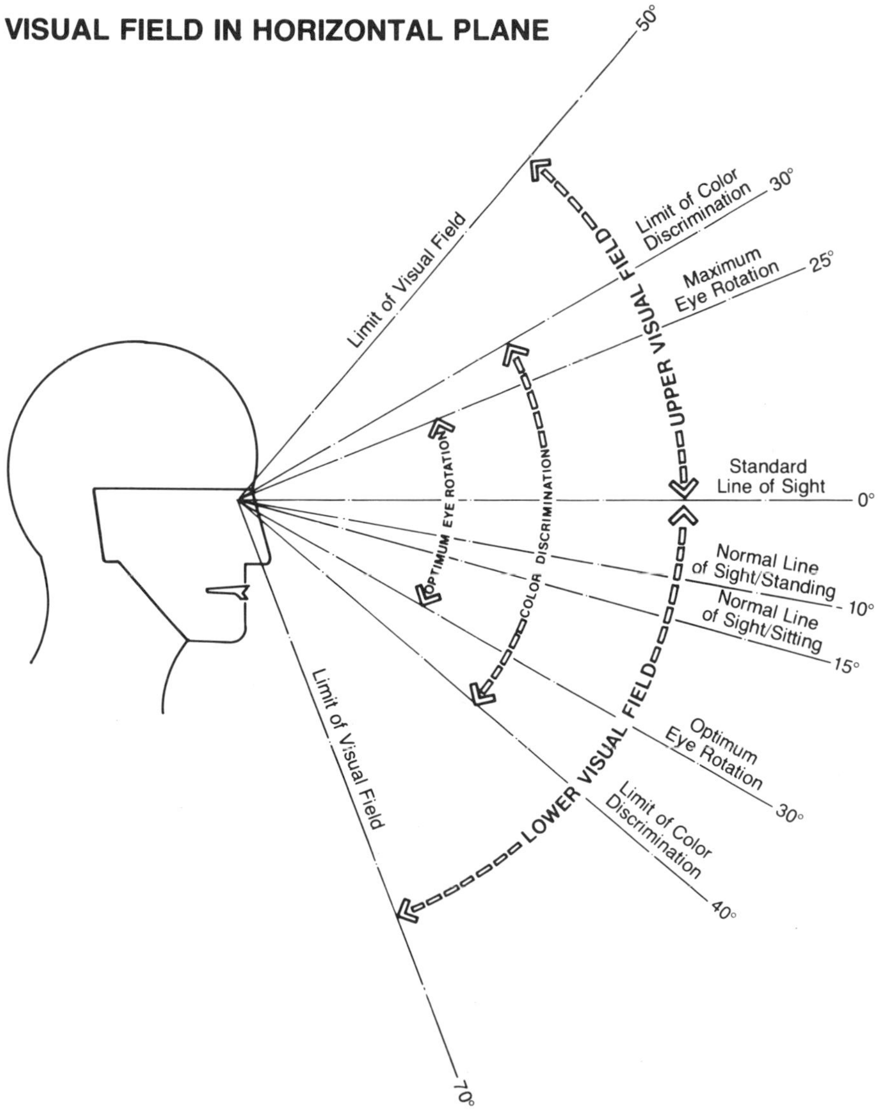
50°
Limit of Visual Field
Limit of Color Discrimination
30°
Maximum Eye Rotation
25°
UPPER VISUAL FIELD
Standard Line of Sight
0°
Normal Line of Sight/Standing
10°
Normal Line of Sight/Sitting
15°
OPTIMUM EYE ROTATION
COLOR DISCRIMINATION
Optimum Eye Rotation
30°
Limit of Color Discrimination
40°
LOWER VISUAL FIELD
Limit of Visual Field
70°

**VISUAL FIELD IN VERTICAL PLANE**

# 9.1 BASICS

The visual field is that part of space, measured in angular magnitude, that can be seen when the head and the eye are absolutely still. The visual field of the individual eye is termed "monocular vision." Within this field sharp images are not transmitted to the brain, causing objects to appear unclear and diffused. When an object, however, is observed by both eyes simultaneously, the visual field of each individual eye overlaps, creating a central field of greater magnitude than that possible by each eye separately. This central field of vision is termed "binocular field" and, as indicated in the top drawing, is about 60° in each direction. Within this field very sharp images are transmitted to the brain, depth perception occurs, and color discrimination is possible. Within this central field, recognition of words and symbols also occurs: 10° to 20° of the line of sight for the former and 5° to 30° of the line of sight for the latter. Beyond these respective limits, both words and symbols tend to disappear. The area of the sharpest focus is actually about 1° either side of the sight line. Depending on the particular color, color begins to disappear between 30° and 60° of the line of sight.

As shown in the drawing at the bottom of the page, the standard line of sight is assumed to be horizontal and at 0°. A person's natural or normal line of sight, however, is actually below the horizontal and varies slightly depending upon each individual and whether he is standing or sitting. If standing, the normal line of sight is about 10° below the horizontal and if sitting about 15°. In a very relaxed position, both standing and sitting sight lines may drift to an even greater angle below the horizontal: about 30° and 38° respectively. The magnitude of the optimum viewing zone for display materials is about 30° below the standard line of sight.

# 9.1 BASICS

The preceding drawings serve to individually illustrate the range of head movement in the horizontal and vertical planes and the field of vision in the horizontal and vertical planes. The drawing here combines both the head and eye movements in the vertical plane involved in sighting at various angles above and below the horizontal plane. Although the diagram itself may be of little, if any, practical use to the interior designer or the architect, it serves to stress the extent to which the area that can be scanned is affected by the range of head and eye movement.

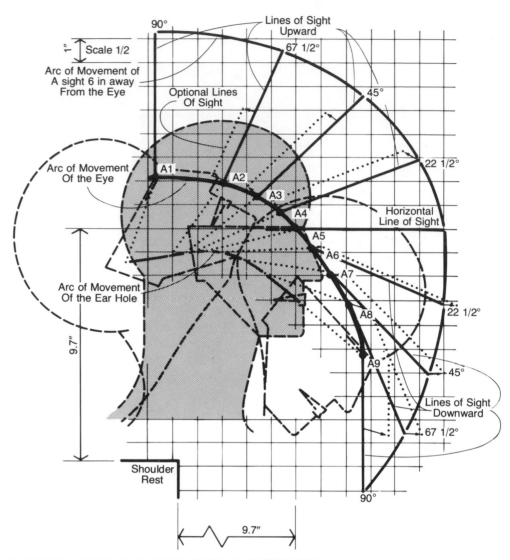

## RANGE OF HEAD AND EYE MOVEMENT IN THE VERTICAL PLANE

Adapted from *Human Factors Engineering*,
U.S. Air Force Systems Command Handbook, DH1-3, P. DN2B11, 19.

| TABLE | SEATED VIEWING | STANDING VIEWING | ACTIVITIES | | ANTHROPOMETRIC DATA |
|-------|:---:|:---:|:---:|:---:|---|
| | | | | **9.2** | **WORKSTATION DISPLAYS** |
| 1B,3C | ◑ | | | 2 | EYE HEIGHT |
| 1F,3G | ◑ | ◑ | | 6 | EYE HEIGHT SITTING |
| 1L,2H | | ● | | 12 | THIGH CLEARANCE |
| **1M,2I** | | ● | | 13 | KNEE HEIGHT |
| 1N,2J | | ◑ | | 14 | POPLITEAL HEIGHT |
| 1O,2K | | ◑ | | 15 | BUTTOCK-POPLITEAL LENGTH |
| 1P,2L | | ● | | 16 | BUTTOCK-KNEE LENGTH |
| 1Q,3F | | ● | | 17 | BUTTOCK-TOE LENGTH |
| 1V,4D | | ○ | | 22 | THUMB TIP REACH |

The interior designer or architect is frequently faced with the design of interior spaces and/or cabinet work that must incorporate a visual communication system of one type or another for an individual viewer. The system will inevitably include display material to be viewed from a sitting or a standing position. The viewing time may vary from a few moments to situations where the viewing task may well be a full-time activity. The display material may be in the form of a television readout, a film clip, or a transparency or x-ray negative to be viewed on a backlighted surface. To design the installation properly, the designer must be responsive to both the anthropometric and visual considerations involved. Eye height, for example, sitting or standing is clearly an anthropometric consideration, yet when applied to a visual communication system design, it becomes indistinguishable from what might be more appropriately categorized as an exclusively visual factor. It is the eye height measurement and the cone of vision springing from it that will help determine proper display location. Consideration must also be given to the problem of a very tall viewer and a very short viewer. Can the location of the display accommodate both users? If the display is to be located over a workcounter or desk surface, will the design accommodate the viewer with the shorter reach? If the design accommodates the reach requirements, will it also accommodate the human factor of the visual field and will the display be legible to the viewer? The drawings and data that follow deal exclusively with single-viewer, short-range displays and contain information that will be helpful in resolving some of the design problems posed. Note, however, that the information presented is not intended as a design solution, but as guidelines that can serve as a reasonable basis for preliminary design studies. When one considers the great variety and types of visual displays possible and the extent to which the visual field can be increased by a simple movement of the head or eye rotation, the data can be placed in a proper perspective. Moreover, it is customary in the design of workstations of this type to have a full-scale mockup of the unit for testing prior to production of the final unit.

# 9.2 WORKSTATION DISPLAYS

The need to include a visual display component as part of an individual workstation is not uncommon. In most cases the display takes the form of some kind of computer readout arrangement. Whatever the nature of the display, the distance between it and the eye and the height and angle of the display is an important consideration. In certain cases displays must be observed from a standing position, in others from a seated position. The workstation must also accommodate people having a wide range of body sizes. The drawings on this and the next page will explore some of the basic visual and anthropometric factors involved.

## Distance of Display from the Eye

Through the process of accommodation, the mechanism of the human eye will automatically focus the eye on the display at the required distance. Most sources place the minimum distance from viewer to display between 13 and 16 in, or 33 and 40.6 cm; the optimum distance between 18 and 22 in, or 45.7 and 55.9 cm; and the maximum distance between 28 and 29 in, or 71.7 and 73.7 cm.

It should be noted, however, that the ranges cited are approximations and vary with the size of the display material and lighting. Moreover, the nearest point to which the eye can focus moves further away from the eye with age. At age 16, for example, it is less than 4 in, or 10.2 cm, away, while at age 40 it is over twice that distance away. By comparison, however, the furthest point to which the eye can focus shows relatively little change over the years. Accordingly, the maximum range of 28 to 29 in, or 71.7 to 73.7 cm, is limited more by the size of the characters and the reach limitations related to the workstation counter or controls. The usual reading distance for printed material is about 18 in, or 45.8 cm.

## Viewing Angle

As a general rule for optimum viewing, a sight line from the bottom of the display to the eye of the viewer should form an angle of not more than 30° with the standard horizontal line of sight. In cases where a seated ob-

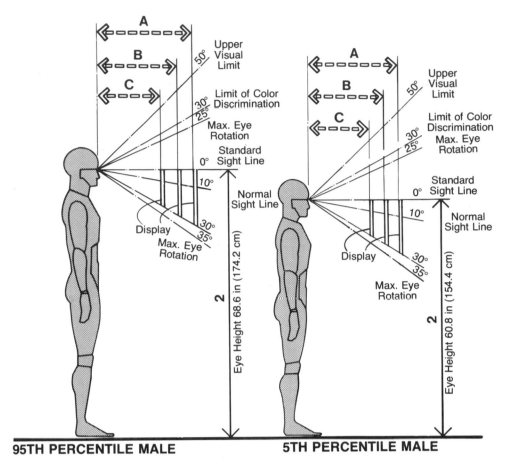

**95TH PERCENTILE MALE**     **5TH PERCENTILE MALE**

**THE STANDING MALE VIEWER / WORKSTATION DISPLAY**

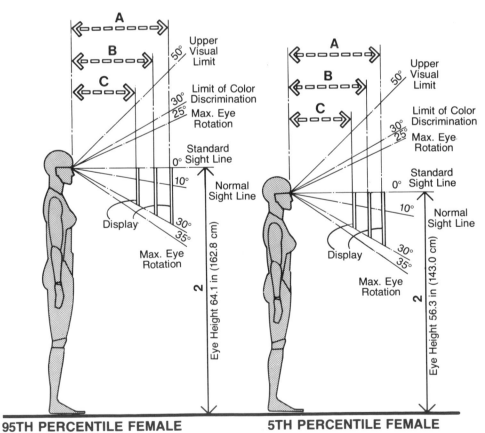

**95TH PERCENTILE FEMALE**     **5TH PERCENTILE FEMALE**

**THE STANDING FEMALE VIEWER / WORKSTATION DISPLAY**

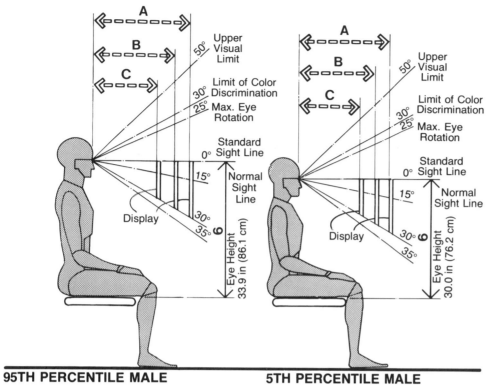

**95TH PERCENTILE MALE**      **5TH PERCENTILE MALE**

## THE SEATED MALE VIEWER/WORKSTATION DISPLAY

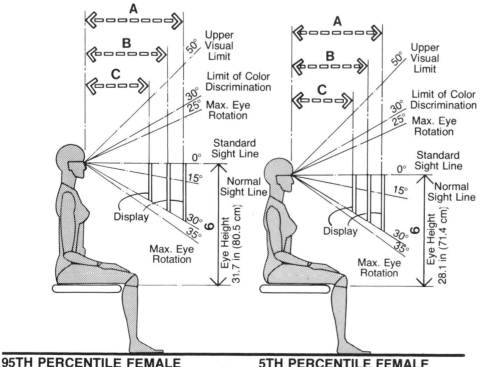

**95TH PERCENTILE FEMALE**      **5TH PERCENTILE FEMALE**

## THE SEATED FEMALE VIEWER/WORKSTATION DISPLAY

server is to function at the workstation for an extended period of time, he would, after a while, assume a more relaxed position, causing his head to rotate downward a few more degrees. The 30° could therefore be increased to 33°.

### Height of Display

Ideally, the height of the top of the display should relate to the eye height of the viewer. The great variability in eye height measurements and in certain cases the size of the specific display may make this difficult. One solution to make the display within reach and within the visual field of the smaller viewer is to increase his eye height by means of a raised platform. Safety precautions, such as a railing, should be provided to prevent accidents. The platform should be movable so that it can be relocated at such times that the workspace is to be used by a taller viewer. Another solution, although more costly, is to develop an adjustable arrangement, whereby the display panel may be raised or lowered to suit individual eye height. Where a seated viewer is involved, the problem is less difficult. The variation in the eye heights of the tall and short seated viewer above the seat surface is much less than that of the eye heights above the floor of tall and short standing viewers. The difference in eye heights of the latter is about 12 in, or 30.5 cm, while the difference between eye heights of the former, as indicated by the drawings, is less than 6 in, or 15.2 cm. Accordingly, the problem of making the display within reach of the visual field of the smaller seated user can be solved quite easily by the use of a chair with an adjustable seat height.

### Display Angle

Where possible, the angle of display should place the viewing surface perpendicular to the normal line of sight.

### Controls

Controls should be placed within reach of the smaller viewer and located so that the body movement necessary for operation of the controls will not obstruct visibility.

|   | in | cm |
|---|---|---|
| **A** | 28–29 | 71.1–73.7 |
| **B** | 18–22 | 45.7–55.9 |
| **C** | 13–16 | 33.0–40.6 |

# 9.2 WORKSTATION DISPLAYS

The top drawing illustrates guidelines for use in establishing preliminary design assumptions for a workstation display console. Since the types of displays and the nature of the tasks associated with those displays can vary considerably, the drawing cannot be taken too literally. The configuration shown, however, is fairly representational. Certain basic factors should be noted anthropometrically. The use of an adjustable chair will permit the eye height of the seated viewer to be raised or lowered to view the display, as may be required depending on body size. An adjustment range between 15 and 18 in, or 38.1 and 45.7 cm, should be adequate to accommodate the eye height sitting requirements of about 90 percent of all viewers. Adjustability, however, will be of little value if the vertical distance between the underside of the desk and the floor is insufficient to accommodate the knee height and thigh clearance when the seat is adjusted to the appropriate position. If such distance is not less than 26.5 in, or 67.3 cm, the majority of viewers will be accommodated.

The location of the top of the display should align with the standard sight line for optimum viewing conditions. Since the eye and the head can rotate within certain limitations and, in so doing, increase the area that can be scanned, displays can be located above the standard sight line when absolutely necessary. It should also be noted that the more perpendicular the normal sight line is to the display plane, the greater the viewing comfort. Accordingly, consideration should be given to sloping the display plane since the normal sight line is about 15° below the horizontal.

The drawing at the bottom is from another source and stresses many of the angular relationships involved in display console design.

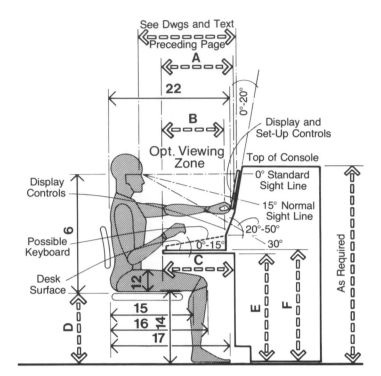

## DESIGN GUIDELINES/ WORKSTATION DISPLAY CONSOLE

Adapted from *Human Engineering Guide to Equipment Design*, p. 393.

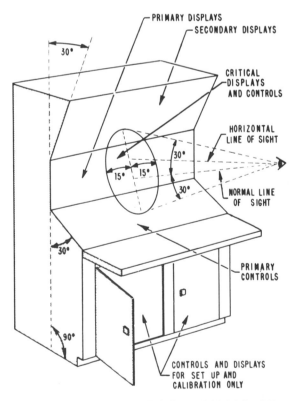

## RECOMMENDED POSITIONING OF CONTROLS AND DISPLAYS ON VERTICAL SEGMENT CONSOLES

From *Human Factors Engineering*,
U.S. Air Force Systems Command Handbook DH 1-3, P.DN2E5, 4.

|   | in | cm |
|---|---|---|
| A | 16–18 | 40.6–45.7 |
| B | 16 min. | 40.6 min. |
| C | 18 min. | 45.7 min. |
| D | 15–18 adjust. | 38.1–45.7 |
| E | 26.5 min. | 67.3 min. |
| F | 30 | 76.2 |

| TABLE | SEATED VIEWING | STANDING VIEWING | SPEAKER | ACTIVITIES | ANTHROPOMETRIC DATA |
|---|---|---|---|---|---|
| 1A,2B | | | ● | 1 | STATURE |
| 1B,3C | | ● | ● | 2 | EYE HEIGHT |
| 1C,3B | | | ● | 3 | ELBOW HEIGHT |
| 1E,2D | ● | | | 5 | SITTING HEIGHT NORMAL |
| 1F,3G | ● | | | 6 | EYE HEIGHT SITTING |
| 1N,2J | ● | | | 14 | POPLITEAL HEIGHT |
| 1O,2K | ● | | | 15 | BUTTOCK-POPLITEAL LENGTH |
| 1P,2L | ● | | | 16 | BUTTOCK-KNEE LENGTH |
| 1Q,3F | ● | | | 17 | BUTTOCK-TOE LENGTH |
| 1W,6B | ● | | ● | 23 | MAXIMUM BODY DEPTH |
| 1X,6A | ● | | | 24 | MAXIMUM BODY BREADTH |
| | ● | | | 28 | ECTOCANTHUS TO TOP OF HEAD |

**9.3 DISPLAYS FOR GROUP VIEWING**

Visual communication systems for group viewing present somewhat different problems than those normally associated with systems designed for the individual viewer. Ideal displays for the latter are located so the viewing angle is generally below the horizontal line of sight. However, due to the size and relationship of a group display, such as a projection screen in a motion picture theater, to the viewer and the obstruction of the visual field of one viewer by another, the display is located so that the upper limit of the optimum viewing angle is situated above the horizontal line of sight. The general layout and configuration of the seating must be planned to ensure the greatest visibility for the greatest number. The minimum distance the front row of seats can be from the display to allow adequate viewing must be considered in the planning of the interior space and general seating layout. Seats must be planned to allow sight lines of one viewer to pass above and between the viewer in front. The distance between rows must allow adequate clearance for circulation and human movement. Provisions for the disabled or wheelchair-bound viewer must also be taken into account. In live situations, a lectern, pulpit, or bimah and the speaker all must be considered as part of the communication system. The design of the lectern should respond to the anthropometric and visual requirements of the speaker. In addition, the lectern-speaker as the display should bear the proper visual relationship to the viewers. The drawings that follow explore various aspects of the group viewing process and suggest clearances and other data for use in preliminary design studies.

# 9.3 DISPLAYS FOR GROUP VIEWING

The design of spaces for group viewing activities requires some knowledge of the anthropometrics of the tall and short standing and seated viewer and the visual implications involved. The top drawing shows that the basic 5th percentile and 95th percentile body measurements of standing viewers are such that the line of sight of the shorter viewer would be obstructed by the taller viewer. When the same 5th and 95th percentile measurements are applied, the drawing of the seated viewers indicates that the line of sight of the smaller viewer just clears the midshoulder height of the larger viewer in front. It should be noted that the difference in eye height between the larger and smaller seated viewers is about half the difference in eye height when the larger and smaller viewers are standing. The minimum distance between the first row and the display can be determined by drawing a sight line from the top of the projected image to the eye of the viewer seated in the first row at an angle not less than 30° nor more than 33°, as indicated in the bottom drawing.

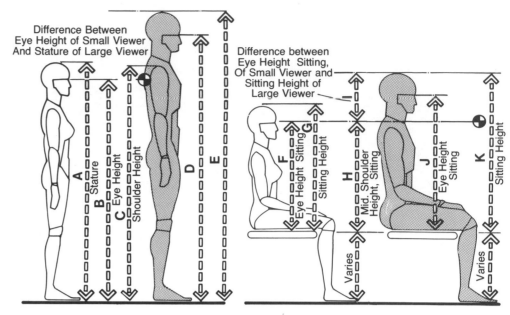

## COMPARATIVE ANTHROPOMETRICS/ STANDING AND SEATED VIEWERS

| | in | cm |
|---|---|---|
| A | 59.0 | 149.9 |
| B | 56.3 | 143.0 |
| C | 57.8 | 146.8 |
| D | 68.6 | 174.2 |
| E | 72.8 | 184.9 |
| F | 28.1 | 71.4 |
| G | 29.6 | 75.2 |
| H | 27.3 | 69.3 |
| I | 9.3 | 23.6 |
| J | 33.9 | 86.1 |
| K | 36.6 | 93.0 |

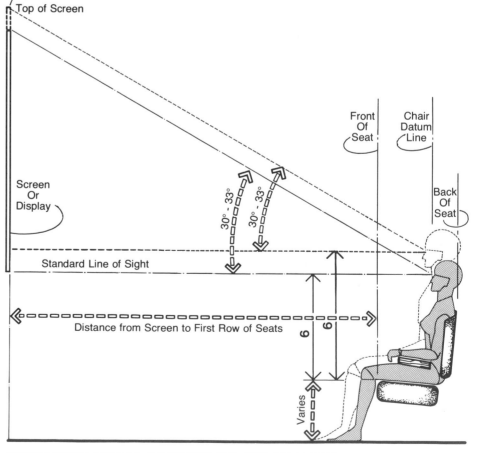

## DISTANCE FROM SCREEN TO FIRST ROW

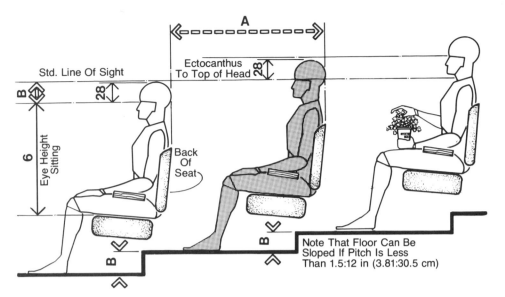

**STEPPED SEATING / ONE-ROW VISION**

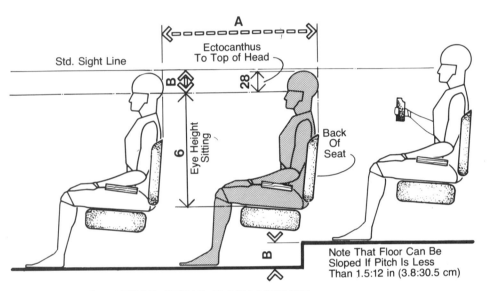

**STEPPED SEATING / TWO-ROW VISION**

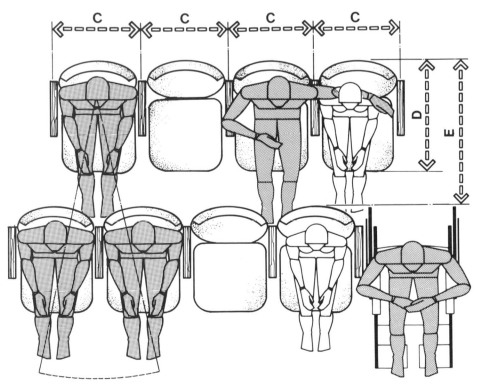

**STAGGERED SEATING**

# 9.3 DISPLAYS FOR GROUP VIEWING

Maximum visibility for the greatest number of seated viewers can be achieved by elevating their eye heights successively from front to back row so that one viewer can look over the head of the person in front. The ectocanthus to top of head measurement is the anthropometric data most useful in determining the actual height by which the floor must be stepped or sloped to achieve this condition. It is the distance from the outer cornea of the eye to the level of the top of the head. The 95th percentile data shows this measurement to be about 5 in, or 12.7 cm, and is the increment by which the floor is stepped. The top drawing illustrates the "one-row vision" method of elevating eye heights so that the viewer may have unobstructed vision over the heads of those viewers in rows immediately ahead. The center drawing illustrates the "two-row vision" method which prevents the heads of all viewers two or more rows ahead from blocking visibility. The advantage of this method is that it minimizes the slope or number of steps. Its disadvantage is that it is not as effective as the one-row scheme. Wider seats and a staggered plan, however, can improve visibility by permitting a view between the heads of those directly in front, as shown in the bottom drawing. In regard to the depths of rows, although a 32-in, or 81.3-cm, spacing is often used, 40 in, or 101.6 cm, is recommended.

|   | in | cm |
|---|---|---|
| A | 40 | 101.6 |
| B | 5 | 12.7 |
| C | 20–26 | 50.8–66.0 |
| D | 27–30 | 68.6–76.2 |
| E | 34–42 | 86.4–106.7 |

# 9.3 DISPLAYS FOR GROUP VIEWING

Unless traffic flow to the pew is controlled, the lack of armrests makes the seat allowance shown in the top drawing somewhat theoretical. Assuming some controlled means of seat space definition, however, a reasonable incremental unit to use as a basis for seat width is the maximum body breadth. The 95th percentile data for larger users is 22.8 in, or 57.9 cm, taken with the subjects nude. The top drawing shows three possible seat allowances: 24 to 26 in, or 61 to 66 cm; 28 in, or 71.1 cm; and a possible minimum of 22 in, or 55.9 cm.

When one considers that an allowance for clothing and ritual-related body movement should be added to the 22.8 incremental unit, the 22-in minimum would not comfortably accommodate the majority of users without some body contact. Economics permitting, the 28-in spacing is recommended. The bottom drawing shows several pew spacing possibilities. All can work, depending on the level of comfort desired and the nature and frequency of ritual-related body movements.

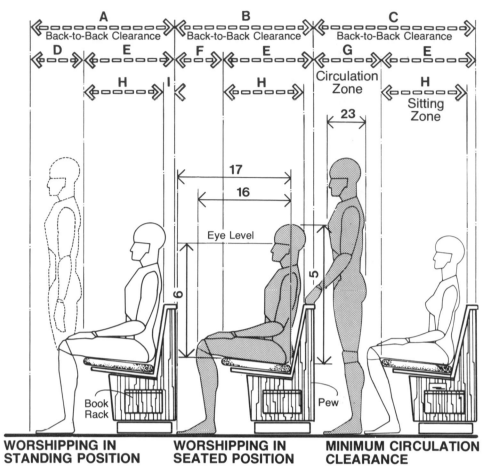

**BASIC PEW CLEARANCES / ELEVATION**

| | in | cm |
|---|---|---|
| **A** | 34–38 | 86.4–96.5 |
| **B** | 34–36 | 86.4–91.4 |
| **C** | 42–48 | 106.7–121.9 |
| **D** | 12–16 | 30.5–40.6 |
| **E** | 22 | 55.9 |
| **F** | 12–14 | 30.5–35.6 |
| **G** | 20–26 | 50.8–66.0 |
| **H** | 20 | 50.8 |
| **I** | 2 | 5.8 |
| **J** | 42 | 106.7 |
| **K** | 22 min. | 55.9 min. |
| **L** | 24–26 | 61.0–66.0 |
| **M** | 28 | 71.1 |
| **N** | 14–18 | 35.6–45.7 |

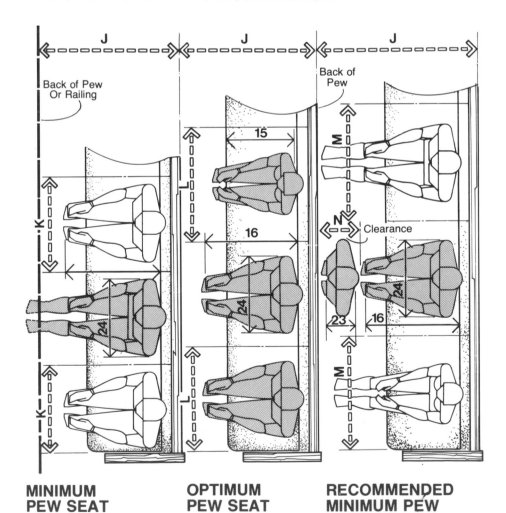

**MINIMUM PEW SEAT PER PERSON**  **OPTIMUM PEW SEAT PER PERSON**  **RECOMMENDED MINIMUM PEW SEAT PER PERSON**

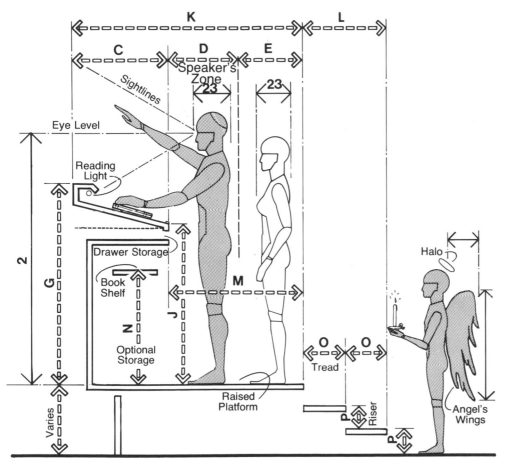

**LECTURN, PULPIT, OR BIMAH**

**SECTION**

A
C D
Speaker's Zone
23
Eye Level
Reading Light
30°
Book Drawer
Optional Storage Below
Optional Footrest
G
H
1

**FRONT VIEW**

B
E F E
Speaker's Zone
Eye Level
J
G
1
2
3
I

When an audience is listening to live speeches, lectures, or sermons, the lecturn, pulpit, or bimah and the speaker should be viewed as the display. With respect to the speaker, the display is assumed to be whatever notes or other written material he may use in connection with his delivered presentation. The top drawing shows some of the basic dimensions involved and suggests some of the visual and anthropometric considerations implied. For optimum speaker viewing comfort, the surface upon which notes are placed should be at an angle of about 30°. When anthropometrically determining the height of the top of the lecturn surface facing the speaker, elbow height should be taken into account. The extent to which the lecturn may obstruct both viewer and speaker vision should also be considered.

Visibility for the viewers in the first row is also extremely important. The bottom drawing indicates a raised lecturn situation. As with any platform, safety provisions should be built into the design.

**RAISED LECTURN, PULPIT, OR BIMAH**

K L
C D E
Speaker's Zone
Sightlines
23 23
Eye Level
Reading Light
Drawer Storage
Book Shelf
Optional Storage
N
J
2
G
M
Raised Platform
Varies
O O
Tread
P Riser
P
Halo
Angel's Wings

|   | in | cm |
|---|-----|------|
| A | 42–66 | 106.7–167.6 |
| B | 48–66 | 121.9–167.6 |
| C | 24–42 | 61.0–106.7 |
| D | 18–24 | 45.7–61.0 |
| E | 12–18 | 30.5–45.7 |
| F | 24–30 | 61.0–76.2 |
| G | 45–50 | 114.3–127.0 |
| H | 4–8 | 10.2–20.3 |
| I | 36–39 | 91.4–99.1 |
| J | 7–10 | 17.8–25.4 |
| K | 60–90 | 152.4–228.6 |
| L | 22–28 | 55.9–71.1 |
| M | 36–48 | 91.4–121.9 |
| N | 29–32 | 73.7–81.3 |
| O | 11–14 | 27.9–35.6 |
| P | 6–7 | 15.2–17.8 |

# D EPILOGUE

# EPILOGUE

NASA is presently planning a space vehicle that will "carry large numbers of people of all nations and races, and of a wide range of body sizes and ages, into and out of weightlessness." It is anticipated that such a transportation system will be followed by "space stations where people will function for long periods, in an environment for which their bodies were not designed." In regard to the design process involved in this massive scientific undertaking, scientist-astronaut Dr. William Thorton writes:

> The quality of the interface which connects man with his machines frequently determines the ability and the ultimate performance of the man-machine unit. . . . The beginning of any man-machine interface is the objective knowledge of the full range of man's size, shape, composition and mechanical capabilities.[1]

Apparently, Dr. Thornton has applied a concept that many of us, as earthbound designers of interior space, for too long have failed to recognize. It is ironic that, as designers involved deeply in situations where the quality of people's interface with the physical environment is paramount, we have, as a profession, failed in our awareness, exploration, understanding, and application of engineering anthropometry—the most basic aspect of that interface.

In the research, writing, and general preparation of this book, we found ourselves both stunned and frustrated at the lack of anthropometric data generally available for use by architects and interior design professionals—professionals who are primarily responsible for the total design of the interior spaces in which people live, work, and play. The frustration was compounded when we observed other professionals, to their credit, impressively involved in the development and application of anthropometric data to the design of equipment and man-in-space environments at a time when the term itself was still relatively foreign or unfamiliar to the majority of us in the interior design and architectural professions. With a few exceptions, we have as a group remained far too passive, when, in fact, by the very nature of our professional mission, we should have been at the forefront of the research in this area. As a consequence we have found that too much of what is being designed today is still based on unchallenged and outdated standards, rules of thumb, intuitive judgments, antiquated trade practices, and manufacturer's recommendations, many of which are insensitive to human factors, in general, and body size and dynamics, in particular. We feel it is incumbent upon the design professions to take immediate action in this area and look forward to the time when architectural anthropometry may possibly develop into a discipline in itself or, at the very least, constitute a basic part of the educational process for interior designers and architects.

Undoubtedly, many may question the level of importance we have placed on the study of body size and human dimension as it relates to interior design and architecture and the sense of urgency we have placed on the accumulation of necessary anthropometric data. Although body size would understandably be an important factor in the design for the cockpit of a fighter aircraft or the limited confines of a space vehicle in zero-gravity, some may argue that problems of fit within typical civilian environments are not as critical and that to apply such an approach to the design of civilian interiors would be like going after a mouse with an elephant gun.

Although military and aerospace design applications of anthropometric data may well involve more and different body measurements and in some instances the tolerances of fit may be more critical, many of the applications have equivalent civilian counterparts. More importantly, however, we want to emphasize that an improper fit between the individual and his environment, whether that environment is in the military, aerospace, or civilian sector, can impact dramatically not only on his comfort but on his personal safety. In some instances the quality of that interface can, in fact, be a matter of life and death.

To reinforce that statement, we must lay out certain facts and misconceptions we have uncovered, as well as insights we have gained, during the research for this book over the past two years. Some of this material may have been implied in previous sections of the book, while some may have been discussed in somewhat greater detail, and certain material may not have been mentioned at all. We hope it will all serve to underscore the present and very real danger faced by the user in his interface with those components of interior space designed without regard to human dimension and, at the very least, the urgent need for additional research and reevaluation of many of the questionable practices and standards in circulation today.

The most shocking information uncovered during the course of our research involves children. A recent study indicated that the death rate of children under one year of age from accidental suffocation related to beds and cradles was 18.6 per 100,000 live births in 1965. The implication is that a strong relationship exists between improperly designed furniture and accidental death and injury. Other studies imply that improper spacing of slats in cradles and playpens, which would permit an infant's head to pass through, is the cause of many of the fatalities—a clear, although painful, example of the importance of human dimension in the design process. Within a larger context, the chilling statistics from the Consumer Product Safety Commission are that upwards of 2 million children are injured each year in accidents attributed to toys, playground equipment, bicycles, and other children's products. One can only speculate how many of

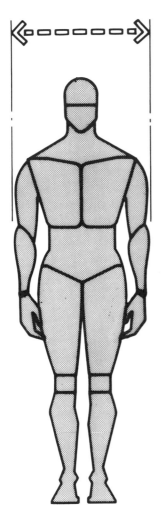

Figure E-1. Maximum body breadth.

these accidents are caused by the designer's insensitivity to human dimension and the poor quality of the user-product interface. So critical was the problem and so essential to its solution was anthropometric data that the Consumer Product Safety Commission funded a three-year study, the major purpose of which was to provide basic selected measurement data on infants and children, particularly functional measurements, essential for the development of adequate product safety design standards.

Perhaps the greatest misconception we became aware of is the notion of the so-called average man. There has been a tendency on the part of those engaged in shaping our interior spaces to design to accommodate the average user and, by extension, to mistakenly assume that in so doing they are accommodating a majority of those users. The reality is that no such human being exists. So-called average dimensions are simply statistical means indicating that in the sample population whose body measurements were recorded, about 50 percent had a specific body measurement of a particular dimension or less. Obviously, any design based on the accommodation of such data would, in most instances, exclude at least 50 percent of the users—a far cry from the majority the designer had originally intended to accommodate.

Moreover, no person is average in all his body dimensions. He simply is not built that way. This has been demonstrated by studies made of the middle range of a sample of 4,000 males, which showed that of ten body dimensions measured, only 25 percent were average in a single dimension and less than 1 percent were average in five dimensions. Despite this, we are constantly exposed to literature suggesting designs to suit the average user. In addition, what little body size data has heretofore been made available to us proudly declares that the dimensions are that of an average person. To further compound the error, the same data, usually in the form of a dimensioned figure, are not limited to a single body measurement, but a host of measurements. The human body, as indicated earlier, is simply not proportioned so that all body measurements are average.

Another misconception, the perpetuation of which could impact on personal safety, if not comfort, deals with a very basic body dimension, that of maximum body breadth, illustrated in Figure E-1. Maximum body breadth is measured with the nude subject standing erect and with arms hanging relaxed at the sides. The dimension reflects the horizontal maximum breadth across the body including the arms. We decided to consult published anthropometric data to determine what the range of dimensions were in regard to this particular body measurement. Based on a study by Hertzberg, Emanuel, and Alexander in 1956, the 5th, 50th, and 95th percentile data were 18.8 in (47.8 cm), 20.9 in (53.1 cm), and 22.8 in (57.9 cm), respectively. Adding an allowance for winter outer clothing of 3 in, or 7.6 cm, and rounding off increased the figures to 22 in (55.9 cm), 24 in (61.0 cm), and 26 in (66.0 cm), respectively. The startling revelation in this data can only be fully appreciated when compared with what the actual maximum body breadth allowances are in the various design standards in circulation regarding corridor widths, door widths, spacing of plumbing fixtures, and motor stair widths, to list only a few.

For example, many local, state, and national codes, in establishing requirements for corridors, passageways, and walkways, use a 22-in, or 55.9-cm, incremential factor. The underlying implication is that 22 in, or 55.9 cm, represents the dimension required to accommodate an additional pedestrian lane. Two additional lanes would require a total of 44 in, or 111.8 cm. According to anthropometric data, however, only 5 percent of the users would have a clothed maximum body breadth of 22 in, or 55.9 cm, or less. Further research revealed that certain other studies concerned with walking patterns and gait indicated that the human body sways from side to side a distance of about 4 in, or 10.2 cm, making 22 in, or 55.9 cm, even more inadequate. A so-called two-lane motor stair has a maximum width at rail height of 48 in, 121.9 cm, tapering to a 40-in, or 101.6 cm, clearance at the tread. Allowing for the taper and recognizing that the body position of the passenger is dictated also by the location of his foot in relation to the side of the stair, we again found that only those passengers with the smaller range of body sizes would, in fact, be accommodated.

Another rule of thumb presently circulating and actually suggested by manufacturers is the center-to-center spacing of lavatories at 24 in, or 61.0 cm. How many of us, in laying out public restrooms, have unquestioningly applied this standard? During the course of our research, we decided to test the validity of such spacing. An application of anthropometric logic proved the spacing to be inadequate. The maximum clothed body breadth measurement of 26 in, or 66.0 cm, clearly indicates an error. A battery of lavatories spaced according to the standard simply would not permit the user, with a larger body size, access to a fixture without displacing the person next to him. It should be noted, however, that maximum body breadth measurements are taken with the subject's arms at his sides, while actual use of the lavatory requires the arms to be extended out from the body, thus increasing the space required in front of the fixture and making the 24-in, or 61.0-cm, spacing even more inadequate. Actually, less than 50 percent of the users can be accommodated by such a spacing standard—hardly a reasonable range of accommodation for a public facility subjected to intense peak loads. It would seem that the spacing requirement was based more on accommodating the maximum number and sizes of lavatory types than the number and sizes of the users it was supposed to serve.

A similar problem, for similar reasons, applies to recommended spacing for urinals, except that due to the nature of the activity involved and even more restricted spacing, the standards are even more inadequate. Present rules of thumb, as well as actual manufacturer's recommendations, suggest spacing urinals, placed in a battery arrangement, between 21 and 24 in, or 53.3 and 61.0 cm apart. Given the maximum clothed body breadth dimension of 26 in, or 66.0 cm, cited previously, the absurdity of such a spacing becomes obvious. Curiously, most sanitary codes dictate the minimum number of plumbing fixtures deemed acceptable, but do not specify any requirements for minimum spacing. The designer may comply with the language of the code, but by not questioning the anthropometric implications, not its intent, since less than 50 percent of the users could actually have access to the fixtures under peak load situations without body contact.

On balance, it would appear that present standards allow the manufacturer the greatest number and variety of his products to be installed in the smallest space possible and the building owner to reduce construction costs and maximize rental area while still complying with code requirements—all at the expense of the user and the quality of his interface with the interior environment. We conclude that most currently used design guidelines which presumably should reflect people's maximum body breadth dimensions, simply cannot be reconciled with published anthropometric data and that the designs evolving from those guidelines are simply unacceptable. Anyone who has used the crowded restrooms at an airport, sports stadium, or bus terminal has observed the percentage of fixtures left unoccupied, despite the great number of people waiting in line to use the facilities. How often have you actually seen two people abreast facing the same direction in a so-called two-lane motor stair or walking through a 44-in, or 111.8-cm, opening? Very infrequently. The reason is quite simple: more often than not they simply cannot fit.

It should be noted that our arguments with present clearance allowances is exclusively anthropometric. In order to present the most conservative argument possible, we did not mention the hidden dimensions. Surely the body buffer zone (and the personal space implied), particularly with respect to the planning of public toilet facilities, should be considered. The fact that people will walk so close to a wall and no closer should be a factor in determining clearances. Human gait and cultural influences also affect clearance allowances. Personal comfort and the quality of life surely are other ingredients to consider. If all these considerations are taken into account, as they should be, present clearance allowances become even more inadequate.

And what of personal safety? In many cases where inadequate standards are used, the larger width of a certain opening, walkway, or stairs, relative to the smaller width of similar openings, walkways, or stairs, may suggest double lane traffic, when, in fact, two lanes cannot be accommodated. The user whose sensory mechanism may not be sophisticated enough to anticipate the inadequacy will attempt entry into the perceived second lane. It is almost inevitable that body contact with the adjacent pedestrian will result, or one of the two will be obliged to side step to allow the other to pass. Either eventuality may result in an accident. During crowded conditions or an emergency such an accident could prove fatal. More serious still would be a situation where a two-lane pedestrian traffic flow was essential to evacuate a specified number of occupants from an interior space of public assembly within a certain period of time. If incorrect maximum body breadth data were used in determining the width of the corridors, passageways, or stairs involved, it could result in a disaster.

We also discovered that present standards for tread-riser relationships are to a large degree based on antiquated rules of thumb. Many codes today still utilize an empirical formula that originated almost four centuries ago. Some of the few studies made recently, both in this country and abroad, indicate that many stair designs and standards simply are not responsive to the anthropometric requirements involved. Present minimum tread dimension requirements in circulation do not provide enough contact surface to accommodate the larger range of maximum shod foot length. Our own limited investigation suggests that where conditions permit a 6.8-in, or 17.3-cm, riser and an 11.3-in, or 28.7-cm, tread relationship maximizes both comfort and safety and that a riser height of 7 in, or 17.8 cm, or more should be avoided if at all possible. When one considers that somewhere in the neighborhood of 4,000 stair-related fatalities take place each year, the need for additional research in this area becomes painfully evident.

While we are hopeful that this book will, to some degree, be helpful in making the designer aware of the importance of human dimension in the design process and in establishing a link between the discipline of engineering anthropometry and the architectural and interior design professions, it is a very modest beginning. There is much we must do and much we need to know.

- We must first fully grasp the fundamentals and significance of engineering anthropometry so that we can engage the anthropometrist in intelligent discussion in order to define our needs.

- We must press for appropriate anthropometric data concerning the civilian population generally, since most of the present information involves the military.

- We must also develop an inventory of data concerning specific groups within the civilian sector, such as children, elderly people, and physically disabled people.

- We must encourage research at the university level and by independent design professionals and firms through professional societies and government and private foundation grants. Studies of the human body in motion should be high on the list of priorities.

- We must begin to question existing standards and guidelines.

- We must insist that anthropometry be included in professional architectural and interior design curricula.

- As the largest specifiers of residential and contract furniture and other components of interior spaces, we must demand from the manufacturers of these products the highest quality of product-user interface. We must encourage the manufacturer to reevaluate product design in terms of responsiveness to human dimension, body size, and corresponding variability. The degree to which elements of interior space can be adjusted should be investigated.

- To implement the foregoing, a committee should be created within the professional design organizations. Lines of communication should be established with the anthropometrist, the educational community, the manufacturer, the architect, and the interior designer. A clearing house for data and research of interest to the designer should be created. Lecture series dealing with anthropometry should be initiated.

To conclude on an optimistic note, perhaps one of the most encouraging developments with respect to the availability of anthropometric data on civilian populations came about during the writing of this book. It has long been contended that the degree to which military data could be applied to civilian design situations was relatively limited. In a paper delivered at the meeting of the American Psychological Association in August 1978, Charles Clauser of the AeroSpace Medical Research Laboratory, Wright-Patterson Air Force Base, Ohio, and Dr. John McConville of Anthropology Research Projects, Inc. of Yellow Springs, Ohio, suggested that military data may have a far greater level of applicability to nonmilitary situations than previously thought. They stated that

> Although relatively fewer and smaller surveys have been conducted on civilian subjects, it can be demonstrated that large segments of the military and civilian populations of the U.S. are comparable in body size and it is our conviction that much of the data from the military surveys are equally applicable or adaptable to non-military uses. This is particularly true of the vast body of anthropometric information which has been assembled, edited and standardized by the anthropology group of the Aerospace Medical Research Laboratory (AMRL) at Wright-Patterson Air Force Base into a facility known as the AMRL Anthropometric Data Bank, a resource which has grown over the last several years till it now comprises a uniquely comprehensive source of both military and civilian body size data.[2]

Although Clauser and McConville concede that certain gaps in data may exist for children and those older than 45, they do not view this as a serious obstacle:

> There are obviously other segments of the population not represented adequately in the data bank and there are undoubtedly data that are required by designers that have not yet been collected. When significant gaps in samples or anthropometry are identified, they can, in all likelihood, be filled by conducting relatively inexpensive studies of less than 500 carefully chosen subjects (Churchill and McConville, 1976).

> Despite the gaps, we believe that the AMRL Anthropometric Data Bank is a uniquely comprehensive and functional anthropometric data base from which a great variety of needed information can be readily obtained in usable form by commercial designers and engineers." (We want to add architects and interior designers to the users of these data.)

The major area of weakness, they advised, "remains at the point of contact between the various users and the anthropologists who are familiar with the existing data."[3]

As a profession we must generate the initiatives necessary to ensure proper contact. Above all, we must define and communicate our needs if we are to intelligently utilize anthropometric data to establish the proper relationship between human dimension and interior space. And utilize these data we must, if we are to improve the quality, comfort, and safety of our interior environments.